SOUTH AMERICA

There was nothing durable on this continent. The people were bound to have dictatorships and to smash them each time. They were resolved to have democracies and they always got dictatorships. They put themselves to all pains to organize, to co-ordinate, to construct, and to mould—but at long last they were bound to wreck it all again. They were unable to endure any one or anything set in authority over them. Nor would they even have endured Christ or Napoleon in authority over them.

RIO DE JANEIRO WITH THE SUGAR LOAF.

SOUTH AMERICA

Lights and Shadows

By

KASIMIR EDSCHMID

Translated from the German by
OAKLEY WILLIAMS

NEW YORK
THE VIKING PRESS
1932

PHOTOGRAPHS BY ERNA PINNA

PRINTED IN ENGLAND

CONTENTS

PART I

CONCERNING THE WEST INDIES, VENEZUELA, PANAMA, COLOMBIA AND ECUADOR

PART II

CONCERNING PERU

PART III

CONCERNING BOLIVIA

6

PART IV
CONCERNING CHILE

PART V
CONCERNING ARGENTINA

PART VI
CONCERNING BRAZIL

PART VII

WHITHER AWAY, SOUTH AMERICA ?

LIST OF ILLUSTRATIONS

Part I

CONCERNING THE WEST INDIES, VENEZUELA, PANAMA, COLOMBIA, AND ECUADOR

SOUTH AMERICAN REVOLUTIONS

THE captain of the *Boskoop* was in a good humour because the ship was averaging 320 miles. In the course of breakfast he recounted, rather piquantly for a Dutchman, the story of Simone Rafaele Urbina, who a few months previously had come to the island of Curaçao from Venezuela. Urbina had taken the Dutch Governor prisoner, shot a few policemen, and had seized the whole of the ammunition depots of the forts of Willemstad. Then, with the handful of his supporters, he had returned to Venezuela intending to start a revolution there on the strength of the captured munitions.

"Since that time," concluded the captain, breaking up the party at the breakfast table with a gesture of almost feminine grace, "there have always been a couple of small Dutch warships in the harbour of Willemstad in Curaçao."

Going up to the smoking-room Goehrs passed the chart of the course hanging at the foot of the companion. He was able to appreciate at a glance what a tiny island Curaçao, and what a big country Venezuela was.

In good weather, the coastline of Venezuela should, he thought, be visible from Curaçao.

In the smoking-room a steward was pouring out coffee for the twenty-one passengers on board.

The *Boskoop*, of the Koninklijke Nederlandsche Stoomboot Maatschappij, was a freighter of 5500 tons, with a very attractive deckhouse for passengers erected 'midships. In the bows were barrels of phosphate made fast by cables. On one side of the stern deck were twenty-four large crates, each containing a cow that gazed, mooing amiably, across to the other side of the deck, where a black Friesland bull of heroic proportions was standing alone in his massive box and noting their charms with an attentive eye.

Goehrs reviewed the passengers drinking their coffee. They were for the most part Ecuadorians and Colombians, at whose ports the big passenger liners did not call. Among them were one or two Frenchmen married to Ecuadorian women, who were travelling to South America, to save whatever they might of their wives' plantations, suffering from the cocoa blight.

The family most in evidence on board were the Patinos. For the mother with her eight children had had to wait in Paris for three months before she found a boat with a sufficient number of vacant berths for her caravan. To this family party there further belonged a cousin who was with child, and her husband, an architect about twenty-five years old, by the name of Hernández—thus making eleven Colombians in all. They were all subject to the domination of Luis Patino, aged nine.

If Mother wanted to go on shore, Luis, with his graceful, rather negroid Murillo head, settled the question. If Luis flew his kite from the stern, his pretty sister held the ball of string for him. If Hernández, the architect, who had at least fifty per cent. of Indian blood in his veins, unfolded a mass of papers on deck to work at the plans for the Basque, Italian, and neo-Dutch villas wherewith he aspired to embellish his native city of Bogotá at an altitude of some 9,000 feet, it was Luis, T-square in hand, who proffered advice.

" I believe," said Urquiza, fairly pecking up the family, as it streamed up the companion, with his keen eyes, " I believe that, if there should ever be a question of reinvesting the Patino family fortune or of marrying off one of the daughters, they would first of all consult Luis."

" I expect so, too," said Goehrs, " but I imagine that even that would be less dangerous than giving Hernández a commission to build you a villa."

Urquiza twitched his left eye like a hen, a trick to which the tall, slim man was particularly addicted. It always meant that he was suppressing the national passion for gesticulating with his hands. He was a man with regular Spanish features, an Ecuadorian living in Paris, who attached great importance to making it clear that he personally regarded South America from a European point of view. Like many other individuals of western South America, he obviously disliked being identified with the curious conditions obtaining in those countries. He had options on gold mines in Ecuador, but his assets, like those of nearly every one on board, were on a modest scale.

"All lads in South America," said the Dutch engineer, Van der Weele, who was going out to Curaçao to take a pipeline through the harbour for the Shell, "are as astute at the age of nine as other people are at thirty. But when they are thirty, they unfortunately have no more intelligence than other people have at the age of nine."

At this moment, Mme. de Merlezun, who was the last, entered the smoking-room. She was by birth an Ecuadorian, quite young still, and really looked like a girl. The Merlezuns had an old estate in the Pyrenees, and Gerald, her husband, was even younger and more attractive-looking than she. They were usually seasick at the same time, which is a rare phenomenon in married couples. The indisposition was less conspicuous in her case because she was usually occupied in knitting pullovers, while he ostentatiously manipulated the *Nouvelle Revue Française*. The young woman was late to appear because after breakfast she had gone to feed her pheasants, which she had lodged in a little coop close to the bull. These remarkable birds—seven of them—were pets of the whole ship's company. They had the wonderful capacity for disposing of both pickled herrings and pêche Melba.

Urquiza surveyed Mme. de Merlezun from head to foot, the while he finished off his coffee with a whimsical gesture.

"Why on earth has that nice little woman taken it into her head to endow Ecuador with an unknown breed of birds?" he asked reflectively. "Her father would prefer her to perpetuate her own species, for which she shows precious little inclination. The average of her family in Quito is between a dozen and fifteen children. They make a point of honour of it. Her father would certainly be glad to double young Merlezun's allowance if instead of pheasants she were to bring him out grandchildren. . . ."

"For shame, Urquiza," the captain interrupted him gallantly. "A point of view that expects fifteen children of that dear little thing is—to put it mildly—unhygienic."

URBINA'S RAID

THE captain lit a big black cigar, holding it straight in front of his face. Like many Hollanders his head had something of Anglo-Saxon impassivity and at the same time

13

something of Roman urbanity. He had previously sailed the West Coast of Africa, but had managed to get in a good deal of reading and had visited every museum, cathedral, and concert that had come his way.

" Well, let's have the gramophone, Duynker," he called to the first officer. The captain had an amazing predilection for tango records that combined singing and whistling.

The *Boskoop* was fifteen days out on her non-stop run to the West Indies, she had spent a day and a night hooting in a thick fog in the English Channel, along with seven other steamers, all hooting and bellowing ; she had ridden out a terrible gale both before and after the Azores—and the captain, now that the weather was at last beginning to grow warm after such a long spell of searching cold, wanted to have all the music he could get.

" They say that Urbina's now lurking in Porto Rico after spending a month or so in Panama," Van der Weele resumed the breakfast-table discussion. " I believe there are a lot of people in Curaçao in mortal dread of his possible reappearance."

" Whose ? " asked Hernández, who had just joined them.

" Urbina's."

" What's it all about ? " inquired old Count Maizzes, who had been sitting at another table at breakfast. With sixty-eight years to his credit, he was the oldest man on board. He was very old in a genuinely dignified way, the delightful type of old wreck that only a Parisian can be. He was going out to Ecuador for the first time in his life with his wife, some twenty years his junior, to visit the no less picturesque wreckage of her plantations.

" It's not a particularly creditable story for us, Count," said the captain, knocking off the ash of his cigar against the sole of his shoe ; he was straining his ears listening to a record of Carlos Gardel singing " El Carretero." " Urbina and five other passengers turned up in Curaçao quite serenely one day, after an eight hours' run from Coro, Venezuela. For four months he and the other five serene fellows who had accompanied him lived in Curaçao without once picking a quarrel with even a fly. All of a sudden one nigth he assembled fifty Venezuelans he had recruited from the labour barracks, near the Shell depot about six miles from Willemstad, loaded them into two motor lorries, and took Curaçao with them—that is to say, he shot three of the hundred police stationed there, seized the fort, and took the Governor prisoner in his own palace. Then he cleared all the depots on the island of all their ammunition and small arms. Revolver in hand, he forced the captain of an American steamer (of 2000 tons belonging to the Red D Line) to take him, his munitions, and his fifty ruffians across to Venezuela. By way of precaution he took the Governor with him on the picnic, but returned him the same evening from Venezuela along with the American. Quite a pretty bit of piracy. Unfortunately, half the world guffawed over it at our expense."

" And the fellow's revolution ? "

" Was a failure," said Urquiza dryly.

" That's a way revolutions fortunately often have in this part of the world," sighed the old Frenchman. " It's different on our side. My grandfather was old enough to have lived under Marie Antoinette—and my people are still full of it."

" Revolutions in South America are, it is quite true, not as old as that," said Urquiza equably, " but to make up for it they are the more frequent. And apart from that, the revolutionaries over here are as a rule actuated by other motives than those of M. Robespierre."

He rose to offer his chair to old Maizzes' wife, who had long ago left Ecuador for Paris at the age of seven and had not since seen that country again. Yet forty years of zealous study of the manners of Marie Antoinette had not, in her case, availed to disguise the fact that she derived from a country lying on the equator, in which very few people could boast of being of entirely white descent.

" Well . . . what about the motives ? " said the old Frenchman."

" Yes, let's consider the motives that made Simone Urbina want to launch a revolution in Venezuela," agreed Urquiza, slowly pouring out another black coffee and twitching his left eye violently. " Urbina was living in the State of Falcón in Venezuela and one day, in the town of Coro, seduced the Governor's wife. Thereupon there was a violent row between the supporters of Urbina, who was nobody in particular, and the partisans of the Governor, who, at any rate, was the Governor. But both of them were supporters of the President. President Gómez therefore himself intervened in the quarrel between his satellites and —gave Urbina an official appointment with a salary. But Urbina considered this insufficient support in the struggle in which he had become involved only because he had seduced the wife of another man, who happened to resent it.

Urbina therefore turned simultaneously on the Governor and on the President. It did not worry him in the least that Gómez was the cruellest, the most savage, the most powerful tyrant in the world to-day. Nor that Gómez had turned the whole of Venezuela into a rabbit warren of military roads and forts, and that all the harbours were fortified for his private warships which were always kept under a head of steam. Nor that nearly every third man was in Gómez's personal employment. All that meant nothing to Urbina. He simply made up his mind to secure some arms, and he hit on the happy notion of trying a raid on Curaçao in preparation for his putsch in Venezuela. For arms are more difficult to get in South America than whisky in New York. Urbina knew that he had only a journey of something between five and eight hours to reach the Dutch colony and so he laid his plans carefully and at his leisure. His raid succeeded, too, in the case of the Dutch, whom he took entirely by surprise. But in Venezuela his schemes were anything but a success. His revolution in Venezuela failed, but a revolution there can hardly expect to be as well organized as Gómez's counter-measures. They are really extraordinarily efficient. In about the same period when Urbina's revolution occurred, Gómez stamped out five or six similar ones."

"One of them was even set on foot by one of Gómez's own sons," said the captain. "Gómez made this son, when he was studying in Paris, an allowance of $40,000 a month— and in spite of that he tried a putsch. The fact is, a revolution in South America is quite a different thing from a revolution in Europe. It has a good deal of a popular sport about it. And what attitudes they do strike! When Gómez's rebellious son finally died in Paris, his father spent £12,000 sterling on his obsequies."

"Yes," said Urquiza with a smile, "if he had not given the youngster such a lot of money during his lifetime, the lad would never have tried a revolution. A revolution is the biggest stroke of business that can be brought off in South America. But it's the most difficult and the most risky as well. It can, like all big business, only be floated with quite a lot of working capital. That's why the objective of every revolution is the national treasury. Every revolution is bound to aim at the national treasury, because in the long run, if it should succeed, a whole system, a whole government, and all its supporters have to live on it. Before he made his first revolution—and that's a long time ago—

Gómez was a poor man. To-day he's the richest man in South America. And on top of that he has seen to it that all his supporters, and that includes the parliament, are also rich. Do you see now why a revolution—that is to say a business venture—that sets out to overturn such strong financial interests must be heavily financed to succeed? The odds differ of course in every State in South America. But in every one of them you require more than a few hundred thousand rounds of Dutch ammunition and a couple of field guns."

"There are close on three thousand Venezuelan exiles living in Paris," remarked Maizzes.

"All of them personal enemies of the President," suggested Urquiza, "only living in Paris because they have a fancy for enjoying life a bit longer ; which no one could guarantee them in Venezuela. Gómez has turned his power for such purposes to very good account. You're not allowed to travel in Venezuela, for instance, without having your luggage searched for arms by detectives, masquerading as customs officials, at least three times a day. In the same way a note will be made of your name ten times a day at every street corner and at every crossroad. The Government of Venezuela knows where to put its hand on every one of its subjects at any minute of the day—and that, with a population of three millions in a country twice the size of France, is a bit of an achievement. As a result the Government can really afford to do what it pleases. It can call up recruits at one end of the country and have them trained at the other, and is free to turn them adrift on to the streets when it has no further use for soldiers ; and on every road in Venezuela you will find discharged soldiers without clothes, without footgear, without a penny, begging their way over the huge distances to their homes. In fact the Government is free, if it so pleases, to seize its nationals' property. It has a free hand with the legislation and can juggle with the law accordingly. Gómez one day seized most of the nation's livestock by putting such high licences on cattle brought from the provinces of the interior to the coast that they exceeded the value of the beasts. Isn't that a brilliant bit of organization ? And an eminent President ? No other State in South America is quite so badly off in the way of Presidents as Venezuela. This brand of President is a Venezuelan speciality. And it is very much the same thing in the matter of revolutions. In Ecuador the President, for example, living in Quito, two days' railway journey up country, will be very shy of enforcing general military service that has been the law of the land for the Lord knows how many years. On the contrary, for fear of a revolution he maintains a purely Indian army. This army is small and it has the advantage that its rank and file do not understand Spanish. If the President were to call up only five lads of good families, they would start a revolution within the week and march the Indian army against the palace. For the same reason Ecuador does not possess a proper navy. If it had a decent navy, its officers would very soon be training their guns on the fort of Guayaquil. A proper navy would be in an incessant state of revolution. Instead, Ecuador owns three neat men-of-war under sails. Isn't that so, Captain ? And when we put into Guayaquil, we shall first of all have to salute some ancient dismantled hulk. And then you will see an Ecuadorian admiral appear in full uniform on the quarterdeck and salute. . . ."

" Oh . . . nonsense," interrupted the captain laughing. " You're exaggerating, Urquiza."

Old Maizzes turned his vulture head with its half-extinct blue eyes on Urquiza.

" You are an eminent patriot," he said approvingly. " But, tell me, why didn't you go in for the only big business to be done in your country ? "

Urquiza was silent for a minute before answering the old man's malicious question. And as long as he delayed speaking his left eye twitched continually, just lifting his left nostril with it.

" Why didn't I embroil myself in any revolution ? " he said listlessly. " They cut off my grandfather's head for doing that. And my father, after losing all his property, had to live in Chile for fifteen years. The gold mines of Ecuador yield about seventy-five grammes of gold to the ton, and Vanderbilt draws about two million dollars a year from a single mine. I'm free to confess that I regard this kind of occupation as a less exacting line of business."

" You are right there," exclaimed Maizzes and resentfully raised a tremulous hand to his snowy temples. " You are right. Revolutions bring no luck. My father was ambassador in Darmstadt under the third Napoleon. Then the revolution and the republic wiped out the prosperity of our family for a second time. Otherwise I really should not have to be taking a long sea voyage at my age on account of a wretched plague in the accursed cocoa plantations and travelling about in a crazy country."

18

"Perhaps, too, you will now understand why I am living in Paris," replied Urquiza politely, and left the smoking-room.

Van der Weele, the Dutch engineer, who was to take the four-million-dollar pipeline for the Shell through the harbour of Curaçao, had been drumming with his forefinger on the smoking-room table for a full three minutes. He had ceased listening to the conversation after it had strayed away from the Dutch political frontier problem. It had lost interest for him. For to a Dutchman the notion of revolution is quite as grotesque as would be the idea of converting the bourse of Amsterdam into a picture palace.

"But the most outrageous thing," he now interposed angrily, "is that this Urbina fellow has addressed a letter to the Governor of Curaçao demanding the release of all the Venezuelans imprisoned for complicity with his raid. He threatened, in the event of the prisoners being interned in the fort any longer, to return to Curaçao and to pay the Governor a rather more disturbing visit than last time. And then came the incredible—the Governor released the gang. If Holland is so weak in the face of every adventurer . . ."

The captain raised his finger with a smile. He had just turned on a dainty tango-like polka and was listening with voluptuous enjoyment to its sweet, lilting rhythm, while he silenced the other with a motion of his hand.

"We Dutch are a sensible nation, Van der Weele," he said when the "Cariñosa" had died away, "and have always behaved like decent people, but we are fond of our money as well. Why should the Governor risk some mad dog of a fanatic throwing a bomb into the oil tanks, with a few million guilders going up in smoke? I should have released the fellows, too."

The Case Against Venezuela

ABOUT the same time two men were standing on the little promenade deck in the stern.

A young man from Curaçao who had been studying tropical medicine in Hamburg, London and Holland was standing beside Goehrs. His mother had been a Spaniard; his great-grandmother a Frenchwoman from Guadeloupe. His ancestors on his father's side were all Dutchmen. His name was Barnveldt.

They were gazing out over the sea into the hot night.

"As a boy I often used to see folk arriving in Curaçao from Venezuela in canoes. Their shoulders and arms, where they came above the gunwales of the boats, were drilled with buckshot."

Barnveldt took a pocketbook from his linen coat. "The dark spots here," he went on, "are the blood of one of the poor fellows whom the Venezuelans had riddled with shot on the occasion of the raid on Curaçao. I took him to the hospital in a car myself. That night Urbina placed a bodyguard and his own car—requisitioned—at my disposal for the purpose. Urbina is a sensitive man with an intellectual face. He behaved handsomely and bravely. But the country he was born in is a damnable place.

"Three years ago I was travelling through the interior of Venezuela to collect plants hitherto unknown. The border country between Venezuela and Colombia is pretty well unexplored still. When they had to demarcate the frontier in a hurry one day, they did it by taking several thousand photographs from an aeroplane. The Indians in these virgin forest zones are particularly fond of picking off white men. The Indians, however, did not put a stop to my intention of travelling in the interior, but the Venezuelan banks did, by refusing to honour my letters of credit on the National City Bank of New York. In Gómez's country anything may happen.

"The monument to him is already unveiled in this country; on it you read :

Viva Gómez y adelante !

"' Long live Gómez and progress !' Gómez was originally a person of no importance. People who want to cut a figure in Venezuela entitle themselves, before they play any part in public life, Doctor or General. Gómez promptly became a general. Almost everything belongs to this general to-day. Venezuela is one of the states with the biggest output of crude oil. Every morning a fleet leaves the harbour of Maracaibo exporting hundreds of thousands of barrels. That means thousands of dollars for Venezuela in export licences. Gómez allows even the most subordinate officials to have their share in this profit. Every book published, every newspaper printed, every piece of paper written upon, grovels before him along with its writer. His parliament, elected at the point of the sword, idolizes him.

"An interesting personality. A few years ago he suddenly

resigned the presidency. On his motion a man of the name of Pérez was elected. This Pérez at once appointed Gómez inspector-general of the army. The whole thing was a put-up job. Gómez resigned so as not to act as a constant personal stimulus to revolution. But with the army under his command, Gómez remained just as powerful as he always had been. This gamble with the country is bleeding it white, dissipating its natural resources to be exploited by foreign capital, and reducing people who love the country to frenzy.

"Unfortunately the people who do love the country would have to adopt exactly the same methods if they were to come into power. For how else are they going to keep in power? Ah, there is no more terrible or more vicious circle than government by might.

"The suspiciousness of the Venezuelan Government is unparalleled. Foreign ships even have to moor eight paces away from the quay at night, so as not to be in contact with the land. There are, the Lord knows, ships that hang a life-size portrait of Gómez in their saloon when they put into a Venezuelan port, and only take it down after clearing harbour. They are ships of nationalities which would cause you considerable astonishment if I were to name them.

"One thing certainly astonished me, and it was in part the reason that at the time prompted my journey—capital punishment has been abolished. I puzzled my head why on earth it had been done since it suited the methods of the Government so admirably. I believe they abolished capital punishment to prevent the country from becoming depopulated. Even the Devil is not altogether a fool.

"But in individual cases the Government achieves exactly the end it desires, although by roundabout ways. Sometimes prisoners who have been kept in the dark for months are brought into the light so suddenly that they go blind. And whether you set political offenders to road-building in the malaria areas or shoot them down out of hand on the beach amounts to very much the same thing. You always remain master over life and death—legally or illegally.

"I put myself to some trouble to see the prisons. The methods of the prisons are, I assure you, inhuman. In Puerto Cabello the water for washing and for drinking is turned on for a short time twice a day. It runs down a trough that extends through six cells. The water passes for a minute through cell No. 1, then for another minute through cell No. 2, and then for a similar length of time through cell No. 3, and so on. It may be all very well if you happen to have cell No. 1; but, as in cells Nos. 1 to 5, every one drinks the water and washes in it, it is bad luck to occupy cell No. 6. In the dungeons of Fort San Carlos they simply let the prisoners be flooded every morning breast-high by the incoming tide.

" Although I came with letters of introduction from very influential Governors, no commandant ever allowed me to put my nose inside his prison. The Governors have really a great deal of power in this country. They can call out troops and arrange for any one they please to disappear. But in this country the prison commandants are far more powerful than the Governors. And with it all, Venezuela is a beautiful country. But human beings do not fare well there. When Alexander von Humboldt visited it, the people were undoubtedly happier and more contented."

Barnveldt put the wallet with the dark stains that he had been holding in his hand back into his pocket. Everything about his head that was Dutch looked firm, big, and powerful, more especially the forehead. Everything southern about him, from the slanting dark eyes to the close black hair, seemed to be ablaze with a passionate sympathy.

At that moment the other man stretched out his arm. A tiny light blinked in the distance.

" We are just passing through the Lesser Antilles into the Caribbean," he said.

" Right," said the Dutchman. " You have discovered the West Indies for the hundred-thousandth time, Goehrs."

The West Indies and Columbus

GOEHRS was, it is true, a man who did not care a tinker's curse about " discovering " anything. He was a writer who hated the word " expedition " just as much as he did the phrase " globe-trotter." The former struck him as too pretentious and almost always wrongly applied, and the latter was simply inept. They were all part of that equally stupid view of travel as purely a matter of relaxation, in which a trip to Nice or Cairo is " travelling." Goehrs had never yet met a human being on a real journey that was being undertaken for pleasure only—there was no such thing because real travelling was a very exhausting and very uncomfortable business and the tithe of the enjoy-

ment derived from beautiful scenery was out of all proportion to the nine-tenths of unpleasantness of which simpletons
who talked about globe-trotters had no conception. Goehrs
held globe-trotters as a type to be, like a good deal else, the
invention of leisurely authors with plenty of naïveté and
innocuous imagination to spare. Goehrs had never encountered a person who corresponded to this Oscar Wilde
ideal of a traveller, but he had met many people who had
undertaken long and difficult journeys for business purposes
or with a bent to educate themselves.

Goehrs was a little distinct even from the latter. He did
not travel, as for example, an Englishman does who is
always engaged on anxious inquiries whether the limbs of his
Empire are still working smoothly in their sockets, and is
therefore always a little harassed. Nor did he travel as a
Frenchman travels who, with his native Paris imprinted on
his heart, looks upon the whole world as an ingenious jigsaw puzzle. And finally he differentiated himself from a
good many of his German fellow-countrymen by the trifling
fact that, when he was confronted by international problems,
he did not rush at them with a war-whoop, only to succumb
to them.

On the other hand he entertained a feverish interest in
questions which unfortunately do not, as a general rule,
interest a German in the least. He was concerned whether
black, white, or café-au-lait coloured races were destined to
fashion the face of the earth, and why the diversely coloured
races confronted one another with an ineradicable hatred.
He was concerned as to the reason why human beings fare
well in one quarter of the globe and ill in another, why they
were more advanced on one continent and more backward
on another. He was concerned with questions of the social
conditions under which human beings were living, and of
the extent to which their good or bad qualities were condi-
tioned by climate, fate, or crossbreeding. Finally, he was
concerned with the question whether their progress, or
their retrogression, was in fact an advance, or a setback, or
only European prejudice.

Goehrs was aware that since the war immense changes
had been going on ; great nations had relinquished the first
place in history, and other nations had taken their place.
England had fallen back from the greatest power in the
world to the status of just a great power, and in her room
the Yankees had stepped into the foremost position in the
world. In addition to this, there were a number of other

nations which, without it being possible to adduce proof of it, had advanced or receded—and Goehrs took this phenomenon into account. He had the idiosyncrasy of falling obstinately in love with countries he did not know and of not growing tired of them until he had picked them to pieces and investigated them. For this reason the study of a map was more interesting to him than a stage play.

He was able to sketch in all the cables between the several continents on a map of the globe or enumerate the twenty States of the republic of Brazil together with their capitals. He knew the tables of altitude, the waterless areas, the exports, the air-line communications, the funicular railways, the numbers of the natives, the constitutions, the harbour facilities, and the sanitary conditions of a good many out-of-the-way countries. He was a theorist with an imagination, which is to say, a positivistic theorist, who looked first of all to human beings themselves for results and for precious little from theories.

Half an hour later, Goehrs was studying, with an odd thrill of excitement, the position on the chart of the course of the Greater and the Lesser Antilles, which, with the Bahamas, make up the West Indies.

Quite at the top was a tiny speck off the Bahamas. It was at this point that a man first struck land on October 12th, 1492, in a ship of barely a hundred tons that could make no more than twenty-five nautical miles a day. The man had the reputation of being a sound seaman, though a notorious dreamer, but he had made many mistakes in his reckonings. He had set sail to find gold and spices and called the new world he found here the " West Indies." His name was Cristóbal Colón or Cristoforo Colombo. The island off which he first moored his ship he named San Salvador, called by the Indians Guanahani.

Then he made Cuba with his sailing ships. For a long time he and the rest of the world held it to be part of the continent of Asia, the Indies of which he was in search. On his subsequent voyages he made the peninsula of Paria. At first he took Venezuela to be an island and later on for the southern extremity of Cuba.

These mistakes show how the most important events in the world, as a rule, occur, quite correctly in principle, quite mistakenly in regard to particulars. Things happened at breakneck speed then. Columbus was one of the greatest pacemakers in history. Dozens of successors explored the New World as a consequence of each one of his voyages. With ships of a ridiculous tonnage, on oceans where a hurricane meant death, with an ignorance that was unparalleled, and guided by accidents that, apart from their deeper significance, were simply ludicrous.

Even Humboldt a few centuries later, when geographically everything was plain enough, only landed in the region of present-day Venezuela by mistake. He had intended to go somewhere altogether different. But the impossible conditions on board a merchantman, and the fact that the captain had no quinine on board as a precaution against malaria, prompted him to disembark in Venezuela by way of protest. And there he stayed for the next few years.

Goehrs held no decided views about chance. On the other hand he held very decided views on the people who took theirs. He looked on the men of Columbus's generation who had reached the West Indies in their cockleshells as the keenest sportsmen in history. He only had to look over the side to realize what a "rough sea" must have meant in the Caribbean. Between August and October the Caribbean is the playground of hurricanes, which romp over an area some hundred miles square at a wind velocity that is greater than the twelve-point maximum. In their centre they have a nucleus of about two miles in breadth. Towards this nucleus the winds drive from all four quarters and hammer down a ship as flat as a plaice.

Goehrs had seen a 34,000-ton steamer, crammed with

American trippers, crawling out of one of these hurricanes like a beaten cur. Ten passengers had an arm or a leg broken ; all the boats had been carried away ; and a number of portholes had been stoved in. To wander into the centre of one of these hurricanes on a sailing ship was tantamount to suicide.

For all that, the Antilles, under the name of the West Indies, were coveted by every country. Spain, which was the first to own them, claimed that the possession of the West Indies gave it all the riches in the world. At that date the trade in spices, silks, and Oriental groceries was esteemed beyond any other in the world—with the exception of gold.

The West Indies were a huge, fabulous possession that never ceased to stir the imagination of nations. They soon developed a vast industry by becoming the clearing-house of the slave trade.

When Spain's energy, frittered away recklessly in European wars and colonial adventures, slackened, all the vultures of Europe forgathered and picked up islands. It was a strange era, when even Holland conquered Brazil. France and England acquired islands of the Antilles. The West Indies became as particoloured as a map of Europe. Finally, several of the islands even declared their independence, which turned out a tragic jest. For their independence amounted to no more than that of certain subsidiary companies of the big trusts, which carry on in business under their own names only for the purposes of dodging taxes.

Goehrs studied the map of the West Indies carefully, from the Bahamas to the southernmost Dutch A.B.C. islands. He made a sensational discovery ; it concerned the advances of the United States of America. The Yankees, from comparatively recent dates, owned practically all of the bigger islands of importance. Cuba, Porto Rico, and Haiti were theirs together with others, overtly or covertly.

Anything belonging to the British, such as Jamaica, Barbadoes, and Trinidad—anything belonging to the French, like Guadeloupe, Martinique, and half of San Martin— (the other half of it belonged to the Dutch) was not worth mentioning as compared with the American possessions.

It was not worth mentioning because these colonial possessions had no system about them. But the Yankee property represented a prolongation of Florida, the half of a huge pair of imperial pincers that North America was pushing out towards South America. And when Goehrs reflected that the independence of the Central American States was extremely problematical—the fulcrum of this mighty pair of imperialistic pincers, of the West Indian possessions of the Americans, must be the Panama Canal. Goehrs was looking forward with intense interest to seeing this Yankee canal, studded with big guns.

It struck him as a most remarkable thing that it was the Yankees of all nations who had, in military parlance, " outflanked " this continent. For they were a race, a power, a nation that was not in existence when these islands were successively discovered. North America, during the era of the discoveries and for a long time afterwards, played a very subordinate part. It was not explored and opened up until comparatively modern times, but then, it is true, at a mad pace. Thirteen years after the war it blossomed out into the strongest—from both the military and the economic points of view—power in the world. Four hundred years ago not a soul would have staked ten gold pieces against a million on this issue.

And what would things look like in a century hence ? Would the Yankees swallow South America, or would it prove to be the destiny of the South American half-breed nations one of these days to make the North play second fiddle ? Goehrs did not know, but he proposed to come to grips with the problem in the course of the ensuing months.

For all that, he prudently remained conning his map for a considerable time. It was too pretty and unique a discovery he had made, ascertaining that the Yankees, who at the time of the discovery and golden age of South America had, strictly speaking, no existence at all, had now grown into the great imperialistic menace of the continent. But at the same time this discovery gave him a shock. It was a warning to him against attempting any forecasts as to the development of present-day States, races, and continents.

Goehrs shrugged his shoulders and turned to contemplate the sea. He then went down to his cabin and, although he could hardly keep his legs in the heavy roll, he stuck a pin in the chart hanging on the inside of his cabin door, exactly between Guadeloupe and San Martin. That was the present position of the ship.

If the action was a little romantic on Goehrs's part, it is evidence of how precise he was.

27

THE *Boskoop* put into Curaçao for a day or two to discharge a cargo of potatoes, onions, wine, cement, transportable houses, motor boats, of anything you like in short. Goehrs had in the meantime changed his address to the Hotel Americano. Before he went ashore Luis Patino had, with the assistance of his box of paints, embraced the opportunity, while the luggage was on the deck, to sketch some striking designs on Goehrs's suitcase. Luis was an unusually gifted lad and, in addition to steamers, could delineate figures such as sailors wear tattooed on their arms.

Goehrs, on returning to his luggage, glanced first at his suitcase, then at the captain, and then at Luis Patino's mother. Madame Patino looked at the mess and was vastly amused.

" If Luis means to be naughty, no one can stop him," she said in English with emotion.

Four days later Goehrs was sitting at lunch with Merlezun in the roof garden of the Hotel Americano. The Frenchman had gone ashore because Paul Morand, whom he knew personally, had spent a fortnight at the Americano in the course of his trip to the Antilles.

They had put the fish course behind them and were busily engaged on a shoulder of lamb when it occurred to Merlezun to ask for a slice of bread.

" A bit of bread," he said in Dutch, because he was very proud of having learnt, on board ship, a language that perhaps only ten Frenchmen speak well.

" We speak English or Spanish only," replied the mulatto. So Merlezun repeated his request in English. The waiter drew a fork from his trouser pocket, crossed the whole expanse of roof garden, speared a slice of bread in the far corner, carried it as far as the table, took it off with his fingers, and laid it beside Merlezun's plate.

" I thought I was in a Dutch colony," said the Frenchman in astonishment. " But at the post office they won't take Dutch money ; in the shops the prices are marked in American dollars ; and the newspapers are in Spanish."

" Keep calm," said Goehrs cheerfully, plunging the fork that had served him for three courses into his pudding. " Nor is curaçao, the liqueur I mean, made here."

They looked down for a while through the shimmer of heat at the harbour, which in the guise of a fair-sized river bisected the island. They watched a pontoon bridge open and close by means of a motor, like the hands of a clock according to whether a big ocean liner was putting out or whether one of the innumerable fifty-ton sailing boats from Venezuela was putting in. The moment the bridge closed again, a crowd of Negroes and cars poured across it. Facing them stood a handsome rococo building, where the Governor resided, and above it an old fort—and then, immediately beyond, as at the mouth of a river, flecked green and white and emerald, with the sleek movements of a beast of prey— the sea.

Merlezun pushed back his plate.

" Everything is a matter of luck," he said, raising his handsome head to look at the Dutch flag fluttering, red, white, and blue over the Governor's palace. " If the Venezuelan coast were not so flat that only small boats can make it, the Venezuelans would be able to exploit and refine their ridiculously rich oilfields themselves. Then the five hundred white, red, and yellow giant tanks of the Shell would not be standing here in Curaçao ; the island would be bankrupt, twelve thousand hands would be out of work ; a fleet of ships with crude oil would not be putting in and another fleet with refined oil putting out every day— and doing me out of my early morning sleep."

Merlezun was in a bad temper. He had been swindled out of a dollar by a taxi-driver the previous day, and the Dutch policeman to whom he appealed had not, as Merlezun expected, bashed the nigger over the head with his rubber truncheon—but had made a note of the names of both parties and had requested the Frenchman to accompany him to the police station. Merlezun had thereupon waived the dollar, but had a poor opinion of Dutch qualifications for colonization.

It was a Sunday. The Negresses filled the street in front of the red-painted, two-storeyed garbage box known as the Hotel Americano with a blaze of colour, with such pistachio greens and raspberry pinks as made the harbour look like a giant bunch of toy balloons.

" Funny ! " said Goehrs. " For the last half-hour I have not seen a single white man."

" Five Governors in three years," added Merlezun. " There's something wrong somewhere. There are 40,000 Negroes, 1,000 Jews, 1,000 white Catholics, 2,000 white Protestants. But the government of the island is Catholic although Holland is Protestant en bloc. And why ? Because all the Negroes are Catholics, descendants of the slaves

29

imported from Africa who were the big business here before oil."

Goehrs leaned over the veranda to wave to Barnveldt, who was swaying across the pontoon bridge in his car, and, like a boat under sail, dividing the stream of Negroes. Merlezun looked glumly down at the Negroes, who were all wearing patent-leather shoes or yellow-and-white American crape-rubber shoes, very wide light trousers, tight-fitting grey coats, Panama hats, and spectacles.

"If I were Governor here I should at once take steps to have all those fellows going about barefoot," he said, and struck a match sharply.

"What would you do, Barnveldt, if you were to be made Governor of Curaçao ? " Goehrs turned with a laugh to the approaching Dutchman.

The other looked at him for a moment.

"I should at once proclaim self-government for Curaçao and independence from Holland," he answered quietly.

A DUTCH COLONY

GOEHRS'S first question in Curaçao was an inquiry for the real natives. For before the Spanish conquest the West Indian islands had been very densely populated by red men.

In the dialect of a redskin tribe Curaçao meant "roast priest," because the Indians had evidently not refrained from the observance of their ritualistic customs in favour of the wearers of the soutane. At the time of the Conquista Curaçao was enfolded in the haze of legend. It was known as the Isla de los Gigantes, because the Indians were reputed to be giants. But that was, of course, some tall story of the Spanish soldiery who whetted the appetites of their audiences in Spain by inventions of this sort.

In any case, as far as Goehrs was concerned the whole question was void. There were no more Indians. The Spaniards had killed them off.

About midday Goehrs drove out to the Barnveldt family plantation for the second time. By this time he had crossed the island, about 45 miles in breadth, six times and had been delighted to realize that one had to find one's way over an approximate area of some 210 square miles by instinct pure and simple. For the island was overgrown with the slender, tall columns of cacti and divi-divi trees, which were flattened down by the wind like big besoms in the breeze. Armies of goats were climbing about this virgin forest of cacti. They climbed about like squirrels and nibbled away the green out of the crowns—but there was hardly any green to be had.

" The island has only one fault," said Barnveldt. " There's no water. It doesn't rain at all for nine months. And for the three when it ought by rights to be raining, it doesn't rain either. Surface water is consequently only struck at a depth of some 125 feet and may give out at any time. To make up for it, the climate is equable, so wonderfully equable. . . ." He inhaled the air with the same devout expression with which a man of deep feeling greets his native soil.

They happened to have stopped on one of those remarkable terraces wherewith Curaçao descends to the sea. The island lies on a column of white coral. This has, once or twice in the course of history, lifted and sunk with its soil, animals, and human beings, and on its north coast has thus laid out a right royal series of terraces. The lowest terrace, some hundred feet high, stood defying the ocean with a rampart of pointed coral halberds. The car stopped on the second terrace, more than half a mile inland—and yet they could see the tossing sea break against the coral bulwark into half a hundred distinct roaring fountains of spray, each some sixty feet tall.

The medley of desert and tropical virgin forest that made up Curaçao appealed to Goehrs for two reasons. It was at one and the same time tropical and dry ; which sounded like a contradiction in terms. It was very hot and very windy—a genuine rarity.

" The paradise of breezes," he called it, taking tea in the plantation surrounded by billowing lace curtains. The plantation had, by virtue of three wells, become a luxuriant oasis of trees for a few hundred yards. But this greenery was only the home park. The plantation did not grow plants. It grew goats. Goats that were hunted every day and brought down with bullets like chamois. Their carcasses were thrown away and their skins sold in Hamburg.

" Paradise of breezes . . ." said Barnveldt's father with a smile. " Paradise of goats."

The old man sat in formal attire, white drill suit and black button boots. With his narrow bald head and commanding blue eyes, he was half like a lean Dutchman, half—he got that from his grandmother—like a French general. No one would have guessed that the youngster with the dreaming

31

dark eyes of a fanatic was his son. Spanish blood had intervened.

"What a queer Dutch that is," said Goehrs, as they strolled about the garden and the youngster spoke to one of the gardeners.

"It isn't Dutch."

"Eh?"

"Our local language, Pagiamento."

Goehrs tried to talk "Pagiamento," but the gift of tongues was denied him. The language of which the educated Dutchmen of Curaçao who were the backbone of the colony were so proud was compounded of only fifteen per cent. Dutch, seventy per cent. Spanish, and five per cent. English and Portuguese. And the balance made up of scraps of Yiddish and Indian confronted him with a task to which he was not equal.

"You are, after all, a man of common sense, Barnveldt," he said in despair. "Well, if an island with two little subsidiary islets, with a population of 40,000 Negroes and 4,000 whites, aims at becoming independent, an island on which nothing except goats will grow, an island to which everything a man needs has to be brought by ship . . . when an island like this wants to set up as a State on its own account, what, in Heaven's name, is going to become of the world? You are after all a man with a brain. A clever, level-headed Dutchman."

"No," said Barnveldt, "I am first and foremost a Curaçaoan. And a Dutchman as well, it is true. It's no fun for us, after living here for centuries, to have governors sent out to us from overseas, whom we have not chosen, who do not understand us, and who are surrounded by advisers whom we have not selected. That is a matter of the blood, Goehrs, and it would be the same in your case."

Goehrs did not answer, but for some seconds thought hard how climate, remoteness from Europe, the incidence of blood corpuscles of another race can change a character he thought he knew as well as the Dutch. He could work out with almost mathematical accuracy what racial influences had turned the scale in the political peculiarities of his curious friend.

On his way back Goehrs again drove cross-country, past many Negro villages. The Negroes of the interior, quite unlike their urban brethren, had made a merry Africa with huts and kraals among the cacti pillars, and were pretty well naked. It was only in their cemeteries that they too

32

had become luxurious. They did not invest their savings in spectacles and Walkover footgear and ample trousers but in marble tombstones. They were more keenly concerned about a dignified death than about a life of ease ; and Goehrs, on seeing the huge churches cheek by jowl beside the Negro huts, ceased to wonder why Curaçao had to have a Catholic government. The roast priest had become the triumphant priest, who, even if the Indians had ceased to be, had taken charge of their descendants to such good purpose that they fed out of his hand.

"There it is," said Barnveldt. And Goehrs, following his outstretched finger, saw the first gables of Willemstad. For days Goehrs had failed to grasp the fact that Curaçao city has, in addition, a name of its own to distinguish it from Curaçao the island. Every one said Curaçao when he meant Willemstad, and Goehrs, too, talked of Curaçao but meant Willemstad.

He was particularly fond of strolling about the residential streets of Curaçao. There was something about these villas closely akin to the character of the population. Goehrs had never seen a garden suburb as natty, as bright, and as fanciful. Their lines were planned, in accordance with the Dutch temperament, on such doll-like and sedate principles, and their façades had turned out so bizarre, so colonial, and so imaginative. Half little Holland, half gaily coloured Portugal. Their fronts gleamed a medley of yellows, reds, greens, and blues, exactly like the gowns of the smart Negresses. They looked just as improbable, just as pathetic, just as attractively baroque.

A few steps from the Hotel Americano Goehrs came to a standstill in front of a monument. It had been erected to the memory of one of the liberators of South America because he happened to have been born in Curaçao. On the pedestal was the inscription : " Der beroemden Curaçaoenaar Petrus Louis Brion, 1782-1821." The date stood for a critical period in South America. In the course of these years all the colonies cut the painter from their mother country, Spain.

Goehrs studied General Brion's monument. He saw a man who, like all his contemporaries, was vainly struggling to get his head above an unduly high military collar.

At this moment Van der Weele, the engineer, strolled out of the Hotel Americano.

" Funny face, eh ? " he said.

" No funnier than mine," said Goehrs.

"Yes, it is," replied Van der Weele with conviction, chewing his black cigar. "Don't you see, everything in life is like that, a bit relative and a bit comical—fame is like that, too. When the sculptor who had got the commission for Brion's monument at length delivered it, some native of Curaçao asked him : ' Has it turned out a good likeness ? ' ' Probably,' said the sculptor. ' Did Brion really look like that ? ' asked the man of Curaçao doubtfully. ' Why not ? ' replied the sculptor. ' Do you happen to know what he looked like any better ? ' After this conversation every one in Curaçao looked at one another askance. They had one and all forgotten to look up a portrait of Brion—and then it turned out there was no portrait of Brion to be had. The man up there with the inscription announcing that he was Brion probably looked more like any one in the world than Brion. And now every one is aghast. And who is to blame for it ? The Makambas."

"The Makambas ? "

"Do you speak Pagiamento ? "

Goehrs shuddered.

"Makamba is a word by which the people of Curaçao designate the Dutch, and it is, the Lord knows, an infernally impudent word."

Goehrs gazed across the narrow river bed of the harbour out to the sea that was tossing about with whitecaps on its green-flecked hide.

"What do you really say, Van der Weele, to your fellow-countrymen setting up a sort of Alsace-Lorraine in miniature here ? "

The engineer winked one eye and rolled his cigar round several times with his lips. Then he said in English with a twinkle :

"If Luis means to be naughty, no one can stop him."

The Americans Fortify Panama

A FEW days later in one of the two hundred Hindu stores of Colón, a town at the head of the Panama Canal, Goehrs met Rosita Patino, Merlezun, and old Maizzes. They arranged to have a swim and to take tea at the Hotel Washington. But before that Rosita, Merlezun, Goehrs, and Nove, a friend of Goehrs, drove out to France Field.

Goehrs had a map on his knees. The Panama Canal Zone was the fateful spot of South America and Goehrs felt as if he were on the trail. For it is at this point that the Continent becomes coquettish and quite slim. The waist of America is less than forty miles in width—but it is a terrifying spot.

Originally this unique strip belonged to the Republic of Colombia when at the beginning of the 'eighties the French, prompted by the Lord knows what idealistic motives, hit upon the notion of cutting a canal through its very narrowest point. They had a man with an international reputation for a job of that kind, whose monument stands on the banks of the Suez Canal : Ferdinand de Lesseps.

In 1881 they floated a company with a capital of over $250,000,000. Eight years later only a part of the roughly forty miles had been cut ; an army corps of navvies had died of malaria ; the capital was spent ; the French had underestimated the bulk of soil to be excavated. There was a scandal that shook the world.

The canal was bankrupt, but the importance of the work was plainer than ever. The significance of the canal was that shipping for the West Coast need no longer pass round Cape Horn and effected an enormous saving of time and money. This affected all seafaring nations to the same degree. However, it affected only one nation to the very marrow of its self-consciousness as a power : the United States of America.

Twenty years previously the Yankees were not wide-awake enough to see the highroad to the south. But they were wide-awake enough to be able to leap with the full force of their imperialistic ideology into the breach in which the French had come to grief. And to what good purpose did they leap !

They did not care a tinker's curse about Colombia's objections to the American scheme for taking the canal through their territory. The Yankees were rich enough and resourceful enough. All of a sudden in 1903 the province of Panama embarked on a revolution against Colombia to which it belonged, and entered into negotiations with the United States as an independent State. Panama received $10,000,000 for its revolution and its canal rights. Thereupon the Americans bought the French out. The French got away with $40,000,000. The Americans then sank another $375,000,000 into it.

The treaty with Panama was signed in 1903. Under its terms the Americans acquired a strip of land five miles on the right and five on the left of the proposed canal. Thereupon they drenched the country in crude oil, killed the mosquitoes that had killed the French, and built a few locks in which the shipping was simply pumped up to the Panama table-land. The Yankees were cleverer than the French, who tried to cart away mountains there was no possibility of removing. The Americans had the shipping simply hoisted uphill (by their system of terrace-wise locks) and lowered again afterwards. From one ocean into the other. No one believed that the scheme was feasible. It was. The altitude of the interior averaged about seventy-five feet. The Americans made light of these altitudes. Inland they turned the beds of the rivers and the lakes to account. A brilliantly clever scheme.

Eleven years later, a few weeks after the outbreak of war in Europe, the Canal was opened. On August 15th, 1914. Fifteen years later, in the course of a single year, 6314 vessels traversed the canal with thirty million freight tonnage. The Canal Zone had an American governor and a population of 14,000 employees and officials.

But all that was only of secondary interest so far as the Americans were concerned. That the trade of the world effected economies, that the country was made habitable, that the mechanical side of the venture had proved a brilliant success—that was all very well. But the point that interested the Americans was altogether different.

They had in the meanwhile effected another wonderful piece of work alongside the Canal : an army corps, hundreds of military aeroplanes, and big-gun emplacements masked by a screen of villas in palm groves and golf links, compared with which Gibraltar was as a marker's shelter on a rifle range. The Americans were at last in a position to fling their battle fleet of the Atlantic into the Pacific where and when it suited them. They had now enclosed Central America and South America in their pincers. The Canal furnished them with an immense fulcrum in their systematic advance. Further, at the entrance to the Canal they built their own city, Cristobal, which grew out of all recognition and in a twinkling had swallowed up the town of Colón.

Gochrs put his map back into his pocket. They drove straight from Colón without any break through Cristobal, a town of bungalows, but built of cement—a cement bungalow town, which plain columns invested with a certain measure of the dignity of the tropics. Informal, but severe, with big guns for a background.

The rainy season had just set in, and the green of the palm trees, of the lawns, and of the hedges was fascinating.

A few miles beyond Cristobal the car took them across a muddy trench.

" That is Lesseps' old canal," said Nove.

" Lesseps . . . ? " queried Merlezun, dumbfounded. " That . . . ? " and he looked back at the bog horror-stricken. " The mention of Lesseps always makes me feel depressed. I once chanced upon his son in a virgin forest in Ecuador. He was even then quite an old man and held some small appointment on some godforsaken farm. I thought of the monument to his father and said : ' Look here, do go back to Paris ; there must surely be a decent job for a man of the name of Lesseps.' ' Perhaps,' he said indifferently, ' but, young man, I should have to trek through the forest for a whole three weeks to reach the railway and I am too old for that.' He had not a penny of money. ' Shan't I drop a word to the minister in Quito ? ' I asked him. ' He should be in a position to make life easier for you out here.' The old man gave a start of alarm, and I saw that he had done with such things as ' ministers ' and ' Europe ' long ago. ' Give me a little alonal, young man,' was all he said, ' to enable me to get a bit of sleep again in spite of this infernal fever.' "

" Poor fellow," said Rosita compassionately.

Nove shrugged his shoulders. " Fame is not hereditary. We shall be at Major Lyon's bungalow in a minute."

A park opened out, more beautiful and exotic than that of the Hôtel du Parc in Cannes. Avenues of coconut palms rose as if cast in bronze, sharply outlined against the beautiful blue sky. Sparkling lawns led along the gracious sweep of the bay. The officers' wooden bungalows, fitted with wire blinds, had plenty of elbow-room. Somewhere beyond this charming bay, on which swans and pelicans ought to have been floating, lay the submarine station. And somewhere behind this beautiful park lurked the big guns.

Goehrs had to admit that the Americans, who by rights had no business to be here at all, had laid out their fortifications with an eye to the charms of the landscape that was unique.

" Hello, Major."

" Hello, Nove."

A man had come out of one of the wooden huts, jumped on to the running-board, and hung on. The car raced ahead. Down avenues. Across golf links, but they had ceased to be golf links. They were aerodromes, quite open, with seventy-five military aeroplanes. A dozen machines were cruising about in the air. The rest stood aligned in their open, gaily painted hangars, like race-horses at the starting-gate.

In the middle of the well-kept lawn of France Field was a machine as slim as a mosquito, as big as a house, quivering with eagerness to take the air under the pressure of all its engines. Its wings were a brilliant yellow. On their under-sides, a blue circle enclosing a white star with a red dot in the centre of the white star. And in black in the space between : U.S. Army. Its tail was blue. And the extreme tip of the tail was cheerfully zigzagged in red and white.

There the thing stood as though made of glass, on the lawn of a country house, so smart, so gay and improbable—a giant plaything.

"That's the biggest bomber in the Army," said Major Lyon.

For the first time he turned his head into the car. A broad-brimmed, olive-drab hat was cocked at a rakish angle on his head, dividing it into the precise proportions of scholarliness and dash that all typically good American faces have.

A dozen boys were squatting cross-legged on the lawn in front of the machine. They were wearing khaki shirts open at the neck and knickerbockers, and had round white sailor caps stuck on the sides of their neat, fresh heads.

They sat there like Buddhas—if Buddhas in this kit with such impudent eyes and a Boston accent be conceivable—and listened. They were not listening to a lecture. They were listening to the machine-gun rattle of the motor running in neutral. They were educating their auditory senses. For hours. Major Lyon gave a signal.

The motors were running at a very high number of revolutions. The scamps in the aeroplane in charge of the controls grinned all over their faces at the din. It really did roar and rattle so merrily. And the twelve boys squatting in front of it and training their ears beamed broadly amid the thunder, as did the lads in the machine. And at the same moment a puddle fifty yards behind went up into the air in spray. The exhaust had blown it away.

"That's that," said Major Lyon cheerfully, "and now you will have some ice cream and a cup of tea at my place."

His name was inscribed in big letters over his bungalow. His bungalow had the look of a club pavilion, and it was very good ice cream, and tea took exactly five minutes. Agreeable and rapid. Really very pleasant.

" Don't you think," said Nove, when they had taken their seats in the car again, "that the Yankees are living too fast ? They're wearing themselves out. Everything runs too smoothly, too rapidly, too perfectly. In three generations they'll be ready for scrapping."

" Possibly," said Goehrs. " But an army corps and a few aerodromes like that one and masses of heavy artillery and submarines and whole fleets in commission, on a strip of territory ten miles wide by forty long—that stands for a military force as concentrated as beef tea, as concentrated as the world has ever seen. That stands for the conquest of South America."

" Perhaps," said Nove, " perhaps. But then again, perhaps probably not. What do you make of it, Rosita ? "

Rosita was in her own way a beautiful girl with improbably big eyes. She was, it is true, not an open-air girl, and her figure was rather full blown, but her skin was so translucent, her colouring so delicious, and she was so enchanting in her movements and so fantastic in her languid, fiery, and exotic graciousness, that there was something fairylike about her, something rich and unreal.

She had succumbed from the moment she had first touched shore to a bad attack of melancholia. Her family had spent two years in New York and a year in Spain and Paris, and Rosita had seen enough to realize that a hell was awaiting her in Colombia.

Colombia is a big, fair, savage country and it takes two days by train to reach Bogotá—and to cover a bit of the distance in between by car and another bit on foot. Bogotá is cold, although it is almost on the equator, for it lies at a height of 8,400 feet. There are very few entertainments and very little society up there—a little painting in oils, a little golf, and still fewer picture theatres, and now and then a bull fight—and precious little freedom along with it. And at the finish, matrimony. It seemed to Rosita that life for her was over. She relapsed, the nearer they came to Colombia, into that state of inertia that overcomes all South Americans of the West Coast on approaching their native land after living in Europe. They shudder at the prospect of living in their native country, with which they are none the less in love.

" What do you make of it, Rosita ? " repeated Nove, and the way in which he threw all the stress on the " i " was very pretty. " What do you make of it ? " He was anxious

39

to wring an answer out of the intelligent young girl from Colombia.

" I think we ought to do some shopping now and then have tea at the Washington Hotel," said Rosita Patino.

THE WHISKY FRONTIER

ROSITA went shopping. Silk pyjamas for two dollars. Heavy silk embroidered kimonos with dragons and birds for four dollars. And perfumes cheaper than in Paris. Colón was a paradise without a customs office. Then, because it was so hot, they all had another ice cream at the drug store and looked about for a conveyance.

"Washington Hotel," said Nove.

" Two dollars," said the taxi-driver.

Nove waved him away.

The black chauffeur replied : " Do you expect me to drive you for nothing ? "

Nove nodded, and they drove to the Hotel Washington.

" Didn't you really give him anything ? " asked Merlezun in the hall.

"No," said Nove, "without a fare the fellow would never be allowed into the hotel grounds. But to be in the hotel grounds is to be sure of a fare if a liner does not happen to put in at that particular moment. And as at this particular moment no liner is discharging, he ought perhaps to have paid us a premium as well to get in at all. Quite a cute lad, what ? "

The Hotel Washington lay facing the sea with a lavish air, with the air of a palm grove that expands as if one of its trees were of itself an act of homage. Goehrs had read on the authority of several writers of repute that the Washington Hotel was the focus of the social world of America on its travels—and that half the world was in the habit of taking up their quarters there for months. He wanted to catch a glimpse of the Canal cocottes.

But an hour later only twenty bathers had forgathered at the swimming-pool. Simple, honest, and obviously moral folk.

" Three of them are French," said old Maizzes, who had been sitting on a bench at the bathing-pool for two hours because at his age *cocottes* interested him more than bombers. " It is a very unusual thing to come upon French people."

"Outside France," Goehrs supplemented.

40

They stayed in the water for an hour because the water was so warm that it took an hour before it began to cool them down. They then gathered on the wall above the pool.

"As a matter of fact," said Rosita, crossing her rather too plump legs, "everything that is pleasant is against the rules here. You are not allowed to spit into the water nor run into the sea—and what have you left?"

She raised both her arms in a plaintive gesture of dismay.

She was right. The hotel with its retinue of palm trees stood facing the sea very picturesquely—but the sea itself had not been included in the invitation when they built the famous swimming-pool. The pool was no bigger than the public swimming-baths of some inland town 500 miles from the sea. And a high wall, against which the sea broke, ensured its privacy against the advances of the ocean.

"Apart from that there are an infernal lot of mosquitoes," added Merlezun, with a pained glance at his snow-white skin. "And what a mob! . . ."

He was wrong, but he could not help himself. After the English, it is the French people on whose nerves travelling Americans jar most of all. He was wrong because all the people bathing and domiciled here were honest, decent folk who had come on shore from their Grace Line and United Fruit Company steamers in badly spotted white knickers and in big panama hats, and were enjoying themselves here, a trifle noisily but in a cheery, straightforward way; decent people—but anything rather than the world of fashion eminent writers had persisted in describing over and over again. Every now and then they took a flat flask from the pockets of their bathing-gowns, sent for soda water, and blended the two. They appeared to enjoy the result immensely.

"The hotel stands on the American side of the line," explained Nove with a smile, "and Prohibition, of course, holds good there. But as conditions are rather quaint here, there is nothing illegal in drinking whisky you have brought with you. Only none may be sold."

Merlezun shook his head.

"It really is a little absurd, the way the muddle has developed to keep pace with the growth of the two towns," said Nove, who was sitting on the wall like a monument of Paolino, the boxer, in his bathing-suit; "even the police are not quite sure which is Colón and which is Cristobal—what is the republic of Panama and what the republic of the U.S.A. There are streets in which alcohol may be dispensed

41

on one side of the roadway but not on the other. There are
houses where alcohol may be dispensed in the garden, but
not in the house itself. The night clubs are so laid out as
to have two exits, one into Panama, the other into the
U.S.A. That has very diverting consequences, for, if a
patrol should come along, an honest American sailor cannot
come to any harm. As a general rule the American soldiers
have drunk their pay by the fourth of every month. That
means that there is a lot of money in circulation, for a
sergeant's pay amounts to fifty-seven dollars a month.
And what a lot of stuff the fellows can put away ! When all
is said and done, every nation drinks hard, but only the
Yankees soak. So there is in reality only one frontier in
Panama—the whisky frontier. For the alleged international
frontier, is of course, a farce. Panama, with its population
of half a million, that is to say of Indians, Negroes, and half-
breeds, is really only a virgin forest State. But the Yankees'
Canal Zone, ten miles by forty long, is a genuine world
empire. Armaments, armaments, armaments—there is
nothing else here."

" So it seems to me, too," said Rosita, slowly dangling her
legs in the water preparatory to her last swim across the
pool, and she looked across to the end where a few young
flying men of the United States Army appeared among the
bathing-cabins. But she drew her legs out of the water
when Nove handed her a banana. She had hitherto sat in
a fit of dumb abstraction, and there was something of the
sadness of an animal about her melancholia, of that sorrowful inertia that appears to be innate in the soil. Even her
blue-black hair had lost its lustre and her figure had lost its
fullness. The moment she clutched the banana, Rosita
stripped off the peel with two wild movements ; her eyes
shone again entrancingly ; she tossed back her head, and
her hair began to glisten. In two bites she was half-way
through the banana.

" Nothing but soldiers," she said, and gazed around the
whole of the pool again.

" And we were trying to hunt for *cocottes*," sighed
Merlezun.

" I believe," said old Maizzes jocosely, " Rosita is the
only one in the whole place," whereupon, for all his age,
that wild little animal Rosita flung the remaining fifth of
her banana at him. Although the girl laughed, she was
furious.

" Well," said Goehrs tolerantly, " I have my suspicions

about the fat Frenchwoman in the shower bath. But for the sake of being on the safe side," he added, looking into Rosita's broad face that was beaming again, " to be on the safe side, we had better, when we get back on board, just ask Luis what he thinks about it."

Through the Panama Canal

TWO days later, Goehrs fared from the Atlantic to the Pacific through the Panama Canal.

The first white man to see the Pacific Ocean while following Columbus's track had covered this same route, though, of course, on foot.

This man had a very short but violent history. In 1510, a young ne'er-do-well, Vasco Nuñez de Balboa, arranged for his conveyance on board ship in a barrel from the island of Hispaniola. The island of Hispaniola is called Haiti to-day ; in those days most of the West Indies were known by other names than those they bear to-day—thus Cuba was in its time called " Juana " in honour of a young prince, but when the prince died without having distinguished himself the Indian name Cuba reasserted itself. Vasco Nuñez de Balboa was one of those keen, daring adventurers who, even in the second decade after Columbus's first voyage, had already pretty effectively overrun such portions of the New World as were known. As the manners and customs of these people were very unruly, the law was correspondingly severe. Vasco Nuñez was fleeing from his creditors, and death was the stake even if this flight were staged on such original lines as Vasco Nuñez was fond of.

Consequently some difficulties with the captain arose when the latter discovered a man to be the contents of the barrel he had shipped. But in the end the captain, who was planning an expedition to the Gulf of Panama, took the outlaw with him for the simple reason that the latter had already once taken part in an expedition, unsuccessful though it had proved, into these very regions. He thought the man might be of use to him. So they disembarked somewhere in the neighbourhood where the Canal has since been cut, and a few skirmishes with the natives proved that Nuñez the felon was a better leader than the man who had fitted out the expedition.

Vasco Nuñez de Balboa believed, of course, as did every one else in the world, that he had landed on the coast of

43

Asia, or at any rate that a huge tract of country, which he would have to penetrate before he could reach India, lay ahead of him. He had no idea that America had a very thin spot at this particular point. Panama at that date was as it still is to-day, an impenetrable, tropical forest with formidable swamps. But that did not prevent Balboa, after he had discovered a shrine full of gold belonging to the Cacique Dabayda, from plunging like a fool into the interior in quest of the metal. The venture with a handful of men was, of course, insane. But luck favoured Balboa.

Balboa's Spaniards were in a curious, ecstatic state. They were obsessed by a mystic devotion composed in equal parts of God and gold—that combination of which Philip II has left such an unparalleled and superhuman record in the lines of his Escorial near Madrid.

The priests who accompanied these expeditions did nothing to prevent the soldiers from enlisting on the quest for gold as for a crusade—but all the gold they found did not on the other hand prevent the soldiers from being genuinely, fanatically convinced that they were seeking this gold for their God. And here at last was a clue, unequivocal for the first time, to those lands of gold, in quest of which one expedition after the other had been sent out for the past two decades. Balboa pushed on. Since he had accidentally hit upon the narrowest spot of the continent, he did not go under but came out one day on the farther shore and saw the Pacific at his feet. Vasco had taken five and twenty days to cover a distance which the little railway, running alongside of the Canal, to-day covers in a couple of hours. He had had a terrible struggle with the Indians, swamps, and fevers, and had throughout been harassed by the notion that he was running his head into a shoreless country. And then he saw the sea.

He fell on his knees, had a tree felled, a cross fashioned of it, and the name of his king cut into the bark of another tree. Then he went down to the sea, halted his men, walked, with his sword in one hand, his shield uplifted in the other, breast-high into the water, and with this ritual took possession of that portion of the world bordering on the new ocean for the Crown of Castile.

Only five years later Vasco Nuñez de Balboa was dead. He died on the block. A year later, on the spot where he had discovered the new ocean, Panama was founded. In another few years ships were being transported in sections from Colon on the Atlantic to Panama on the Pacific.

Expeditions were fitted out from Panama to find the land of gold, Peru—and did find it. . . .

Goehrs stood on the deck of his ship, which was being towed into the first lock of Gatun at 6.30 a.m. He had heard a great deal about the operation but had never understood it when he had heard it because it had always been described with too much verbiage and with too much technical detail. What happened was simple enough. The Gulf of Panama suddenly narrowed down to a dock not much larger than the vessel herself. When the ship was inside this dock, which was closed at the far end, two huge iron gates shut behind her. She was lying as snug as in a spectacle case of steel and cement. And then the effect of a pumping action from below came into operation. The inrushing water gurgled and swirled until it had risen in the dock about twenty-five feet.

After the ship had by this method been raised by some twenty-five feet above sea-level, the huge iron gates opened majestically in front of her bows, and the ship slid into a new lock, a new spectacle case that was waiting for her at this level by virtue of the distant enormous hydraulic machinery. Again the huge gates closed behind her by electricity and the same operation proceeded—and again the ship was raised. She thus climbed some eighty to eighty-five feet by means of a lift.

Neat little electric locomotives on the right and left banks towed the vessel from lock to lock. The locomotives climbed wonderfully—like tanks, like broad stout beetles of steel that could crawl uphill vertically. After the vessel had been raised a few times in this way, she reached the elevation of the inland plateau, which was full of river beds and lakes, along which she quickly proceeded on her journey. By dint of this ingenious notion, the realization of which had cost some tens of thousands of lives and some $750,000,000, the ship set out on a five hours' course through the canals and lakes of the interior, the beauty of whose tropical luxuriance was only enhanced by a light warm rain. On the right and left banks, almost within reach of one's hand, lay the impenetrable, green, iridescent jungle, just as Balboa had seen it in his day, peopled, just as in his day, by many Indian tribes, the ruins of whose huts stood scattered about. After a short spell of this adventurous progress through the primeval forest, among climbing parasites and palm trees through mazes of islands and backwaters, the ship again came to a standstill before another lock like a well-trained

45

beast. Again the huge iron gates opened—and the ship dropped from storey to storey. The lift was going down this time. This time the water was being pumped out instead of into the spectacle cases. And finally she had come down to sea-level again and was floating in a gulf. But this time it was the Gulf of Panama. And this time it was the Pacific. And this time it was off the town of Panama that she dropped anchor.

An International Celebrity

A FEW years ago, a nice lad, Richard Halliburton by name, swam the whole length of the Canal. He reduced the Canal authorities to the verge of despair because they had to open the locks for the young man, set the giant mechanism in motion, and shift enormous volumes of water. An ordinary merchant steamer pays nearly a dollar a ton for this privilege and many of them are of anything between 8,000 and 12,000 tons. But they had to wash the youngster through because he had a permit from the Governor in a pouch round his neck and was escorted by a boat, on board of which stood a non-commissioned officer of the United States Army with his rifle at the ready on the look-out for sharks or crocodiles.

" Hold on," said the official at the first lock, and inspected the permit. " In accordance with the regulations, I have to weigh you all the same. Further, you are not allowed to be outside the boat in the locks, otherwise you will be drowned in the whirlpool of the water rushing in."

" Right."

Halliburton, who had already burnt his shoulders in the sun while swimming in Limon Bay before a pretty girl had brought him a sunshade, weighed in.

" You're the smallest craft that's ever passed through the lock," said the official. " You only weigh a fraction of a ton, and there's twenty-five cents to pay."

Halliburton paid.

He then swam through the three Gatun locks. Or rather he was rowed through. He swam with his sergeant and the loaded rifle across Gatun Lake, past the islands of Tiger Hill and Lion Hill, across the whole of the big artificial lake on the plateau of Panama, past Pena Blanca and past Buena Vista, past San Pablo and Juan Grande, through the old narrow river bed of the Rio Chagres, into the even closer narrows of Culebra Cut where the heaviest blasting had been done in the hills. He arrived swimming, with his sergeant and his rifle at the ready, to the single lock of the Pedro Miguel and was lowered to the double compartment of Miraflores lock and thence was again pumped down into the Gulf of Panama and into the Pacific.

Halliburton took quite a number of days doing it and his " story " describing his journey had continuation, thrills, and dramatic incidents. By day the sergeant, along with his rifle, held the young lady's parasol over Halliburton, and in the evening Halliburton with his sunshade, his boat, and his sergeant went ashore and spent the night on the fringe of the forest. On the morrow he rowed out to the spot where he had quitted swimming the day before—and began swimming anew. When Halliburton had left the last gate of the Miraflores lock and was swimming on close to his goal, the town of Panama, the sergeant grabbed him by the scruff of the neck and hauled him on board, for one or two giant fish of the Pacific had set their hearts on devouring the sportsman just before the completion of his tour.

Halliburton's achievement has become the epic of the Panama Canal. On the handbills and among the memorials to the tens of thousands who died on the Canal banks, Halliburton's name always crops up. Goehrs remembered standing on the spot whence Byron had swum the Dardanelles in order to repeat a classical deed in the classical spirit, supplemented by a dash of English athletic fanaticism. Goehrs knew that every century has other heroes and other conceptions of heroism. Years previously he had read a delightful book written by Halliburton at the age of eighteen when he had run away from home with a dollar in his pocket and had travelled round the world as stoker, able seaman, and anything that came along.

The book was quite attractive, but it never had the remotest prospect of ever being mentioned in the same breath with two lines of Byron. Indeed, the whole difference between the two swimming exploits is that Byron's swim across the Dardanelles became celebrated only because it was the fame of Byron's immortal spirit in general that recalled this little record ; whereas the new heroism of the American did not require a background of the spirit. Halliburton's era definitely dispensed with it. Facts were facts and records records. To be the first to swim, the first to have hit on the notion, the first to have carried it out in a sportsmanlike way. Three cheers for international celebrity. " International celebrity," thought Goehrs. " Is there anything cheaper nowadays than just that ? "

GOEHRS was confronted by the same difficulties in Panama that had met him in Colón. Here, too, a new American town had grown up on the territory of the Canal Zone beside the town of Panama, and two towns had again become inextricably tangled. The name of the American town was Balboa.

And again there was only a whisky frontier.

Old Panama was in essentials a Negro city, with girls who wore white stockings rolled up just below the knee, showing an expanse of black skin until later on it was draped by those pinks and greens such as pretty Negro girls wear all the world over. They had moreover intermarried with Chinese, Malays, Hindus, whites, Indians, and Syrians and produced an extraordinarily attractive variety of shades, eye angles, and nasal formations. In the heart of the Negro town stood the old churches ; in the streets, laid out on the lines of those in Seville and Cadiz, Negresses stood on balconies carved in the Spanish style, and in front of the houses lay piles of gold and green fruits : alligator pears, bananas, pineapples, and papayas.

An old-world Spanish town populated by the hybrids of every race. Folk who ought to have been talking Spanish but were talking with a terrific Yankee dialect. That was the Panama part of the tangled town. It encompassed the President's palace.

Goehrs looked out from the inner courtyard of the palace on to the street. He could not see anything because the bayonets of the guard of the Panamanian soldiery formed a regular grille between him and the sea. In the inner court-yard a pretty fountain was playing. In the basin of the fountain some big white cranes were standing and gazing up motionless at the Moorish decorations of the hall. A big tortoise was lying placidly among them.

Since 1903, when the country proclaimed its independence, twelve presidents have occupied this idyllic Oriental retreat and ruled over a country peopled by 50,000 whites, 35,000 Indians, 80,000 Negroes and 300,000 half-breeds, a country as big as Ireland, a country with a constitution and a National Assembly with forty-six members. . . . Twelve presidents have ruled over this idyllic spot among American troops, bombing squadrons, big-gun emplacements, and submarine stations.

People were well aware long beforehand that every one of

these presidents was going to be elected. There was no election campaign worth mentioning. There was not even any betting. The presidents were nominated by the lords of the big aeroplanes and the big guns. Infallibly as fate. And round the peaceful white cranes and the big tortoise lay the most vulnerable and most dangerous point in the whole continent.

At the same time one of the most beautiful. As the guard fell in for a minute to salute, the bayonets fell apart and Goehrs looked out from the hall of the thirteenth President for a moment. The view over the bay of Panama and the virgin forests and the mountain ranges was enchanting. More beautiful than Monte Carlo.

BALBOA

ON the other side of the whisky frontier of Panama the Americans have built a new tropical town, Balboa. A marvellous park of a tropical town with unreal-looking lawns, with parrots and syringa, with palm-bordered streets and villas in between, with bungalows and palm trees round about. Huge beautiful palms at measured intervals and a scent over all from twenty varieties of flowers, all distillng a lavish fragrance. Ebony trees, hibiscus hedges, cocoa bushes, and clumps of bamboo, and the bay in the background as on the Riviera. Though the parallel struck Goehrs as cheap, it was nonetheless apt. It was true of the softness and sweetness of the light, of the spare and disciplined strength of the palm-tree avenues, of the quivering graciousness with which this tropical scene itself revelled in its own extravagant, lucent beauty and lavished it on its inhabitants. Even the hospitals in this palm grove of a town showed like English country seats. Even the skies looked at times dull, so radiantly green, so like streaks of light were the mysterious green shadows of the lawns. And the streets were wonderfully clean-cut through these lawns.

Goehrs counted four condors and eighty vultures in the air. The club houses looked like colonial country mansions, all suffused by an intoxicating atmosphere of almost unreal lightness. Everything seemed especially made for the well-being of mankind. The headquarters of the Canal administration looked like a convalescent home. And in the heart of this park-like town were golf links, as if a golf links took no more room than a tennis court. Where people in

D

other towns are in dread of being run over, men in white knickers were wielding their golf clubs. The men in the motor cars drove in their shirt sleeves and the women discarded hats.

Goehrs could think of no other town laid out so informally, so indifferent to the limitations of workaday life, so full of everything that really brings relief from urban life. It was uncannily like a stage setting that apes reality and overdoes it. Even the fire-brigade engines, standing in open sheds, ready to dash off, looked as if they were painted. With spick and span young fire-fighters standing in front of them. In the open air riding-school horses with gleaming coats were pirouetting across the emerald lawn. And in front of the stadium, Kaffirs were exercising a team of greyhounds under mango trees in full fruit.

In all these places men had, thirty years ago, been dying of malaria like rats in the swamps. Wonderful how hard the Americans worked. No one in the world works like that to-day, thought Goehrs. But to what end ?

A CHAUFFEUR PHILOSOPHER

NEITHER Panama nor Balboa, which encircles Panama, was built on the site where the first Panama had been founded. The first Panama had been entirely destroyed one hundred and fifty years after its foundation by one of the genial buccaneers who ruled the seas like dynasts, by the Englishman, Sir Henry Morgan.

Old Panama stood a goodish distance away along the coast from the two new towns.

As Goehrs was driving past the harbour of the new Panama on his way to the old, he saw that a whole covey of shipping had been pumped through the Canal. There were two boats of the " Great White Fleet," the handsome packets of the United Fruit Company, which sail partly under the American flag, partly under that of Honduras. This turned Goehrs's thoughts on the remarkable problem of what influence such considerations as customs, tolls, and similar matters may exercise on the question of the national colours. There was a liner of the North German Lloyd, a Greek vessel, a Grace Line steamship and its Chilean competitor of the Compañía Sudamericana de Vapores, a Ford steamer, a little yacht that was throwing the lead in the bay for depth, a Norwegian merchantman, a vessel of the Dollar Line, an Italian and three British tramps, and a big English ship of the P.S.N.C.

After half an hour's run in the car the French chauffeur from Martinique pointed to the sky-line. Goehrs saw a town of mighty ruins with big square towers among which a grove of handsome palm trees had grown up.

As everywhere else in the world, the conquering race had displayed the keenest sense for natural beauty in the lay-out of their town. The site of the ruins on the coast was beautiful. The Spaniards had built here, hundreds of miles away from the mother-country on a spot they had reached through the primeval forest with sectional ships, a fortress town of titanic size such as only the Crusaders had erected in Palestine before them. They had devoted all their clerico-military architonics and æsthetic genius to this strongly fortified town, fantastic in design, incredible as an achievement.

Sir Henry Morgan, who demolished the town a hundred and fifty years after its foundation, had made a thorough job of it. He had among other things carried off a convent garrison of two hundred and fifty virgins, but he had failed to destroy a number of the towers.

Beyond it on the beach, palms dropped their coconuts into the sea in sheer exuberance of wealth and, farther out in the bay, lay little islands with fascinating sugarloaf hills. At his feet, Goehrs saw an army of ants that in its march had unconcernedly taken its Grand Trunk road straight through the old castle. Every ant, with head erect, was bearing a fragment of green leaf that was exactly ten times the size of the ant itself. It was about the same thing as if Goehrs had loaded one of the town walls, the chauffeur from Martinique, and the car on his head and had carried them back to Panama. The parallel, it is true, only held good in regard to the relative expenditure of energy, so Goehrs told himself, in fact it did not hold good at all. For his strange porterage, assuming he could have done it, would have been purposeless, whereas the work of the ants was subject to some strictly logical or biological law or other.

The spectacle gave the chauffeur from Martinique an idea, too, but a different one from Goehrs's. He had a dog in the car, a beautiful collie. He ran off and fetched the dog.

" He is so fond of ants," he explained, and the dog did in fact at once set about licking up a part of the army with his tongue.

"Extraordinary!" said Goehrs, flabbergasted.

"Why, sir?" the chauffeur asked. "Everything that has to do with food is purely a question of the imagination. At one time this is normal, at another that. In my young days no one in Martinique would have eaten a banana. Bananas were only fit food for pigs. It was only when they hit upon the idea in Europe of importing bananas that people in Martinique began gingerly to eat them. If Europe were to conceive the notion of importing ants for food to-day, I assure you not a soul in Martinique would refuse to eat ants with relish."

The driver was an old man and had seen neither Paris nor Europe. But, although unsophisticated, he had imbibed in French Martinique that half devil-may-care, half philosophical spirit which even bootblacks acquire in a French atmosphere with their mothers' milk. He stood there laughing, with a cigarette in his mouth and stroking his dog's neck. Goehrs, gazing at him, wondered how many people outside of Europe talked of Europe in exactly the same way as Europeans usually did of exotic countries.

"Where did you get that beautiful dog?" he asked, and stepped a little to one side because a few coconuts were descending from overhead.

"From Admiral Byrd's uncle—you know, Byrd the airman. He lives in Costa Rica, and has a kennel of them," said the chauffeur. "I was with him and worked for him."

Goehrs inhaled the aroma of sea and vegetation that clings about this district with almost velvet voluptuousness to the full extent of his lungs.

"Well, he made you a present of a beautiful beast in that dog," he said enthusiastically, studying its faultless head and the lines of its body.

"I bought him," answered the driver, "and paid for him. The Yankees don't make presents, sir. And even if you were to save their lives, they don't give anything away."

COLOMBIA

GOEHRS had seen Rosita, together with her mother, her cousin and her brother-in-law Hernández, her six sisters, and Luis safely into the train at Buenaventura. Buenaventura is the harbour that Colombia, which touches the shores both of the Pacific and the Atlantic Oceans, pushes out into the Pacific. It is the port for a big stretch of coastline, the port for a country that is two and a half times as big as Germany.

Two days ago the boat had sailed from Panama, but how great was the change already !

At the sight of this harbour Goehrs had understood why Rosita had looked miserable as she stared out of the train. Buenaventura was a hole of a place with Negroes in galvanized iron sheds who played billiards, but until recently had had no electric light. And the train that was to take Rosita and the ten other members of her family more than three hundred miles inland to the capital, Bogotá, at an altitude of 8,400 feet, did not even run through. In the event of bad weather or a landslide, Rosita would have to cross a dangerous pass on muleback or on foot.

Goehrs recalled that members of the diplomatic corps had at an earlier date often had a sixty days' journey before they reached the capital. It befell one man to chance to see a hat on the left of his path. Although the ground was very swampy he dismounted and picked up the curious hat and, to his astonishment, a handful of hair with it. He tugged and a head emerged.

The head said : " Thanks, sir. I got entirely bogged here. I am on my way to Bogotá. Please extricate me entirely." The man was pulled out completely and stood for a while in some embarrassment. After a while he said : " Would you kindly help me to get out my horse as well ? It's still in there."

If, however, one should wish to reach Bogotá from the other side, from the ports on the Atlantic, from Barranquilla or Cartagena, he has, if he does not fly, to entrust himself to a river steamer that in maybe ten, in maybe twenty days would deposit him somewhere near Bogotá. How long it takes depends on the head of water in the river—and that is entirely on the knees of the gods.

Hence the long way round through the Panama Canal is still the shortest to Bogotá. For from Buenaventura the journey, after all, only takes two days, with a bit in between by car, by mule, or on foot. So Bogotá still remains the most quaintly isolated capital in the world.

Rosita had a certain amount of justification for feeling depressed. She found a little comfort in the thought that all her friends, male and female, would come to the railway stations to welcome her. For, of the eight million population of this tropic and mountain land, probably only 50,000 were really white, and these 50,000 knew one another well and did not mistake one another for Negroes, half-breeds, and Indians.

53

Rosita had departed by the train with her family, waving her pocket handkerchief like a lasso for a while, and Goehrs was now sitting on the gallery of the Buenaventura Hotel with Rosita's friend, the harbourmaster. And with Señor Correa, a botanist from Ecuador, and a Mr. Wells, agent for Goodyear tyres in Colombia, an American.

It was low tide, and the sea had laid half the bay bare. The mangrove swamps facing Buenaventura stank atrociously. They lay, facing the hotel and the gallery surrounding the hotel, like a marsh on which since time immemorial the little narrow Indian canoes were drawn up.

" How do you manage to get on with a Colombian army 6,000 strong ? " Goehrs asked the harbourmaster, who sat beside him with a glass of whisky at his elbow. His slack, yellowish face was dominated by an eagle's beak of a nose and in his white drill suit with the big Colombia cockade in his cap he made a glorious patch of colour.

" Why shouldn't we manage ? " asked the harbourmaster in his turn. " We are on good terms with our neighbours."

" So every one is. But your neighbours are not, as a rule, with you."

" In our case your amiable views are mistaken," replied the other with some amusement. " There really is no friction. Chile has come to terms with Peru, Peru is on a friendly footing with Bolivia, and Bolivia has come to a settlement with Paraguay. What more do you want ? "

Goehrs knew that history was not made on such sentimental lines as Rosita's friend imagined and he missed any mention of Ecuador. But he emptied his glass in silence. It was beyond everything else a relief to him to strike a continent where, by way of a change, there was no talk, either in mysterious whispers or in dramatic secrecy, of a coming war with any rival, but where war was regarded as a ludicrous and silly business.

" Buenas tardes."

" Buenas tardes."

The harbourmaster got up and went down to the piers to be taken across to a vessel that had just dropped anchor in the roads and was hooting for all she was worth. Shortly afterwards his motor boat shot out with the horizontal yellow, blue, and red stripes of its flag fluttering from its stern. The same colours as Venezuela and Ecuador, except that the Venezuelan flag had some stars in its centre, while in the Colombian flag the yellow panel was as broad as the blue and the red put together. The three States had in the

HARBOUR TOWN IN COLOMBIA.

first instance, a century ago, during the revolt against Spain, made up a single realm, but shortly afterwards, still a century ago, had split into three countries.

"On what terms is Colombia with Panama?" asked Goehrs after a pause during which the white-jacketed hotel waiters had turned on a gramophone in the gallery that all but outbid the bellowing steamer outside.

It had struck Goehrs that the harbourmaster, in his general declaration of peace, had omitted to mention the latter State, which existed barely thirty years and had come into existence thanks to a revolution financed by the United States, in the course of which Panama had rather violently and on somewhat strained terms parted company from Colombia. Goehrs thought that he could in this case realize the feelings of Colombia, especially as he knew by experience with what almost feminine supersensitiveness the nationals of South American republics cherish their national pride. He therefore put the question about the terms on which Colombia might be with Panama purely as a matter of form.

"On very good terms," said the American to his amazement.

"Really!" said Goehrs, and looked across with a sceptical smile to the little Ecuadorian, behind whose spectacles a bright Indian eye sparkled. Dr. Correa had been sent by his Government to New York and Europe for two years for the purpose of study.

"Certainly," said the little professor. "Very good. After all Colombia has received compensation to the tune of many millions of dollars from the United States."

"But one does not settle a point of honour in that way."

"Oh, yes, one does in the long run," said Mr. Wells, crossing his legs.

"First of All, a Refrigerator"

"JUST try one of these," said the little professor after a while. "They are uncommonly fine. They are called aguacates, or avocados." He cut a big fruit like a pear in half and removed the thick kernel. Then he scooped out the soapy flesh after mixing it with pepper and salt and oil and vinegar. "Mangoes are rather small in these parts, but the pineapples are very fine. The sweetest in the world grow in Ecuador. Make a note of the name. They are called piña there. That is a chirimoya," he pointed to a green thing that looked like an artichoke; "it is ice cream to the life. True, the subtropical variety is better than the local tropical kinds. But the best after all are aguacates. In Peru they call them paltas."

"What is the population of Buenaventura really?" asked Goehrs, who was afraid lest, having mounted his hobbyhorse, the professor would continue to ride it.

"Ten thousand," replied Dr. Correa.

"If you include the cemeteries," laughed the American. "All figures of this kind are only estimates. And people display a wonderful imagination in estimates."

"That is so," said Correa, "but the main point is that it is possible to reach Bogotá nowadays without dying on the road." Correa was going to pay a visit to Bogotá when the next train left in three days' time. "Last time I went from Cartagena—from the Atlantic side. The boat took thirty days. And the fare was two hundred dollars."

"A rather inaccessible capital," said Mr. Wells, "but attractive, very attractive. Quite black with persons by the way. The Church has the last word in Colombia on almost everything. But there are golf links and tennis courts, too, up there with ample room for its population of 200,000 and over a dozen music halls. And some quite nice old houses and even a few new ones now. But this port—this port here is a scandal whether it's old or new. It will only grow into a proper harbour when we take it in hand. Buenaventura will then be the finest port on the West Coast and will eat everything else up. I guess we in New York have given Colombia credit enough to justify us in taking over Colombia just as we've taken over Panama. The Colombians could, of course, go on hoisting and pulling down their flag the same as to-day; it doesn't matter a hoot to us. I don't believe the Colombians would really dislike being swallowed up. And why not? Our administration would mean peace and quiet—no revolutions—and ready money.

He crumpled up his straw and wound it round his fingers.

"Do you know how the Yankees would 'make' Colombia?" Dr. Correa asked sarcastically. "They would first of all install a big refrigerator for their drinks. Then golf links. They would then exterminate malaria on the coast by flooding it with American oil—and then they would build convenient motor roads and club houses."

"Sure thing," smiled Mr. Wells agreeably, "and then they would send a few brainy people along who would erect real storage docks and would regulate the import trade, then exploit the country on an intensive scale, and finally in

56

their great big trading business buildings would turn out a hundred times more than these monkeys in their sheds do."

Mr. Wells squeezed the skin of his empty aguacate until the skin writhed like twisted rubber in his grip.

" Yes," he said grimly, " before the war you, all of you, laughed at the Yankees ; you took them all for eccentric, comic characters. The United States is the power whose decision goes to-day, not only in the President of Panama's policy. It decides what is going to happen in Europe as well. Europe herself is half American nowadays."

" We certainly have not very much money left," said Goehrs glumly, " and you may be right, Mr. Wells, as far as trade and industry and one or two other things are concerned. But there are still things that, in the long run, cannot be settled on a cash basis."

" Don't overestimate those things," said the American.

" I won't," said Goehrs with a smile, and got up.

He really did not overestimate anything that went to constitute the real significance of Europe. Nor did he, God knows, overestimate the people with the refrigerators who figured out a country and its people like a guano bed before they took it over as a latter day " conquista." He honestly did not overestimate these methods.

Four Indian Canoes

GOEHRS went down to the cement tank lying close beside the hotel in the reek of the mangroves. It had been built as a trap for the sea. The sea had meanwhile receded half a mile or so, but the sea water was retained in the swimming-bath until the following morning. So Goehrs was able to have his swim. The hotel was really a luxurious establishment for this Negro village, but if the Yankee should prove right in his reading of future history, it would rank as a primitive hamlet in twenty years' time. Refreshèd by his bath, Goehrs walked up and down the wooden gallery on the first floor. He lit a cigarette and seated himself on the railing.

It was half-past five. It was by this time getting on for midnight in Europe. Buenaventura was only a few degrees away from the equator, where the sun has had enough of it at six o'clock. The sun was going down into the sea. The sky was actually ablaze. The misty patches beyond were a bright gold, in between an almost hard turquoise. The virgin forests of Colombia on either shore of the gulf extended their vivid verdure as far as the eye could reach. The forests were so green that the palm trees towering above them looked dull. Only the crescent of white beach was bright. The native huts and the canoes, drawn up on it, stood out from it like insubstantial delicate shadows.

Close behind, the mountains of Colombia began to rise, deep blue, shimmering, ever loftier. They were mysteriously interlaced with broad streamers of white mist. Then these ribands began to glow, green one moment, red the next, then purple. It was breath-taking. In between a beautiful, broad rainbow glowed motionlessly.

The virgin forest zones of the coast remained a brilliant green amid the uncanny quick changes of the evening light. An indescribable feeling of happiness and of restfulness radiated from this green stillness, a sense of bliss that almost made the heart it gripped ache. Inland, above the hundreds of pointed, purple mountain tops, thunderstorms that never reached the coast were raging. Their lightnings never reached the gold of the sunset but their pale shadows hovered like dragon shapes for a while over the gulf and dissolved at length into the purple of the last streak of daylight, of that royal sheen of gold that stands for twilight in the tropics.

At this brief moment an ordinary freighter of the P.S.N.C., with a brown crew in white sleeveless jerseys, low cut at the throat, drifted into the bay from the roads like a fairy barque, and its approach at this particular moment seemed to be at once the weirdest and the most delicate thing imaginable. At last, when the light was, for two or three heartbeats, mother-of-pearl, four Indian canoes laden with turtles that were turned over on their backs flitted across the bay. The slim bronze figures of the Indians, who stood erect as they paddled, vanished with the last glimmer of light, as though blotted out. Night had fallen.

Goehrs went quickly to his room.

He now heard the mosquitoes buzzing everywhere, reacting to the stroke of twilight as if to a concerted signal. Goehrs took a gramme of quinine and went down into the hall. All the windows were wide open. So there was a hint of a draught. To the clamour of the gramophone and under the caress of the zephyr, Goehrs pondered over the Indians for a long time. The features of the Indians encountered him here from every face that was not negroid. They had not been exterminated here as in North America. They had been absorbed.

58

That explained a great many things in favour of, and a great many against South America.

The Panama Hat Industry

GOEHRS was even more exercised in his mind about this problem when a week later he reached Ecuador. Ecuador was a State lying on the equator. Hence its name. Ecuador was a State lying south of Colombia. It was perhaps half the size of Colombia, perhaps only a quarter—that, by reason of certain remarkable circumstances, not to be determined offhand. Ecuador blazoned some rather striking things in its coat of arms : the sun, the first steamer to serve the State, the chimborazo, one or two constellations, the condor, and the fasces—emblems of enterprise, of good order, of imagination, of nature, and of progress.

Goehrs happened to be in a little town, Monte Cristi. This town was one morning made famous all over the world by Edward VII at a watering-place in Bohemia. Monte Cristi was, when Goehrs was there, made up of a couple of hundred houses. The houses started at a height where houses elsewhere usually stop, mounted on four very tall tree trunks. These lofty bungalows were perched precariously as though on four toothpicks and were furthermore woven of bamboo—as light as paper.

From a distance it looked like a Japanese dream town. It rarely rained and it was very hot, for the town lay cosily close to the equator, and the town lacked shade. It procured shade by building its houses on piles—and among the piles, black pigs with long aristocratic faces, donkeys, and calves lay in shadow and in comfort, while the bamboo huts swayed to the breeze overhead. The town was hedged in by a jungle of palm trees, cacti, and bush, and this jungle was overrun by a convolvulus, which clutched everything, swamped everything, and penetrated everything, and like a sister of the lianas smothered the cacti, the palm trees, and the swaying bamboo huts in a sea of flowers.

From the bamboo balcony of the bamboo hut on which he was standing, Goehrs looked up the mountains, where the green tropical floodtide of vegetation flowed up to Quito, the capital, to almost Alpine heights and made it a tropical and at the same time a tempered paradise on the equator. Then Goehrs turned round and went back into the interior of the hut.

In the empty main room an Indian woman was sitting on

a wooden saddle. On the floor in front of her she had a hat, as round as a top hat, the edges of which still consisted of thousands of silky straw fibres. She was working at one of those hats that Edward VII had made famous and are known as panamas, although they are made in Ecuador.

Goehrs carefully studied the way in which they are made.

The woman was leaning with her head bent down low to her knees. Her breasts, supported by a wooden strut, were pressed up almost to her shoulders. And thus, in an almost horizontal pose, lying in the saddle as if at a gallop, she was plaiting the hat over a wooden form on the floor in front of her.

The hat was on the floor because the straw had to be kept moistened while it was being plaited. The woman wove the thousands of silky threads with the marvellous dexterity of a piano-player, dampening the straw out of a cup and weaving it with the same movement. For this she had to adopt a position with a cramped chest and a head bent below the hips that was humanly unnatural.

In one corner of the room hung a hammock, in which her sister was swinging. She was having a rest. Another sister was working in each of the other rooms.

" How long does a hat like that take you ? "

The woman did not look up.

" A month and a half."

" How many hours a day ? "

" From seven in the morning to ten at night."

" What do you earn a day ? "

" A sucre." (Not quite a shilling.)

Goehrs remembered that panama hats figured on the list of exports to the value of between $750,000 and $1,000,000. He knew that the best panama hats, such as the one on which the woman was engaged, fetched anything between a hundred and two hundred dollars ; in fact, that there were some that cost five times that amount. Goehrs knew that all these hands belonged to an export agent ; he saw that these conditions of work, the roughriding of Indian women, meant one of the most terrible postures in which a human being was ever forced to work. It was the perfect treadmill ; forced labour that wrecked the lungs quickly ; it was unscrupulous, mean brigandage.

Goehrs picked up one of the hats. It might have been made of silk. He could have put it in his breast pocket like a pocket handkerchief.

There was no furniture in the house, only three beds and

60

a table in one corner. A bit of string held a big round crab tied by one of its legs to a leg of the table. Some Indian children with slanting black eyes and copper-coloured hair were playing with the crab.

In every house of Monte Cristi, in the same ghastly fashion, panama hats were being solemnly woven at the height of the tree tops in rocking bamboo huts.

The Indians rarely had a red skin. Their complexion was lighter, bronze, yellowish, brown—with here and there a light copper tinge. They had, to some extent, a Spanish strain. They one and all had slanting eyes and looked for all the world exactly like Mongols. Quite different from anything Goehrs had imagined they would look like.

When Goehrs drove to Manta to take ship thence to Guayaquil, he saw the whole district swarming with them. They were trotting through the bush on little donkeys.

Goehrs drove to Manta in an antediluvian Ford. A little Indian boy stood on the left and a little Indian boy on the right running-board. They held on by gripping the door and, while Goehrs raced through ponds, through sandpits, across dried river beds, upon impassable tracks, the Indian boys gave the convoys of donkeys they encountered on the road (more imaginary than real) a kick to drive them to one side. That appealed to them as a great lark. As they had bare feet, it did not inconvenience the donkeys.

Whenever the pitfalls in the road became impossibly obstructive, the provincial authorities had had them patched with the shells of the tagua or ivory nut. The tyres gripped this improvised surface excellently well. The tagua nut, together with cocoa, coffee, and panama hats represented one of the principal exports of Ecuador. The kernel of the nut looked like ivory when it was polished, and many a man, without being aware of the fact, is wearing these kernels elaborated as buttons on his coat.

Goehrs reached Manta in the thick of a swarm of Indians on galloping donkeys. Manta was Monte Cristi on a big scale, planted on tall toothpicks on the beach. The vultures came down vertically out of the sky and walked the streets as scavengers. They cleared up everything there was and had their regular hours.

The bay was beautiful and southern, overflowing with an exuberant green. Flocks of black pelicans rose constantly from the water, circling round once or twice and looking incredibly comic with their highbrow heads darting down, alert as falcons, to catch their fish.

ago. And many of the countries, bordering on ours, are very vain. For the sake of their prestige they paint half a State that does not belong to them at all on to their own. The small folk are exactly the same. Even if they can neither read nor write, they will paint the biggest national coat of arms on their wretched fishing smacks."

" But your constitution provides that every one has to be able to read and write," said Goehrs, who was annoyed that Urquiza only referred to the vanity and lust for prestige on the part of other States, while his own State allocated to itself tracts of country that could by no possibility belong to it.

" Don't be so pedantic," replied Urquiza nonchalantly. " We have had twelve constitutions in one century. One of them stipulated that every citizen was to be Roman Catholic."

" Then are schools really established everywhere ? "

" I believe so," said Urquiza. " But the Indians prefer sucking sugar cane to attending them."

" Pity for the Indians."

" Why ? " asked Urquiza. " They make quite good fishermen."

Urquiza's brain always seemed to be busy with some other subject. They finished their coffee, went out of doors, and took their seats in the middle of the street in basket chairs in front of the lamentable erection that for some unknown reason calls itself the Hotel Ritz.

Goehrs looked meditatively down the street. He had been strolling about Guayaquil for the last three days and marvelling. Along the sea front ran a pretentious promenade, but the town itself only boasted a few asphalt streets with a drainage system. The rest of the streets were nothing better than picturesque swamps. In the middle of the boulevards motor cars climbed dunes covered with six-foot grass, like tanks, clawed their way down again, and then tried another dune. On top of which, these streets were unlit at night. For a city with a population of 100,000, extremes met with startling abruptness ; the Middle Ages with modernity ; squalor with capital expenditure. Outside the attractive hospitals lay deep, swampy marshes, reeking cesspools lay round the new villas, and beside attractively dressed ladies almost naked Indian children disported themselves complacently. In the shops painted plaster-of-Paris busts of doubtful Tyrolese origin were on sale for ninety dollars, and in other shops pictures of all the saints in the world were displayed on the friendliest terms with anatomical diagrams of the human frame.

INDIAN HUTS IN ECUADOR.

Nor was life easy for the townsfolk. While the villa quarter was plunged in the mangrove swamp of the malaria zone, the cemeteries lay on the rising ground to enable the dead rather than the quick to have the benefit of the sea breezes. The cemeteries were redolent of the pomp of old Spain : glorious avenues of majestic palm trees ; baroque vaults like the portals of churches, in which the dead in lead coffins were stacked in two storeys above one another, and side by side by the hundreds. In this country with five inhabitants to the square mile, land was obviously too expensive. They buried their dead above ground, and the sweetish smell that corpses and flowers have in common floated over the palm trees on which the black vultures were perching silently and moodily.

"Just as well," said Goehrs, "that there is nothing going on and so we cannot go out ; otherwise we should be breaking our necks."

"The town is in a transition stage," said Urquiza languidly. "In five years Guayaquil will be a delightful town."

Since Urquiza had had the soil of Ecuador under his feet, he had become a changed man. Hitherto Urquiza had been very critical of Ecuador. Now he insisted on admiration only. He had lost his sense of proportion, had shed his cynicism, and was now just like all the rest of his fellow-countrymen who used to strike him as so comic.

"The times," said Urquiza, "are really over when people poked fun at Ecuador. There was indeed a time when there were only ten ladies' hats and three fireplaces in Quito, the capital, and when a beaver of the Louis Philippe era cost five English pounds sterling. The young people nowadays play tennis and go for picnics with their friends just as if they were living in Europe. And the present President is one of the few really clean men there are in South America."

Goehrs knew that any young man who was seen twice in the company of a young girl was morally bound to marry her, and that a young man who had seduced a girl was bound under quite other than moral suasion to marry her—and finally that a young man who was seen in the company of a lady of not quite unequivocal reputation was ruined. What was the matter with Urquiza to talk rubbish like that ? But he continued to gape up at the sky.

"What about your own plans, Urquiza ?" Goehrs asked.

"The country has struck a streak of bad luck. I met two of my friends to-day who had come back from Paris, one because his cocoa plantation was being ravaged by the blight, the other because his plantations were swarming with crocodiles and he was no better off."

" But you haven't any plantations," said Goehrs. He had no great sympathy to waste on men who lounged about Paris while the Indians were working on their plantations at twopence a day at the risk of being devoured by crocodiles. " You haven't got any plantations, Urquiza," he repeated.

Urquiza beckoned to a waiter and had his legs sprayed with Flit. A cloud of petrol vapour enveloped him for a second. He then put his hand in his pocket and gave a coin to an individual that had crawled on all fours out of the blackness of the street into the zone of light round the basket chairs.

" I ? " said Urquiza, and for the first time looked the other in the face. " I failed to raise the money I want for my mining deal in Paris and, if I fail to raise it here, I shall buy two mules and go into the mountains and put a bullet through my brains."

He twitched his left eye like a hen.

" By the way, be careful with matches. They have a monopoly. You might be held up and searched, and, if you should have any matches or oil lighters about you, the fines are very heavy. The firm with the contract demands these barbarous methods and our Government—but it would be a mistake to tell you that because you might be making notes of it. They ought not to admit writers into a country that is undergoing the throes of transition. Do you know what Mexico did when Blasco Ibañez proposed to visit Mexico ? Mexico offered Blasco Ibañez money if he would stay away and not write. . . ."

THE QUALITY OF THE RACE

NOTHING was further from Goehrs's thoughts than to be fatuously facetious at the expense of countries that a century ago had had the misfortune to take over, together with their freedom, the heritage of centuries of mal-administration. As long as South America belonged to them, say for some three hundred years, the Spaniards had segregated it from the rest of the world with asbestos, fire, and fortifications. South America was a colony for the purposes of exploitation only. The Spaniards admitted no one and let no one out without having passed him through a pretty fine sieve, and South America was not permitted to trade except with Spain.

Even Alexander von Humboldt, who a century ago had himself reached Quito, the capital of Ecuador (except that the country was not called Ecuador at the time), by an adventurous route, had needed not only the good offices of a very powerful Spanish minister, but the introductions of a number of foreign diplomats to procure his passport for South America at all. South America had endured this state of being a Spanish penal colony for exactly as long as history in general has put up with like conditions. When the French Revolution broke out, the blaze spread to South America, and in the course of the long wars in the early years of the nineteenth century the South American provinces rid themselves of their Spanish administrative officials and made themselves independent. Please note, Spaniards, Spanish half-breeds, and Indians expelled the European Spaniards. So far South America had had only one galaxy of heroes, to wit the contemporaries of Columbus, Balboa, Pizarro, Valdivia and the rest of the discoverers, conquerors, and Indian butchers—all three occupations amounting to much the same thing. In the struggle at the beginning of the nineteenth century against the Spanish mother-country and its governors, the insurgent Spanish colonists set up a second galaxy of heroes, generals such as Bolívar, Sucre, and San Martin.

After the Wars of Liberation the several Spanish administrative districts suddenly cropped up as independent States. Things did not develop quite as smoothly as might appear from the map to-day. States such as Colombia, Venezuela, and Ecuador were one State to begin with ; Bolivia too was united with Peru. But in due course they fell apart.

In any case States suddenly arose that had previously never aspired to the honour. Their sense of nationality is only a century old. All the States arose on a common basis —on a very thin ruling caste of Spanish immigrants. So thin was this veneer that the big battles of the Wars of Liberation were often fought with a few hundred men on either side.

The Spanish immigrants, more especially in the early days, had been quite immune from every kind of prejudice, inter-married with the Indians—so freely that there are probably not any well-established families without some Indian blood. The whole population of the west and north consists mainly of half-breeds and Indians.

Since the Spaniards had, in the several parts of South America, intermarried with different Indian tribes, and as, in this land which contains all the climates of the world, they had developed on different lines, great differentiations—differentiations of character, of language, and of initiative—were bound to arise between the several countries, though they were no greater than the differentiations that obtained between, say, the Germanic peoples at the time of the Thirty Years' War. Even if the South Americans loathe one another, they are none the less the same race with the same language—even if with varying dialects of it. It was, however, on these shades of difference that all sorts of issues hinged, more especially nearly all the quarrels, wars, and troubles that had occurred.

Goehrs had observed that all South Americans became bitter as soon as there was any allusion to the admixture of the Indian strain. They slurred it over in some embarrassment because they knew they were all more or less guilty on this count. In doing so they acted very strangely. It was the most crucial problem of South America. It was a problem in which Goehrs was keenly interested. For whether South America was going to play a great part in the world or not depended on the race inhabiting it—not on its mineral or vegetable resources.

Of what was this race capable and of what was it not ?

Goehrs was aware that there were people who condemned the half-breed race root and branch. And on the other hand there were people who maintained that out of this intermingling of Indian heroism with Spanish daring the new heroic race of the earth would spring.

It was precisely this that made Goehrs thoughtful when he compared the streets of Guayaquil with the demeanour of the men who lived at their ease in Paris while the Indians, whom no one ever thought of treating otherwise than as niggers, went about their work in conditions that were damnably akin to slavery.

Was this thin layer of half-breeds and this thin veneer of white men capable of genuinely creative initiative ? Had they the capacity for moulding and conserving States ? Or would this source of initiative be discovered one of these days in the lower Indian layer that still made, in the main, "quite good fishermen," cattle herders, plantation hands, and pack animals ?

Or would the mystic force that avails to elevate a people, not come at all—and would the work of development simply be taken in hand by the Yankees ?

How was Goehrs to form an opinion when everything
68

throughout the country was still in a state of topsy-turvydom ? There was no more a social problem than there was a definite policy on the part of the ruling caste towards social questions. The country was one of illimitable possibilities ; politically it was in a state of chaos and geographically it was a fairy story. There were people who assessed its population at three and a half millions, and there were others who claimed that the birds and the crocodiles must have been included in this total and that it amounted to perhaps a third. A country that rose from the tropical to the arctic zone and, at an altitude of 9,000 feet, had plantations in lieu of snow. A country that did not even offer its millionaires in Guayaquil the luxury of a motor road, but, to make up for it, had a glorious coastline which remained inaccessible because, over an expanse of some thirty miles, it consisted of swamp, however picturesquely the palm trees might be growing in it.

For the entertainment of its inhabitants there remained a picture palace, a little tennis, no golf, and perhaps a little yachting. But plenty of malaria and yellow fever to counterbalance it.

The climate on the coast was awful. Office hours were from eight until eleven and from one to six—with a stout railing round the cash desk. From one until six—that means until nightfall. Work all through the hours of tropical heat. When with the dark it became cooler, there was nothing to do except go to bed. For the employees life held no further prospect beyond the hope of earning some money and of keeping their health. The odds were against either.

THE TELEGRAM

THE morning Goehrs intended to start for Peru he tried to hand in a cable. People, cabling from South America to Europe, usually make use of a code. There were hundreds of codes, official codes and private codes. These private codes are so cleverly compiled that one word might convey five sentences. For the rates were very high—more particularly for codes—and every one cherished the secret ambition of wording his cables in such a way that they read like telegrams in clear and not in the considerably more expensive codes. For no writer in the world is paid at such high rates per word as the cable companies for telegrams in code.

On the other hand there were cables the cable companies had arranged—cheap telegrams that took two or three days and were called week-end telegrams or L.C.O. or L.C.W., but the use of code words was prohibited. And every one handing in a cable of this description had to declare in what language his message was drafted—for the purposes of checking because there were, of course, many languages in the world the clerk did not know.

Goehrs drafted his cable in code, which he wanted to send L.C.O., but put it into his pocket again on the protest of the clerk at the counter. He turned away to write out another.

"Why don't you simply go to another counter and declare on your form that it is written in Bulgarian? There isn't a soul who knows Bulgarian here," said a man at his elbow who was sending off a despatch.

"I should not care to do that," said Goehrs, tearing up his first telegram.

"That is very decent of you," said the young man beside him. "Nor should I care to do it, but a lot of people do. It certainly cannot be right to defraud these confiding people."

"Certainly not."

The young man told Goehrs that, when President Hoover paid his visit to Ecuador, the President of Ecuador had some difficulty in carrying on a conversation with him, because he did not speak Spanish and the Ecuadorian did not know English. But both of them spoke German.

Goehrs was unable to check this story, but it appealed to him. It appealed to him in general to have found a continent after the many countries he had visited, where, for the first time after the war, German counted for something.

"The President is a very decent man—and that says a good deal for a South American President. He was a surgeon, and it is still the fashion to call him in to operate."

The young man accompanied Goehrs in the direction of his ship.

"How many Germans are there in Guayaquil?"

"About eighty."

"Decent club?"

"I don't know."

"What do you mean?"

"I was not invited to become a member," said the young man. "I am a Jew."

THE BANANA BOATS

GUAYAQUIL lay some thirty miles beyond the bar that interposed at the mouth of the River Guaya between it and the sea. The shipping had to cover thirty

70

miles upstream after waiting at the bar for high tide, and only small craft and freighters could do it.

The river was delightful.

Goehrs's ship lay off the market place. The market was a wooden erection built down to the river in tiers. All the fruits of the tropics were stacked on its broad terraces—chirimoyas and paltas, bananas and pineapples, melons and oranges—and unfolded all the wealth that colours ranging between gold, red, and green can display when they ripen in a tropical climate. All the sailing boats coming downstream from the interior of Ecuador laden with fruit make fast to these timber terraces on the river. They were swarming with parrots flitting and chattering among the fruit and the sails.

Over the banana boats hung broad awnings so loosely stretched that it looked as if even the sails had dropped off to sleep in the heat of the sun. When a pitch on the terraces above was sold out, files of Indians appeared with loads of fruit on the swaying gangways between the boats and the shore and carried them up. When they returned and had finished their job, they almost always plunged into the river and swam about among the bamboo rafts with water flashing like silver from their bronze skins.

Goehrs spent hours watching the broad river.

Its water was soft and rapid. It was yellow one moment, purple the next, green a third. And on the tropical gentleness of its iridescent waters little miracles floated past. Incessantly, all day long, little meadows of exquisite beauty would float past—little meadows, self-supporting, fertile as hothouses, and so vividly green that they might have been made up of delicate green flames. They passed all through the night, too, like green, glittering ice floes, from Ecuador down the Guaya into the Pacific.

On his arrival, Goehrs had spent two nights on the river and another two off the bar on his departure. These days were among the most restful of his life. The moon was shining ; the stars were flat and deep and hung very gently over the water. The primeval forests gleamed in an almost blue light under the rays of the moon. These nights were of an infectious charm. They were immune from the cruel magic which nights in the tropics often breathe ; they were immune from supersensual spells of splendour and phantasmagoria. Theirs was a gentler magic of mystery and melancholy ; tender and seductive and unutterably strange. During the daytime tropical rain would occasionally fall for half an hour and envelop everything in dense water as if the rain were a fog. It conveyed that impression. But it was fog of a different kind. It was a warm fog that looked like mother-of-pearl. For months afterwards this glamour of the landscape through the fog of rain seemed to Goehrs like the only dream without desire he had ever known in his life.

Just before the ship cleared, a square banana shelter of bamboo, which had been rigged up in the bows in an hour, was being packed. When the boat hooted a signal of departure, twenty Indians rushed back on board their lighter, to which a narrow swaying gangway led from the boat. Only one man insisted on making his way up it. He was not a pure-bred Indian. He was a Zambo, a lad crossed with a Negro strain. He was carrying a bough of some two hundred bananas, in three clusters round the stalk, on his head. He was naked to his middle and only wore a loincloth round his hips. As, to the hooting of the steamer, he rushed up the gangway with his arms raised high above his head to steady the splendid green bundle of fruit, his skin shone in African and in Indian bronze. His bearing was in every way distinguished. It was so free, so naturally beautiful, so young and yet so tragic ; it was so gallantly impetuous and yet so gentle at the same time that it impressed Goehrs as the one and only movement in accord with the scene and the brilliancy of its atmosphere, both of which he was inhaling with a deep sense of blessedness. As the ship rode over the bar and headed for the Pacific, another movement recurred to his mind.

Between Panama and Buenaventura Rosita had been eating a mango on the deck. She was holding the half-squeezed rind in her left and the sticky yellow pulp of the fruit in her right hand. She called after Goehrs, who was running down the companion to his cabin : " I should like to give you my hands to take down for a wash." Rosita had made a movement that raised her firm little hands into the air and literally threw them away from her body. It was a strange movement because it was so entirely in harmony with her figure that was a little too rounded but of a spontaneous animal gracefulness. There was something listless, indolent, delicately sensitive, and, in spite of its melancholy impetuousness in this raising of her hands, it was a movement like that of the banana porter, final of its kind and typical of the spirit of the country.

As typical as those meadows that came floating down the yellow Guaya in hundreds of green eyots.

Part II

CONCERNING PERU

THE GRAVEYARD OF PUERTO CHICAMA

GOEHRS had been travelling down the north coast of Peru southwards for the past fortnight. The coastline is about as long as the distance from Amsterdam to Constantinople. It took all this time because his coasting tramp put into many ports, took in and discharged cargo, coal, timber, and guano. Into insignificant little harbours with not much more than a few wooden sheds but which served some districts up country.

The coast of Peru was close to the equator, cut off from the tropics as if by a knife and burnt dry. Immediately beyond the fertile virgin forests of Ecuador, a desert zone of majestic beauty opened out. A belt of sand studded by the towers of the oilfields and wells, lit by a moon that shed a green light, and chilled by the frigid Humboldt stream that wherever it came fretted the tropics like acid into sand.

Yet for all that Goehrs became attached to this chilled, disenchanted coast. The dunes, with the triangular mountain giants behind them, this whole landscape on heroic lines, glowed of an evening like Greece. It was the counterpart of Ithaca, Naxos, and Santorin, barren, rocky, treeless, choked up with sand—and in the evening light shining clean, aloof, unearthly above the wild splendour of the Mediterranean.

Goehrs spent days in Payta, Pimentel, Eten, Pacasmayo, Salaverry, Supe, Huacho, in a dozen little harbours. One day he went ashore in Puerto Chicama. He went to the sandy beach on a lighter. The lighter was all but circular and as shallow as the half of a nutshell. There was a village of clay huts among the dunes, inhabited by a hybrid race of Chinese, Indians, and Negroes. Somewhere beyond the dunes lay Casa Grande, one of the most prolific sugar provinces of the continent, but it was out of sight because

73

the belt of desert lay between. Goehrs walked about the dunes to stretch his legs. As he was returning to the port he saw that a patch of desert was fenced off by a few bamboo stakes, but fenced in such a slovenly way that one or two donkeys had made their way in and were rolling about on it. It was the graveyard.

The natives had driven some ship's timbers into the sand here and there and painted an initial on them. That was all.

They had not buried the dead, only laid them out on the ground and fashioned a crust of clay over them. These crusts were lying all about the place like mummy coffins. The vultures had, however, pecked open the thin layer of clay and devoured the bodies even before the candles in the oil tins on the graves had burnt out. Two months later in Chile Goehrs was talking to the owner of a big sugar plantation—about half the size of Belgium—behind the dunes. He told Goehrs that on two occasions he had given the natives proper new cemeteries but that they had made no use of them.

The natives are very conservative.

They were fond of the hundreds of vultures that perched on the gables of their wretched huts in dense black clumps and considered the custom of having the dead devoured by vultures to be a more sanitary arrangement than to allow them to putrefy. The natives entertained very close relationships with the vultures. They threw everything that was dead and that they did not want to keep out of doors to them—fish, fruit, and donkeys—and the vultures descended and made away with it all.

By the same simple method the natives disposed of their dead. They thereby both honoured the rites of their religion and followed their habits. They buried their dead, and at the same time had them consumed.

Goehrs, who spent three days in Puerto Chicama while his boat was taking cargo on board, studied this strange coastline every evening. It lay under the Southern Cross. The green moon made its dunes and hills appear spectrally great and beautiful. The steep rocks gleamed, smothered under guano, as white as sugarloaves. The reek of the guano the ship was taking on board is the most concentrated stench of putrescence in the world, and it lay like an acrid miasma over the bay that never quite lost the apocalyptic splendours of its sunsets.

Not a tree, not a shrub. Thousands of miles of desert. Every evening Goehrs reflected that exactly four hundred

GRAVEYARD IN NORTHERN PERU.

years before, over the selfsame course from one natural harbour to the next, the mightiest, the greatest man of South America—Francisco Pizarro—had sailed. What a stout heart must have upborne Pizarro to have endured this solitude when, after sailing it for three years, ever disappointed afresh, ever finding desert over again, he had sought the golden land of Peru here. What privations and what disillusions must this coast have imposed on him ! His good ship must have dropped anchor all along it only to find uninhabited country. In spite of all, following the gold myth, Pizarro had sailed on and had eventually reached his goal.

PIZARRO

AMONG the company who had won through Panama with Vasco Nuñez de Balboa had been one Francisco Pizarro. Born in Estremadura in 1478, the bastard of a Spanish nobleman, he had at first, together with two illegitimate and his only legitimate brother, herded swine before he made his way to the New World. He had been of the company when Balboa plunged into the water and claimed possession of the South Seas for the Crown of Spain. He was of the company when Balboa died. He was of the company, and the part he played at Balboa's death was purposeful but not unequivocal.

He was, like all the great conquistadores, half a religious maniac, half a coldblooded imperialist. God and gold ! He loved God and he loved his King. But that did not prevent him from behaving in the service of his God like the most savage bloodhound in South America and, when it suited his purpose, from deposing and beheading the King's viceroys, in the service of the King. After he had watched Balboa, whom he held to be half a huckster and half a play-actor, conquering a whole ocean, the Spanish officer Pizarro was imbued with the ambition of completing a discovery of which this was only the beginning. In his eyes, Balboa's exploit hardly counted. No fame was won thereby, no power shattered, no fortune gained. There they were at Panama, on the edge of a New World, almost blindfolded, without knowing anything about it. Pizarro, who at that date was well on in his forties, became obsessed by this vision. With callous greed he envisaged what masses of gold remained to be discovered and what a number of nations to be converted to Roman Catholicism. This mystical conception of conversion inspired all these frays and invested them with their grandeur and their treachery. Everything that stood for the lust of power in these ruffianly Titans of the Conquest was masked by this spirit of their times.

Pizarro was in the sway of this ambition when he arrived at the threshold of his fifties, when men, as a rule, become sedate and prudent. About this time he at length reached an agreement with the Crown, or with the Governor of Panama. In accordance with this agreement the Crown was to receive the customary fifth of the proceeds of the expedition. At the same time Pizarro enlisted two partners. One of them was Diego de Almagro, a man of sound judgment and of unknown origin. The two were made for one another. They soon found the third and the capital they needed.

On November 14, 1529, 112 Spaniards left Panama and set sail on a pitifully small craft for the south, along an unknown coast with as fantastic a purpose as has ever prompted any enterprise in history. Three years passed in misadventures, in cruising to and fro, in returning to Panama on board worm-eaten ships, in incredible privations, until they discovered Ecuador and then Peru. It was here that Pizarro stumbled on something that took his breath away, on the land of gold. And on the Inca Empire. On more gold than he had ever dreamed of and on an Indian race more gifted than any one had believed possible. He found not a tribe, but a State.

Moreover, fortune favoured Pizarro.

The twelfth Inca ruler, Huayna Capac, had just died and, contrary to custom, had divided his realm. He had left the more settled part of his country to the successor whom every Inca ruler had to beget with his own sister. But he had left the part of the kingdom in which Ecuador lay to one of the sons of his harem, Atahualpa by name. Shortly before the Spaniards landed, Atahualpa had effected a *coup d'état*, had taken his brother prisoner, and had removed all potential pretenders, his father's legitimate and natural sons thereby for the first time splitting the Indian empire into two hostile factions.

The Indian State was an immense empire of such a notable construction that it would not stand division. This was Pizarro's one great stroke of good fortune. He grasped the situation at once and turned it to account without delay. On November 15, 1532, he entered the city of

Caxamalca with 110 foot and 67 mounted men and a number of regiments of the opposition faction. Without them Pizarro's expedition would have been a ridiculous fiasco.

Atahualpa's army, 40,000 strong, was encamped beyond Caxamalca. In the middle of the camp rose the temporary structure of Atahualpa's tent. It was not so much a tent as a mansion that had been rapidly run up round a patio. It had been built with a flower garden and running water, hot and cold, that had been hurriedly brought down from the hills by pipes.

The odds again were slightly in the Spaniard's favour in the way of equipment, dogs, horses, and ordnance. But they were not decisive odds. Pizarro was well aware of that. He assured Atahualpa that he was approaching in a friendly spirit and invited the Inca ruler to pay him a visit. Pizarro waited with bated breath to see whether Atahualpa would come. A day. A night. Fortune was again in Pizarro's favour. The Inca emperor came.

First of all came his advance guard in cotton harness of chequered patterns. They tidied up everything, straw, twigs, peel, littering the road. Then came musicians and singers. There followed the officers of the Inca court in gold and silver mail. Then came Atahualpa's litter. It was upholstered with tiny, many-coloured parrot feathers and decorations of beaten gold. A retinue of litters and hammocks followed it.

Pizarro, who knew that there was strategically only one single chance for him and his little force in this vast empire that he meant to have, seized his chance forthwith. He had laid all his traps. But true to his character, he could not spring these traps without having God for his accomplice. No Spaniard of Pizarro's type, who perpetrated the most hideous crimes, could die without having made his confession and always saw to it that God was on his side when he was scheming some particularly dastardly iniquity. And that not from guilefulness, but in keeping with the whole spirit of that era. They believed that God must be on their side and that it was all done to do Him honour.

Pizarro, who was standing behind the window when Atahualpa's litter arrived at his house, sent out Brother Vincente, and the priest went up to Atahualpa with the cross in one hand and the Bible in the other, reading an address of which the latter could not understand a word. Not only as regards the language, but as regards the matter of the

77

address as well. For the Inca sovereign, who ruled over half South America, knew to all intents and purposes nothing of Europe. For example, he thought the horses, then unknown in South America, were carnivorous beasts of prey. How was he likely to know anything about Christianity ? What had he been able to learn of Christian ethics ? That Christianity stole at any cost, hanged his Governors, ravished his women, cut off his subjects' hands, and marched along a road of impaled and half-charred men.

The monk handed the Bible to Atahualpa. The Inca tried to open the book but failed, because the Incas had such an original method of record that they did not understand books. The monk meant to help Atahualpa, but the Inca, whom no human being may venture to touch, misunderstood the movement, and pushed his arm aside. Thereupon he dropped the book, of which he could make nothing, on to the ground, and told the monk that, if his master desired to negotiate with him and really had peace at heart, it was for him to show it in deeds, to liberate the prisoners and make amends.

The monk went back into the house ; Pizarro had seen Atahualpa throw the Bible on to the ground and now had a pretext for destroying one of the most notable empires of the world. He now had, as he had hoped, God himself for his justification. He flung himself into his mail, thrust the Indians in their golden armour aside, grasped Atahualpa by his arm, and, dragging him from his litter, shouted "Santiago !" The cannons roared out. The ambush closed in. Pizarro maintained his grip on the Inca until his retinue had been cut down. Outside the city his men added a few thousand corpses to these.

Pizarro then went back into his house at once. Fortune had again favoured him.

Pizarro was a big, powerful man, very ascetic in externals, nearly always wore a plain black cassock girt about the waist and reaching to his ankles, and with it white riding boots and a white hat. It was only during his spells of fury that on very ceremonial occasions he donned a robe of fur. He had only one relaxation—playing tennis. He played the game no matter with whom. He would have trained a horse to return the ball if he had been unable to find a human opponent.

After the massacre of Caxamalca a vast empire fell piecemeal into Pizarro's hands. He became (in the service of his King) wealthier than any dynast. He had a number of children by Indian women (Inca princesses brought up in the palaces). In pitched battle he overthrew his partner Almagro, who threatened to become troublesome, and had the old man strangled. He founded Lima, the capital. And, when Almagro's bastard ran a sword through his throat, he was an old, but vigorous man, though poor as a church mouse. He was poor because he was lavish. When on June 26, 1541, he fell, he had acquired all the honours a man of his day could hold. He was Viceroy, Marqués, and Knight of the Order of Santiago. All this because at the right moment he had had the courage to have the whole of the ruling caste of a worldwide empire put to the sword when the ruler of this empire dropped the Bible. The empire whose ruler had dropped the Bible comprised the Colombia, Ecuador, Peru, and Bolivia of to-day, together with parts of Chile and Brazil.

Such slight occasions, Goehrs reflected, determine the splendour and misery of an empire. At the same time he knew that this was only a shallow reading of the lessons of history. Trivial incidents do not determine the splendour and misery of an empire, but destinies based on the un-riddled plinth of tragedy.

For the Inca empire, built up on lines as intricate as they were attractive and daring, as grand as they were para-doxical, had forfeited its existence before a sterner tribunal than that of a brutal and dæmonic bandit leader, long before it was ordained for the Spaniard to appear to give it its *coup de grâce.*

And Atahualpa ?

For weeks after he had been taken prisoner, convoys of llamas from all parts of his country poured in to ransom him. Atahualpa was thirty years of age, well built except that he was a little too stout, with frank, handsome, dis-traught features. Pizarro assembled a court martial one fine day and had Atahualpa found guilty and sentenced to death for " intrigues." He was sentenced to be burnt at the stake.

Atahualpa was reduced to despair by idea of such a death. Pizarro gave him a chance of escaping from it.

" What is it ? " asked the Inca.

" Baptism."

Atahualpa suffered himself to be baptized, for in his realm that stood for five centuries of success, for five centuries of war, renown, military rule, and the enlargement of its borders, in his realm success stood for so much that he acknowledged the victory of the white god over the brown god and everything it implied.

Thereupon Atahualpa was again sentenced to death on a new count and hanged.

In this matter as in others Pizarro went his way with great precision—with the same unreasoning certainty, with the same daring, sober imagination, with the same dæmonic steadfastness with which he had always clung to the legend of a land of gold all the while he was wasting time as a subordinate colonial officer in Panama, with which he had finally discovered the country, and with which he was conquering it now.

God was again called into court to furnish a justification for Atahualpa's execution. Atahualpa was sentenced on ethical, not political grounds. For the cruelties he had practised on his own kith and kin before the Spaniards had landed. Pizarro had the assassination of the pretenders to the crown in mind. It was on these grounds that Pizarro, who could neither read nor write, murdered Atahualpa in the name of divine justice, whose functions Pizarro therewith assumed in Peru.

THE INCAS AND THEIR CONQUERORS

APART from the fact that Atahualpa's cruelties were no concern of Pizarro, everything of which on matters of principle he accused the Incas was not even half-way right. The two races simply failed to understand one another. The Spaniards from the outset failed to appreciate everything that distinguished the Incas, the aristocratic passivity of their State, the exclusiveness of their ruling caste, the luxuriance of their mythology, the intricacy of their civilization, the beauty of their cities and their life.

Of what indeed, apart from military matters, were these Spaniards competent judges ? These Spaniards ! Grand adventurers and splendid soldiers, but otherwise the scum of humanity. One hundred and eighty superb scoundrels, led by a few officers who were, like wolves, ravening for gold and power, who happened to be magnificently equipped mechanically for achieving their ends. In the eyes of these idolatrously Catholic Spaniards, prepared to perpetrate any abomination on behalf of Crown and Church, the Indians were pagans pure and simple. In the era of the Inquisition that meant being something lower than a dog.

In the eyes of the Spaniards the Indians were strange creatures, whose lower orders had intercourse like animals in the field, fellows who begot children of their own sisters, whose women roamed about naked with only an acorn hanging from a thread, whose daughters had before marriage either slept with all the young men within reach or, on the other hand, were so chaste that at their wedding rites their own mothers had to deflower them, and whose men wore their organs in a sheath made often of gold and emeralds.

The Spaniards saw that whole tribes were homosexual, that in many districts the bridegroom, on marriage, allowed all his friends to sleep with the bride before he went to her himself ; they saw that men slept with youths in the temples and that boys were sacrificed, their lungs and their hearts burnt in honour of their deities. The Spaniards saw that cannibalism was beyond all doubt being practised, that prisoners were bound face to the wall, slices being carved from the rounded portions of their buttocks and calves while the victim was yet alive, and that the blood of these victims was used as the Spaniards' own priests used holy water. The Spaniards saw that the flayed skins and heads of prisoners were filled with hot sand and suspended in the public places. They learnt that human heads were boiled in the Indians' cooking pots and that idols were set up in many places. . . .

Goehrs laid aside Friederici's massive, magnificent tome in which the ethical justification for the Conquista was argued with admirable industry from the diaries of Pizarro's men-at-arms and thousands of other sources.

The Spaniards' judgments were, beyond doubt, crass barbarity. Pizarro's Spaniards would have passed much the same sort of judgment, if by some obliging scene-shifting in history, they had discovered, not Peru but the Egypt of the first Rameses or the Mycenæan model State in Crete. They would have found the union of brother and sister accepted as the highest principle of eugenics ; they would have seen the riffraff procreating in the fields ; they would have, as in Peru, confounded ancestor worship with idolatry ; they would have mistaken sacrifices in the highest phase of the most complex religious mysteries for cannibalism, and regarded pæderasty, such as every myth evolves, as sodomy, a crime which the Catholic Church of that period looked on as more heinous than manslaughter.

Pizarro would cheerfully have had Rameses executed for a nigger and, with a general's sphinxlike smile, have looked

F

upon the pyramids as quaint, meaningless ant-heaps of stone.

Nor would the Spaniards in Egypt have conceived the notion that the fellahin were human beings any more than it had dawned upon them that the Indians were human beings. It was only Pope Paul III who some time later conceived this idea and in his bull " *Veritas ipsa* " laid down a very humane declaration on the point. No doubt about it, the Spaniards would have treated the Egyptians as animals and would have melted down every scrap of metalwork in Egypt, smashed every work of art, and carried off every precious stone. They would have done this, in the first instance, to collect gold for the financing of Spain's continental wars and, in the second, to appease their Catholic conscience, which would have regarded even such works of art as the seated figure of the Princess Nofret, the delightful wood carvings on the ancient Ra-Nufer of Sakkara only as hideous idols. They would at most have left the pyramids standing because they could no more have overturned them than they could certain strongholds and palaces in the Peruvian highlands.

All that, including the fact that the Spaniards were such scum, was fate. But the judgment of this scum was by no means right on that account.

What were the Incas really like ?

THE INDIAN EMPIRE

THEY appeared on the scene somewhere about the year 1000 and had united many flourishing Indian civilizations and states into a closely knit military monarchy. Perhaps they came, as all Indians probably did, from the north across some land bridge or other from Mongolia. Perhaps they were an Aymara tribe of Lake Titicaca which, like the Macedonians under Philip and Alexander, suddenly and inevitably came to the front and conquered half the world.

In any case they suddenly appeared, a military race with a taste for poetry, like the Cretans, with palaces full of paintings like those of Minos at the foot of Mount Ida, a race with a sense for natural beauty, of delicate decadence in sentiment, of forceful energy in political thought. Their religion, too, was musical and lyrical. They imagined they were descended from the sun and the lion. They made a great cult of astrology. They had virgin priestesses. They had within the inner circles of the court a society that was fond of the drama, athletics, and poetry—all of it within the spell of a priestcraft whose priests were military leaders as well, just as were the princes of Knossos three thousand years before them.

They staged comedies and tragedies, but the actors were exclusively amateurs of the ruling caste. Their dances were controlled and reticent, and only the men danced. They had a scrip consisting of coloured ribbons that were knotted in some insanely complicated fashion. Yellow stood for gold ; red for soldiers ; and the knotting of them denoted verb, simile, and adjective. They had, in addition to the jargon of the vulgar, a particular precious court language. One of their wonderful aqueducts was called Silver Snake. The names of the quarters of their cities were Clove Hall and Lion Beam. Their poems were as fragrant as the Japanese :

> Whilst thou art singing,
> Thou wilt fall asleep,
> But at midnight
> I will be with thee.

> Cailla llapi
> Punun qui
> Champi tuta
> Samusac.

The rising generation of esquires were on a given day dubbed knights. After a six-day fast. After tests in keeping vigil and the endurance of pain. After six days of athletic contests. After Indian Olympic games. For this festival they appeared crowned with flowers in beautifully woven fabrics, very delicate, very warlike, very self-disciplined and with the same sweet, fatal love of beauty as the Cretans.

For centuries, it is true, the drums in Cuzco, the capital situated (and situate) at an altitude of over 10,000 feet in the Cordilleras, never ceased to send ever fresh regiments to war, to overthrow ever new nations, to organize them, to incorporate them into the cell system of the Inca State, and therewith to raise them sociologically, but . . .

But when they celebrated their high festivals and worshipped " Pachacamac," who was perhaps the sun, perhaps the spirit of the sun, they did it in the manner described by Garcilaso de la Vega, himself an Inca prince and Pizarro's contemporary : they drew in their shoulders, bowed down, raised their eyes to the skies, lowered them again, and, laying their open hands on their right shoulders, blew kisses into the air.

The Inca State was organized on remarkable lines.

There were neither money nor property fines, nor taxation. But compulsory service. Every one without exception had to work. A third of the State lands belonged to the Inca sovereign. A third belonged to him in his capacity as priest (officially, to the sun), and the remaining third belonged to the people. The people had to make no payment ; they were given as much land as they wanted—but they had, in addition to their own land, to cultivate that of the sovereign and of the sun.

So, strictly, there was no private property.

In return, all measures were adopted to ensure the people's welfare. They were protected by military and police forces (who were relieved of agricultural work). They had the benefit of a splendid network of roads, messenger posts, bridges, waterworks, and a system of irrigation which at that time had turned many of to-day's deserts into fertile districts. The country was organized on a system, clear as crystal, of provinces, districts, and communes. It was served by insurances against old age and sickness and against famine by State granaries. It was governed as a State by laws of a severity only equalled in the Islamitic realm of the Wahabis : by loss of a hand for theft, by death for adultery. Public health was safeguarded by hygienic measures, by licences to work the gold mines, by prohibition to work in the quicksilver mines. The Inca's obligation to work was so strictly enforced that there were neither beggars nor paupers. Any man who, for whatever reason, was temporarily incapacitated from work had, at any rate, to send in two hornfuls of lice collected in evidence that he was engaged on a task for the common weal.

The staple food was vegetarian. There was meat on festivals only. Cattle and water were State property. The State administered and distributed them. Everything was organized ; a most efficient bureaucracy. A cubic, clearly ordered system of cells. An army organized on basic units of hundreds into regiments and divisions.

Even the individual distribution of work of the masses was specifically scheduled and regulated. When, for example, the season was so far advanced that the plots of the sick and the incapacitated had to be tilled by the hale, the parties concerned were advised by an official. He mounted the rostrum, gave a signal and announced : " The work on behalf of the sick and disabled will begin to-morrow. The persons appointed for the work will assemble at seven o'clock."

But the laws were not only severe, they were common sense as well. And, above all, they were far-seeing. "Any man incapable of managing his domestic affairs is not qualified for a State appointment."

What else was this State, thought Goehrs, than pure communism, the purest but most peculiar communism in the world ? Yet it was coupled with an upper stratum of big capitalists, supervised, controlled, and ruled by a small section made up of gorgeous princes, priestly athletes and generals, vestal virgins, and semi-divine sovereigns—people who acted in theatres and conquered provinces, and who could leave the most powerful governors of great States, unless these, too, were the issue of the brother-and-sister wedlock of the court, outside the gates of the temple when they entered the inner shrine.

What a daring, what a perilously balanced fusion of two antagonistic political systems ! What heroic incompatibility, but at the same time what almost criminal daring in the structure of the State !

This race perished together with its ruling caste, and hence wholly and utterly, on the advent of the Spaniards. The Incas suddenly saw 180 mail-clad men with horses disembark from their ships, organize disaffected Indian regiments, and march against their capital. Prisoners had their hands cut off and were then liberated to spread the terror. The Spaniards trained bloodhounds and unleashed them on the Indians. Indians had their heads forced into millstones and their trunks were then torn away. These 180 men and their allies sent a wave of panic to precede them. Pizarro had the wife of the Inca prince Manco riddled by arrows. She gave orders for the remnant of her body to be thrown into the Yucay for her corpse to float down the river to join her husband.

The Indian people did not understand how gold and God were concerned in actions such as these. They could not understand why the white race should invade them with such unprecedented savageness and bloodthirstiness, in such a welter of inhumanity, yet, to all seeming, protected by the gods. On the other hand, the condottieri of Pizarro, the tennis player who disliked having to wear a full-dress coat, understood no more of the Inca Empire than they would have understood a kingdom of ants ; to the intricacies

85

of which they were always bound to be blind and which could mean nothing more to them than an ant-heap to be kicked out of their path. True, they did their ghoulish work, for which fate had ordained them, with astounding zest. They left nothing but ruins in their wake. They left them behind to show that high in the Cordilleras the daintiest of despotisms and the most charming of communisms had once held sway.

The Fate of the Indian Rome

"BUT how did it come about?" thought Goehrs, standing on board his ship in the beautiful bay of Puerto Chicama. "How was it physically possible for 180 Spaniards to be strong enough to smash so highly organized a State of such unusual size?"

He knew the answer.

In the first place it was a mistake to take numbers into account. It was a mistake, too, to talk of armaments—which, in the main, were not so very far apart. The issue hung from quite another matter. It was the over-centralized weakness of the Empire of the Incas that enabled the Spaniards to win their victory, not the overwhelming strength of the Spaniards—terrible fellows as they must have been—for, soberly considered, 180 men would not have been strong enough to conquer a small province, let alone a State.

The Inca Empire was too delicately poised to stand a severe shock—not in a military, but in a sociological sense.

The Inca Empire simply had no moral strength in its structure, no national solidarity, no national spirit. "The birds cease to fly," said Atahualpa, "if I will have it so." But his Indians, instead of raising a fiery national resistance, began to commit suicide when the Spaniards came.

The interplay of poise and counterpoise in the Inca Empire was too intellectually subtle. It consisted of forces that elsewhere in the world have always fought one another tooth and nail. On the one side tyranny—on the other, mutual aid; on the one side fantastic wealth—on the other, elimination of private capital. It was like an attempt to fuse the Russia of Lenin with Charles V and his aristocracy. The Inca State held together for five hundred years, but when the hour of danger came the equipoise of its component elements proved too paradoxical to offer any resistance. The base of the pyramid was not the people, but the small ruling caste. The pyramid was standing on its head and toppled over. The people, it is true, had previously always been content because the people's interests had been safeguarded. But there had, none the less, been something wrong.

"Even if it is only a trifle," reflected Goehrs. "But the despatch stations, the broad mountain roads, the relays of runners from the coast to the interior had not served the interests of the people, but to convey fresh fish for the Incas from the coast into the interior as fast as possible. That is symbolic. A people will only stand that kind of system as long as history will stand it and, when once history refuses to stand it, the State falls to pieces. The occasion for it does not matter. It does not matter whether, as in Crete, it was an earthquake, the collapse of a nation as in Teutonic Ravenna, or a racial clash as happened at Caxamalca ; or whether the work were done by a premeditated revolution as in Paris and Moscow. It was not the bloodthirsty Spaniards but fate that overthrew the Inca Empire, built up on too aspiring lines. . . ."

Shortly afterwards Goehrs, on board his boat, was coasting on farther southwards. The temperature continued to fall, but it was still hot.

It was on this coast that Pizarro's Spaniards had one day captured an Indio who was out fishing. The man was quite dazed, for he had so far never seen a white man, and a great deal about them was strange to him. Before the Conquest the Indians had never seen either horses or poultry, dogs or cows, and they had neither olives nor oranges, vineyards nor wheat. The Indian was bewildered by people who possessed all these things. The Spaniards cross-questioned him about gold. He thought he had to give his name and said " Beru." They pressed him with inquiries about gold. The Indian answered " Pelu " which was meant to convey that he lived on a river and was a fisherman. The Spaniards in their turn misinterpreted that again and assumed that the name of the country was Peru. " Peru " thenceforward was the equivalent term for gold. It was the Yukon and Kimberley call for the adventurous spirits of 1532 and the succeeding years. In response to this call, one of the most gracious, marvellous, and beautiful empires of the world was wiped out, its aristocracy butchered, its cities destroyed, its works of art melted down, its mines exploited at the expense of the mass of the Indians who passed into Spanish slavery.

Peru ! Peru !

Goehrs studied this coast thoughtfully. The people inhabiting, opening up, and ruling this country to-day were descendants of the issue Pizarro, his officers, and his men had begotten by the Indian women of the Incas.

It was the heart of South America.

A few days later Goehrs reached Lima, that Pizarro had lived long enough to found and that became the capital of the continent for centuries.

LIMA

GOEHRS was put on shore with two men and with them climbed into the launch that was to take them to Callao, the port of Lima. The two men had often afforded him some entertainment during the course of the voyage. He had played shuffleboard with them on a tiny space and therefore knew them well, for there is nothing that lays bare the baseness of human nature more ruthlessly than shuffleboard.

One of them was an Ecuadorian of the name of Naboa. He had published a sumptuous work on Latin America in many volumes. He himself believed everything it contained.

The other was half Peruvian, half Frenchman. His grandfather had in his time run away to sea from Biarritz because his Spanish mother had treated him with undue severity. He had drifted to Lima, the Lord knows how, and later on had officially introduced the French into the country, discovered the oil wells, and sponsored many mining enterprises. His grandson who was then going on shore had been sent to Paris at the age of ten to be brought up there ; at the age of seventeen he had made a discovery of an especial use for crocodile skin. He bought an option on all the crocodiles in Madagascar. His patent consisted in removing all the humps on crocodiles skins, which he regarded as unsightly, and importing them as heels for army boots. This invention had cost his family in Lima such a lot of money that they recalled the young man to Peru. To his regret Goehrs lost sight of both these notable men at the customs office.

He was ushered into a private compartment and searched from head to foot for firearms.

On a wide, handsome asphalt road Goehrs then covered the eight miles between the port of Callao and Lima. Like every one else, he paid the toll of a shilling for the use of this road. He worked out that the road must have yielded a revenue of at least $12,500 per month.

There was a monument by the roadside : not of Bolívar, Martin, Sucre, or any other hero generals of the War of Liberation. It was a monument the Rotary Club had erected. A massive pedestal, and on it a wrecked motor car. The inscription beneath it was an admonition to be sensible. Goehrs had many opportunities for wondering whether this invocation were addressed to motorists only or to every one living in the country.

Goehrs drove with his pile of light luggage (he always travelled with portable luggage only) to the Hotel Bolívar. The Government of Peru had had this hotel built a few years previously for the centenary celebrations of the independence of the republic, in order to house ambassadors and ministers of all the nations bidden to the festivities in what it imagined to be a first-class hotel. The whole hotel with its 200 rooms and 200 bathrooms had been delivered ready made from England—with English furniture, tables, utensils, beds, baths, and w.c.'s. The hotel had cost the Government half a million dollars. Goehrs had to pay five dollars for his room. An egg cost twenty-five cents, an orange eighteen cents, a palta fruit growing close at hand seventy-five cents.

" Your prices are unusual," Goehrs remarked to the Swiss head porter.

" Everything is dear in Lima," the latter replied with a smile straight from the Bernese Oberland. " A salute from a straw hat costs five dollars here. Only the newspapers are cheap."

Goehrs had three letters of introduction in his pocket. One to President Leguía's son : the President's son was in Europe on the track of a man who had swindled him out of 30,000 pounds. Goehrs had a second one to a deputy : the deputy had recently got into President Leguía's black books and had been replaced out of hand in parliament by his brother. Goehrs finally had a third letter to a minister : the minister had had to resign a month before because he had made money by unconventional methods. The minister had had the administration of an estate. He had been administering it for a long time. After his trusteeship had long ago expired, he had gone on placing big orders at the charge of the estate. Although for the last ten years or more not a newspaper dared print a word against the

Government, this had proved too much of a good thing for the President.

" What has become of the man ? " asked Goehrs.

" He is gone to Europe as an ambassador."

" Where ? "

" To the Vatican."

Lima struck Goehrs as intoxicatingly beautiful. The city of 300,000 inhabitants was situate as in a park of palm trees. Of an evening the new quarters had twice the amount of light of the metropolitan cities of Europe. Even the zoo lay fragrant and green in the centre of the city. From his car Goehrs saw the black-and-white condors with their comic turkey combs hanging over their aquiline beaks. They were sitting on their perches. Lions and elephants were roaming about ; they were, it is true, not particularly big specimens.

And in between lay the old quarters and the old mansions —Pizarro's Lima. The façades of the bright houses were broken by the carved, filigree screens of their balconies, balconies that were closed in like coffins to prevent any one from seeing the women behind them, balconies full of bizarre figures—like Gothic lace turned into black timber.

The modern quarters were built in very similar style, only more affected. The old baroque colonial style was reproduced here with fantastic flourishes. The villas rose through the foliage of magnificent boulevards in hundreds of variations. The history of these new garden cities was, it is true, even more striking than the impression they themselves conveyed. It was not nearly as attractive. The most attractive house in Lima was built with the money embezzled from prisoners' food rations. The pink illumination of an avenida from delicate glass globes was a legacy from a man who had made huge profits by speculating in building sites under the said glass globes. The asphalt road was built by the owners of the houses under legal duress, and many a man who could not pay had had his house sold over his head.

This modern new town was built by force, at enormous expense, under fantastic acts varying in their degree of injustice. But built it was. Some one or other was carrying out a scheme to build the only modern metropolitan city on the West Coast with mysterious persistence and by uncanny methods.

The reason was clear.

Ninety per cent. of the population of Peru lived up country, that is to say, three or four of its four or five million inhabitants, according to estimates. There may perhaps have been six.

They did not take any interest in politics, being half-castes and Indians. Everything that occurred and was rendered effective happened in Lima. Lima was Peru. And this Peru in Lima had been inflated as rapidly as it was humanly possible to inflate it, more especially when one remembers what a one-horse town old Lima was. A sleepy hollow with glorious old buildings, it is true, and with four hundred years of history. With sixty-seven churches. A township through which the flower of Spain had passed for four hundred years. The portraits of old viceroys were hanging in its museums, where the state coaches of the nobility with their coats-of-arms were also on view, as were cannons, standards, bloodstained armour—signposts of a Peru that is no less as proud of having been founded by the Spaniards than it is of having kicked these same Spaniards out three centuries later.

There were two Limas : the dingy one with the aroma of history, and the new city that had dramatically sprung up by the other's side—just as if modern Barcelona were to seat itself beside Old-World Seville.

" South America All Over "

GOEHRS was standing one forenoon in the cathedral of Lima with a young English mining engineer, through whose hands passed a lot of copper and tin ore produced in the Cordilleras.

" Over there," said Mr. Hill and beckoned to an Indian. They went into a dark corner of the cathedral, founded four hundred years ago, to see its founder lying there. Pizarro's coffin was let into the wall at about the height of the line of vision.

" Have you any matches, Señor ? " asked the Indian.

" No," said Hill and gripped Goehrs's hand.

The Indian lit a match and, standing on tiptoe, they saw Pizarro's mummy through the glass slit in the coffin lid. There, preserved in rather slovenly fashion, rather meagrely, in its old chest, lay the bones of the man who had conquered this quarter of the globe. The skeleton was covered in yellow, parchment-like flesh. It was about six feet in height. The head had hardly any teeth left, but in spite of that the old mummy had its mouth agape. The skeleton was that of a man in his sixties. With cotton-wool in his eyeholes and with cotton-wool in the holes that Almagro's bastard had once carved in it.

There Pizarro lay, on consecrated ground, of course, but preserved no better than a dead cat. To the left Pizarro's panegyric was inscribed on the cathedral wall, to the right that of President Leguía. . . .

On their drive to Hill's bungalow, lying outside the town near the suburb of Miraflores, Goehrs asked : " Why did you clutch my hand a minute ago, old man ? "

" Because you were all but blundering into an old booby trap," said the Englishman. " The rascal only wanted to see whether you being a foreigner, had any foreign matches. Then, after pocketing his tip, he would have laid information against you to the police and you would have had to pay a couple of pounds fine. The informer gets half of it."

Goehrs had to admit, abashed, that he had a box of foreign matches in his pocket.

Hill's bungalow was almost smothered in greenery. As far as Goehrs's eye could range from its windows, a grove of olives opened out, more extensive than those he had seen either in Delphi or the garden of Gethsemane. These olive trees round Lima are as much like the cultivated olives of the Greeks and the Hebrews as domestic animals are like beasts of prey. Pizarro himself had planted these olive trees.

" Considering the fact that you and your mines are sooner or later going to plunge this unhappy country into class warfare, you really have a very attractive pitch here," said Goehrs ; " even the crickets are chirpy."

" They are," agreed Hill, " but they're brutes none the less. They've just eaten my third dress suit. Everything here—and not only human beings—is busy devouring. You can only have mahogany furniture here. Mahogany is too tough for the ants. They eat up any other furniture like butter."

On the way back to town, a few hundred yards outside Lima, they drove past blackish-grey masses of clay, millenary clay ramparts by which the outlines of fortifications could still be clearly traced.

" That's pre-Inca," said Hill. " They had to blast the ramparts with dynamite when we were taking the road out here ; the stuff's as solid as that."

All along the coast there were heaps of the wreckage of

this " stuff." That was the third Lima that Goehrs had discovered, the Indian Lima.

Hummingbirds were flashing from leaf to leaf in the public gardens of the new Lima as they drove in. And the black vultures were perching on the new villas and palatial buildings exactly as they did in the desert. Goehrs saw that a great deal of what he had at first sight taken at its own value was, at a second glance, a little stagy. Many of the façades that looked like houses were in fact only false fronts, masking a bar or cinema in the open air or in a wooden shed. Many two-storeyed houses consisted only of a ground floor with the frontage for the second built on to it. There was plenty of faking everywhere to confirm the impression that the place was bigger than it really was. Not that it was in the least necessary. They were just driving across a huge square, on one side of which rose a vast building in its scaffolding, like a Titan at the stake.

" That is South America all over," said the Englishman. " That is going to be a Palais de Justice bigger than the one in Brussels. They pulled down a whole district to make room for it. And now the whole show has come to a standstill because they've run short of money. But perhaps the old man will put it through yet."

" The old man ? "

" Leguía."

MUMMIES WITH PARROTS' HEADS

GOEHRS, after a while, told himself that it was time for him to cease visualizing the Indians as they used to be in schoolboy storybooks. The Red Indian type of romance might no doubt apply to a few barbarous and unimportant tribes of North America. But it had pretty well died out with the tribes to which it might have applied. As for the many millions of Indians who had lived and were still living in the civilized Indian States of South America, and who made up almost the entire population of several States of the west and north, this romance, this setting, and the whole of this literary buncombe had never had any meaning at all.

Lima seemed to Goehrs to be peopled by Japanese or by a cross of Japanese and Malays, in any case by a broad-faced race. There was doubtless a great deal of cross-breeding, but the main characteristic strain was Indian.

Indian broad faces were now beginning to cut his hair, to

93

sell him fruit, to wait on him, and to black his boots. But for all that it took a little time before he had rid himself of the muddleheaded misrepresentations of Fenimore Cooper and Karl May. He was not a sentimentalist, but at first it hurt him for some reason or other that the heroic figures who had peopled his imagination before he knew the facts were now confronting him with the functions and in the aspect of honest traders.

The only warrior aspect the Indians still retained was in their capacity as policemen when at night they turned back their red coat collars over the shoulders of their blue capes. But in the daytime, standing quietly at street corners in their peaked caps and pressing the buttons that operated the red and green lights of the traffic control, there was nothing heroic about them. They were officials.

And the soldiers in their khaki were simply Mongols.

Goehrs then went, in order to see something tangible of Indian history, to the Inca Museum that a man of the name of Victor Larico Herrera had built. In this museum Goehrs realized at once that everything he had credited to the Incas as evidence of their civilization had been in existence for many epochs, for thousands of years, before the Incas. He saw gold shields and gold masks, ornaments and rings, mirrors, and glorious coloured vases and marvellously beautiful fabrics that had defied time. From a dozen civilizations, from a dozen territories—from the coast and from the highlands. From their highlands the Incas had imperialistically linked up these dozens of cultures, just as they had linked up into an empire the States from which these cultures came. Magnificently, with imagination, by routine organization, in tragic, heroic decadence. Exactly like Egypt. Many of the images, many of the ornaments, and many of the paintings might have been discovered in Egypt. Goehrs stood meditatively for a while in front of a glass case of trepanned skulls. The knife of the Inca surgeon had peeled the bone like a fruit, the incision was just as accurate, just as smooth, just as clean. In the centre of the part trepanned was the aperture of a wound. All round it the last scrap of skin, looking as if it had been polished, was left. In fact the Inca doctors used in their day to remove a fragment of the skull to look for a splinter of bone as if their craft was akin to the sculptor's art. Beside them lay the scalpels. The Incas had no steel, but they had a process for hardening bronze that made it at least as hard as steel. No one to-day knows how they did it, but do it they did.

94

But the most sensational exhibits were their mummies. They gave Goehrs one of the most startling surprises he had anywhere in South America. They were the mummies of princes and chieftains, and the dry soil had kept them in a state of perfect preservation. The most remarkable thing was that the mummies were not lying down but squatting. They were squatting in fabric coffins, in huge prisons of wool which were in part modelled on the human form, with a horrible exactness and an indescribable weirdness.

They were half-lifesize cones, composed of innumerable strands of wool knotted together, on to which the Indians had sewn sleeves and which they had surmounted with heads of fabric. Clumsy monuments of wool, but how they were clothed! With fabrics more splendid than the Coptic, in a vivid terra-cotta colour, varied, veined, and patterned in blue, green and black. Wearing their ornaments, girt with their weapons. And then the faces!

The faces were covered in fluff of green parrot feathers— like silk. And the nose, the eyes, the eyebrows, and the mouth were outlined by black and white parrots' feathers. Real, long, tightly plaited pigtails, crimson switches, falling across the shoulders, were sewn on to these wool heads with their masks of parrots' feathers. And on their heads they wore a feather circlet of the most delicate plumage imaginable. A turban of feathers. There they stood as heavy as sacks, but breathing a majesty as of the gods, tender and strange as that of another planet, a majesty that was half that of the primeval forest, half of the finest flower of art— half princes, half birds. The Indian chieftains in these prisons of moulded wool crouched in a squatting posture with their knees drawn up under their chins. The folk who had interred them thousands of years ago had been very concerned about their posture. They all had their arms raised, with their hands pressed against their cheeks. They had in the first instance been squatting decorously and rigidly in their fantastic parrot-headed cages, but in course of time the muscular tissue had contracted. Now they sat crumpled up, with raised arms like melodramatic actors of some tragic fate, panic-stricken, with upturned faces, their mouths agape, gnashing their splendid teeth, frenzied, struck down as they shrieked.

There they sat, half the size of their fabric coffins, arrested in ghastly gestures, their chins on a level with their knees ; in their big, silent monuments of wool, the cones with the arms cobbled on and heads with human faces superimposed,

95

never-to-be-forgotten faces of parrots' down, with only the circlet of feathers on their skulls left to attest the magnificence of their lives. A spectacle than which few others in the world are more macabre.

When Goehrs looked up, he saw the Indian lad who was acting as custodian lounging against the wall with half-closed eyes. Ninety per cent. of the population of Peru, a country three or four times the size of Germany, looked exactly like him. The Indio was a simpleton, picking his nose to pass the time. Beside him stood half a dozen half-bred Indian students, poking fun at the mummies.

"I wonder whether any one," thought Goehrs, deeply stirred by the incident, "whether any one coming from some foreign and half-civilized continent, who had read widely about our heroic epochs, who had studied our cathedrals, had admired our royal suits of armour, had heard the story of our Crusades . . . and who then came over and caught us at our work to-day, at our occupations, with our manners and characteristics, just as we are and not as we imagine ourselves to be . . . I wonder whether a visitor of this type would poke fun at us?" Who can tell?

Goehrs passed the young students on his way out. These lads were making a strenuous effort to be smart. Everything about them was a little too tight. And if they had a tailor who had carelessly dropped one sleeve lower than the other, they carried this particular shoulder lower and with more of a droop—for the sake of being smart at all costs.

As Goehrs left the Larico Herrera Museum, a shrill whistle blew. It was at once taken up by another whistle and ran like machine-gun fire down the whole avenida. The motor cars pulled up. Then came a heavily armed officer on a motorcycle, with a side car occupied by another heavily armed officer. Then came a heavily armed officer in a car. Then another car. Thereon followed a heavily armed officer on a motorcycle with a side car, again occupied by yet another heavily armed officer.

"Who was that?" Goehrs asked the Indian lounging against the door.

"President Leguía."

UNDER A DICTATORSHIP

THE Cordilleras come down like animals quite close to Peru's narrow strip of coast, with groups of outposts, behind which the mass of the herd huddles. Even the outposts are shapely and high. They tower up like giraffes and peer down on the cottonfields and on Pizarro's Lima.

During the Peruvian winter, which is as hot as our summer and covers about the same period, Lima wears a pearl-grey veil that is quite luminous, quite unique, enfolding the city as in a fairy-tale atmosphere.

But in an hour's motor run the people of Lima are over 2,500 feet up in the Cordilleras, in Chosica where there is always sunshine. They then lounge about the railway station, which is the same building as the hotel, and wait for the trains and for the newspapers with all the winners. For in the long run they get to feel very chilly in Lima's dainty veil, which leaves everything in full visibility, but makes everything look a little secretive. It always looks as if it were going to rain in half an hour's time although in Lima it only rains—what you can really call rain—once in every thirty years.

As Goehrs drove up into the Cordilleras, he saw on every side, among the ever loftier triangles of the mountains, the ruins of old Inca cities which had been built up the mountain sides on terraces, cities that had had populations of tens of thousands.

" These settlements are very ingeniously planned," said Hill, raising his hand from the wheel. " Up the hillsides, where nothing will grow. The Indians kept the fertile lowlands free for tillage, because the valleys are simply absurdly fruitful. This road is an old Inca road—macadamized, of course, and asphalted. Almost all the roads in Peru are Inca roads. They actually go to altitudes of 10,000 feet and beyond. Leguía has revived that programme. As rail transport is so terribly expensive—you can tell that by the price of eggs ; an egg from San Francisco is cheaper than an egg from the Cordilleras of Peru—and as railroads are few, Leguía is trying to open up the country by road transport. Along with irrigation and small holdings ; nothing new, but an innovation in these parts. Most of it, it is true, hangs fire, because the funds keep on running out. But the Yankees keep on chucking money into it again. And the whole thing is at any rate a programme. And you have no idea how valuable even a programme can be."

" Why does every one shirk giving an answer when one puts a question about Leguía to him ? "

" There are reasons for it."

" What reasons ? "

Hill raised a gauntleted hand from the steering wheel and made a very vague gesture in the air.

Goehrs left Chosica in the early morning and by midday was at a height of 13,000 feet. He travelled via Oroya in hairpin bends by the highest regular railway service in the world, the Central Railway, up into the Cordilleras. At La Cima he reached a height of some 15,000 feet, and had passed through 63 tunnels and over 67 bridges to cover about 300 miles. From the terminus, another spell by car, and Goehrs reached the skirts of the vast virgin forest that extends as far as the Amazon and right across Brazil to the other coast of the continent. Impenetrable.

As Goehrs was returning to Lima, the Peruvian who had left a past behind him in Paris culminating in the option on crocodiles in Madagascar got in at Oroya. His name was Leonidas Arena. His family had property in the Oroya district, which happens to be an immense mineral field. When he got into the carriage he was raging against the Yankees—like all Peruvians.

For Peru's incredible mineral wealth was being exploited by two big American companies, the Cerro de Pasco Copper Corporation and the Northern Peru Company.

"The Cerro de Pasco people," said Arena, dropping peevishly into a corner seat, "have put up a blast furnace near Oroya, and this furnace develops gases, and every head of cattle has died and every blade of grass has perished within a radius of some thirty miles. My property is practically valueless. I have heard that a German company has made an offer to the Yankees to take the gases fifteen miles away to treat them there. They've offered the Yankees a wad of money for the rights, it's said, and the Yankees have turned it down. The land, thanks to their gases, has become as valueless as real estate on the moon, and they'll be able to buy it up for next-door to nothing. The Yankees in Peru behave as high-handedly as if they were dealing with a nigger settlement. And before long . . ."

The young man was very angry and Goehrs hardly recognized the shuffleboard champion again. When Goehrs got out at Chosica, where Hill was spending the week-end in a little villa and told him the story of Leonidas Arena, Hill remarked :

" That sort of story shows you how yarns get spread about in Peru. For it's all just a trifle different from what your noble friend represents it as being, though the Yankees are, of course, the very devil. For they've put up the furnace in Oroya with incredible carelessness, and it didn't matter a hoot to them if everything did die off—barring human beings, who, by the way, benefited by these gases, more especially if they were tuberculous. The Yankees didn't worry as long as the previous President was in office. ' Here's the dough—O.K.' But when everything died off and more than everything, there was a row at last. The Yankees had to pay compensation, quite juicy compensation, too, and that won't do any harm either. Your friend the crocodile-stalker was probably trying to get rid of his land above its market value and burnt his fingers over the deal and is now spreading the yarn the other way about. And that, of course, is the way with all the reports one hears in these parts—inevitable in a country with a Press censorship."

" Is the censorship very severe ? "

" The severest in the world."

" But there's a Parliament and a Senate."

" No one's elected to them, unless the President cares to have him there."

" And the army ? " inquired Goehrs incredulously, and indicated an officer in a French uniform who was teasing a fighting-cock with a straw in his right hand and supporting himself on his murderously big cavalry sword with his left.

" Don't you make any mistake," exclaimed the Englishman. " They're Indians, one and all. No self-respecting man is a soldier—although he ought to be according to the constitution. The officers are trained pretty efficiently but that's for the protection of the President. And even then, he allows them to run about with only that long, useless skewer stuck in their belts—they haven't got a single cartridge. The real bulwark of the State is the police force. They are amazing. A father doesn't know whether his son is a member of it. A husband doesn't know whether his wife is. The Old Man is unrivalled, superb as an organizer. Perhaps you'll understand now why no one answers you when you ask questions about him."

" Perhaps," said Goehrs.

SOME RACIAL STUDIES

ONE evening Goehrs went with Arena to one of the few places of popular entertainment there are in Lima to watch the dog-racing. The stands were empty, but there

99

was a crowd round the oval course. Eight Indios led eight greyhounds past and stuffed them into a box that had eight apertures closed by glass panes.

An electrically driven hare then buzzed past on a rail round the oval course, and just at the moment when it was passing the box containing the eight dogs the eight glass windows opened, the greyhounds dashed out, saw the hare whizzing past—and were after it like streaks. After the first round a canvas barrier was set up in front of the dogs and they bounced into it like tennis balls, were caught up, and led off. White discs with the winners' numbers were then hoisted. It was only then that Goehrs realized that behind him there rose a big barrack with many ticket-office windows and that three times the number of people were assembled there as on the course. But they were nearly all of them Indians and not a man had so much as cocked an eye at the racing. They, one and all, had only been betting. At window 5–6 Arena was standing beside a young lady.

" What did you put on ? " Arena inquired.

" Nothing," replied Goehrs.

" Then what did you come for ? " asked the girl laughing.

Goehrs answered that he came to watch the dogs and the Peruvians, but she did not take offence.

" The dogs are no good," she said. " They're the survivors of hundreds of dogs a few ladies in Lima acquired because it was said to be *the* thing to race dogs. But that didn't last long, and, after they'd seen their names mentioned in the newspapers several times, their interest in it evaporated. These dogs are simply the dregs. People only come here to bet now."

She laughed, went to the ticket office, and asked for number twelve.

" You put something on now," she said.

Goehrs went to the ticket office and backed number seven. Ten soles on number seven. He had an unaccountable fancy for this number. Dog number seven, however, let his fancy down badly. He made a poor showing and took not the least interest in the hare he was supposed to be running down.

" What did you back ? " asked the damsel.

" Seven."

" Didn't you have a look at the dogs before the start ? "

Goehrs shook his head.

" You've put your money on the only dog that hasn't even got a tail." Goehrs was inconsolable.

" Have you had dinner yet ? " Arena asked her.

As she had not had dinner, a little party of five drove back into the city and, as there were only two restaurants in Lima, they hit on the idea of supping in the Chinese quarter. Though the young lady had the escort of her brother and a cousin, dining out in the evening was, strictly speaking, from the Peruvian point of view, neither proper nor fashionable. People did not dine out, just as they had not dined out under the reign of the Viceroy Amat y Junient.

The Chinese quarter was very crowded, but at last they found a table in a very dirty restaurant at the far end of a courtyard. Eight little bathing huts were built round a little garden, in the centre of which was a pool of crayfish. The cabins had no doors ; only at the height of five or six feet there was an attachment like a wooden flap.

" First of all pisco," said Arena, " and then camarones."

Pisco is in Peru what a cognac is in Europe. It is distilled only from the skins of pressed grapes. And camarones are crayfish.

While they were having supper a hut full of Peruvians amused themselves by throwing things through the ventilation holes into an adjoining cabin of Chinese ; to which the latter objected. This gave the Peruvians such offence that they invaded the Chinese hut and seized the Chinese by the throat, whereupon the Chinese screamed exactly like geese. The arena was then transferred to the courtyard, and there the two sides had it out. Quaintly enough, one of the combatants was a policeman who had nothing on except his shirt ; at the beginning of hostilities, he had hurriedly added his policeman's cap to his outfit.

During this racial war, staged before the public gaze like a shadow-play, Goehrs noticed that all the rest of the huts turned out inquisitively. Chinese family parties emerged, and many of these families were half-breeds. The men were Chinamen and the women Indians. Or both already mixed. The girls of this cross were extraordinarily pretty.

" I thought," said Goehrs, " there was a law prohibiting the immigration of Asiatics."

" You get round it at the rate of ten pounds per head. That's just the awful part of this country, that everything, absolutely everything, has its price under our government," said the young lady's brother.

This remark had the effect of an open sesame on the others. They discussed their government as Russian émigrés talk about the Bolsheviks. But they talked about it without mentioning names. Not a single name was mentioned. President Leguía's government, which depended on the support of the little fellows, the Indios, the dock labourers, and the Cholos-Mestizos, was a very well-hated government in the eyes of all the great old white families who had shared the government between themselves for the past century.

"When we were children," said the young lady, "we were allowed to hit at the Chinese if we came upon them in the streets. That was very nice. But we didn't dare do it to the Japanese."

Goehrs stared at the gentle philanthropist in amazement.

"The Japanese are a dangerous crowd," said her brother gravely, "and when one knows the tricks the Yankees and the Japs are up to to get a naval base in South America, it wouldn't surprise me if many of the yellow Japanese labourers who are now being smuggled in at the rate of ten pounds per head should, one day, in the event of war, turn out to be something very different from manual labourers."

"A naval base for the Japanese!" exclaimed Goehrs, for this theory struck him as a little too far-fetched. But the young people took it seriously and nodded. "And yet they are still letting the Japanese into Lima?" he asked.

"At the rate of ten pounds per head," said the young man. "Well, what do you think the officials, who are paid 800 pesos a month, run three cars, and live in houses that cost them 600 pesos a month in rent, are going to live on?"

He was the first man to speak his mind bitterly and acrimoniously against the Government and not run away. For some reason it struck Goehrs at once.

"Have you, by the way, got a Peruvian passport?" he asked the young man.

"Certainly," rejoined the latter calmly. "True, like Arena, I have a French one as well. The Peruvian is quite handy in Paris. But the French one is a hundred times more useful in Peru. Thanks to it they can't very well just have me disappear."

"COMPARATIVELY GOOD . . ."

ON the way back through the Chinese quarter Goehrs scrutinized the faces very closely. The Indios were really very like the Japanese. But they had a different look. Delicate, slightly arched noses. This nasal arch was the fateful dividing line between the two races, which in

Goehrs's opinion, backed by all the intuition he possessed, must have derived from one and the same stock. In the Hotel Bolívar he threw up the wide window and the "wintry air" of 68° came in together with the scent from the palms in the patio, round which the wings of the hotel were built. Opposite him a young American lady was lying in bed with her knees drawn up, on which she was reading the New York *Herald Tribune*. All the others had their windows closed. Peruvians feel the cold at this temperature.

Goehrs did some hard thinking.

Had the domination of the old Spanish coterie of a few thousand white families, who had simply oppressed the Indians, and had now been cold-shouldered by the Government, been better than the present Government? Or was Leguía's Government better, which was directed against the old families and was aiming at raising the status of the Indian, at encouraging the small holder, and at opening up the country by road traffic, and which as an earnest of its good intentions, had conjured the amazing new Lima out of the soil?

The answer would have been easy if it had not been necessary to omit rather arbitrarily one or two considerations, such as that of freedom, without which a European cannot even think. For the present Government was a dictatorship. But the other system of government had been a dictatorship, too. But not such an efficient dictatorship.

On the other hand, from a purely economic point of view, it seemed to Goehrs to be a mistake to join in the howl of Leguía's opponents, who maintained that Leguía's Government had gone mad building and making roads and ruining the country as Louis XIV had ruined France. Peru, they claimed, was like a beggar in a golden chair. Peru was going to ruin itself on Lima.

"What would modern Munich be," Goehrs thought, "without its mad king? A provincial market town. And where would the money saved be? Gone to the dogs during the years of inflation or in some other way."

If it came to a choice between a Government that did a great deal (without even breathing the word "socialism") and was only incidentally corrupt and thievish and another that did nothing, but was corrupt and thievish as well—if it came to a choice between two such governments, Goehrs would, without hesitation, plump for Leguía's, although it seemed to him to be, considered all round, a pretty fair outrage against humanity.

But European standards, including those of morality, appeared to him to be entirely meaningless in this case. Good in this quarter of the globe stood for comparatively good. And bad in this part of the world stood for comparatively bad. He had at any rate learnt that much. Any other attitude here would be sheer lunacy.

A Bull Fight

ON the following Sunday, Goehrs was sitting with Hill and two ladies on the stone seats of the ancient Plaza de Toros, the circular bull-fighting ring. The two young ladies were Englishwomen and yet, as a matter of fact, they were not. They were native-born and only their grandmother had been an Englishwoman, and that still clung about them a little. They still remembered their grandmother telling them that a few decades ago, before the Peruvians had developed their sense of nationality so strongly, Peruvians when addressed by Europeans in the street would stand still, hat in hand. All that, it is true, had changed a great deal, because the Peruvians were driving about in very fine cars nowadays and were quite self-possessed, but they still hankered after dancing with English people at the Country Club.

The two young ladies were not only not Englishwomen, but their Indian blood, to the extent of 15 per cent., showed in their complexions and their eyes. They were very petite, well proportioned, like toys—but, like all Peruvian girls, not really pretty. But they were, again like all Peruvian girls, convinced that they were very attractive and expensive toys and, as all South Americans do not marry for the settlement, because the majority of the families are very big and do not give dowries, they had great prospects of marrying well, unless they should previously lose their reputation, which no South American girl can afford to do.

They lived with their mother in a bungalow next door to Hill's, in Pizarro's olive grove. Like all Peruvian girls, they were obsessed by the idea of marrying a European, an idea before which Europeans grow astonishingly shy. For when a European marries a Peruvian, he marries along with her a family of anything from five to ten members, who with touching artlessness would settle down in his house when and for as long as it suited them. He married a very devil of a family, who never left him alone, not even in his bedroom.

In addition to Hill, a fair-haired young man of thirty joined them : John Compton, commander of the flying squadron of the Peruvian army.

The bull fight for which they were waiting was being held in aid of a remarkable cause. It was being given for the benefit of distressed men of letters. At popular prices. But it soon became clear that it was not a bull fight but a novillada. No fighting bulls turned out, but young animals. No professional toreadors, but amateurs, aficionados, youngsters of good (but not too good) families and business men of important (but not too important) concerns. It was a bull fight in mufti, without the feverish atmosphere of the corrida, without its valour, without its fatal, wonderful beauty, and without its rigour of rules, in accordance with which one of the adversaries was bound to be left lying on the sand in the sun, the man or the bull. There was nothing Spanish, nothing Moorish about it, the mingled character-istics that in Seville constitute the monstrous fascination of the bull fight. It was a burlesque.

The bulls were skeletons covered in calfskin, and even their horns were half cut off as a precaution against any harm befalling the amateurs. This was unfair because it raised the odds against the bull. The fairness of the bull fight lay at any rate in the fact that the chances of winning it were, if not quite equally divided, fairly level between man and beast. Goehrs had seen many a bull in Spain far more than a match for its adversary in fighting spirit, in joy of battle, and in craftsmanship, led off reprieved to spend the rest of its life at pasture, while the bullfighter, hissed out of the ring, was relegated to outer darkness—with a career, which in Spain is only second to that of the head of the State, closed to him.

If the odds were unevenly matched, they were levelled up by the amateurs being so perishingly inferior. As soon as they took up the sword, after all the preliminaries of waving their cloaks about and baiting, to give the bull, eye to eye with it, its *coup de grâce* by a direct thrust to the heart through the vertebræ of its neck ; as soon as the amateurs were supposed to be directly up against the bull and expec-ted to run it through, they were in such a flutter that the animal was not in any very great danger.

But what were the bulls about ?

A real Spanish fighting bull has, as the result of centuries of breeding, on entering the ring, only one desire : that is to reduce anything human and alive in the arena to pulp. The childlike bulls of Lima had only one desire and that was to get out of the arena again with all possible speed. They did not put up a fight ; they simply ran for all they were worth for the gate at the far end and, by tossing their heads, made it abundantly clear that they had urgent appointments outside. No butcher in Spain would have taken the least interest in dispatching such cowardly brutes.

But the bullfighters of Lima approached these miserable beasts with pride in their bearing. They unfolded their scarlet cloths in front of them and excited them to one or two freakish bounds, but they themselves committed blunder after blunder in their performance. The movements of the Spanish bullfighter have been prescribed for centuries. They consist of countless steps. The steps are the figures of a sombrely attractive ballet. Every spectator in Spain knows every movement exactly, every pose, and judges from them whether the toreador has pluck or is showing the white feather, whether he is clever or dull-witted or a genius. The spectators in Lima did not know the rules well. They overlooked any number of mistakes and even passed quite vulgar, conceited movements of extreme ungainliness such as would have cost a toreador against a slightly better bull half of his hindquarters. But in the long run this tomfoolery by fatuous oafs became too much of a good thing even for the onlookers of this type, and they began to grow noisy. Two bulls had already been led off because the amateurs were simply incapable of finishing them off. One of them looked like a pin cushion. When the third bullfighter instead of running his sword up to the hilt into the third bull only jabbed a couple of inches of it into the animal's neck for the fourth time, the hubbub started.

" You poor cripple ! " shouted a man from the highest tier to the bullfighter, a corpulent, no longer very young man, Suito by name, who ordinarily used to lounge about in Lima a good deal and consequently enjoyed a measure of popularity which, however, he forfeited entirely that day. Suito was wearing leather guards on his knees and a Cordovese tall hat.

" Caricature of Canero," roared another between his hollowed hands, comparing Suito, on account of his leather guards, with the famous toreador who used to bring down his bull from the saddle.

There was a devil of row with every one whistling and yelling, and Suito left the ring in dudgeon, pale but shrugging his shoulders.

" Beastly mess," remarked the flying man. It was the first remark he had made that day.

" It is almost always the case," said Hill. " Even the bulls degenerate in this climate. The bullfighters as well, of course, but that is less astonishing."

" Extraordinary thing ! " said Goehrs. " In Spain the fate of the monarchy or the republic depends more on the attitude they adopt towards the bullfighting than on their economic policy. The Spanish enthusiasm for bullfighting is the most fanatical enthusiasm there is. The Spaniards would simply die for it. In Lima this enthusiasm seems to have become a farce. Otherwise they would have torn the amateurs to pieces."

" Yes, even enthusiasm degenerates in this climate," agreed Hill.

" A quarter of the seats are empty," said one of the young ladies regretfully.

" If we had gone to the football match," said Hill, " we should have had a crowd of 30,000 and we should have had a really sporting game."

" No. No football," protested the other young lady as, juggling with a mirror in her left hand, she gave her little hat a tilt.

" Let's go on to the Country Club," suggested Hill, " and have a dance."

" Not a bad idea that," said the two Peruvian girls.

An hour later they were at the Country Club. Hardly anywhere in Europe outside of England was there such a club with so many overlapping facilities for outdoor games, what with golf-links and perfect greens, with tennis-courts and swimming-baths and a paddock all round it. Thirty years ago after the street-fighting they had piled up the dead in stacks here and burnt them. In the lounge twenty-five couples of English people, Germans, Italians, and Peruvians were now dancing.

" How do these people all happen to meet ? " asked Goehrs as he drank his tea and watched the dancing.

Hill swallowed his whisky sour, and lounged back in his chair.

" First of all," he said, " there are a few people from the legations here, but they're not the people who look as if they were, whereas the people who look as if they were will be selling you your ticket for the boat to-morrow. They are only guests, because the dues are high. There are a few Peruvians, and they are Peruvian snobs, sons of newspaper proprietors, and a few deputies who like their daughters to be seen dancing with Englishmen. They all dance a little too strenuously. I think you ought to be drinking coffee instead of tea, Goehrs. Peru has the best coffee in South America. For three centuries it used to be reserved for the exclusive use of the Spanish court. As a matter of fact the coffee plantations here are still privately worked, not by mass-production methods as in Brazil. Quite small beans. They're roasted in the shell with a little butter and sugar. And then a tremendous quantity is used when it is ground. As everybody knows, people only drink water in Europe."

" We shall have to invite you to take coffee in our bungalow one of these days," said the young ladies.

" Don't you go," said Captain John Compton—this was the second time he opened his mouth that day. " Everybody arrives at eleven instead of at eight and everybody brings five people with him."

" And they only give you cocktails to eat," sighed Hill.

" You are odious," said the two young ladies. " We will invite you two all the same. And now what about a dance ? "

THE INQUISITION

THERE are exceptions, thought Goehrs, on making the acquaintance of Señora Molfino in her own house, in which there was no husband but a great deal of old furniture and coats-of-arms dating back to colonial times. The husband had been a moving spirit of the National Club and had been banished. Señora Molfino was not only descended from one of the few old families who had settled in Lima three hundred years ago ; she was, too, the first human being Goehrs had met to express her opinions without reserve. She obviously was taking risks in doing so. Wives ran exactly the same risks as their husbands if they disliked dictatorships, though they were not, it is true, in the same degree of danger—for there were wives whose husbands disappeared if some one or other took an interest in the wives. Señora Molfino certainly seemed to be unconscious of danger. Nor had her husband disappeared because she was an exceptionally beautiful woman, but for purely political reasons. Señora Molfino was a woman of uncertain age because—as is the case of the majority of Peruvians when they have lost the first bloom of youth—it was an open question whether she was 28 or 45. But Señora Molfino was an educated woman and far cleverer than most of her compatriots, who were not very different from the girls Goehrs had met at the dog-racing field and at the bull fight.

" Lima is very puzzling," she said one day, " and hardly any one succeeds in keeping its three epochs distinct. I should like to make you really realize that. Have you ever seen the old streets called ' Smite the Jews ' and ' She was great with child ' and ' To the desperate ' ? "

Goehrs shook his head.

Señora Molfino smiled. Her mythological first name, Diana, did not altogether suit her but, when she smiled, a cold expression came into her eyes which did fit the name.

One day they were in front of the Palacio Torre Tagle, in which the Ministry of Foreign Affairs was housed. The palace was a plain, two-storeyed building, but it was only the aloof Spanish style of architecture that made it so plain without, in order to emphasize all the hidden wealth of its interior. The only striking features of the palace were two wonderful filigree balcony boxes, elaborately carved wooden coffins through the black whorls and flourishes of which the ladies of the house had for a century or two looked out on the narrow street without themselves being seen. Within, the palace consisted of a wonderful Moorish court-yard. Its interior was the most beautiful of any colonial building in South America. With flights of stairs, arcades, saloons, portals, terraces. It covered the whole of Spain of the era of the conquests. Instinct with taste, with dignity, with aloofness, with intimacy, with catholicism, instinct with life and with asceticism, with wealth and solidity, full of overweening arrogance.

Señora Molfino pointed across the street through the balcony cage to an unpretentious house.

" The house over there is very similar. Only the people living in it had as their motto, ' After God, we.' "

" After God, we," repeated Goehrs. " Seventeenth to eighteenth century. That was a motto true to the spirit of those days."

Leaving the palace, Goehrs observed that the pillars of the entrance hall were propped up by cannons planted aslant. He had already been puzzled by all sorts of things in the rooms ; for example, by what means they had con-trived to transport building material, the furniture, the coaches, the silks, and the pictures to Lima in small hundred-ton sailing ships.

In the middle of the Moorish courtyard stood a man's bust on a slender pedestal.

" Who is that ? "

" Legíua," said Señora Molfino.

" He looks like Briand."

Diana Molfino shrugged her shoulders. " You will see other portraits in which he has a likeness to other people."

The car then drove to a suburb and drew up outside a gateway where privates and officers were standing about in groups in the courtyard. In the middle of a garden, gay (in midwinter) with flowers, rose an airy, delicate palace made up only of flights of stairs and columns. From all the terraces of this dainty plaything, from all its oriel windows and stairs, roof gardens and alcoves, Goehrs looked out over the country in front of Lima—on that narrow strip of flat ground forming the coastline. The vultures were floating above it. And closing in round it, alarmingly close, rose the Cordilleras, almost always with the silver grey veil about their heads, until one after the other, as if granting a favour, they ever and again raised the veil for a second in the play of light and shade.

" Delightful."

" Charming places the people used to live in, aren't they ? " said Señora Molfino. " To sit on this terrace with wax candles of an evening . . . delightful. A viceroy built this dainty bandbox for his mistress. The viceroy's name was Dom Manuel de Amat y Junient. The people called his mistress the Indian bitch—*perra chola*. She was evidently a witty woman and shaded the name off into Italian—she probably had Italian as well as Indian blood in her veins— into Perricholi."

She threw a rapid glance at the tide of tropical verdure streaming up to the purple Cordilleras. The scent of the flowers was almost overpowering. Going back, they saw long lines of stabling.

" Nowadays," said Señora Molfino with an accent of contempt she took no pains to disguise, " the President's police guard is quartered in the little palace."

The palace was certainly not adapted for military occupation—on the contrary. But it did not strike Goehrs as exactly contemptible. On many an occasion troops had been billeted in palaces where at other times voluptuousness had reigned—that happened to be one of the little ironies of history.

Señora Molfino had a definite plan of operations. She then

took Goehrs to the Senate—the old seat of the Inquisition. The session hall of the Inquisition was all in red. All the doors leading into it were of iron and had a hole just big enough for a mouth to cover. When the defendant was summoned before his judges to make his defence, he stood in this red room. But his prosecutor, whom he never saw, stood outside and laid his indictment through the hole in the iron door.

" Here is another portrait of the President," said Señora Molfino, and pointed to a portrait depicting some one in evening dress with a broad sash across his chest. Amid the stagnant atmosphere of the Inquisition that had sent thousands to their doom hung the portrait of President Leguía in a white shirt front. . . . " Now I'm going to show you something awfully nice of General Bolívar," said Señora Molfino.

She drove Goehrs to the outskirts of the old city. There stood a one-storeyed house of quite a preposterously insignificant exterior. " It is forbidden to enter with head covered," read a printed notice on the door. This did not mean that the author of the announcement was afraid lest visitors might carry off purloined articles under their hats ; the notice merely called upon every one to enter a shrine that embodied the spirit of national dignity bareheaded. True, they struck matches on Pizarro's coffin, and laid information against strangers who might happen to have Ecuadorian matches in their pockets, and bedded down horses in the Palacio Perricholi, the architectural gem of South America, but the Lima of the Wars of Liberation and of national consciousness means a great deal more to the Peruvians of to-day than the Lima of the people who had made it, founded it, and conquered it three hundred years before. Pizarro and the viceroys were still Spaniards—in sentiment, at any rate. The generals of the War of Liberation after 1800 were, even if descendants of Pizarro, at any rate Peruvians. A whole world divided them—a political world.

In the house that Goehrs entered, hat in hand, General Bolívar had lived for a time in the decades after 1800. Bolívar was born in Venezuela, but he had liberated not only Venezuela, but Colombia, Ecuador, Peru, and Bolivia as well. The Wars of Liberation had indeed been a concerted action of South America, but the hottest fighting had been for Lima and Peru, for Peru had always been the jewel of Spain, and Chile and Argentina were at that time pretty insignificant as compared with Peru.

III

All the rooms in the house were stuffed full of pictures, furniture, proclamations, mementos, letters, weapons, camp beds, sashes, and uniforms that had belonged to Bolívar or to one of his generals. A very personal museum—private and discreet. A narrow, delicate head showed from all Bolívar's portraits. At the back of the house lay a garden with cloisters round it. A fairy-tale garden with fig trees, with syringa bushes, vines, palms, and hibiscus—a fairy-tale garden, a poet's garden, not at all the garden for a general.

"What do you think of Bolívar?" asked Señora Molfino, snapping-to a work-box which some enthusiastic lady had presented to Bolívar.

They passed into an annexe where a big wall space was filled by a huge fresco in commemoration of the first centenary, celebrated a few years ago, of the independence of Peru from Spain. It was a very highly coloured picture, and Goehrs made out several well-known faces in it. In the centre stood President Leguía, and, grouped round him, portrait sketches of the members of the diplomatic corps, of generals, ministers, and of a popular French general who happened to have been on a visit to South America. In addition, flags and emblems. In the right-hand corner was an aeroplane with a portrait of the President's son in flying kit. A commemorative, horribly painted picture.

It struck Goehrs that everywhere—beginning from Pizarro's mummy to Bolívar's underwear—whenever a historical incident was recorded, Leguía's name figured.

"We will have a cup of tea now," said Señora Molfino when they were back in the car again.

The lawns of the Country Club were like pile carpet. It was a perfect day, and the view extended far out to sea. The figures of three men playing golf in white knickers stood out on the skyline. Beyond them two huge blocks of rock of a soft metallic blue, like the plumage of a pigeon's breast, rose against the pink of the Peruvian sunset from out of a sea invisible from where they stood.

"What islands are those?" asked Goehrs, a plate of strawberries in his hand. He saw Señora Molfino's face turn dead-white. At the same moment he realized that he had been guilty of a blunder.

"That is San Lorenzo," said Señora Molfino. "Many people have their arms broken and are tortured before being transported there. For years no one who has been banished there has come back. No mail reaches them either."

Goehrs realized horror-stricken that the wife was talking of her husband.

" You must hate Leguía very bitterly," he said without really being able to grasp that in this European setting all this could be fact.

" I do," said Señora Molfino quietly.

" In some respects things have not changed much since the times of the Inquisition," said Goehrs, picking to pieces a syringa blossom standing in a vase in front of him.

" There are a few more new roads," replied Señora Molfino, " but what good are roads ? "

She was sitting with her back to the islands and had not even turned round to glance at them.

THE HEADHUNTER'S TROPHY

ON his way home, Goehrs ran through what he knew about Leguía. Peru was a country about four times as big as Germany (perhaps not quite so large) with perhaps four or five or six million inhabitants ; so big a country that single estates were as big as fair-sized English counties. It had a coastline of over 1400 miles, about 2500 miles of railways, 113 provinces, 873 districts, 13 bishops, 9000 telephones, and 6000 motor cars. A country with the finest cotton outside of Egypt, full of ore, full of oil, full of tobacco, full of sugar. The only country with a genuine colonial hallmark, with the savour of conquest, with old Spanish traditions. With a narrow, flat coastal zone of from 40 to 65 miles in width ; with Cordillera highlands about four times this width ; and then the zone of the primeval forests of the Montaña extending all the way to the Amazon. With innumerable tropical valleys between mountain ranges ; orange groves among glaciers—a topsy-turvy country.

A country that since its declaration of independence a century ago has waged unsuccessful wars, has lost territory to Chile, and of late years has come to terms with Chile again. A country where more of the inhabitants speak Quichua than Spanish, in the main an Indian country full of Cholos, half-breeds, with perhaps a few hundred thousands who might be called " white." A country that has recovered from State bankruptcy. A country with inexhaustible resources, and hopelessly lacking in enterprise.

A country with a constitution, a Senate, a Congress, an army, and first-class cruisers. In 1930 this country was ruled by Augusto Leguía, a man with sons and brothers, a white man of good family. It was being ruled by him in his fourth term of office, although constitutional law forbade any one to govern for more than one term without an interval. He was governing it now for the fourth time, three times in succession.

Leguía ruled as dictators had ruled in Rome ; with a Senate, with a Congress, but with all the seats in these bodies occupied by men whom he wanted to have there. The army ? Not over-spoiled, so as not to become a weapon against him. The little navy ? In the hollow of his hand.

On his side ? An insignificant section of people devoted to him to the death. Sixty of the old families who had become impoverished and had deserted to his side. And then the masses.

Against him ?

Goehrs was just then driving past the National Club in the Plaza San Martín. Its columns and bow windows stood out snow-white against the foliage. Footmen in livery were standing on a broad flight of steps. Against him, thought Goehrs. Practically speaking, almost every one that counted, because practically almost every one who had ambition, influence, money, and brains desired to be in power himself.

What was it then that kept Leguía in office—kept him there so firmly established and for so long a time ?

His personality. He had for a decade been the most interesting, toughest, and most attractive figure of a dictator in South America. One incident in his life recurred to Goehrs that was at the same time associated with a national holiday. Leguía had had to survive many plots, and on one occasion of an attempt against his life one of the conspirators had betrayed everything at the last moment. Ten minutes later, therefore, the revolutionaries had to strike ; they went by tens to Leguía's palace, where nothing was as yet known of the conspiracy, and dragged him out, hauled him across the street, and in the square of the Inquisition confronted him with the alternative of resigning or of being riddled with bullets. A gigantic Negro held a pistol to his head. But the old man was a tough customer.

" Death rather than the loss of my honour," he said, and drew himself up. The Negro raised something above his head. At that moment a volley crashed.

The volley was a sheer mistake, for the officer in command

of a patrol that happened to be passing gave orders to fire on the Negro only because he thought he saw a simple case of assault upon a white man. He acted without recognizing any of the parties concerned, purely in the interests of law and order. The army was at the time probably involved in the conspiracy against Leguía, but the plot was unorganized because the rebels had been compelled to strike prematurely. In any case the officer had given the command to fire with a result disastrous for the Negro. Leguía, on the other hand, grasped the situation with the quick resourcefulness of the tyrant, promoted the lieutenant on the spot, addressed the soldiers, mounted a horse, and rode back. " That is the fate of every one who attempts the life of Leguía," he preached the selfsame day.

This date had become an official holiday. It was thenceforward known as " the day of character."

There were people in Lima who compared Leguía with Cavour, with Christ even. And there were people in Lima who cleverly hinted that he was nothing more than a *caudillo*, a bandit chief in patent-leather boots, a criminal like Gómez in Venezuela—only more discreet and more intelligent.

But as against this latter view, there was the work Leguía had accomplished ; a new Lima, an effort to develop a new Peru by means of roads. The only question was whether this work, belittled, naturally enough, even by Señora Molfino, rested on sound foundations. For there were people, too, who reproached Leguía with having become a very wealthy man during his term of office and of having a family and a following that was brazenly corrupt. This was ugly but it seemed to be true, yet it appeared to Goehrs, comparing South America with South America, not with Europe, not to be as important as it sounded.

So what manner of man was he ? Could this country, three-quarters of which was still in a state of savagery, be governed other than by the methods of the dictator ? But how did Leguía contrive to govern it in the teeth of the factions who had ruled it for a century, under a system that depended entirely upon his own personality ? Was this a petty or a big man who sweated everything out of Peru that did not suit his book, who banished thousands, transported hundreds to San Lorenzo, who caused people to disappear every week, every night, and was surrounded by an unrivalled network of espionage ? Who was this man whom many people honestly maintained to be charming, who, in his late sixties, was still a ladies' man, and of whom others claimed that on his island over there he had his enemies tortured and the arms of his opponents broken ? This man who governed a country, in which there was not a trace of a socialist party or socialist movement, in a spirit of socialism ; a man who set himself up like a Roman tribune looking for support only to the masses, without a programme, on the strength of his personality, and whose propaganda aimed at raising the standard of the Indios, an unheard-of proposal ; of the Indios, seventy per cent. of whom did not know what it was all about because they did not understand Spanish.

What manner of man was he ? Good or bad ? Great or petty ? Probably a little of both. . . .

Immersed in these thoughts, Goehrs reached his hotel. A head was hanging in the showcase of the cigarette merchant's in the hall that had not been hanging there that morning. A Sansa. A head no bigger than the space you enclose between your thumb and middle finger if you keep the tips of both closed. A head from the Montaña on the River Amazon. A headhunter's head. A rare trophy.

The Indios in the virgin forests have the knack of removing the bones out of their enemies' skulls, of preserving the formation of the head and of drying it with herbs and hot sand so that, reduced to a tenth of its original size and with waving hair, it still remains the likeness of the man on whose neck it had once sat. A really daring perversion of valour.

The export of and traffic in these heads was prohibited by law. Goehrs went into the shop.

" What is the price of the Sansa ? "

" A hundred dollars."

" That's absurd, my lad."

" Beg pardon," said the Cholo nonchalantly.

" What is the price of that tiger ? " asked Goehrs, and touched a tigerskin lying on the floor with his foot.

" Twenty-five dollars."

Goehrs left the shop. The image of the head of the man, hacked off and reduced to the size of an egg, haunted him for a while. Amazing country. An enemy's head four times the price of a tigerskin.

At this moment the wish to make the acquaintance of the man who held this country in the hollow of his hand possessed him. On the following morning he went to his ambassador, an able, quiet, clever gentleman, and requested him to present him to Leguía.

AT six o'clock on Monday evening Goehrs's car pulled up at the back entrance to the President's palace. A number of soldiers with fixed bayonets crowded the dark, narrow passage. An officer saluted. They walked rapidly through the passage and came out into a green garden round which the four wings of the palace were built. The palace was only a two-storeyed building. You stepped straight out of the garden into the ground floor. You reached the upper storey by a steep wooden staircase. It gave on to a wooden gallery running round the four wings.

Two men were standing in the gallery, which was painted a dark red, at the top of the wooden staircase.

One of them was a man in dark-blue trousers with a red stripe. He had heavy gold frogs across his chest and a French military képi. The chief of the military council.

" Colonel Basso."

The colonel bowed. He was a man with a big, black, slightly drooping moustache. The other man was about thirty, fair, with a narrow head and spectacles. The master of ceremonies. A mere boy.

" Señor Arramburu."

Goehrs threw a glance past the colonel's gold frogs into the garden. Pizarro had built this palace four hundred years ago. He had lived in it himself. He had laid out the garden. In one corner of it a fig tree was growing. Pizarro had planted it. Fountains of old azulejos tiles of a delicate blue decorated the lawn. Pizarro had seen those glazed tiles every day.

They passed from the dark-red timber gallery into a room. French furniture. The door leading on to the gallery was left open. Just as in a country house. The colonel disappeared. The young master of ceremonies had been educated at a German school. He spoke German with rather the same accent as a Frenchman does.

" The President will be ready in a minute," he said. " I have just come across from the Foreign Office and am only here on duty. Have you see the Foreign Office—the Palacio Torre Tagle—charming, is it not ? There are some quaint stories about it. Do you remember the slanting cannon against the columns in the courtyard ? In medieval times they formed a fence—any one who crossed it could claim sanctuary. Did you like the interior ? "

" There are few houses of the seventeenth and eighteenth centuries in Spain in such an excellent state of preservation."

" And so secretive. And so well built. On the occasion of the centenary celebration of Peru's independence we had a company of 3000 there. You remember the big wooden lion in the courtyard, holding a pair of scales in its mouth ? They used to weigh the silver in them in the old days."

" Very massive scales."

" Massive times, too. Every now and then they would pass a rope through the lion's jaws and hang some particularly interesting individual to the end of it."

The door of the adjoining room opened. A tall, fair man pushed the gilded screen back and went up to the table in the middle of the room, on which he had left his tall hat. He was carrying an attaché case. He wore a little, fair toothbrush moustache. The British Minister. He pushed his case under his arm, just waved his tall hat, and went out. The door behind the gilt screen, which had closed for a moment, opened again. The colonel with the gold frogs stood in the doorway and beckoned.

The room into which Goehrs passed was a little bigger and fairly lofty. It contained four old shabby arm-chairs with high backs. A leather sofa stood against the wall. The walls were bare. A writing-table with a few sheets of notepaper on it was stood in the window. On its top casually rested an ebony elephant from Zanzibar and a little marble lion.

A man, very slight and very neat, was standing in the middle of the room. The tunic of General Bolívar the Liberator, hanging in the Bolívar house, would have fitted him. Almost childlike shoulders. His feet in button boots a woman might have worn. In the face, too, there was a look of Bolívar, a likeness, not of the several features but in the composition of the head and the expression. Bolívar's face, that as the face of the most distinguished man of his times a century earlier had to adapt itself to many expressions and is handed down in hundreds of engravings as a general's face, a popular idol's face, an intellectual face— just as the tastes of his day would have it, and with just as much in it as his contemporaries read into it—Bolívar's face was sharp, cameolike, and a little womanish. Bolívar had Byron's eyes and forehead, but they were the eyes and forehead of a southern Byron, born in Venezuela. Bolívar's nose and chin were different from those of the Englishman. Bolívar's nose was thin and long ; his chin was small.

Leguía's face was on similar oval lines. There was something delicate about his face that masked an intense energy. Just as there was something very soft hiding in Bolívar's features behind his impassive commander's face. But this girl-like man had one advantage over him that Goehrs had so far not observed in any other man's face—deep, dark eyes of an animal, beautiful eyes, subject to very strange changes.

Leguía invited Goehrs to take his seat against the wall. He himself stood with his back to the windows. The garden formed the background.

They began to talk about Peru at once without preamble.

" Since Johannesburg, I have not seen a city," said Goehrs, " that has developed in accordance with a definite plan and with a given style like Lima. In ten years' time—how was it done ? "

" Yes ! Lima had to grow into a great new city," said Leguía, playing with his delicate hands, " but my programme for the irrigation of the coastal desert and my programme of colonization by small holders are much more important. You always have to have the climate in mind here. Do you really sleep well in Lima ? "

He smiled in a charming way. Goehrs leant forward.

" What is your view of Mussolini ? "

Leguía hesitated for a moment. For a second a streak of lightning flashed through his feminine smile. His dark eye swept appraisingly, like that of a fencer, over Goehrs.

" How can I with such a small task pass judgment on so great a statesman with so big a work ? " he said ; then with some reserve : " Mussolini has done everything he could do for his country."

" I only asked you, Mr. President," said Goehrs smiling, " because I thought that this European would interest you more especially."

" Undoubtedly, he does interest me," said Leguía evasively, " but why more especially ? I am equally interested in your old President Hindenburg. I admire seeing an old general like him becoming such a fine statesman. What difficulties, great Heavens ! But America—how old do you take Peru to be ? "

" One has to pin one's faith to men of science and they are arguing about it. I believe a lot of thousands of years."

" You cannot give it a date," said Leguía. " Nor need one worry to do so. Two thousand years is a very long spell of time. Just remember that the Spaniards have only been here for the last four hundred years. And that I have now been President for ten years in succession. And that I have not taken a single day of these ten years off duty." He smiled broadly.

"Ten years—and not an hour off. People always form certain expectations of a man and of his work, and one has to live up to them, and in the long run one adapts oneself to them. But two thousand years—what a spell of time! When President Hoover of the United States was on a visit here I presented him with a piece of Indian fabric that was two thousand years old. A glorious bit of stuff. What colouring! What draughtsmanship! What a highly cultivated folk there must have been even then! Remarkable folk, these Incas and the tribes and the civilizations before them, eh? Yes—my whole will is set on raising the status of the Indios."

"Seventy per cent. of the population," said Goehrs, and remembered that half of them more or less were still living the life of slaves. And that Leguía espoused their cause, that the President who ordered the arms of his opponents to be broken was the first man to take up the cause of the Indian with real sympathy.

Goehrs rose and realized at that moment how quiet it was and how eerily green and dark the garden suddenly became. As he got up, he was looking straight at the fig tree in the corner of the garden Francisco Pizarro had planted. Immediately above it he saw the window of the room in which the bastard of his friend and deadly enemy Almagro had plunged his sword into Pizarro's neck.

Goehrs shook the President's feminine hand. Leguía kept his left hand half-way in his pocket. Leguía's whitish grey hair lay in a smooth parting over the tan of his forehead. Leguía smiled the thin, alluring smile of a woman. But he remained standing, easily and yet alertly in the middle of the room. Sixty-eight years of age. The sole dictator the civilized world accepted at the moment.

NIPPED IN THE BUD

GOEHRS had worked out a scheme to travel to the terminus of the Oroya line up to the edge of the virgin forest and ride on muleback via Ayacucho through the Cordilleras to Cuzco, the old capital of the Incas. He had estimated four days for the journey as the crow flies. But at this point he came into collision with the whole problem of traffic in South America.

" You'll never get there," said Hill. " True, the distance is short enough. I have been asking my *mineros* about it. You'll either be caught by a snowstorm in some Indian hut 16,000 feet above sea-level, or you'll get malaria in one of the deep tropical valleys. The country is practically un-explored—and it doesn't make a good impression if all trace of you is lost for a bit. Not a soul will believe that you didn't want it to be. There have been one or two bad cases of self-advertisement among travellers of late. Ask your minister about them."

Goehrs was annoyed.

" Apart from that," Hill went on, " you'll want five mules. They'll cost you five-and-twenty pounds a head, and in Cuzco, supposing you ever get there, they'll only give five pounds apiece for them."

So Goehrs bought a steamer ticket. So he had, instead of travelling the much shorter, direct overland route, to go two days south to Mollendo and endeavour to reach Cuzco by rail in a few days' time from there. But it was more businesslike because knocking about with mules for weeks only for the fun of aping an " expedition " struck him as childish.

Hill gave him a farewell lunch in his toy bungalow. He mixed the cocktails himself. Cocktails icy as a glacier stream.

" Have you read what *El Mundo* said about the bull fight the other day ? " said Hill, handing round the glasses. " It did make the journalists sit up that people from the crews of eight ships should have attended the knockabout with these poor beasts, among them the officers of two American cruisers that brought the new American ambassador over."

" I read it, but the paper was not writing against bull-fighting but against the spectators who, as they neatly put it, turned a national celebration into a jamboree. That is the wrong line of argument. The public have, of course, the right to protest if it gets idiots like those dished up to it as bullfighters. They have paid their money. If amateurs want to make an exhibition of themselves and are no good they should invite their friends. . . ."

" Don't get excited about it," interposed Hill. " Better try some *seviche*."

He served the dish himself. Little oysters with red beards like tiny lobster claws—a dainty for which any man on the west coast would go to his death. In spite of the condiments

121

of green and red peppers and onions, the tang of the sea was full-flavoured.

" Nice, that oysters should be called *señoritas*, little ladies," said Goehrs and raised one in his spoon. Hill's Indian was waiting. Hill had not succeeded in teaching him much Spanish, but the Indian, during the two years he had been in his service, had taught him a good deal of Quichua. He brought in a big dish of crayfish soup.

"It's made with rice and cream," said Hill, who, as a case-hardened bachelor, knew all about cooking. "Have you ever seen such big crayfish ? And yet they're as full-flavoured as little freshwater crayfish, or rather they have three times the flavour. And how did Leguía impress you ?"

Goehrs looked out over the thousands of old olive trees. Was something new brewing in Peru, or had, as he sometimes thought himself, nothing changed ? True, there were aeroplanes ; towns were springing up like mushrooms ; roads were being surveyed ; and one oil-borer after the other was sprouting up. But did these make any odds to the human beings ? The Indios were free now, had all the rights that any one can have in a State, but what use had they had from these rights ? There was no Indian problem, and there was no Indian movement. The Indio was a beast of burden. Just as under the Incas the Indio had been a beast of burden. Not because he was brown, but because he was an Indio.

Goehrs longed to get to the highlands and see more of the Indio. He took a chirimoya that was as big as a coconut and looked like a huge green strawberry. He cut it in half and spooned out the white nougat-like inside, a white flesh full of pips, a soft flesh like a *chaudfroid*. The fruit exhaled a fragrance that beggars description. Too strong, but it might have been distilled of strawberries, pineapples, and peaches. That is what the fruit tasted like, too. And the same scent was wafted in from the garden. The Indian came in with a newspaper.

" Hurry up the coffee," said Hill. He looked at his watch. The boat was due to leave at five.

Hill opened the *Crónica*, whistled between his teeth, and handed it across the table to Goehrs. Goehrs saw a big headline. " Attempt on the Life of the Head of the State." The *Crónica* reported that forty persons had been arrested in Lima the previous evening and transported to San

Lorenzo. The moving spirit of the conspiracy was the Chief Magistrate Urbina, who lived somewhere up country. Urbina had for weeks been training a wretched illiterate Indio like a dog to stab Leguîa in the public streets.

Goehrs did some calculations. If the people had been arrested at eight o'clock p.m., Leguía must have signed the warrant for their arrest at six o'clock, that is to say, before his audience. During his conversation with Goehrs Leguía had been quiet and cheerful ; he had been always smiling and talking about Peru as if Peru were a country as peaceful as a kindergarten. And yet Peru was bristling with revolvers itching to have a shot at the dictator. Leguía did not dodge them. He was in the public eye everywhere and not only with the " hares," the heavily armed officers on the red English motorcycles. Leguía appeared in public at the beauty shows, at the races, at the bull fights. He knew that a few thousand revolvers were sighted on him. And why did they not go off ?

There was some mysterious force about the little man, who was old and in bad health, but a real man for all that.

"Urbina, by the way, has confessed," Hill read out. " Well—that means to say he has been put to the torture. But hurry up and get into the car. It's four o'clock. I'll run you round to the quay by the beach."

ADVENTURES IN MOLLENDO

GOEHRS steamed southwards off the coast of Peru again for two days and two nights. He saw numbers of seals and schools of dolphins, but he had never seen so many birds. Millions of them over the water linked up into a chain straight across the path of the steamer. They were flying out to sea and would not allow the ship to break their chain.

They flew for hours round the vessel's bows, and she ploughed a salient into their originally straight front until in the end a huge streamer of birds was fluttering on the right and left of the funnel, twenty miles of birds straining to fly round her bows, and then to fly back the twenty miles they had come. They would not give in, they would not break their chain although, if they had broken it for a second and closed up again astern of the ship, they would have saved themselves hours of flight.

They are very logical or very stupid, reflected Goehrs, who had watched their breathless chase for the whole of a fore-noon until all these heavily flying divers, ducks, and pelicans had passed—but perhaps their sole condition of life depends on being both at the same time. They simply cannot risk trying an experiment just to save themselves trouble, and adventuring on the ocean of intelligence by breaking away from their acquired instinct. That is a preserve of the human animal.

The coast was of mythological beauty. Rocks, desert, always half veiled. White guano rocks on a blue sea. Shell-like jellyfish, brown as toadstools, iridescent as amethysts, measuring a yard across, surrounded the ship, kept her company, and trailed strands of evil-looking, luminous orchid tendrils from their umbrellas.

By midday Goehrs reached Mollendo. The steamer lay out in the roads. Goehrs was out of humour because all the shipping companies calling here, including the Japanese, had formed a combine to make this little run so expensive that he might just as well have covered it by air. But he did not want to fly because he was anxious to see one or two things which cannot be seen from the air.

The seas at Mollendo, even in calm weather, run so high that they always break with a roar of thunder. No one lands on this coast in the normal fashion. At this spot the rocky coast has a lateral inlet that had been dredged out like a canal—that was all there was in the way of a harbour, but it did not facilitate disembarkation because the swell rose and fell yards high.

Goehrs was shot in the launch through a few breakers between the reef and was just in time to see cows with slings round their middles whisked out of a swaying lighter into the air. Then he was sitting on board his launch in a frame that had fallen from the skies. Then the frame ascended. Five Indians were standing on the cross-beams, and each of them held one of his bags. And thus like Rameses on his throne surrounded by a bundle of dangling natives Goehrs shot up in the air and was conveyed by the steamer crane in a wide arc on to the coast of southern Peru.

Mollendo was the port for the railways running through the interior of Peru to Bolivia ; it was its sole *raison d'être*. A little township of a few thousand Indios and a handful of whites dumped down on the beach.

The hotel was a one-storeyed square wooden box like a bathing establishment. It took up a quarter of the town all to itself. You passed straight from the street into your room. Goehrs was given No. 34 and had to go round the corner to unlock it. As the rooms had no windows, he, like all the other denizens, propped his door open to get some light. He stood a little canvas screen in the gap. The door had once had a glass panel, but that had been replaced by cardboard long ago. Goehrs then enveloped his room in a cloud of Flit, for it was distinctly dirty. He then went into the town and strolled through it, a matter of five minutes' walk. He encored this performance ten times before nightfall and was always meeting the same people who, like himself, had had the bad luck to arrive on a day on which no train left up country. On the fifth occasion they exchanged greetings. Fellow-sufferers, companions in misfortune. The official in charge of aliens saluted, too. So did the customs officer. They sympathized. In the dusk towards evening all the young people of Mollendo forgathered at the hotel, walked round the four sides of it, and took stock of what was going on behind the screens. Their evening stroll. Their sole recreation. It was diverting to discuss what the individual inmates of the hotel were wearing or in what stage of *déshabillé* they happened to be.

Goehrs joined in with the parade round the hotel. He saw a solitary woman and about six men standing in their cabins and changing. But it was not very exciting. He therefore felt gratified when the Indio waiter called upon him to go to the police station to have his passport stamped. The poor passport was by this time chock-full of stamps. Every town had its police officer for aliens. But this time he was glad to go to the station. The officer there, with whom he had exchanged salutes five times, told him he knew him by sight now and that he had himself suggested his coming, to save him bother. Goehrs thanked him heartily. But the whole thing only took ten minutes.

Goehrs then espied a very high chair with broad foot-rests in front of the hotel. He at once climbed into it and had his shoes " shined." The Indian in charge of the operation did it with only a taut-stretched cloth, which he manipulated with remarkable zest. This lasted twenty minutes. By his action Goehrs provided entertainment for a dozen Indians lounging against the wall of the hotel shanty. In fact every one here seemed to be consumed by the sole desire of being permitted to look on—but there was so little to watch. The fellows really looked on with positive passion. Mollendo was indeed the ideal town for the *voyageur*. What other vice could very well have flourished here? If you set out to stroll down a street, it petered out in two minutes. You were out among the rocks and the desert at once. Not a shrub, not a blade of grass.

At last Goehrs set out once again to lay in a stock of candles because he did not trust the electric light. The shops were almost all owned by Chinese or Japanese. The attractive square with strongly scented flowers in the middle of the town stood round the monument of the Peruvian General Bolognesi. The inscription recorded that the monument was presented by the Chinese colony. Goehrs had frequently been struck by the fashion of presenting monuments. He had been surprised in Lima that the Spanish colony should have presented the Peruvians with a magnificent Moorish arch to commemorate the centenary of the day on which the Spaniards had been expelled from the country by the Peruvians. It was unconscious humour. The Asiatics' monument was a little bribe. By their presentation of a national hero the Chinese were aiming at protecting themselves from pogroms and at making themselves popular. "By no means stupid," thought Goehrs. "Wily dodge!"

After dinner Goehrs made another attempt to go to town. He argued that of the thirty tolerable houses in Mollendo the one without the coat-of-arms of a consulate was sure to be a picture theatre. What is more, he found this house, too. Instead of windows it had wooden shutters. But about eight o'clock the place was still in darkness, and so it was at half-past. The same thing at nine. At half-past nine it was still in darkness, but something was buzzing inside. Goehrs went in. A big hall. Goehrs paid an Indian girl some trifle. He then joined the audience of five Indians in the big barn. The picture was some propaganda or other for the colonization of the virgin forests of Peru. Life, so it seemed, must have been very gay there. But you were only able to guess at it because the film was so bad that you were not even able to make out the figures. Evidently they danced there continuously and made merry. Goehrs knew that there were colonies there, including one for Tyrolese, but also that these colonies were not suitable for Europeans. The climate was dangerous, and they were cut off from all communication with the outside world. And, as they were too inaccessible to hold out any prospect of marketing their products with any hope of profit, there did not appear to be much occasion for such a lot of dancing. The five Indians in the cinema with him went to sleep forthwith. After half an hour one of them woke up, ascertained that there was nothing discernible on the screen, and began to whistle. The others joined in, but even that did not make life in the virgin forests any more intelligible. So Goehrs went to his hotel to go to bed.

The door of the room next to his stood open to the street, and he saw about ten young ladies sitting in the room over their needlework. Goehrs unlocked his cabin, disinfected it with Flit again, and undressed. By a back door he let himself out into the courtyard where there was an open-air shower bath behind a wooden partition. He had his shower bath and went back into his room, and got into bed. He heard a noise going on at the door connecting his room with that of the ten ladies engaged on needlework all the time. But he did not worry about it. Goehrs read the Mollendo newspaper from the front page to the last and back again from the last page to the first for a while and then switched off the light. At the same moment he chanced to glance at the door opposite. It was shining from at least fifteen holes. All these holes had been artificially bored. He had an explanation for the full attendance of young ladies now. The damsels had all attended his evening retirement. He stayed quietly in bed for half an hour. Then he rose and in his turn went to the door and looked into the adjoining room. It proved quite entertaining.

When he was back in bed again, he noticed that there were two holes in the ceiling above him. There was no means of locking the front door ; there was no bolt for the back door ; and the door to the ladies' apartment was off its hinges. He had a thousand dollars in his wallet and an excellent night. Subconsciously he heard the sea crashing against the white cliffs of Mollendo all through the night.

The next morning half the town was again parading round the hotel and watching its inmates at their toilets behind the screens. Even the black vultures with their red heads took part in the inspection. And a few big pelicans came up especially from the sea and perched on the railing to make sure of not missing anything. It really was an ideal town for *voyageurs*.

After Goehrs had finished dressing, he, too, strolled round the hotel to superintend the operations of others. He disliked holding aloof from the customs of the country. His train for Arequipa left at two o'clock that afternoon.

THE Cordilleras traverse Peru from north to south in three big ranges, like the three horses in a troika. They traverse the whole of South America from Panama to Cape Horn—an incredible distance, full of folds and humps. They are always equally remote, equally serene, equally overpowering, with broad tablelands in between, in wonderful, untiring sweeps. They are plain, without boastfulness, without picturesqueness, as simple as only mountains that are unending can be. They are quite smooth, as if they were wearing hides. The desert had been turned into mountains.

During the ascent, between the twists and turns of the line, Goehrs for hours saw the sea lying below him like a tossing bar of silver. The first scene of his entry into the Cordilleras came to an end when he was rolling over a vast plateau. Flat as a drawing-board for miles, smooth as marble. Endless golf links, enormous aerodromes. Hard desert flooring. As beyond Cairo.

The second scene of the Cordilleras opened with the same restfulness as the first. The same treeless, beautifully rounded, grandly planned mountain composition as in Palestine, the same suggestiveness in the landscape as in the neighbourhood of Jerusalem when you climb the Hill of the Temptation or descend into the Valley of the Jordan. Only on a rather dramatically bigger scale.

Then Nature again interposed an interval. Another plateau again. Again as if designed for golf links and aerodromes. But varied by one of the wonders of the world.

Thousands of great sickles, each one fifty yards in length, green in colour like the green of Portuguese oysters, with tall, with steep backs some fifteen feet high and sharply cut ridges, were lying at intervals of about a hundred yards over the reddish plain. On the windward side they were like zebra skins, but far more delicate, as delicate as the enlargements of the lines of the human thumb. Marked off to the hundredth part of an inch with such uncanny accuracy as no casting could ever reproduce. These delicate, giant toys of Nature lay strewn like marine monsters on the desert floor, the scrupulous smoothness of which looked rough and untidy as compared with green ice formations—ice formations of dust.

The wind had built these green geometrical designs by depositing a lava dust from the volcanoes that falls in accordance with definite laws over a given distance. A wind,

MACHU PICHU, INDIAN RUINS IN THE PERUVIAN HIGHLANDS.

always blowing in accordance with immutable laws from the same quarter at the same strength for centuries with the same plastic purposefulness had erected these green, exotic monuments.

Difficult to grasp. But further :

These green monuments increased with the same precision with which they had been constructed. They grew with the precision of an hour-glass. Goehrs compared the measurements that had been taken of them during the past decade. The differentiations were so infinitesimal that, if Goehrs were to have betaken him about half a mile away from any of these dunes, the dune to his eye would be exactly as big as it had been fifty years ago. But if he were to have retired some five miles away, it would, though still a conspicuous dune, resume the shape it had had at the time of the Inca Empire, when the runners of the Indians were plying from the sea to Arequipa and Cuzco.

So there stood the dunes now, green and delicately chased. Nature's unchanging, silent clock of destiny. What would the world look like, Goehrs thought, when the ridges of these oyster-coloured sickles, instead of being as to-day fifteen feet high, had reached twice that height ?

At this moment the Cordilleras rang up their third scene. They rose to tragic heights. Misti appeared, narrowing gently to a summit like the mountains on Japanese prints. To the right and left of it Pichu-Pichu and Chachani with snowy crests. The foothills of the third Cordillera range still lay in front of these graceful shapes, but the three mountains soared above their foothills as if there were a deep atmospheric layer between them, that mysterious distance that even in Nature still separates by a vast gulf the great from the sublime.

The lower hills now flushed a rosy pink, with marblings of green that ate into the red like mildew. But the upper half of Misti, still overtopping them by three times their height, gleamed in purple samite. The snowy crest surmounted it, a real crown, quite simple, of almost childlike majesty. To the right and left of this peaked, gentle crest the ridges of the Pichu-Pichu and Chachani flowed down like buttresses—as if the snow had become melody. So care-free, so simple, so inimitable in poise—Switzerland a hundred times over. Mountains 20,000 feet in height. Within a space of three minutes, night had swallowed them up.

An hour later Goehrs got out in Arequipa. He shouted " Garzia " down the platform. The platform was dark and rudimentary. An Indian with a broad, round face appeared, " I am Garzía, señor." He drove Goehrs through the whole of Arequipa up to the Quinta Bates.

AREQUIPA—C'EST MOI

A FEW days later Goehrs was sitting under a big parasol of black, red, green, and gold stripes, among palms, indiarubber trees, and hibiscus hedges, on a genuine English lawn. Beside him sat three big English bulldogs. One was white, the other grey, the third brindled ; Biddy, Muffins, Sally. Facing him sat Mrs. Bates, the mistress of this country mansion, a lady of fifty-five, long in the leg, white of hair, with a massive head and an imperious chin. Her eyes were blue.

Behind her a flight of stairs led straight from the lawn into the Quinta. It was always so highly polished that it could only be approached at risk of life and limb ; Mrs. Bates, in view of the normal dirty state of Arequipa, regarded it as fulfilling an educational function. The mansion was entirely overgrown by a dozen varieties of climbing plants. Beautiful vicuña and alpaca blankets lay on the beds in the rooms and there were lilies in vases. In the small hall was a portrait by Lawrence and a little picture by Monticelli. In the dining-room hung a picture that looked like an El Greco, but was by one of the last of Inca princes whom they had confined in a monastery.

In the open-air, unroofed lounge, the English woman-secretary of a mining company, in riding-breeches as spotless as if they had just been laundered, was making an appointment by telephone, also installed in the open air. Everything at Quinta was in the open air, even the baths—a marvel in the Indian city of Arequipa. A highly cherished marvel. A marvel famous throughout Peru.

Birds with little heads and rotund tummies perched in pomegranate trees and made noises like frogs, while humming birds of the size of dragonflies flitted in and out among the rose trees and syringa bushes and quivered over the mimosa like shimmering insects with incredibly long tails.

" I am Arequipa," said Mrs. Bates with a gesture that ranged from the attractive secretary in riding kit to the towers of the cathedral. The gesture embraced her whole realm, including the ten young Englishmen and Mexicans who had been sent by their families interested in mining ventures to the highlands of Peru and for whom she had created this oasis—if they happened to find favour in her eyes. She was very eclectic.

Goehrs thought of the drawing-rooms of the old Spanish families, where the chairs were all aligned against the walls with a spittoon beside every chair. . . . He nodded at Mrs. Bates.

Mrs. Bates was one of the most notable personalities in Peru. She had married a Scotsman and had accompanied him hither ; she had seen him disappear into the mines and emerge again occasionally ; she had brought up his children by her and by other women, white and red, and had seen them married and die and had seen her husband die and had brought up his grandchildren. A marvellously indomitable woman. On the highlands of Peru, with her three dogs and her inexhaustible originality, she ruled Arequipa, the second biggest city of Peru, a city full of old Spanish mansions and of ten times as many Indian barracks, with a beautiful cathedral and a square of colonnades that conjured up Venice.

Goehrs looked up into the air from the tropical garden. The magic of the light in the highlands made the tightly packed foothills of the Cordilleras, which came half-way up the palm trees, appear nothing more than a gentle ridge Mrs. Bates had thrown up to screen her garden and her dogs. There lay the high Cordilleras like a neat moraine. Still free from snow. To an altitude of 13,000 feet. Perhaps ten miles away. But—all that was only half-way up the palm trees, was only foothills. But above them, above the crests of the palm trees, hung on the left the broad back of hachani as peaceable as the brown bulldog lying on the lawn. And then beside it, in the gap between the palm fans and the mimosa tree, floated, gently and peacefully, the narrow peak of Misti with its restful, fairy-like crest of snow. The magic of the light made it look as if it were a couple of hundred yards beyond the garden. But it was 13,000 feet above the garden, which itself was nearly 10,000 feet above sea-level. Misti is higher than Kilimanjaro.

The atmosphere round the mountain was thin, a steely blue, high and dark, a deeper blue than the skies of Italy. The air was not as joyous. But more mysterious and purposeful.

Goehrs looked across the high plateau, half-parched for want of water, half-green with the artificial garden of Arequipa and its population of 50,000, and surrounded on every side by the barren, pointed little volcanoes of the Cordilleras, as by a bevy of unknown, kindly beasts.

"Sparta," he thought. Sparta was like this, severe, war-like in its oasis of greenery in the barren plain of Lacedæmon, under the steely snowfields of Taygetus.

"Yes, Sparta!" thought Goehrs. "Sparta and a bit of Zanzibar and of something else—of something else."

But he could not unriddle this something else—anything wherewith to compare it; it felt as though the plumes of the Indians who had reigned here were still suffusing the air with a faint fragrance of exotic and delicate grandeur that eluded words.

Señor George

MRS. BATES came down the stairs, that were polished to the slipperiness of an ice-shute. She had doffed the black silk gown and hat she had inexplicably been wearing for breakfast at eight o'clock in the morning in the garden. She was in a cotton dress and apron and looked as if she would like to slay all the Indian women who had been waiting for her for the past two hours in a corner of the garden. Mrs. Bates changed six times a day and (with the exception of the evening) always into something that seemed to be inappropriate to the time of day. She had her own noteworthy ideas on pretty well everything.

Thus she had laid out her garden into twelve little gardens separated from one another by hedges and trees, which was not English but Mauresque-Spanish. And there she commanded half a dozen Cholos, half-breeds, and full-blooded Indians, who appeared in turns, as in a comedy, as gardeners as bootblacks, in white jackets as servitors at table or attendants at the bath. One of the two outdoor baths, on the way to which it was so pleasant of a morning to encounter the rest of the company in bath gowns, for there were no bells. It was all very English and all very free and easy.

In two or three of these twelve gardens stood little buildings sunk deep into the soil, of timber and glass, with running water and electric heaters—dolls' houses which Mr Bates occasionally let. In two of them were domiciled nice young couples from Mexico and Brazil, who had mines and haciendas on the Puna but preferred to live here. The Puna was the adjoining tableland, about 12,000 feet in height where the big sheep-runs were situate and where things were rough and life unpleasant.

In another of these subterranean bungalows there also lived a bachelor of about thirty. An Indian who had just been engaged came rushing from this bungalow and yammered : " Mrs. Bates—there's a naked man in the garden over there."

" Stuff and nonsense," said Mrs. Bates imperturbably. " That isn't a man, that is Señor George."

Señor George had been sent to Peru by one of the biggest ore companies in Germany, in which his family held shares, to serve his apprenticeship on the spot. He had been there for two years by this time, first in Bolivia and then in Arequipa. At first he had found it stimulating to draft estimates for the shipping of 2000 tons of tin. But after six months it began to pall on him, for he was a clever, well-educated, and spoiled man with any amount of capacity, a man who might just as well be secretary to a cabinet minister and whose imagination debarred him from going on shipping tin for years. In deference to his imagination and to his family, they therefore gave him an appointment in Arequipa, where he was representative of a very big concern, an appointment not unimportant in itself, but in which it did not matter very much whether Señor George put in an appearance at the office or not. The mining concern of Cerro de Pasco was one of the biggest in the world, and it was not of very great consequence whether a distinguished young man with family connexions did or did not work his fingers to the bone.

Señor George was, none the less, far from slothful in business and still found time enough to woo the favours of the ladies of Arequipa, but what was a man like Señor George to make of such discreet and carefully chaperoned favours ? He became bored. And he succumbed one day to the apparition of a red shawl and red hair that suddenly appeared, together with the young English lady belonging to them, in the Quinta Bates gardens. This interesting damsel had arrived with an expedition on its way to the high-lying mines of Bolivia ; and so it came about that Señor George became involved in one of the most remarkable frauds in history. He was gullible, of course, as Parzival, and credulous as any dozen other lads, and credulous, finally, as the English capitalist who financed the expedition to the tune of 200,000 pounds sterling and floated the shares on the Stock Exchange.

Señor George had now come back from his expedition and had been recuperating at Mrs. Bates's for the past three months by walking about lightly clad in the dwarf garden of his subterranean bungalow. Mrs. Bates looked upon this tall boy in much the same light as she did on one of her three bulldogs. She trained him. She fed him. She mothered him, she loved him, and she declined to take him seriously. She need never have done anything else than to say of this big, athletic young man with an adventurous past, who was breaking his heart anew every week : " That isn't a man, that is Señor George," to adduce evidence that she was the most amusing and dominating person in south Peru.

It was the end of May. The rainy season had lasted from December to March. So it was winter-time in Peru with the thermometer at 95° F. from 8 a.m. to 6 p.m. From 7 p.m. until 6 a.m. it was between freezing-point and 40°. Some difference. But one hour after sunrise it was as hot as at midday. Crazy country ! With a coast that equalled that of Arabia. With a city like Arequipa situate almost 10,000 feet above sea-level, and brilliant with flowers in mid-winter. With a Puna plateau as high as the Jungfrau where flocks of sheep were grazing. With valleys in between and with a primeval forest in the east as tropical as Dar-es-Salaam.

Goehrs stayed on in the garden all day long and gazed at Misti. He was making friends with the mountain. Towards evening Misti draped itself in a cloud that hung like a cloth of dazzling white over its crest.

" Funny fellow ! " said Mrs. Bates. " Now he's having his head shampooed with snow but no one's allowed to see it."

Goehrs felt a severe pressure on his skull. He was sensitive to changes of weather ; he felt a storm the day before it broke, but it felt quite different here. He told Mrs. Bates about it.

" Nevada," she said. Goehrs guessed that " nevada " ought to mean very much what " fochn " does in the Alps and " chinook " elsewhere. Nevada really means snow. Very neat.

Although the temperature was 86° and Misti was having its head discreetly shampooed under a towel, the atmosphere was so charged with electricity that one had only to brush against the skins on the floor for big sparks to leap out of them. When Goehrs went to bed, the alpaca skin on it emitted sparks like a battery.

By the following morning Misti gracefully unveiled itself of its flag, which had worn very small and thin. It had had a new snowfall and disclosed it serenely. Everything was in the best of spirits. The dogs on the polished stairs threw their muzzles up, snuffed the air, and gave a bark or two.

THE INDIAN PROBLEM

GOEHRS came back through the Indian villages in the neighbourhood of Arequipa and was a little depressed at having found them so incredibly neglected, dirty, and unfit for habitation. He had observed the same thing within the purlieus of Arequipa, in fact within ten yards on either side to right and left of the Villa Bates. The villages beyond were clustered against big clay walls facing the road. A house against this wall was only a receptacle for clay, fire, dirt, stench, children, women, and animals. The trail had been adventurous. Twice Goehrs had had to repair it with stones piled into the big pools to get on at all. He had driven through an avenue of mud huts—studies in grey—compared with which the Kaffir kraals of Africa were pleasant summer residences.

It struck Goehrs that the higher he climbed the Cordilleras, the more conspicuously did the Indian type vary. The people here were not quite pure-bred Indians but they had a much darker skin than the Indians on the coast. There was a big bastion of cheekbone immediately under their eyes, and beneath this a narrow, thin second face, consisting of nose, mouth, and chin, was appended regularly. Two faces—that was the most striking feature of these Indian heads that gazed up at him from every quarter with long noses and the eyes of kicked and dying dogs. They sat crouched in front of their huts like their ancestral mummies and gazed blankly into space. The women were wearing panama hats that suited their plaits and ravaged faces oddly enough. Every now and then a red rag on a pole announced that *chicha*, a liquor distilled from Indian corn and replete with fusel oil, was on sale.

The drive through this country, where cars cannot get on at all, had lasted a good many hours. It had nearly broken up an obliging Ford, and had taken them into the first Cordilleras triangle, where the high tableland in turn runs out, where green gives place to brown and where cattle, donkeys, and dogs, bellowing and yapping in unison, had given chase to the car.

The Indians inhabiting Peru were for the most part Quichuas who, together with the dozens of other big tribes, had been conquered by the Incas nine hundred years before. The Incas had governed the Quichuas as a guardian might have administered an estate. They had been made to work in the mines ; they had been made to till the soil, while the Incas looked after their welfare. The Spaniards had dealt with the Quichuas on the same lines. They had ruled the Indians from 1535 to 1820, had made them work in the mines and till the soil but—they had failed to look after their welfare. They had decimated, tortured, and maltreated them as a race has hardly ever been maltreated. The Indians had put up with it with hardly any rising worth mentioning. Forty years before Spain for ever lost its colonial empire, a descendant of the Incas had brought about an Indian rising—but not very successfully. The Spaniards had bound him hand and foot to four horses and torn him to pieces.

Forty years later, the few hundred thousand Spaniards there were in South America, descendants of Spaniards and Inca half-breeds, raised the great rebellion of the Liberation against Spain. San Martin swept from the south northwards through Chile and Argentine, Bolívar from the north through Venezuela by way of Colombia and Bolivia to the south. They liberated every country and last of all Peru, the land of gold, the heart of South America, the first kingdom of the Conquistadores. The descendants of the Conquistadores in their turn expelled the Viceroy and established their independence. And what was the emblem they chose for their flag in this War of Liberation by a great colony against the mother-country ? The old Sun of the Incas ! They—that is to say, a handful of white families, a few hundred thousand half-breeds and several millions of Indians—resolved to liberate South America under the battleflag of the old, royal, fighting Indian race.

And what had Peru, the heart of South America, the only country with old-established traditions of colonial civilization, subsequently, after its liberation, done for the Indians ? Goehrs had in several places seen the small beginnings of social services for the Indios and he had made a note of Leguía's goodwill. But what he had seen in general and as a whole was awful. Alcohol, exploitation, and slavery.

After this trip Goehrs was sitting at the tea-table in the

gardens of the Quinta Bates with a young Brazilian who had
a hacienda on the Peruvian Puna, with Señor George, and
with an American mining engineer of the Northern Peru
Company. The quinine trade, so far as Peru was concerned,
was past and done with years ago ; the rubber gamble had
been hopelessly bankrupt for years ; what people were
interested in was sheep and llama farming and ore. Peru
was rich in copper and silver, and no one knew how brimful
Peru was of ore in undiscovered spots.

" What do you pay an Indian in the mines ? " asked
Goehrs.

" Three soles," said the engineer. That amounted to five
shillings. That was double the amount " boys " were paid
in South Africa. But only a very small fraction of the
Indians was working in the mines.

" And what do you give an Indio ? " Goehrs turned to the
rancher.

" Indian corn," said the Brazilian, and patted Biddy's
neck.

" Isn't there really any one whose business it is to see that
these people are at any rate a little better housed ? "

" Whose should it be ? Good Lord ! " said the rancher.
" And why ? Not even the clergy have hit on that notion."

The Brazilian was a good fellow, but the idea there was
any need for housing an Indio in hygienic conditions was as
astonishing to him as a recommendation to bed down his
cattle in his dining-room would have been to a substantial
farmer in Europe. That had been bred in the bone for
centuries. And he failed to understand why a man like
Goehrs should worry about it.

" What do you expect them to do ? " asked the American.
" It would mean putting up money to make these people
clean, and then they would only demand higher wages at
once. Why can't you leave the Indians to their lice ? After
all, they like them."

" Yes," said Señor George sarcastically. " If the sanitation of Indian houses were a business showing a profit, there
would be ten companies ready to take it up. But the
proposition would have to show a profit. Money is dear
in Peru, my dear, good fellow-countryman, and people
will only put up money where it is sure to go with a
bang."

At the same moment as he said the word, " bang," the
sound of shots was heard outside. But no one took any
notice of it. Only Señor George, in answer to Goehrs's

inquiring glance, remarked cheerfully : " Indians firing in honour of a saint's day. They do an astonishing lot of firing when they are feeling really devout."

" Could you, as a matter of fact, get on without Indians ?" Goehrs asked the sheep-rancher. The latter shook his head. " And you ? " he asked the engineer of the Northern Peru Company.

" At an altitude of more than 13,000 feet—couldn't be done," said the American. " White men can't as a rule stand heights, least of all in the mines."

Goehrs watched the hummingbirds flitting about in the stillness. Peru has two problematical alternatives. Either to raise the status of the natives, representing seventy per cent. of the population, and thereby to raise social and political problems—or to exterminate the Indians and therewith go bankrupt.

" And what is your opinion of the Cholos—the half-breeds ? "

" They are especially the dangerous crowd," said the American. The Brazilian nodded.

After this answer, Leguía's dictatorship appeared to Goehrs in a far more kindly light. In a country with seventy per cent. or possibly three quarters of Indians, and only very few whites and a good many half-breeds, where they were exterminating the Indians as in Spanish times and looked on the half-breeds as dangerous—in a country of this kind, was not even a dictatorship a good thing if it espoused the cause of the Indians ? Of course, it was. But this, it appeared, was by no means the opinion of the minority of the country that controlled its wealth (and was exporting it to the United States). They looked on the Indians, as they had always done, as cattle.

" Are you for or against Leguía ? " Goehrs asked the American. The answer took his breath away.

" For, of course," said the Yankee beaming. " It's arithmetic, just figure it out. The gang round Leguía has gorged itself and grown fat. If a poor man should succeed him as President with a poor set that has to gorge itself full again—my God, they'll be after our money like rats. Long live President Leguía ! "

" Poor Peru ! " thought Goehrs.

The Indians were firing again, like men possessed, in honour of some saint or other, who at bottom did not concern them in the very least.

THE nevada was back in Arequipa. Misti showed a thin column of smoke and was pouring a great quantity of electricity over the tableland. Every one was cross when you shook hands with him because he usually got a shock. Only the dogs were attacked by a curious seizure of love's young dream. Biddy, the white monster with a pink shot hide, who normally only stirred when she was petted, all of a sudden raced about the garden, jumped, a quaint ungainly figure, into the hammocks, and by virtue of all the blandishments of which she was capable tried to incite the worthy Muffins, who, foolishly enough, responded ; which proved very exhausting and that was about all he had out of it.

Señor George appeared above the edge of his hedge and was watching these proceedings just as Mrs. Bates was coming in from the road.

" Why, for Heaven's sake," he asked in alarm, " are you wearing a mantilla on your venerable head ? You surely haven't become converted or a Catholic, dear Mrs. Bates ? "

Mrs. Bates certainly did look odd with the high Spanish comb and veil on her blue-eyed head. She looked as the late lamented Queen Victoria might have looked if, instead of the saltcellar of a crown she used to wear, she had donned the high-peaked black veil of the Spanish dancers for a head-dress.

" Don't you worry about me, George," said she acidly. " It wouldn't be a bad thing if you were to adapt yourself to the customs of the country a little, instead of running about half naked in a solar topee, as you did this morning in the public highway, when every one is dressed in black."

Mrs. Bates was cross because she was annoyed with herself. For she had had to attend a christening in church and wear the prescribed costume for the purpose—which she, as an Englishwoman, did not consider altogether appropriate.

" I believe there is going to be an earthquake," said Señor George guilelessly, taking off his solar topee and studying the inside of it as if it were a newspaper.

" I don't mind," said Mrs. Bates. " I have a record of over fifty of them." Five minutes later, she came back into the garden for breakfast, all in white.

" You promised to tell me the story of your expedition

the other day," said Goehrs, taking a piece of toast which had some local cheese baked into it.

"That was a quaint little show," said Señor George, "but the story would bore Mrs. Bates since she took part in it."

"Not in the least," said Mrs. Bates, "because you tell it differently every time, my dear."

"The man who set the whole thing going," said Señor George, ignoring Mrs. Bates's interpolation, "worked at the scheme for fifteen years—that, I think, is the most original feature of the whole thing. That is why everything dovetailed so wonderfully. First of all, he bought a document containing a secret report from an Indian woman in Oruro. The parchment was of a date when the Spaniards were still governing South America as a colony and were very much scared of the Jesuits. The Jesuits at that time had built up a big power of their own, with an army and so forth, on rather communistic lines in what is Paraguay to-day and the State of Misiones. The Spaniards finally evicted the Jesuits, but, before they left South America, the Jesuits hid a quantity of gold—there is no doubt about that. As little doubt as there is that the Incas in their day removed so much gold that it would be possible to fill whole goods trains with it to-day.

"In short, the parchment was a secret report and addressed to the Society of Jesus. It was, in addition to the fact that it was genuine on chemical analysis, genuine from the psychological point of view. For it stated that all the Indios that had effected the transport of the gold had been removed subsequently to prevent the spot from being betrayed. This was the customary procedure, and the Jesuit would not have recorded it if it had not been meant for his Society. Its indications on matters of facts were very precise. It became possible to assess the value of the buried ore at about four million pounds sterling. The name of the man who had bought this document was Samuel Brix and he spent a big sum of money on organizing an expedition to Bolivia and on identifying the spot. He did actually sink a shaft there and found a crucifix with the inscription : ' Get thee gone or thou wilt be dead in five minutes,' or words to that effect.

"Brix had trustworthy people to vouch for his story. The shaft they had sunk had fallen in, so there was nothing to be done at the moment because it would take a lot of plant and a lot of money to get on with the work. Brix went to London and, by virtue of his document and evidence

MISTI, VOLCANO NEAR AREQUIPA.

and convincing manner, raised 200,000 pounds in shares. The shares soared at once on the Stock Exchange ; every one became enthusiastic about Brix—he had a wonderful manner—hadn't he, Mrs. Bates ? "

" Don't you think Biddy has a wonderful manner ? " replied Mrs. Bates, and pointed to the pinkish white siren, successfully laying herself out to wheedle evidence of her charms from the other dogs.

" No doubt, but, if a man raises 200,000 pounds in London for treasure-hunting, he has to display rather more initiative than you give him credit for, dear Mrs. Bates," said Señor George equably. " It is the best evidence of good character for a man to raise such a substantial sum of money for such an adventurous purpose in the City of London. It is even more eloquent of the good impression Brix made than the fact that eventually I personally took a hand in the venture. Which is another bull point. Well, a magnificent expedition was fitted out. He sank 50,000 pounds in its equipment. He came to Arequipa with a trainful of boring-machines, steam hammers, tents, tinned foods, dynamite, and the like. It was very jolly there then, wasn't it, Mrs. Bates ? "

" I believe it was a very exhausting time for you," said Mrs. Bates darkly.

" Sometimes there is something of a bright young bull about you, dear Mrs. Bates," said Señor George irritably. " You simply cannot stand red cloaks."

" Not when they are draped across the shoulders in a certain way, my child," agreed Mrs. Bates with meaning. She closed her eyes and folded her hands across her breast.

" In addition to me there were ten other youngsters engaged when the expedition left for Bolivia," continued Señor George. " The expedition had to pass through Arequipa because it is the only tolerable railway connexion with Bolivia and the whole show was close to the Peruvian frontier. And, well, since I had done some work in the mines up there, Brix asked me to join them, and, of course, I was glad to do so, more especially as they gave me a decent interest. The business side of the show was beyond cavil— simply beyond cavil, and of course I knew, too, who was putting the money up. Simply A.I. Not a soul had a shadow of doubt about that and in any case no one stood to lose anything.

" So we started off, went to Lake Titicaca, crossed, went to La Paz, trekked to the mining district—it was only then that the expedition really began, when everything was conveyed by pack mules. For six months we grubbed about up there, 16,000 feet up ; it was terribly cold ; in tents, too. The shaft was there, of course, but it was always falling in, and progress was slow.

" Brix suddenly went off for a few days, but did not go to La Paz but to Arequipa—was at any rate away for four days. No one knew why he went to Arequipa. I know now he went there because he could use the telegraph wire from there without causing comment. Ten days after his return, the whole expedition bust. We struck rock, the shaft ran out, and the whole show was a wash-out. Brix had wired instructions from Arequipa to sell his holding. The shares at that date were quite a decent price, for the results were most promising—they had cleverly issued information for publication every week, and every one interested in stocks and shares thought we were close to the gold. There was a full-dress row, more especially as they could not prove anything against Brix. Not the least thing."

" Hang it all ! But all the documents must have been genuine."

" Not likely. He probably had buried the cross with the inscription up there some ten years previously ; it was undoubtedly an old cross. The parchment was probably not genuine either. You have no idea how well you can fake things if you take fifteen years to do it."

" But to have buried the cross would have required an expedition at least ten strong."

" He probably dealt with these people in the same way as is described in such meticulous detail in the document," suggested Señor George dryly.

" I have seen the parchment," Mrs. Bates interrupted. " I have seen a lot of old parchments in the course of the thirty years I have been living here. The parchment was undoubtedly genuine."

" I daresay," said George calmly. " But the share deal was a brilliant bit of work and the cross was undoubtedly a swindle."

" Good Lord ! " exclaimed Mrs. Bates chuckling. " I have seen the fellow sitting here and felt convinced that he did not believe a single word in the whole yarn. But the parchment was unquestionably genuine. Lord ! Supposing the fellow had actually stumbled upon the treasure in which he had not himself believed. I should have liked to have seen his face. Probably have gone into a fit."

" What a beautiful, gentle imagination you have, Mrs.
Bates. I never realized that," said Señor George, rising.
" But I believe there is going to be an earthquake, my dear,
esteemed Mrs. Bates."

An Indian Procession

GOEHRS was standing in the Plaza de Armas, which
was full of palms and red flowers, watching a humming-
bird. The bird hovered in the air for a moment with
quivering, flashing wings over one of the big red blossoms,
then plunged its long, pointed beak into the calyx, tugged at
it hard once or twice, drew back its head, stood poised for a
while with shimmering wings on the same spot, only to hurl
itself afresh into the nearest flower.

Goehrs turned to his companion.

" What is the reason, Señora Albago, why you have such
a tremendous number of churches here ? "

" Very simple," said the Brazilian lady from Goehrs's
boarding house, who had been living here for two years and
whose husband was the rancher on the Puna. " There is
such a demand for them."

" It's the only town I know where the churches compete
with the picture palaces," said Goehrs meditatively.

" And it's probably the only one where it's considered
more fashionable to go to church than to the cinema."

Goehrs had found the town studded thickly with
monasteries. They were particularly thick on the outskirts
of the city, reminding one of mastiffs with their mighty walls
and dazzling white stone ordnance on the ramparts ; their
walls as thick through as houses normally are, huge strongholds of the faith.

Everywhere, wherever you least expected it, a cloud of
incense would break through the reek of the suburbs. Big
baldachins were frequently erected in the open air under
which, beside the figure of the Crucified, all the furniture of
the tragedy, as recorded in the Bible story, was displayed
life-size : the cloak, the dice, the spear with the sponge of
hyssop, and the cock. In front of the convent gates the
wretched ragbags of Indian women were lying crouched in
the dust.

The nuns of the several orders floated through the streets
like the figures of princesses that had descended from Gothic
cathedrals. When they spoke to any one, the person

143

addressed began to tremble. When they appeared with a collecting-box neither officer nor lawyer (although every second man in South America was a lawyer) dared to say no, but testified with every manifestation of zeal how happy he felt at being privileged to pay. The priests adopted the demeanour that officers of the General Staff are fond of affecting on active service. And the bishop, who used to drive through Arequipa in a handsome car, gave one the impression not of a high ecclesiastic, but of a statesman representing the authority and the power of a sovereign State. The representatives of the Church looked less like the servants than the rulers of the Faith—instinct with medieval dignity, with the pride of place of a privileged estate.

Señora Albago beckoned to Goehrs. The procession was approaching, and they had to move a few paces forward. The cathedral of Arequipa occupied the whole of one side of the Plaza. It was not built on the lines of a fortress for the purposes of military offence and defence ; it stood quite exposed, the heart of the city, its pride, its jewel generously proffered. It was very broad-chested but symmetrical, well proportioned and designed, graceful and strong, its main front supported by a second colonnade, its two towers strong, pointed, and graceful, and finished off by two mighty arches, springing from its flank, as if to enclose the square with its palms and flowers as well. It was not old but it looked as if Charles V had built it.

Goehrs walked past with Señora Albago to watch the procession enter a little church.

" Don't you, as a Protestant, experience any difficulties in this environment ? " asked Goehrs, for both the Brazilian and his wife were non-Catholics.

" No," she said laughing. " The days when Protestants were not allowed to read their own liturgy and had no funeral service are over. If the priest forbids any one of my little Catholic friends to come to see me, I admit she stays away. The young girls are, of course, very emancipated, but once they are married, that is all over with."

" What are those fellows rushing for ? " asked Goehrs. The Indios suddenly broke excitedly from the procession and rushed to the church, each man holding his saint high above his head and shouldering each other ruthlessly.

" Every one is trying to be nearest to the altar with the saint he is carrying," said Señora Albago with a smile.

" They all believe that whoever is standing nearest to it will profit most."

" Do the Indians then really believe . . . ? "

" Not a bit of it," said the young woman. " Somewhere or other they entertain a veneration for their ancient gods— in spite of four hundred years of Christianity. They believe in Christ at most when He is ' Lord of the Earthquake.' They have a brown Indian Christ, the ' Señor de los Tremblores,' in Cuzco. They have something approaching trust in him because he causes the thunder. When the Pope presented them with a new white Christ in its stead, they refused it. The Lord of the Earthquake had to be reinstated in the cathedral."

" But the Indians blaze away all day long out of sheer devoutness and never miss an opportunity to show what good Christians they are."

" Because they are afraid."

" Afraid of the saints ? "

" No," said Señora Albago smiling, " afraid of the priests."

" What harm can the priests do the Indians ? The Indios hardly have a poncho to cover their shoulders, not even boots."

" They still have some trifle or other—a llama, a few head of poultry. The Church is immensely powerful. That is why all governments come to terms with it."

" All . . . ? "

" All governments. One of Leguía's predecessors in his time had the crucifix removed from the table of the parliament—well, he had to pay for it when he came to die. And Augusto Durand, who at one time led the revolutionary army and laid a heavy hand on the Church, made his peace with her later on, once he was in the saddle. Government is very powerful and the Church is very powerful, and both are too well advised to tear each other to pieces. The Indians are beginning to shoot again. I can't stand any more of their banging. If you've had enough of it, come with me and have a cup of tea. My husband is unfortunately up there on the Puna among his sheep, but the tea is quite all right."

Goehrs had hardly taken his seat in Señora Albago's garden-room among her tiny old-Spanish furniture, armchairs and images, when he leapt to his feet again.

" I'm afraid I am boring you terribly, but why are those fellows blowing their bugles again ? "

It was a march. Like an Indian Sambre—et—Meuse.

" They're the soldiers. Do let them go on bugling," said Señora Albago. " What on earth else is there for soldiers to do ? "

" Are the officers held in respect ? "

Señora Albago shook her head. " No member of a good family becomes an officer."

" But supposing Peru should be involved in war ? "

" Who is it to be involved in war with ? " she asked in astonishment. " The army is much too bad to be able to risk going to war. It consists only of Indians. I do believe the young men of good families would, if it really came to fighting, take to the forests instead of joining up and being shot down by, say, the Chileans. . . ."

Goehrs was standing in front of a cabinet and turning over a little collection of Inca figures, necklaces of teeth, and little gold images of gods and goddesses.

" Don't touch that," Señora Albago suddenly exclaimed, and snatched back his hand from a piece of cloth, painted with a human face. " Indian death-masks are nearly all poisonous. . . . When you go to Cuzco next week, I'll give you a garlic root to take with you. It has a horrible smell, but it's the best specific against mountain sickness. Within a few hours in the neighbourhood of Crucero Alto you will reach a height of over 15,000 feet. And the *soroche* is as dense as fog round Crucero Alto. It's an extraordinary sickness, you'll see."

HOSPITALS AND ORPHANAGE

MRS. BATES had a habit of bustling through the charitable institutions of Arequipa from time to time and, once she was about it, she would polish off half a dozen at a time. Goehrs escorted her on one such occasion. At the bottom of her heart Mrs. Bates was astonishingly generous and gave any one capable of earning money the chance of doing so. She had distributed pocket handkerchiefs among the nuns in the orphanage to be embroidered, some table-centres for the children to embroider at the foundlings, and she was going to leave something particularly nice at the hospital.

French nuns were for the most part engaged in all these institutions. They drove first to the Franciscan convent, where eleven nuns, all in white from the soles of their feet to the top of their heads, were bringing up sixty children. Half the children were dressed in white, too, the other half in grey. Goehrs inquired about the reason for this differentiation in the colour scheme because he suspected some racial differentiation. He learnt however that the children in grey had once committed a theft. This struck him as rather severe, and the Mother Superior agreed with him entirely that the punishment degraded the children too much and for too long.

"But we have to retain severe punishments," she said. "You can have no idea what bringing up children in this country means."

"You can have no idea," endorsed Mrs. Bates, with a little frown.

They drove to the hospital. The hospital of the second largest city in Peru had in its time been founded by wealthy people. It had five hundred beds. Arequipa was impoverished now, and the wealthy people who had become poor could not afford to maintain it. The sisters worked like horses. They were hardly adequately dressed. Goehrs would not have cared to come into contact with them.

"How much do the patients pay a day?"

"Thirty centavos." Sixpence.

Goehrs looked out of the open window on to the hot street.

Two men were dragging across the square a third man seated on an ordinary chair, holding his arms above his head, and howling like an animal. From the other side came a big man bearing another on his shoulders in the same way as the carcasses of game are carried.

Mrs. Bates benevolently patted the back of the sister standing beside her.

"If it wasn't for the sisters," she said gravely, "the people would die in the public streets."

Goehrs looked out into the square, where people were being brought in from every quarter. It was a genuine Breughel. Exactly as the Middle Ages had depicted these scenes.

Mrs. Bates drove to the foundlings' hospital where she had a commission to discharge. The most interesting feature of the foundlings' home was the turn-table by which the babies were surreptitiously deposited at night, some with, some without a mark of identification. If it were not for this device, these children would probably be thrown into the stream. Three hundred children, of all shades : Indios, Zambos, Cholos, tinted Asiatics, little Negroes, whites with blue eyes. They leapt to their feet like soldiers and shouted : "*Buenos días.*" At a nod from the Mother Superior they sang as a compliment to Mrs. Bates and Señor Goehrs a song of such length that both the persons they were delighting to honour were put to a considerable amount of embarrassment.

" The best thing for the babies is to come here without any mark of identification," said the Mother Superior, delighted at being able to talk French again, " for when they have marks and reach the age of ten and have learnt a certain amount of needlework, the most repulsive relatives crop up and want to drag the child back into the gutter again to make money by its accomplishments."

" What is the meaning of the blue, red, and yellow bows the children are wearing ? "

" They are the marks they have earned."

" One never sees the children about outside," said Goehrs.

" They would come back from the streets in a verminous state. They stay here for good. It's the happiest time of their lives. Later on, when they grow up and we cannot keep them, Heavens ! what's to become of them in this country, where even the good families in Arequipa are so poor that they can't afford to keep domestic servants ? "

" Where are the babies ? " inquired Mrs. Bates impatiently. She had been commissioned to buy a child for a friend. Many good families that were childless, but were fond of children and wanted to have one, obtained their children here.

The Mother Superior signalled an order. " The very latest," she said in another ward, pointing to a bed. A tiny scrap two days old was lying on the pillow.

" Without any identification mark ? "

" None."

At the head of the bed was the label, " Irma." But for some reason or other the scrap did not find favour in Mrs. Bates's sight. Goehrs did not understand why, because as he saw them, one infant of that age was exactly like another. She shook her head. Then a grand, emotional scene was enacted in the sewing-room, in which Mrs. Bates rose to great heights. A table-centre had been embroidered for her in pink and white instead of in white, and Mrs. Bates loathed pink from the bottom of her wholesome, sturdy heart, which the French sister, who loved pink beyond all else, failed to realize. It was the rivalry between the Union Jack and the Tricolour over again. So two nations who never have understood and never will understand one another fought out their old quarrel over the table-centre.

In the car on her way to Quinta Bates, Mrs. Bates said :

" I happen to have heard that a daughter of one of the best Peruvian families is expecting to have a child by a young fellow before long, and I assumed that they would have deposited it in the foundling hospital by this time. But probably it's being sent into the country or is there by now. That little imp of the name of Irma can't be the child, but I'm going to find it. One may as well have something well bred if one adopts a mite like that. The sisters do a whole lot of work, don't they ? Without getting anything out of it for themselves. Yes ! the Catholic sisters are splendid. I'm a Protestant, nor am I a very devout one. But fair is fair. Don't you agree ? "

" Undoubtedly," said Goehrs.

The Heart of the Inca Empire

GOEHRS was sorry to leave Arequipa, to leave the palm trees of the Plaza de Armas, Mrs. Bates's garden and fleshpots, Señor George, pretty Miss Johns in her riding breeches, the American, Señora Albago and her husband, three aristocratic Peruvians, and a newly arisen Señorita Isabelita, Señor George's latest inamorata.

Misti that evening was putting up a white, ominous, thick column of smoke, had piled up a dark-blue cloud for a background, and had dyed its snow-cap an amaranthine crimson ; its white plume looked particularly menacing.

Every one in Peru goes to the railway station when any one he knows sets out on a journey, because a journey ranks in the same category of importance as dying or loving. Goehrs left all his friends on the platform with two tubers of garlic from Señora Albago wrapped up in tissue paper in his hand and climbed into the sleeping-carriage of the Ferrocariles del Sur del Peru.

Many people in Europe, who ought to have known better, had assured him that to travel on unknown South American railways on the benighted West Coast was as restful as spending the night in a cellar with dead rats. People in Europe are always very cocksure, and on the strength of many an experience Goehrs had learnt that they were usually wrong. Besides, he hated the superiority of the type of European who treats everything non-European with condescension. The superiority of this type of individual is only based on the fortunate accident of a rather older organization, which is no fault of theirs, and not on the superiority of their intelligence, which is usually more suburban than the intelligence of many people in less well-organized countries.

Goehrs thought the sleepers of the Peruvian Company delightful. They were clean, had better bed linen than is common in Europe, were comfortably heated, had running hot water, convenient lighting, and practicable doors with locks. Not at all bad for a private company that practically served only Indian country.

Goehrs woke up at about 2 a.m. in Crucero Alto at the altitude of the Matterhorn. He deliberately tried deep breathing exercise. He had no trouble. It is at this spot that the majority of people travelling into the upper Cordilleras are overtaken by the *soroche*. Generals, athletes, women—without distinction, as they had one and all told Goehrs. The soroche is a mountain sickness akin to sea-sickness. It attacks, stupefies, and leaves its victims wishing they were dead. These symptoms are the sequel of the fight the heart is waging against a sudden decrease in the supply of oxygen with which the lungs supply it. And they are the consequences of the rapidity of evaporation in the atmosphere, which one man's physique may stand well and another's badly.

But there is something else involved in it as well, something mysterious emanating from this volcanic, highly charged soil, because some ranges induce the soroche, and others do not. There are some people who begin to bleed, others who suffer from high temperature and cramp, and yet others who, if they are not prepared to die, have to return to the plain forthwith. There were singers who had to give up singing on the Puna and officers unable to speak.

Goehrs had none of these symptoms. He did not pride himself on his immunity any more than he plumed himself at not being seasick. He knew it only meant that some convolution in the brain centre affecting equilibrium, perhaps in the region of the auditory centre, was just a tiny shade differently and better constituted than in the case of other people and that this was the determining factor—not he himself. A matter of luck.

Goehrs cast a friendly glance at the garlic root and dropped off to sleep again.

His route took him to within a few miles of Lake Titicaca and then swung round for another day's journey in a northerly direction. When he woke up again, his sleeper was standing high and dry. So this ought to be Juliaca.

The carriage was standing in a yellow cornfield white with frost. The train had, without his being aware of it, gone on to Lake Titicaca, across which its passengers would take boat for Bolivia.

Goehrs got out. The ground was frozen hard. The windows of his sleeper were frosted. The sunshine was wonderfully warm. The harvest was ripe. It was winter on the Puna at a height of nearly 12,500 feet. About as high as the summit of the Alpine Piz Palü. And there were cornfields.

That was at six o'clock. At half-past eight a neat little Pullman train with arm-chairs turned up and took him on to Cuzco.

Goehrs had once travelled without a halt through Cœle-Syria—on his left the purple Lebanon, on his right the carmine-red Anti-lebanon—through the granary of the classical Roman world. Similarly, he was faring through the tableland of the Cordilleras, the harvest home of the Inca Empire that had been at least as big as the Roman's. About the size of the torso of Central Europe. The valley along which Goehrs was travelling led straight to the very heart of the Inca Empire—to Cuzco.

A curious landscape. Altitude nearly 13,000 feet. A steppe fenced on either side by pretty hillocks, which appeared to be some sixty feet high, and were snow-covered —newly fallen snow—to the spot where they ran into the steppe. Herds of llamas were galloping merrily up and down the plain among the hills.

The steppe soon ran out and the course was uphill again. The scene became more familiar, more fertile. The Tyrol in summertime. With a gleam of exotic, livid light over it all. Rich in waving, ripening cornfields. Golden. In the depths of the Peruvian winter. In June. Full of lush, emerald meadowland. Full of pools and lakes and foaming white rivers. Full of cattle standing knee-deep in water and enjoying life. Full of herons, of black-and-white Puna geese. Full of swanlike gulls. Full of long-legged waterbirds. They floated multitudinous on the pools, rising every now and then for a quiet flight. Trees in blossom in between. Agaves. Yellow grain.

Goehrs only took in the full significance of this uncanny idyll by drawing in his mind's eye a line from the Dent du Midi on the Lake of Geneva by way of the Diablerets and the Wilderhorn to the Mönch and the Eiger and pictured the country through which he was travelling as a plain superimposed on the summits of those peaks. A little Holland in the middle of it, to which snow mountains ran down on a visit—the snow mountains of a *fata morgana*. Only there were Indian villages in this Holland. Built of a whitish-brown clay with striking patterns in their perforated walls as though built by children, sometimes cones, sometimes squares, or fanciful dovecots.

Snow lay on the thatched roofs of these clay huts. The women sat in front of them as only Indian women can sit. They would stare dully for hours with that inimitable animal look, with something half of vanished savagery, half of wistful fatalism. Melancholy about it—half Tibet, half Fenimore Cooper. They were selling little live fish, clay horses that looked like Chinese modelling, and round, white cheeses. They looked exactly like Mongolians, like Chinese, and sometimes like Malays. Perhaps most like Chinese with narrow noses.

They wore knee-breeches, and violently coloured ponchos. These glorious ponchos were made of llama wool dyed in natural colours—pieces of fabric, with a slit in the middle through which they pushed their heads, draping the poncho like a short sporting toga over their shoulders half-way down their bodies. Surmounting this, Chinese hats. Pointed at the peak. Like lampshades. Goehrs could have imagined himself back in the Yangtse Valley.

It was as hot as Hades. Here and there the Indian children had built snow-men about the market gardens.

By this time the train had reached the village of La Raya. Altitude 14,000 feet, higher than the highest peak in the Bernina Alps. Somewhere near was a model farm managed by an English colonel who was going to educate the sheep to yield a threefold crop of wool.

For some hours past an Englishwoman had been lying in the train in a state of lethargy, pale as wax, half dead. An hour previously Goehrs had offered her his garlic root. A garlic root is composed of ten little bulbs, folded up like the calyx of a flower, and every little bulb looks like a tiny banana. The lady had been sitting for an hour holding the garlic root in her long slender hand with its big aquamarine ring—and sniffing at it. A quarter of an hour before reaching the highest point she felt better. Her pulse was normal. She no longer wanted to die. But she smelled of garlic.

" It is sure to hang about one's clothes for a week," she

said with a smile, " but I promise you I don't mind.   Lord, how ill I felt ! "

So Señora Albago's quaint gift had fulfilled its mission.

At the station where she was to alight, an antediluvian monstrous motor car awaited her.   Ladies and gentlemen in antediluvian monstrous habits, in smartly shabby garb with the heads of thoroughbreds and pearl necklaces—the staff of the model farm—were standing in it to bid her welcome.

From La Raya the railway slid some 3500 feet downhill in a quarter of an hour.   Sicuani !   The rest of the journey was covered by car.

Indian villages everywhere.   The whole plain full of Malay-Indians in gaudy ponchos.   Goehrs, who was now watching the Indians moving about on their native heath, far from all white men, and noting their gait and their odour, felt disposed to accept the theory that they had crossed the Bering Straits into North America and thence had reached South America by way of Mexico.   As a general rule, theories of this kind had, in Europe, struck Goehrs as rather fatuous.   The men of science, to his way of thinking, were often inclined to treat races a little too much as horticulturists treat varieties of flowers they propose to cross.

Every twelve miles or so another tribe would crop up. Different ponchos.   Different colours.   Different hats.   All of them of the Quichua race, the nucleus of the Inca rule. The women were wearing the pagoda hats.   The brim was raised on either side and two little curtains hung down over their ears.   Very pretty.   The hats were blue outside and yellow inside.   Or red outside and green inside.   Flaring colours in this setting.   They often, too, wore red skirts and green waists, and sometimes all colours intermingled.   The men preferred to be all in red.   Many in blue and red.   With rainbow ponchos over all.   And headgear like round tin hats.

They were not all moving at walking pace.   Some were trotting.   With bent knees—more especially when they were carrying loads.   Exactly like coolies.   None of them spoke Spanish.   The handful of white men on the Puna addressed them in Quichua.   " No wonder," thought Goehrs, " that Lima is Peru."

The Indians sometimes addressed a lady who bought something of them as " Senoracha," instead of Señorita— giving it an almost Russian turn.   Many of the Indio women were wearing fur caps.   Almost all the men were wearing nightcaps like a ski-ing cap with a peak falling over the head and earflaps attached to it.

Earflaps. But bare feet. Almost without exception bare feet. On frostbound ground. At the height of 12,500 feet. Higher than Etna.

Goehrs had with difficulty gradually to accustom himself to the fertile confusion that prevailed here between what are to the European the distinct facts of summer and winter. Tropical waterfowl flitting about, buffaloes standing in the pools, herds of llamas and alpacas galloping about, snowmen here and there, waving yellow wheat and snow mountains which just impinged on the ears of corn, frozen puddles on the ground, idyllic lakes with agaves on their banks. . . . In this landscape the Indians squatted about like Buddhas or they stood about motionless as statues in their fields or they trotted along on their llamas against the skyline like everlasting clockwork figures. Goehrs saw the mountains, piled up above them sometimes at a gradient of 45°, parcelled out, like a chessboard into meadows, market gardens, cornfields. Glorious terraces, smothered in foliage, until the snowline blocked their path and cut them off short. These terraces and their irrigation works were, from a technical point of view, quite as bold bits of architecture as are the latter-day bridges linking one bank to the other. The forbears of the Indians had laid out these terraces on the slopes of the snow mountains. They were the Incas' work. And they were the work of tribes settled here a thousand years before the Incas.

Amid those terraces Goehrs pushed slowly into the heart of the Inca country, into the valley of Cuzco, which, in the Indian tongue, is called " the Navel." The navel of the world.

GARCILASO DE LA VEGA'S HOUSE

WHEN Goehrs woke up in Cuzco, he felt a cold he had never experienced before, a cold that penetrated through his fingertips, into the bones of his whole frame. A niche less than five feet in depth was hewn into the wall beside his bed, an apse with one or two pegs for hanging clothes. In the wall opposite was cut a niche more than six feet in depth, with water pipes and a neat little w.c. Almost Moorish. With many red damask draperies. But the wall of the adjoining room was more than eight feet in thickness. Goehrs had to pass through this adjoining room to reach an anteroom. This anteroom had no door ; it gave on to the staircase. Some other guest was sleeping in the adjoining room.

The hotel, for some inscrutable reason, was called the Club Pullman and was fairly large, but on account of the waste of space on masonry it had only three rooms. Nor was it a regular hotel—it looked more like a harem, and its proprietor was a notable of Cuzco. It was a hobby of his to keep a hotel, but he kept it clean. The hotel was only a fragment of a big, old block of buildings. This building had, in its day, been built for protection against the cold and against enemies. That is why it was so massive.

The single window in Goehrs's room was made, not of glass, but of wood, and was not easy to shut entirely. The cold streamed in unimpeded. But when Goehrs threw it open there was gloriously warm sunshine outside, while icy cold prevailed in the room in which he was standing shivering.

The Indians, barefoot, but in ponchos of glowing colours, streamed into the town through the old streets below from every quarter of the Puna. Their bare soles flapped rhythmically as they trotted past. They wore their felt lamp-shade hats on their heads, and two llamas trotted in front of them at the same pace. Cuzco was a city with a population of 30,000, the biggest but two in Peru, and every more important house was a facsimile of the one in which Goehrs was lodged. It was a very old house. Four hundred years ago Garcilaso de la Vega, the Inca prince, son of a Spaniard, the sensitive half-breed who chronicled the history of the Incas, had been born under its roof.

THE BISHOP OF CUZCO

SEÑORA ALBAGO had told Goehrs that there were convents of nuns in Cuzco who had taken lifelong vows of silence, nunneries straight out of the Middle Ages, and Goehrs had telegraphed from Arequipa to his friends in Lima on this account. The latter had put themselves in communication with the Archbishop and the latter had wired to the Bishop of Cuzco, and the bishop had, long before Goehrs's arrival in Cuzco, sent a priest to call at the two hostelries in Cuzco on this matter, and Goehrs therefore had first to pay his respects to the bishop.

For this purpose Goehrs had to cross the town from end

to end, and on this walk Cuzco struck him as being more beautiful than any city in Spain.

The bishop lived, like every one else, in a little palace built round a courtyard. On the inner gallery there happened to be standing twenty Indians who had just arrived in Cuzco after a week's trot from some remote tableland to pay homage to the bishop. They were just being admitted and were slipping from the gallery into the reception-room. Bare legs, blue-black hair, ponchos of green, red, blue, white, and yellow stripes to their waist, and lampshade hats. As they pulled off their hats on entering, Goehrs was conscious of that aching pity that he always felt in the case of elephants, the sense of being confronted with beings that had been adapted to the modern world only by a mistake, and not very successfully

Three minutes later a man with a purple skullcap over his tonsure and a purple-braided cassock entered the room, a man with keen eyes and an Indian profile, the Very Reverend Bishop Petrus Parfan. The room was furnished with green and pink rococo upholstery. A light wallpaper with designs of ears of corn and coats-of-arms. A modern Madonna, in a candy-scarlet cloak, and wearing a childish, high, little crown, was standing on the table. Tigerskins on the floor.

Goehrs learnt that there were neither nunneries with vows of perpetual silence, nor convents under " purely medieval " conditions in Cuzco ; on the contrary that the regime there was not in the least Spanish, but very humane and enlightened. Bueno ! The bishop, by way of compensation, proposed to give him leave to view the episcopal treasury. He rang the bell. A Cholo in spectacles and a blue suit entered. The bishop measured him with his eye and told him to give instructions that the cathedral treasury was to be shown to Goehrs at four o'clock.

Taking his leave, Goehrs saw the Indians still waiting on the gallery, kissing the topaz in the big ring of the bishop, who had gone out to them. They were oddly pagan as they did so in their animal-like movements. So gentle, so wild, and so subdued.

All the Indians had a lump in the left side of their mouths. They were all chewing coca. Goehrs had never yet seen an Indian without his coca and never saw one later on without his coca. Coca is a shrub with thin leaves like dried laurel. These leaves yield cocaine. The Indians, of course, consumed not the chemical distillation, but the drug itself, the

QUETOHA INDIAN IN CUZCO.

actual leaf. Every Indian carried it about with him in a pouch. Coca is a stipulation in every agreement, in every contract. If a man were engaging a number of Indians as porters, labourers, or guides, the Indians would quote a sum and a given measure of coca.

Coca is not so deleterious as cocaine. It deadens the nerves of the stomach. It deadens hunger. It is a stimulant. It enables the organs to endure enormous exertions. But acting on the central nervous system it destroys the organs. It has been degenerating a race of millions for centuries ; it has been drugging whole tribes for tens of centuries. The rulers of the Indian nations used to dope their mobs with it. The Inca conquerers doped theirs with it. The Spaniards doped them. The Peruvian did the same thing—and the American mine-owner was doing the same thing.

" You can exploit a mine without dynamite, without water, without plant, without maybe drills," the young Yankee in Arequipa said, " but not without coca."

When they got hold of alcohol on top of it, the drugged race was simply doomed.

Goehrs liked watching them for hours as they streamed into Cuzco from the mountains in long trains in their flowery garb, accompanied by their llamas and alpacas. Dear, charming creatures with unutterably sad faces. With their purplish yellow complexions. From some mysterious world.

Cuzco was an Indian city but not overcrowded with an Indio proletariat as in the case of Arequipa, but a town full of Indios who went about in it exactly as they had gone about in it a thousand years ago, who drifted about here exactly as they drifted about their native Puna. Seven or eight days' journey from their highlands at an altitude of anything between thirteen and sixteen thousand feet. When they set out for Cuzco, they were going down the valley. A valley situate at the height of the crests of the Dent du Midi.

Conditions as of a moonscape.

Cuzco at first glance appeared to be an old Spanish town lying behind its rampart of hills, warlike, savage, studded with cathedrals, barbarically beautiful, like Burgos of Castile, storeyed, severe, with spacious squares in front of the churches that rose in groups and did not hide away as in Arequipa, a genuine city of churches—an ecclesiastical town puffed up with arrogance.

That was the first impression. But it was wrong. It was all true, but it was incidental. Cuzco was an Indian city, but not only by reason of the Indios passing through it. For everything that was Spanish about it, its palaces, its churches, the façades of its houses, were still standing on Indian groundworks. After Goehrs had walked about its streets for ten minutes, he knew that Cuzco was one of the wonders of the world—perhaps the most marvellous pre-historic city of which the world can boast.

So at four o'clock that day Goehrs went to the cathedral to have the treasury shown him. Eight padres were seated in the carved stalls chanting the office. Then they disappeared each into a different chapel. Goehrs caught one just as, after disrobing, he was leaving his chapel again, but the man he had intercepted was not the treasurer, for he only pointed mournfully to two fugitive black cassocks which, evasive as escaping swallows, were disappearing in the glowing sunshine of the old narrow Indian alleys. So Goehrs never saw the treasury. It was, too, a matter of the most supreme indifference to him.

SAXAHUAMAN

IT was a matter of supreme indifference to him—because what was purely Spanish about this old city, even if it were Spanish in a better state of preservation than in any of the ancient cities of Spain, had failed to engage his interests in the Cordilleras. Since he had woke up that morning, Goehrs had succumbed to that feverish state that always attacked him when once he was anywhere near a spot where outstanding riddles of the history of mankind were challenging solution.

Immediately after his call on the bishop, Goehrs had found a little Cholo in front of Club Pullman with a horse on a leading rein. It was a delightful mount, powerful, but as shapely as a classical charger, saffron-yellow with plaited reins. Señora Albago, who owned a big hacienda a little above Cuzco, had placed the horse at his disposal. Once Goehrs was mounted, it went off like a goat in the curiously lopsided trot peculiar to mountain horses, and with a pair of lungs that seemed untiring. It galloped a few hundred yards up the hillside in the thin air without turning a hair.

On the ridge of the hill lay the great fortress of Saxahuaman, the key of the Inca Empire.

The hill crest was fortified on either side in three terraces. A huge wall ran right round the summit of the hill ; stones twelve to fifteen feet in length were fitted together in it by methods that the destructiveness of no Spanish conqueror, no earthquake even, nothing in the world had availed to destroy. But this was not the most notable feature of the fort.

The most notable feature was the fact that these Cyclopean stones, partly hexagonal, partly octagonal, over quite long stretches, fitted into one another without the use of mortar. They fitted into one another so smoothly, so elastically, so easily, and so powerfully, that they hardly showed a crack. The seeming roughness of the structure proved on closer examination to be the most superb craftsmanship Goehrs had ever seen. What immense talent it must have taken to calculate the millions of planes and angles, to work out their harmonic position, and with all this dovetailing that fitted it together like the cogs of a machine for hundreds of yards, to erect one of the strongest fortresses in the world. Sixteen towers as well. And an extension of the rampart to enclose half of the town of Cuzco below. The Capitol—the Acropolis of the red race. Goehrs sat meditatively in the saddle.

How old was it all ?

De Vega, the scion of the Incas, at the beginning of the sixteenth century attributed the fortress to the Incas. The Incas had not appeared in South America much earlier than the first Crusade, less than a thousand years ago.

Goehrs, however, reached Peru at a date when men of science were despoiling the Incas of almost all merit and importance and, except for their arrogance, left them stripped of well-nigh everything that had been attributed to them. Science was about that time dating most of the public buildings far further back before the Incas. Goehrs, who had learnt from experience in other cases that science is capable of exaggeration and is not competent to differentiate very much more finely between 40,000 and 20,000 years than a flower woman can between two and four million dollars, was not unduly impressed. He believed that there was definite palpable evidence that these walls were thousands of years older than the Augustan age of the Inca Empire. Fourteen thousand or four thousand years—the figure was fantastic enough.

The city of Cuzco was so incorporated in these fortifications that, if the fort stood for the head of a puma, the city represented the body, and finally the course of the river furnished the animal's tail. The puma was cut into the rock everywhere as an emblem, and the Indians believed that they were descended from it. They therefore had laid out Cuzco on the lines of this beast. All round the fort rose hundreds of clusters of tall rocks. Not a foot of them was rough. Full of steps, full of niches, full of rests and arm-chairs. The rock was as smoothly polished as if it had been worked by a chisel. The tallest pinnacles of rock had been reshaped into towers, with altars and incised thrones of mysterious dignity.

For what purpose ?

Nations of the past only submitted to work of such scope on military or religious grounds, or for reasons connected with the food supply. These hundreds of armoured towers of huge rocks would have served no military purpose. Nor could they have had any connexion with the food supply. There therefore only remains some ritualistic object for these conspicuous works. Everything here obviously aimed at achieving the acme of display. Goehrs remembered that one of these rock towers was called "the Seat of the Inca." Steps led up to it from a polished rock. The stone throne overtopped the fortress. It had probably really furnished the Inca emperor with an open-air dais. The Inca might well have held his court in the open air from this natural state box. On the occasion of festivals, sacrifices, receptions. With the tiara round his brow. With the black-and-white condor's feathers in his hair. Cuzco, the metropolis, at his feet, the serried snow ranges of the Cordilleras facing him.

How simple ! What an eye for stage effect ! What zest for power and pomp.

Goehrs tethered his horse, which was just beginning to flirt with a herd of passing llamas, gave it a pat, and looked for the entrance into the fort. It was not very easy to find, but at length Goehrs discovered it at one side, quite narrow, quite low—a square gateway narrowing towards the top. And over the gate lay an enormous stone slab. It was inconceivable how such a slab could be conveyed to its site, raised, and placed in position as a roof of the gateway. But this mechanical problem was by no means what at the first sight gave Goehrs such a shock.

It was something else. For Goehrs saw himself with the clock set back by a few years, standing in excitement outside the Lion Gate of Mycenæ in the Peloponnesus. The Lion Gate of the Mycenæ citadel resembled this Indian gate as one pea resembles another. Saxahuaman displayed the same monumental labour in rock as, in the case of the fair-skinned Mediterranean race, did Mycenæ, of whom Homer tells as of a tradition and a myth. Homer who has himself lapsed into a legend.

Goehrs further looked back on Luxor and saw exactly the same gateways leading into the Egyptian as into these Indian temples. He saw the same pylons, roofed by the same slab of rock. He saw himself standing in Luxor under the pyramids of Sakkara and Giza wrestling with identical problems—with the same mechanical puzzles. It remained inconceivable to him here as it had been there by what means such masses of stone could at that date be moved at all.

Goehrs looked back on Knossos in Crete and saw himself standing in the palace of Minos, that fairylike palace of pre-classical times with its halls of state and baths for the princesses, with its theatres, its bullrings, and boudoirs, made fifteen centuries before the Greeks began to roughhew their first rude statues. He looked back on Knossos, where the double-headed axe was incised everywhere as the puma and the condor were in the Indian palaces here. Everywhere the same ceremonial, the same military might, the same gentle decadence, the same fusion of king and high priest, the same deep religious sentiment, the same appetite for sensuousness and the same exaggerated luxury in the planning of palaces that were at the same time strongholds ; and Goehrs remembered that from the fortress palace in Knossos there were two immortal vistas—one on to the Mediterranean and the other on to the snow-capped peak of Ida, mountain of the gods—vistas similar to those here.

Goehrs saw himself standing in the Alhambra in Granada : the same abundance of water, the same costly water-supply here in Cuzco as among the Moors in Granada, the same miles of aqueducts, the same conduit pipes sunk into the rock, and the same tropical gardens at the foot of the snow-capped Sierra Nevada of Spain as here on the foothills of the Cordilleras. Goehrs recalled that, when they came into the cities from the desert, the Druses in Damascus and the fellahin in Nubia ran about hand in hand exactly as the Indians ran about hand in hand when they descended from their fifteen-thousand-foot mountain fastnesses to Cuzco, which was only a little over ten thousand feet high—though this was the altitude of the highest summit of the Sierra Nevada in Spain. And he remembered the peak of Taurus glittering in the regions beyond Damascus. All these similarities startled Goehrs. There almost seemed to be some common principle that caused all these ancient nations to have some likeness to one another and their customs and cities to have a kindred trend—the Phœnician ruins, the Mesopotamian sites, Babylon, and the ruins near Bulawayo in South Africa.

But, though Goehrs did not profess to be a man of science nor desire to pose as one, an even more striking feature of this similarity dawned on him, not the similarity of the problems to be solved but the kinship in the atmosphere— the atmosphere of a world so wildly amazing, so ancient, so alien, so inconceivable, that it seemed as though it must pertain, not to this universe, but some other planet. He had no evidence to support his thesis. But he fairly winded it. There was the same atmosphere, the same mystery, the same link in common between all these ruined cities and some constellation which we have ceased to possess.

He was as far cut off from it, so it seemed to him, as from Saturn. As he rode around them, he gazed at the ramparts of the strongest, the mightiest fortress ruins of this continent, at this kernel of a vast empire of exotic splendour, at this cupola of an Indian Rome, with a feeling of wistfulness. As amid no other ruins in the world was he conscious of an atmosphere, firmly associated with this soil, of majesty, of civilization, of prehistoric languor, that was almost palpable here. Goehrs felt it like a gooseflesh over his skin, more stimulating, violent, and strange in its intensity than anything he could remember.

He drew rein with the intention of riding back to Cuzco.

THE HIKER

A MOUNTAIN horse's paces are like a circus pony's, it has an entirely different motion from that of the ordinary horse, and a mountain horse pirouetting about among rocks and pitfalls, as if it were in a riding ring, will delight the eye of any man.

Half-way down the Saxahuaman hill, a man stopped short and fairly devoured the yellow horse with his eyes.

" Hello, señor," said the man. Goehrs pulled up.

" Are you riding through Peru ? "

" What has that got to do with you ? " asked Goehrs, laughing.

The man standing in front of him had four dogs in his train. A monkey was riding one of the dogs. The man was wearing a green shirt and khaki shorts; his knees were bare and he had an enormous cowboy hat. He was carrying a flag, a long pole flying a pennon.

"I beg your pardon, you're right, it has nothing to do with me," said the man, " but I'm so profoundly interested in the methods by which people travel. For my own part, I hike."

"Why?" asked Goehrs, with a glance at the menagerie at his heels, which was having a rough-and-tumble among itself and beginning to make his horse restive.

"There are such a lot of liars about," said the man, " I want to see the world as it really is."

Goehrs looked at the man with some curiosity. He had a smooth, hard face, sallow rather than tanned. A fanatic, thought Goehrs.

"Are you running about the world for the fun of the thing?"

"Yes."

"Spaniard?"

"Yes."

"Who's financing the show for you?"

"The railway travellers," said the man smiling. " I'll throw in the journalists. They're the worst liars."

"No doubt," said Goehrs.

"All travellers are liars," said the man. " That has irritated me ever since I was a small boy. I grew up on a farm and can neither read nor write."

"That may be a great advantage," said Goehrs politely.

"But just the same I can check everything. There's no need to be able to read or write, señor, you only have to go on foot. You see now, there's a river somewhere between Brazil and Uruguay. Some one described it as fifty yards broad. Not a soul can tell the man that he's a stupid swindler. But I, who hiked there on my flat feet, know that that river is only twenty yards across. I know he's lying."

Goehrs laughed.

"I once met a famous man," the stranger went on, " who told me that he was in the Chaco with an Indian, who fell from a tree one day and broke his leg. Then the Indio tried to stab himself, but the famous man stopped him. Two hours later a knife flicked out from the bush into the Indian's

163

back, and two minutes later the Indio was dead. The famous man dashed into the bush to find the murderer and, when he got back, the dead Indian had disappeared. He found him three days later on an ant-hill, but he was already a skeleton. The famous man explained that the Indio's friends had killed him because after breaking his leg he could never become a great hunter and therefore was useless. They'd done him the favour that the famous man had denied him and then they buried him in their own way—among the ants! There, you see! Who would ever have dared to tell the famous man he was lying except I—I who have hiked all through the Chaco? The man must have read some non-sense like that and then invented a yarn to match it. Damn it all, not a soul in the Chaco would dream of buncombe like that. Have you ever yet seen a sentimental Indian in the Montaña—you on horseback? "

"No, I haven't," admitted Goehrs. "How long have you been hiking? "

"It's two years since I left Rio."

"And what are you going to do afterwards? "

"Write a book," said the man in the green shirt, the yellow neckerchief, with the bare knees, the flag, the four dogs, and the monkey on one of the dogs.

Goehrs was dumbfounded for a minute.

"But you can't write."

"I've got a good memory."

For a moment Goehrs turned his eyes away. Then he met the hiker's gaze.

"If you take to writing," he said softly, " I'm afraid that one of these days you'll have to take to lying."

"Never," said the man, and laid his hand over the horse's nostrils.

"It's a pity," said Goehrs slowly, "but that's what happens."

"How do you claim to know that? " said the man in vexation.

Goehrs smiled darkly. "Look out, man," he said, " the horse may lash out. Good luck."

The horse had become restive under the man's hand covering its nostrils. Goehrs reined it in, and then the horse in double-quick time parted company from the menagerie and from the man who tramped through virgin forests because the world was too untruthful for his liking.

Goehrs rode down to Cuzco to have a look at the Incas' palaces.

FOR the ancient Indian buildings were still standing. They were still on their ancient groundworks—enormous groundworks. For this reason, and for this reason only, the whole of the Spaniards' triumphant display in Cuzco looked tawdry. For this reason, the niches in the Renaissance churches, where warrior saints flaunted it ; for this reason, the clusters of cathedral domes, their towers, their colonnades, the fantastically baroque porticoes, the pretentious width of the monster churches, had a suggestion of being merely the work of a crude parvenu. And for this reason, the most beautiful, the most perfect, in fact, perhaps the only genuine Spanish city in the world—Spanish Cuzco with its exquisite choir stalls in the cathedral, with its ideal convent of La Merced—for this reason, old Spanish Cuzco only looked like the product of barbarism as compared with Indian Cuzco.

For the old metropolis of the Indians was still in a state of some preservation. Half and half. The Spaniards had only half demolished it. It was still standing well above ground-level. And the Spaniards had built their houses, patched their clay roofs on these lofty foundations.

Goehrs looked down the mighty streets, cut as if out of iron. Their twilight conjured up the atmosphere of the days when the Indian aristocracy passed up and down them : prefects, the governors of great States, nuns, princes, generals, borne in litters with the same easy motion with which the Indian coolies were swinging past him to-day as they trotted out of the city behind their laden llamas. These poor serfs were all the Spaniards had left alive of the race. They were the descendants of the slave race that had brought fresh fish for the Inca emperors from the coast, that had waged their wars, that had built their mansions and temples. The Spaniards had butchered the flower of the race, the brain of the State, the ruling caste, and the pride of the empire, butchered them much more effectively than they had razed their palaces and strongholds, which were indeed less easy to wipe out than the Indian princes.

Goehrs continued to study these palace walls day after day. He gazed at them with a fluttering at his heart-strings that never ceased. For this purpose it made no odds whether the palaces be labelled Inca or pre-Inca. When he said Inca, he meant simply Indian—whether the ruling caste some five thousand years before our era were called

Aymara or Quichua, or whether six thousand years later, when the Spaniards arrived, they were called Inca. What fascinated Goehrs in these surveys was the general atmosphere, the privilege of treading the soil of an Indian metropolis, the urban complex of the yellow-red race. These palace walls illustrated, as he saw it, more clearly than any inaccurate traditions could, the vision, the greatness of the conceptions, and the measure of the coincidences that had conspired to make the greatest Indian State.

He learned to distinguish two types of masonry. One type was exactly like the construction of the fortress above, Cyclopean, irregular blocks of stone pieced together like a mosaic over long distances, a mosaic of huge proportions. The other type of massive masonry was built of square blocks that looked as if they were cast in metal of such uniformity and accuracy that the wall spaces were as refreshing to the beholder as well-trained plants, a delight to the eye, which was stimulated in the same way as by the sight of well-balanced columns and well-trained palms.

The rectangular palace walls slanting a little backwards were subdivided as if by razor cuts and had a solidity and charm that surpassed the Cyclopean palaces by a good deal.

Perhaps there were as many thousands of years between the two types—between the mansions on one side of the street and those on the other as lie between Cologne Cathedral and the Tower of Babel. On one side of the street among the Cyclopean palaces Goehrs was maybe confronting the most ancient and well-balanced structures in the world. And the mansions on the other side of the street, built of the little dressed stone cubes, perhaps represented only the gracefully decadent style of the Incas; in fact the Inca Empire might well have been only a sort of Byzantium, which did not flower until the close of an epoch of culture many thousands of years old. Perhaps the striking, military piety of the Incas was the epilogue of an era when the ruler had always been conqueror and priest at one and the same time—a demigod, fashioned by blending steel and poetry in one.

In any case it was through these narrow streets, with foundations unmoved for unnumbered centuries, in which the ghost of that mysterious, primitive epoch of humanity still lingered to this day, that the Inca princes had passed after receiving the accolade with the lance in one hand and a posy of flowers in the other. Princes, generals, prefects, statesmen, ædiles, vestal virgins, priests—slim-hipped

QUETOHA INDIAN IN CUZCO.

creatures like the princes portrayed three thousand years ago in the frescos on the walls of the temple-palace of Knossos in Crete, athletes and poets in one, singers and organizers in one, State-builders and garden-lovers as well—music-loving creatures of an unceasing inbreeding, which always divided the nation into two worlds, and which allowed the Spaniards to kill off the thin ruling caste and to enter into the heritage of their wealth, of their power, of their way of life, if not of their standard of civilization as well.

Cuzco in the grip of the Spaniards was the symbol of the fall of the Indian Empire. Even if the most beautiful castles and fortresses like Machu Pichu stood in the open country beyond, all the Indians' sentiment, all their pride, all their good fortune and sense of nationality focused on Cuzco. This State was over-centralized in Cuzco. Cuzco stood for everything. The State was nothing more than a chessboard dominated by Cuzco. Cuzco was Rome, and at the same time more than Rome for the Inca emperor was more than Cæsar; he was Apollo and Alexander in one. God and myth and to some extent a human being. How could a State on such lines hold together when so unnatural a gulf divided the sovereign from his subjects?

THE TEMPLE OF THE SUN

GOEHRS again stood in the middle of Cuzco, in front of a new quadrangle of Indian masonry, on the tall ruins of which the Spaniards had built a few hundred medieval houses. This quadrangle was all that remained of a palace for the vestal virgins of the red race, for the sacred maidens whose chastity was inviolable and who occupied a curious intermediary position between the Incas and the heavenly bodies they worshipped. They were isolated and honoured in an inimitable fashion. These fifteen hundred maids, attended by fifteen hundred other maids were never seen by the eyes of man. These spouses of the Sun, these virgins of the Moon, had an unparalleled aloofness, a unique position. Only the wife and the sister of the Inca were permitted to see them. The Inca emperor himself, who alone might perhaps have seen them, waived his right.

The Inca himself waived it, although everything was permissible for him. And because everything was permissible for him, he never came in conflict with the laws. An

167

Inca emperor never stood in a court of law for breach of his own commandments. Since he owned all things—all treasure, every human being, and every realm—his heart was immune from all temptation and his character the more easily attuned to renounce gladly. For all that, the Inca was not beyond the reach of mishap. For the first matter in which he wholly failed was bound to destroy him, since he lived among the laws like a demigod. And his first failure did in fact destroy him, and he fell into headlong ruin, together with his empire and the rash challenge to fate inherent in his position.

The Indian State was overrun by cloisters of this nature, not only with military posts and official dwellings of the administrative officials. All the links in the chain of dominion were faultlessly interlaced in the Indian State—sanctity, power, and beauty. Tens of centuries had lavished their whole yield of golden ornaments on temples and institutions. Cuzco must have been dazzling with gold. What wonder that the Indians, coming from afar, took off their hats as soon as they were in the magic zone of their capital !

Goehrs looked up at the citadel of Saxahuaman. The Peruvians had set up a big Christian cross with electric lights. He turned on his heel and made his way towards another quadrangle. On either side of the streets were hundreds of little vaults—shops where the Indians of Cuzco sold coca to the Indians from the mountains.

In the middle of this quadrangle Goehrs saw a church from which white-robed monks were trooping : Santo Domingo. The quadrangle out of which a church peeped shyly today had once been the centre of the Inca Empire. It even eclipsed the palace of the Inca emperor by the awe that death exercises over life and the sacred relic over the shrine. This quadrangle was the Temple of the Sun, the Holy of Holies of the Indian Empire.

Goehrs gazed along the partition wall upwards. The Inca wall was still intact, huge and beautiful. Only, just at the top, there was a clay attachment, from the windows of which monks were looking down on a narrow, vast street of overpowering impressiveness.

Goehrs rang the bell and entered. He would never have found his way about in the confusion of ancient temple and latter-day church if Father Christoforus Vásquez had not been his guide, a black-bearded monk with a keen nose and thick lips under a white cowl.

The church had been built over and into the wreckage of the ancient Temple of the Sun with a measure of insolence, of arrogance, and of resolve that left the significance of this wicked destruction beyond all doubt. But with what inferiority of style had this Spanish church been built, with what inferiority of proportion, with what decadence in the treatment of its material! A contemptible political make-shift above a royal giant. In spite of it all, the august halls of the Sun Temple were still in a state of preservation, as were the dozens of their pylon doorways, which, broader at the base and narrowing towards the top, led directly from court to court. So too were the blocks of masonry, often a yard long and polished like marble, that frequently furnished the cornerstone or the keystones of arches, supported, a marvel of architectonic craftsmanship, without mortar, only by their own weight.

In the main hall in which Goehrs was standing, the image of the Sun had once been set up. The Spaniards had been in time to see it. The sun was so big that it extended from one wall of the hall to the other. Along the walls to the right and left, the mummies of the Inca emperors were seated on chairs of gold—the whole dynasty. Only one of them, the most virtuous of all, was sitting opposite the Sun, confronting it full face. Not a single one of these mummies had been preserved, not a single mummy of an Inca emperor has been found.

Goehrs passed into the adjoining hall.

The Moon had held court here. Along the walls the mummies of the principal wives of the Incas had been ranged. Only one of these, the most virtuous of all, had sat opposite the Moon, facing it. Every one of the women sitting here had been the wife and at the same time the sister of the Inca. Wife and sister. As in Egypt. The Moon was the consort and the sister of the Sun—and mother of the Inca emperors.

Goehrs was conscious of an indissoluble, wondrous nexus of interrelationships and affinities between the heavenly bodies, human beings, and the symbols worshipped here and regarded as the most natural bond in the world. And they did seem natural under the Cordilleran skies, in which the stars seemed studded thrice as densely as in those of Africa, Europe, or Asia.

Goehrs passed through the walls that led to the third and fourth halls, the Hall of the Rainbow and the Hall of the Lightning. The Lightning, in the eyes of the Incas, was the

Sun's beam of power, and the Rainbow was the beam in which he sent before him his forgiveness.

Goehrs gazed at the walls. There was nothing left now of the splendour and the wealth that had made this temple symbolic of the Indian race. Nothing left except the shell. But what walls they were! At the farther end of the temple they stood, like bent bows, against one another as though cast in bronze, the noblest display of masonry that this noble building held.

"The Spaniards were very wanton in their destructiveness," said the monk, looking out on the fertile tableland that stretched to the mantle of freshly fallen snow on the opposite mountainside.

"They were warriors," said Goehrs.

They walked to the entrance. The monk showed Goehrs one or two frescos he had found under the Spaniards' plaster and had uncovered. He was the type of priest who, deeply moved by the grandeur of such immortal work as was that of the Indian temple, condemned the action of the Spaniards without a trace of narrowmindedness—even if the work of destruction had been prompted for the greater glory of his own Church. He discountenanced the destruction of the temple, at a distance of centuries it is true, at a distance and from an era when the Church had no further need to be on terms of war against pagan religions.

"The Church was more tolerant in her attitude towards great work in Spain," said the monk. "The Church incorporated the Moorish mosque in Cordova so happily into the cathedral that the thousand columns of the mosque were left unscathed. And it remains, too, the most splendid mosque there is outside of Mecca."

"No doubt," said Goehrs with a smile, "but the Moors had been driven from Spain. There was no longer an Islamitic peril. And it was a more prudent policy to be magnanimous than destructive."

They were just then walking through the hall where the Inca emperors had sat along the walls as mummies on chairs of gold. Goehrs pointed to the spot where the giant image of the Sun, outlined in flames and rays, must have stood.

"You must bear in mind that the men who conquered Peru were more or less criminals," he said. "What's become of the image of the Sun? A few days after the taking of the city a man of the name of Mónico Serra de Lequizano gambled it away to a halfwit, who melted it down. That was the type that overthrew the Indian State."

"Spaniards," said the monk. Goehrs glanced at his face quickly. His expression betokened pretty plainly that the monk had Indian blood in his veins. But the monk was not thinking of his Indian blood. He considered himself a Peruvian as did every one else in Cuzco, and, again like every one else in Cuzco, that he therefore belonged to another stock than the Spaniards.

"What is a Peruvian?" thought Goehrs as he groped his way back through the fantastic Indian streets to the Club Pullman. "What is a Peruvian? A man deriving from Spaniards and Indians. And a man who will have nothing to do with either Spaniards or Indians. A mongrel breed that has neither the good qualities of the Spaniards nor those of the Indians. And what good qualities of his own otherwise?"

Goehrs looked out sadly on the wondrous city that was still quite "old," still quite immune from excrescences of iron and glass, still unspoilt medieval Spain built on the site of an Indian metropolis.

As long as Goehrs looked across towards Cuzco, he heard the silent hum of the town, the savage rhythm, the patter of the bare soles of the Indians driving their llamas in front of them and tramping across the cold ground of the streets. The pattering went on to the same relentless tune and rang to the same accompaniment of poverty as it did when the proletariat used to throng through these same streets on the occasions of the Inca emperor's appearances in the public squares to celebrate "Raymi," the feast of the summer solstice, and "Sitna" the close of the rainy season. Nothing had changed, so far as these poor wretches were concerned! On the contrary. Life had become harder.

SERFS AND LLAMAS

A FEW days later Goehrs was riding across three snow peaks. He rode muleback for two days up farmlands as far as the snowline and then down farmlands—across pampas with herds of llamas and through torrid valleys. He was riding cross-country through the Cordilleras that run from Panama to Cape Horn in one or two big ranges and have thousands of little folds in between the big ranges, folds of virgin forest—the Montaña, tropical valleys at an altitude of 6000 feet.

Goehrs was riding to pay a visit to a young man named Bellamy who owned a *finca* up in the Puna. He arrived by daylight. They were just having their supper in the dusk in front of the house. Five minutes later, Goehrs, too, was supping. Farmhouses at that height do not boast much in the way of comfort, nor do they stand on ceremony. Bellamy was a nice lad, barely thirty. He had taken over the property to breed an especial kind of llama wool—it was his obsession and his ambition.

"Had a decent ride?" he asked, and helped Goehrs to a potato breadcrumbed like a veal cutlet.

"Very fair, thanks," said Goehrs. "I spent the night in an Indian's hut."

"At these heights there are fortunately no bugs," said Bellamy.

"No—but just the same you have to become acclimatized to llama meat, roasted on llama dung."

"No matter, at any rate you kept warm," said Bellamy. Goehrs thought of the entrance about twenty inches high and of ten people lying round the fire, and had to agree with him.

"I sometimes have to spend five successive nights like that, when I inspect my estate on muleback," said Bellamy. "You become accustomed to it and the people are always so pleased when you turn up."

"What's the size of your hacienda?" asked Goehrs.

"The finca is 150,000 acres," said Bellamy, "not including snow mountains."

Goehrs had asked what the acreage of the "hacienda" was, Bellamy in his answer had spoken of the "finca." A finca is a small hacienda. A hacienda is a big finca. The visitor always refers to the hacienda—the owner always talks modestly of his finca.

"Good Lord! Not including the snow mountains," repeated Goehrs.

"Distances don't count, and square miles still less," said Bellamy and handed round the white llama-cheese. "A day's ride here is the equivalent of an hour's trip in Lima. In a week of mule and tent you can reach the eastern rim of the Cordilleras, where the boundless primeval forest in the Amazonas direction begins. In six days you would be among the savage Indian tribes, whom even the Incas never subdued. In two days' time you are in Cuzco, but two days away in the opposite direction lies the nearest hacienda. It's in a fold of the Cordilleras that's so hot that in spite of being

172

over 6000 feet high, it's full of snakes and tigers. Everything's a bit at the end of the world up there. My finca varies in height from six to twenty thousand feet ; it therefore contains everything there is to be had at such heights : abandoned mines, corn, llama herds, herds of alpaca and pacoche, potatoes, and coca. But it's getting cold now. Let's turn in."

Goehrs slept on a wooden bedstead set in the clay floor on the first storey. He closed the window that consisted of a wooden shutter but suffered terribly from the cold all the same.

On the following morning, even before he went down to coffee, Goehrs watched herds of llamas galloping about over the tableland. Bellamy was in riding-kit. He had to be away the whole day to supervise a bit of road-making that was profoundly uninteresting.

" You may as well have a look at the way we carry on here," he said to Goehrs, and beckoned to an old Indian standing in the doorway. " You will take the llamas down to Cuzco to-day," he told him. The Indian made some reply in Quichua that Goehrs could not follow. Goehrs only saw that Bellamy, shaking his head in annoyance, sent the Indian away and called up some one else. Half an hour after Bellamy had left, Goehrs saw this man and a woman with a train of llamas, laden with sacks, setting off across the Puna in the direction of Cuzco.

Goehrs spent the whole day among the llamas. These curious animals had interested him for weeks. He knew that they were only clipped every other year and that they grumbled when they were hungry. They were able to live in comfort only at considerable heights, were graceful and stupid. To judge by the specimens he had seen in the zoological gardens, he would not have recognized them. In cages they had been malevolent, sluggish beasts. Here they were like deer and as frolicsome as ponies. They belonged, too, to the camel tribe, but looked like giraffes and behaved like sheep. For some reason or other—and that impressed him particularly—they reminded him of the Indians. They had exactly the same gait, an easy trot with bent knees. In many respects they were quite as feckless as the Indians. That morning Goehrs realized that the Indians had remarkably close relationships with the llamas. Once or twice he saw the Indians helping the alpacas in the act of propagating. The animals, left to themselves, lacked initiative.

The alpacas were at times snow-white in colouring and a

little smaller than the llamas. They throve only at great heights. If they were given no hard food to grind, their teeth, so Goehrs had heard, grew right out of their mouths until they died. Curiously degenerated animals living in a state of touching monogamy. Goehrs saw them roaming about between the snowline and the barren Puna. They really did look like creatures from another planet.

When they dashed up at a gallop—and they were delightfully playful—they were quite fascinatingly pretty to watch, because, in spite of their ungainly bodily structure, they were full of dash and grace. At first sight they seemed to be only fat sheep, sometimes overgrown with thick wool to their hoofs. But their legs had the pace of those of antelopes. The giraffe-like neck rose from the sheep's body, supporting the arrogant camel's head with the eyes of a fallow deer, and the mettle of a thoroughbred horse quivered in their every fibre. When they were moving at walking pace, they looked quite different again. Holding their heads horizontally on stiff, straight necks, they looked highly bred, bewildered, hesitant, and shy, like offspring of a very ancient stock, a little like human beings—but at the same time rather inbred, without guts, a little too much of external finish only, a little too much all breeding without brain. Goehrs, however, became very fond of them.

That evening Bellamy brought back Señor Cubano with him, his neighbour of the tropical finca, who was on his way to Cuzco and whom he had met on the road.

The old Indian whom Bellamy had at first thought of sending to Cuzco that morning was waiting at table in the evening. Something reminded Goehrs of the incident that morning, and he asked Bellamy what the meaning of it was.

"I had forgotten that the old fellow has lost his wife," Bellamy explained, "so, of course, he could not go to Cuzco with the beasts."

"Lost his wife . . . ?"

"Well, I can hardly expect him to marry again at his age for the sake of a load of potatoes, can I ?" said Bellamy.

Goehrs was quite at a loss. Cubano laughed.

"No Indio is allowed to be in charge of a team of llamas without his wife," he said, lighting a cigarette, "and that for a peculiar reason. . . ."

"The devil," said Goehrs with sudden understanding. "Is that really true ?"

He had frequently heard the story in Europe that an old Inca law prohibited the Indios from travelling with llamas

174

LLAMAS IN THE CORDILLERAS.

without their wives because the Indios used to sleep with the female llamas and frequently became horribly infected. The Incas were very much concerned over matters of public health and looked out for the sanitary conditions of the masses.

Goehrs had always looked on that as a yarn, more especially as he had read on authority that llamas in general were immune from syphilis. All the same, he had seen for himself in Peru that llamas did suffer from a skin disease that made their coats fall out and in consequence of which they died.

" Is this—this prohibition still in force in law ? " he asked.

" What do you mean by ' law,' Señor ? " returned Cubano. "Laws change so frequently. But the query you are raising is custom. Bueno ! Custom is more binding than law."

" Apart from that, it's rot," said Bellamy. " How are you going to infect an Indian worse than he already is ? "

They were all tired and went to bed early.

In the course of the following days, Goehrs rode in and out among the Indian settlements round the hacienda a good deal. Bellamy owned in all about three hundred serfs. He had taken them over when he bought the finca. He had three hundred Indians on his estate who were under indentures to work for him for given periods, in the mines, road-building, on the farm, in his homestead, or as porters. In return they received Indian corn, a few acres for their own cultivation, and permission to pasture their llamas on the vast estate. Everything was organized on much the same lines as under the Incas, but not so efficiently.

Goehrs observed that the higher the altitude at which the Indian lived, the better his bodily condition was. The colder the district in which they were domiciled, the better the climate suited them physically. The nearer the snowline they lived, that is to say at an altitude of about 15,000 feet, the cleaner and alerter they were, and the more water they had for their tilth when the thaw set in, the better their crops in the way of potatoes and vegetables. And finally, the better was their bearing and self-possession when they passed, with their peaked nightcaps on their heads under their lampshade hats, their ponchos with the old patterns over their shoulders down to their knees, with bare calves and thin sandals. Goehrs soon arrived at a stage when he was able to sort and distinguish the Peruvian Indians purely by the way they bore themselves. Six thousand—nine thousand—twelve thousand—fifteen thousand feet up. He was able to read it off at once.

But even the brightest of them from the greatest altitude had a trace of that melancholy and abstraction that overcast every member of the race and the oppressive influence of which no Indian is able to escape. There was something in the nature of a tragic exhaustion about them, of the end of a chapter, of a non-resistance to a destiny that held them maimed.

One evening, when Cubano was on his way back from Cuzco again, and they were that evening having their supper in the dusk in the open air the three men engaged in conversation.

" What is the real reason why there is no Indian question, if Peru has, let us say, five million inhabitants, four of which are Indians or all but Indians ? " he asked.

" For one thing," said Bellamy, " the Indians are too inert to take any interest in their own social problems. And for another, they would not be able to exist at all in the plain where politics are brewed."

" A few leading men could live in Lima without any difficulty at all," said Goehrs. " But why haven't they any leaders ? "

" Because every Indian who has had a vestige of education has argued himself into believing that he has ceased to be an Indian. It is the same as with Jews who have once been baptized."

" And the half-castes ? "

" Yes, the half-castes," exclaimed Cubano laughing. " The half-castes, of course, imagine they are white. The half-castes, whatever happens, do not want to lead Indios ; they want to rule them and look down on them."

" And the whites ? " asked Goehrs, horror-stricken.

Bellamy shrugged his shoulders.

" Pure-bred whites—I believe there are very few of them. And if there are any, they are scarcer than Inca princes used to be. And they are anyway shrewd enough to know that an Indian rising would mean the death warrant of every white man."

" It seems to me," said Goehrs, " that no one in this country knows what he is."

Cubano drew a breath through his teeth. Bellamy rapped the table with his riding-crop. The Indian brought in a joint of *venado*, venison roasted over the embers. And with it a dish of small potatoes which were not potato tubers, but grew on a sort of clover.

Cubano carved the joint thoughtfully.

" Supposing you are right, and we are all fools," he said slowly, laying down the carving knife and fork and looking up at the snowy crest overhead that was just beginning to turn pink. " Supposing we none of us know where we are, at any rate there's one of us who knows his place for a certainty and that is this—this fellow here."

Cubano pointed to the Indian who was trotting in and out like a coolie on bent knees. The blue streaky hair escaped from under his peaked cap that covered his ears as well, and was like a chain-mail helmet of the Middle Ages. The poncho in blue, green, and yellow stripes that covered his arms reached to his knees, where his breeches ended up in knee-guards. His calves and feet were bare. He had a protuberance on his left cheek—the quid of coca he chewed incessantly, from birth to death. The coca quid he had in his mouth, as every Indian had had for thousands of years, was compounded of leaves of the coca shrub mixed with potash, and Goehrs, deeply concerned in the chronic doping of a race, had never been able to ascertain whether this admixture of potash with the leaves intensified or tempered the effect of the drug. He had heard both alternatives argued.

Goehrs gazed intently from the Indian to Cubano and from the hacienda rancher to the Indian.

" After all, what does the man know about himself ? " he said.

" He knows that he is a slave, that he always was a slave, and that he must always remain one."

" That's impossible," replied Goehrs. " Better wean the man of his coca and alcohol and that chicha stuff."

" No use. The race has been addicted to cocaine and alcohol for centuries. If you were to deprive the Indians of their narcotics, they would go to pieces on the spot. It is the only thing that keeps them going. They are so degenerate that sudden abstinence would simply mean murder. They would die like flies."

" I should try it for all that," said Goehrs. " Because from the way they're going now, they'll go to pieces in any case."

" They'll go to pieces in any case. Very true, señor. But in the way they're living now, they'll go to pieces decently and as it is ordained they should."

" Ordained . . . by whom ? " asked Goehrs, deeply stirred, and he looked at the Peruvian, who poured out a pisco and then quietly lit the lamp. It was an exceptionally mild evening, and in an overcoat it was possible to sit out of doors for a bit in the dusk. Goehrs saw Cubano's profile wavering indistinctly in the lamplight between the half-extinct snowfields. Goehrs was indignant at the callousness with which this man condemned a whole race to death and refused to see that this death sentence must be annulled and fought. Cubano was in other relationships of life a kindly man, decent towards his dependants, towards the Indians, towards animals ; he was travelled ; in addition to Quichua and Spanish, he spoke English and French and a certain amount of German, was courteous and energetic, had, in addition to Ibañez, read a good deal, if aimlessly, Gide, Werfel, and Michael Arlen, and tried to profess himself a Christian.

" As it is ordained they should," Cubano repeated, shaking his head slowly and without qualifying his statement— just as if he were not pronouncing his own views but the mortal purpose of a fate that he had accepted, that was inexorable, and resistance to which would be simply ludicrous.

Goehrs knew that the death sentence of which Cubano had spoken was written in the face of every Indian he had seen —but in spite of that it struck him as inconceivably cruel to acquiesce in it. Tired, sad, refusing within himself to accept a tragedy that, while involving millions, was beyond reason to solve, he turned to go to bed in the finca where the air was icy cold.

A CORDILLERAN FINCA

THE finca was in a state in which a finca was bound to be after remaining untenanted for thirty years. Before Bellamy had bought it a year ago, it had belonged to a wastrel family that had put in a cousin as its bailiff. The cousin was supposed to have lived on the finca but did not. He lived in Cuzco and only spent a week in the course of the year on the finca. In consequence, on transferring the finca, nothing had tallied. It was short of a few hundred llamas ; it was short of an irrigation system ; it was short of agricultural machinery ; and it was short of a w.c. and some floorboards.

But to make up for it, it had a chapel, a chapel with big images of saints, and the chapel was the room adjoining the one in which Goehrs slept. Every morning Goehrs was awakened at sunrise by the Indians, living near the house, tramping up the staircase and along the outside gallery of the house to reach the entrance of the room converted into a chapel. They gazed in through the open aperture that ought to have been a window. One of the many missing windows on account of which Bellamy had gone to law with the former tenant, during which all the latter's relatives took Bellamy's part, for they were jointly liable and all rounded furiously on their former bailiff—a regular family feud out of which some three dozen lawyers were sucking profits.

"We shall have to put a stop to that," said Bellamy, who was no less incommoded by the men tramping about, although he slept on the ground floor. "I shall have a chapel built for these people next door. But first of all the water supply, then light, and then whitewash."

On the following day Bellamy left for a two days' tour, and therewith forgot something he had no business to forget.

On the day in question, Goehrs was waked by a devil of a din. He saw a handful of Indians approaching across the pampas sharply silhouetted in their red-and-white striped ponchos and lampshade hats against the morning light. He stayed in bed, for it was bitterly cold. The Indians came right up to the house playing music and performed some dances. Their orchestra was composed of some flute-players and a fellow blowing a giant conch. The music they evoked was one of the most dismal noises in the world. It was characterized by an awful monotone. There are a lot of countries in the world that affect this monotone. But the Arab is at any rate erotic and the African is insinuating and warlike in its monotony—and, apart from that, both Arabian and African rhythms are inspiriting. But the Indian music was depressing enough to make one howl. Only the dusk of departed vigour. Foredoomed to death.

The Indians finally came into the house and, as they hunted for and failed to find Bellamy, they at length reached Goehrs's room. They scattered flowers on the head of that thoroughly nonplussed individual, and a man with a curious staff, the *alcalde*, barked an address in Quichua, of which Goehrs did not understand a word.

Goehrs rang the bell like mad. The old Indio who waited on him appeared. Goehrs gave him to understand that he was to give the Indians some money, not too much money. Thereupon they retired.

When Bellamy returned, he thumped his forehead.

" I had forgotten that it was the patron's day," he said. " Every one in South America stands sponsor for something or other, of a child, of an apse in the church, of some business, of a building. Every one stands sponsor, and the Church draws the most astonishing conclusion from people who are connected by sponsorship. In this case it is a matter of sponsorship for a house."

" That's settled," said Bellamy who had gone out for a bit and had come in again. " You have given the Indians a tip for an ovation meant for me." He laughed chaffingly. " They never got anything out of me, not because I am stingy but because I don't want them to invest too much money in alcohol and coca."

Goehrs gazed out of the window for a long time.

Two days later Goehrs learnt that the Indians were grateful. He received two small children as a gift. A woman had come to the finca in his absence and had left them for him.

" If you should make up your mind to go on living up here on the Puna, the two blighters will serve you faithfully for the rest of your life," said Bellamy, inspecting the little yellow wastrels.

" Have the children taken back at once," sighed Goehrs. This Indian music, this making presents of children, this doping of a whole race—all this on the pitilessly cold Sierra, fiercely scorched by day, made him feel sick at heart.

The longer he studied the Indians, the more clearly he realized that, at bottom, they still had the habits of primitive peoples. It was impossible to get them to sit down on a chair ; they preferred to squat on the floor. If they came from the forest districts, they preferred, as he had seen them do in Cuzco, to curl up to sleep in a pouring rain on the cold ground in the open to going under shelter. Many of them, in spite of this way of life, obviously lived to quite an old age, although it was only possible to estimate their age, for no one knew how old he was. In the case of very old men at any rate, the coca bulge they were chewing was more tautly strained in their cheeks than in the case of the young. The girls had children at the age of twelve and were grandmothers by twenty-five. They made use of the most astounding medicaments in the case of sickness. They frequently kept their urine, dried it, and made use of the powder. Their sleep was lighter than that of animals. As a consequence of the stimulation of the use of coca, they never really went to sleep at all. They went on chewing in their sleep and were always half awake.

One day Goehrs had ridden out with Bellamy on mules to a village settlement that was five hours' ride away. Bellamy was anxious to make sure that the Indians were doing some road-mending they were pledged to do. When they approached the village, Bellamy's brow became overcast. A convoy of Indians was moving out towards them. An Indian woman headed the convoy with an open coffin containing a dead infant in her uplifted hand. She was dancing, revolving round herself and her coffin.

Close behind her came the band, the band with the conch-player and the flautists. And behind them a couple of dozen Indians hopelessly drunk, reeling and revolving in their gaudy ponchos.

" We shan't get them back to work for three days," said Bellamy crossly. " They'll keep high revel for three days now because the child has joined the angels."

The dance was awful.

" Quaint brand of Christianity," said Goehrs as Bellamy, after a fruitless attempt to make the *alcalde* see reason, turned his mule's head.

" Christianity ! " said Bellamy. " Not a bit of it. That is some old perverted Inca custom. Like everything else of the Indios."

This remark threw a searchlight on a whole batch of the impressions Goehrs had stored away. He recalled the savage brown Christ of the cathedral of Cuzco, wearing a blue silk loincloth embroidered with flowers, the Indian Christ, Lord of the Earthquake, the Señor de los Tremblores. What other was he than the Lord of the Lightning, whom the Incas had worshipped in the third hall of the Temple of the Sun in Cuzco ?

Extraordinary how deeply, how restlessly, how dæmonically, tradition survived unchanged in the race ! Goehrs had often seen the Indios, on arriving with their llamas from the Puna and suddenly seeing Cuzco in the valley below them, falling on their knees to worship it. And when they left Cuzco again, they would pull up on the last height from which the city was still visible, holding their llamas' leading-reins in their left hands while they laid one stone upon another in farewell greeting to the city.

Their holy city !

And all of a sudden, amid the chatter of a rising flight of Puna geese, Goehrs heard through the deep stillness of the Sierra, the sound of bare Indian feet pattering through Cuzco, this terrible, humble sound of thousands of years, and he understood why the Indios still did homage to this city, on the Inca foundations of which Christian churches rose to-day, not by reason of the cathedral bells droning across the city, but because from deep down out of the twilight of their once heroic blood, out of the deep-seated and sorrowful subconsciousness of their race, there rose this wistful salute of a people foredoomed to death.

PUNO'S SPECIALITY

ON the following day Goehrs rode on muleback to Urcos ; and the day after caught the train to Juliaca and returned over the tracks he had come to Puno. And that same evening, shortly before his arrival, he saw the blue sky with white clouds mirrored in little lakes before Puno, so softly, so etherially, so sweetly as no real mirror could ever have reflected anything no matter how delicate.

Puno, though still in Peruvian territory, was on the shores of Lake Titicaca.

The town was famous for its old men and children who sat in the plaza all day long, caught their lice, and reared the young insects under their armpits until by the evening they had grown fat and sweet-savoured enough to eat. The inhabitants of Puno would not sell their celebrated lice even if you were to offer them twenty centavos apiece for them.

Goehrs did not see Puno, the settlement of some 6,000 souls, nor what its inhabitants were doing with their lice, but went to roost in the bowels of a tiny little white boat lying off the quay. She was a boat of 300 tons, which, seventy years ago, had been split up into her component parts and had been thus conveyed by hundreds of mules over the vast distance from the Pacific to the heights of the Cordilleras to an altitude of about 12,500 feet.

On board this tiny white antique ship he went to sleep in a freezing temperature. On board this jolly little ship Goehrs crossed Lake Titicaca on the morrow.

Part III

CONCERNING BOLIVIA

CROSSING LAKE TITICACA

ON the day Goehrs was crossing Lake Titicaca, President Augusto Leguía, in his own country, Peru, was celebrating the " Day of Character "—the day on which Leguía had chosen to be shot rather than resign. The ambassadors and envoys of all the Powers in Lima appeared at Leguía's palace to offer their congratulations. Flags were hoisted throughout the country. The " Old Man " received two thousand people and shook hands with them. The newspapers published especial editions. A despatch-runner even started, quite fatuously, to run through the trackless Cordillera passes from Arequipa to Lima in honour of the occasion. All this meant absolutely nothing to Goehrs. He was cold.

Lake Titicaca belongs half to Peru, half to Bolivia. On the day Goehrs was crossing Lake Titicaca, the Bolivian President, Hernando Siles, resigned in his fifth year of office. The Council of Ministers, to whom he entrusted supreme power, accepted the sacrifice in the national interests and proclaimed a general election in a few weeks' time. President Siles's decree of resignation and the manifesto in which the Ministerial Council acknowledged the decree were particularly impressive. They were in fact suspiciously impressive. But all this meant absolutely nothing to Goehrs. He was cold. He had been cold for weeks. He was suffering from a cold such as was entirely new to him. Goehrs had experienced every kind of cold ; he liked cold weather and snow, but this kind of thin cold that he found on the Puna he had never known. It was a cold that ate its way through to the bones like acid. Now he was even cold in the daytime, when the sun sometimes blazed with almost tropical fervour—in short, he was cold morning, noon and night, when it really was pitilessly cold.

He crossed Lake Titicaca in a slight curve. The shores were always in sight. About 140 miles in length by 40. Brownish red shores on rising slopes with terraces and corn-fields on them. Light-blue water bearing strange craft. Boats like wooden clogs in shape but made of reeds. With a single mast to which the reed sail hung like a window-blind. Very picturesque. Old-world Indian boats. Those boats took in water in time and, when they became quite waterlogged, the Indios pulled them ashore and emptied them out. Very neat and very primitive.

All round about a lavish expanse of distant snow mountains.

Lake Titicaca was for the Indians what the Rhine is to the Germanic race, the centre of their mythology. It was probably on its shores that the folk of a particularly vigorous tribe of the Aymara Indians rose and in a few decades conquered the middle of the realm, made Cuzco its capital, and bore the name of Incas. Here, too, the legends of the Indians and their story of the creation had their source. Hither there came one day, by order of Intis, the Sun God, the first wayfaring man and woman, Manco Capac and Mama Oclo, to raise the race, living like animals in caves. Manco bore a golden club in his hand and he was bidden to settle wherever the club should, of its own accord, strike the ground. Starting from Lake Titicaca, he set out on the legendary journey that finished in Cuzco, where the divine club struck the earth. Manco Capac was the first Inca. All the heroes that people Indian imagination are bound up with the glamour of the waters of Lake Titicaca: Roca— and Viracocha, Pachacutec and Tupac Jupanqui.

And there was some savour of it in the air—Goehrs was conscious of it even after making all allowance for the unusual circumstance that he was on board a ship at a height at which glaciers were sparkling in Europe. Goehrs was afloat on the highest navigable lake in the world. At the level of the loftiest peak of Piz Palü. A lake larger than a third part of Ontario and almost fifteen times the size of the Lake of Geneva. Goehrs, in all truth, had no appetite for records. But when the sun began to blaze and the ice of the previous night to thaw on the decks and, in spite of the broiling sun, an icy cold wind to sweep the waters, he could not help wondering for a moment how many Europeans had travelled by steamer at very nearly the altitude of the Jungfrau. But even this reflection hardly stirred him. He was cold.

The train from the Pacific had that morning disgorged into the boat a dozen passengers from the coast. They had been rushed up to this height in two days, and were now lying about on deck, newly imported off their Grace liner, gasping for breath like fish out of water and feeling about as miserable. " Deck " was a relative term, for the steamer was very small, so tiny that if you had seen her at a distance of only fifty yards you might have thought you could put her in your pocket. She was called the *Yavari*.

There was only a single man who strolled about the deck, sturdy and erect, and cursed his luck. A man carrying a Ciné-Kodak, the Bolivian representative of an American motor-car firm. He was quite upset at having to go back to La Paz.

" Two weeks ago," he said, " I was still out camping and fishing with friends in upper New York State. It was warm and snug. And now . . . just look at this boat."

The man was unfair. The boat was small but well found, and the Peruvian company kept her spick and span, in excellent condition.

" You might make something of this lake," the inexorable spokesman of the Yankee trusts went on. " You might, since it's so cold, stock it with sturgeon and market caviare. But this Government won't move a finger. It doesn't even build roads to make Bolivia an automobile country and give us a decent market. You can't get anywhere by car. The country is just about 3000 feet too high. Ah !— if the main plateau were, say 7500 feet instead of almost 11,000—say ! what couldn't you make of the country ? But, at this height and with its population, Bolivia will never make good. The Indians are simply useless for civilization. And every white man that has a drop of Indian blood in his veins is, down at the bottom, a lot less use. And who is there around here that hasn't got some Indian blood ? No, sir, Peru and Bolivia are played-out countries. You wait until you get to La Paz. Good God ! and when I look back at my cabin on board the *Santa Clara* . . . ! "

The *Yavari* was drawing near the Bolivian shore. The forenoon passed. Goehrs never ceased from pacing the five yards of deck. He wore his thick fur coat, but even so he was cold. He recalled Bolívar's tight, narrow-chested tunic he had seen in Lima. The story goes that Bolívar died of a broken heart because he failed to unite the five nations he had liberated (Venezuela, Colombia, Peru, Bolivia, and

Ecuador) under one rule. His character, Goehrs reflected, like that of most great commanders, was not translucent and, to all appearances, not unequivocal. But beyond all doubt, Goehrs thought grimly, he did not die of the idealism of his disposition, so much as of congestion of the lungs. In a climate like this—quite unequivocal.

Bolívar was the first President of Bolivia, but resigned in favour of Sucre, who was himself a general and a hero of the Wars of the Liberation. The armies that took the field at that date were very small ; usually the troops in the field were at most a few thousands strong. The commanders were called upon to brave the most severe privations in this climate and at these altitudes. For all that, they got off some splendid gestures, while they fought amid superhuman exertions for two decades after 1800 to eject the Spaniards from whom they were descended. Bolívar on one occasion said to Sucre : " Your sword. You are not worthy to be an officer."

Sucre took the musket from a private standing beside him, fired it into the air, and said : " Then I shall at least be worthy to serve under you as a common soldier."

" No," said Bolívar, overcome, " you shall be a general," and gave him his own sword.

In short, Bolivia, which at that date was still part of Peru, fought gallantly side by side with the future Peruvians against the Spaniards. Indeed it was, when everything seemed to be going well, reconquered by the Spaniards who, after all, could contend that it was they who had discovered and conquered Bolivia and on Pizarro's order had laid out its towns. The Spanish general who reconquered Bolivia gave expression to his indignation at its apostasy by cutting off the hands of the men and flogging the women when he did not find it more convenient to have them shot down from behind. Neither the one party nor the other could deny that, in their methods of warfare, their traditions as well as their persons derived from Pizarro. In the end, however, the Spaniards were kicked out, and, in settling up the accounts of the War of Liberation, Bolivia parted company from Peru.

Bolivia had an area of over 500,000 square miles and was therefore almost three times as big as Germany. It was one of the richest countries in mineral deposits in the world. It had certainly a population of two, and probably no less certainly, of three million inhabitants. Eighty per cent. were Indians more or less, fifteen per cent. half-breeds, the

rest whites.   Bolivia had at one time a coastline which it
lost in the course of unsuccessful wars with its neighbour
States.   To-day it had only a harebrained frontier, without a
harbour, and was wedged in between Brazil, Paraguay,
Argentine, Chile, and Peru.   Its trade passed through the
free ports belonging to Peru and Chile, an indignity that
made the Bolivians very savage.   Bolivia lay in the heart
of the continent, a grim highland block cut off from the
sea, a country almost unknown to the rest of the South
American world.   Ninety per cent. of its inhabitants lived
at an altitude of over 9,500 feet, higher than the Zugspitze,
the highest mountain in Germany, as high as Mount Hood
in Oregon.   That alone explains a great deal.

Bolivia was governed by a long succession of Presidents
and underwent an equally long succession of revolutions,
which were about as frequent as general elections in other
countries.   At times they were quite entertaining as inter-
ludes, and in every case characteristic.   In 1864 for example,
a general of the name of Malgarejo rode out to the barracks
of the rifle regiment, fell in two companies and shouted in his
cheery way nothing more than :

" Lads, I am your friend.   Three cheers for Malgarejo."
The result of it was—so simple was the whole thing—a
dictatorship of seven years.

When Goehrs recalled this episode, it struck him that the
retirement of President Siles, that had just occurred, was
no more difficult than a jigsaw puzzle ; the motives ought to
be easy to piece together once one was on the spot.   The
important consideration was to be on the spot.   Even as
viewed from Peru, Bolivia was as opaque as a fogbank.
And as from Europe entirely impenetrable.

At two o'clock the boat passed the Island of the Sun,
where one of the most celebrated of the Sun God's sanc-
tuaries was situated.   One of the most beautiful and
aristocratic convents of vestal virgins used to stand here.
Baths and pleasaunces led down to the lake amid pergolas
of vines and gardens.   At an altitude and in an atmosphere
that was like the moon's.   An extra-terrestrial retreat.
Snowclad mountains flushed in pink on the skyline.   Arctic
and tropical in one.

Towards evening Goehrs was privileged to witness one
of the most bewildering spectacles in the world.   Beyond
one of the seemingly bare bays, there suddenly appeared the
Cordilleras of the Bolivian shore.   Descending with their
glaciers to the water's edge the Cordilleras suddenly aligned

as if in review order. But what a review! As if an untamed herd had charged up, panting, with glorious vigour, and had suddenly come to a halt for a second's breathing-space, revealing all the unstudied play of its muscles and contours. A range—glowing, titanic, frigid in its splendour, and fashioned wholly by the untrammelled genius of Nature.

At its finish the chain of mountains broke off for a heart-beat—for two measures, for three—and at the end of this interval there appeared, isolated and vast, Illimani. Illimani, a spectral, unearthly white, its dazzling colour already tuned down by the twilight . . . as though fashioned out of a translucent amber with a dash of green. An amazing mountain. In the middle of its sweep its outline broke off abruptly. And on this side there was nothing but the gathering night. But so eerily was the movement of the whole Cordillera range involved in the sweep of the Illimani, and so awesome was the might of this mountain suddenly broken off short, that it seemed as if the whole universe were falling into a bottomless pit.

When at length the evening glow slowly faded, no pink suffused the glaciers, but a silvery green, and in this hue the snowfields gleamed for a good hour after sunset.

But astern, aft of the *Yavari* and behind Goehrs's back, all the bays along the lake had caught the flush of the sunset and drawn a sharp line of it along the shore. In the background was the turquoise-blue sky that deepened into a dark green overhead. And in the foreground, glassy, motionless, the olive trees, the eucalypti, the rubber trees, and fields of Indian corn, every leaf clear cut, for miles.

The moon stood high in the sky like burnished silver, a cold, flaming star. Far away in the distance its light fell on the Indians' Island of the Sun, which rose low out of the pink flood like a maiden's breast. The island of the Indian maidens had a virginal, alien radiance that eclipsed the brilliancy of the moonlight.

It rose in the dusk like a black sun.

TIAHUANACU

LATE at night Goehrs, on board his little craft, reached the Bolivian harbour village of Guaqui and slept in his cabin. On the following morning, shaving with chattering teeth, he watched, through his porthole, the sun rise in an

CORDILLERA IN BOLIVIAN ANDES.

unreal, thin light over the snowy mountains in the hues of a primeval world. The Bolivian clocks were an hour in advance of the Peruvian. With a touch of wistfulness Goehrs realized that it was summertime in Central Europe now, that the woods were green and languid, that the birds were singing in the morning and the meadows breathing fragrance. He went up on deck.

The red-white-red tricolour of Peru was no longer flying overhead, but a flag in horizontal red, yellow, and green stripes—the flag of Bolivia.

Goehrs drove at once some eight miles beyond Guaqui to the ruins of Tiahuanacu. Amid the sparse fields lay the ruins of a temple ; tall, striking monolithic figures towered above them. In between rose an ancient gateway of the Sun. In an earlier age it all must have been situate on the shore of the lake itself. It was now about a two hours' walk inland amid ridiculous Indian huts. Goehrs, who had thought he had escaped from the cradle of the red race, could not shake it off. Here were ruins of the first import-ance, perhaps the most ancient of any in the world ; ruins of great extent, and the exotic gods that, hewn from a single block of stone, rose towering above the scene, were as stirring as were the gateway of the sun and outlines of the temple.

Of what age ? What age ?

Indifferent as might be the attitude Goehrs had learnt to adopt in the matter of exact years and date, a sense of awe overtook him here, for one thing was plain : these ruins went far further back beyond anything he had ever seen before. Most enigmatic, more enigmatic even than the yet undeciphered inscription in the palace of Minos, were the symbols inscribed on the upper portal of the gateway of the Sun.

Goehrs felt that with these symbols he was entering an epoch that was only linked up by innumerable blanks to history as he knew it. Between this Indian culture and the cultures of the Incas, worlds of time had elapsed. The Incas themselves might well have confronted these ruins in the same state of bewilderment as he did.

These ruins were far more unaccountable than the desert cities he had seen in Asia, more incomprehensible than the African ruins near Bulawayo. For they were standing on a desolate plain on an inhospitable plateau twice the size of Germany, and higher above the sea than the summits of the Tyrol Alps, in a solitude and desolation, in an arctic melancholy, that made their huge expanse only the more fascinating.

Later on, in La Paz, Goehrs heard the theory propounded that the symbols for the cross block of the gateway of the Sun were designed to serve as a calendar. This theory originated from a strange man and was very arresting. Quite as arresting as the life of the man who, once upon a time, had ideas of earning his livelihood with two motor boats on the east coast of South America. He had soon been forced, when war broke out, to dress them up as naval gunboats. He was taken prisoner on board one of his gunboats, made his way to Bolivia, became the builder of factories and striking postage stamps and queer museums and celebrated instruments.

This man contended that the symbols on the gateway of the Sun were a calendar. He further maintained that the temple had been laid out astronomically. He ascertained the incidence of the sun's rays and compared the difference of their incidence to the axis of the temple with the date when the sun's beams must have fallen direct on the temple's axis.

This date was some 12,000 or 13,000 years ago.

There were people who championed this fascinating and brilliant theory—and there were others who did not think much of it. The theory appealed to Goehrs as striking, plausible, and daring. But it did occur to him that the symbol on the gateway of the Sun might stand for something quite other than a calendar.

For the whole run to La Paz the past and its riddles kept him enthralled—what races, what antediluvian folk had, in their day, built these temples, these gods, and this city ? How had they lived ? What were they like to look upon ? What was going on in their brain ? What was their attitude to women, to their enemies, to their beasts, and to their gods ?

The plateau was of a sublime evenness now. The railway ran as if it were laid on parquet flooring. Quite smoothly, as if a heavy roller had been taken over it. Full of gravel, a little scrub, and a few llamas, alpacas, sheep, and yawning Indio boys in charge of the herds. A biblical landscape, so simple, so brilliantly and supersensuously bright, so unobtrusive, and yet, thanks to mountains that rose with three hundred snowy summits exactly on the rim of the tray, hedged about with austere serenity.

The tableland suddenly fell away. A ring like a crater

190

opened up some 1200 feet below. The way in which this trough plunged down and then checked itself repeated all the peculiar topography that Goehrs had seen in the dolomites of the southern Tyrol, in the alternating sinkholes and ridges of the Karst, and the rock had all the colours from white to green, from blue to red and yellow—a jumble of cones, spikes, pyramids, capitals, columns, and arches. And below, curled up amongst all, lay the capital of Bolivia, idly basking in the sunshine like an animal sprawling in a titanic arena.

La Paz was playing in the sun and flashing the sunshine back again a thousandfold. It was like a bombardment by rays. Goehrs closed his eyes. It seemed as if thousands of mirrors had been ranged to flash up the mountainside, through a thin haze lying over the town. It looked like a battle in silver ; a noiseless battle, an uncanny, silent beam attack ; an indescribably animated and gentle scene amid this wild lunar landscape—the galvanized iron roofs of La Paz.

La Paz

THERE was a hotel in La Paz in which every one had to stay who had a position to keep up or had anything to sell. Not a ray of sunlight penetrated to it. No one came when one rang the bell. The food was unspeakable. A chilly, cheerless tank of a place that was indeed no gilded haunt of luxury. But all the ambassadors and business men had to stay in this hotel. The prices were double those of a first-class hotel in Europe. Goehrs contemplated it cheerfully. He was not a diplomat and he had nothing to sell. He had no occasion to put up at this hotel.

He put up at a small German hotel occupying the first floor of an old house adjoining the National Bank. It was built in a quadrangle round two courtyards, in Spanish fashion. With German flowerpots in the windows. A room ran down the centre across the two courtyards after the style of a drawbridge. This room caught the sun from nine o'clock until four. None of the others had any sun. There were hardly any houses in La Paz that had any sun.

When Goehrs looked out of his window into the court, he saw an Indian before a hollowed stone, in which he was grinding corn with a second stone that fitted into it.

Goehrs put two questions to the proprietor.

191

" My dear sir," said Goehrs, defrauded of his hopes of catching sight of a glimmer of fire after weeks in the icy vault in which he had to dwell, " why is there no heating in your house ? "

" Because the air is too dry at these altitudes, and if there were any heating you would only catch cold," said mine host affably. " There are only four people in the whole of La Paz who have had inflammation of the lungs and have survived."

" And tell me why does a taxi charge four passengers seven shillings for taking them a distance of fifty yards ? "

" I can't tell you that," said mine host no less affably. Wherewith the conversation languished.

A HEATING PROBLEM

IN Cuzco, Goehrs had made the acquaintance of a South American diplomat who had paid a visit to Cuzco (which was a very noteworthy exploit on the part of a South American diplomat). Goehrs rang him up and they agreed to dine together. José Pacheco was the representative of a South American State that most decidedly was not Paraguay, but he wanted to have the fact acknowledged that things were done by methods of law and order in his republic—not as in others—and that things that might well occur here could, of course, never happen . . . and so on. Goehrs thought this harmless national vanity very charming. He knew, too, that people of this type of mind were regular treasure-troves of information. Before dinner, in the course of the afternoon, he took his first walk abroad in La Paz. La Paz is the most uncomfortable city in the world in which to take a stroll. Many people domiciled there can only walk quite short distances, and, as La Paz is always built up hill or down dale, the majority of people newly arrived at La Paz run short of breath after the first few steps—but most of them were in bed for days with the soroche.

Goehrs passed down the main business street. It was short and provincial for a city with a population of 150,000. Four loudspeakers were shouting against one another. In this street Goehrs thought he had lost his way into a capacious gramophone store. Then he reached the Plaza. He realized at once that this square simply was La Paz.

La Paz took its walks abroad here, and here were its public buildings. That was all.

Originally he had visualized La Paz as an exotic town—with an atmosphere of virgin forests and expeditions that set off into the unknown. He was bitterly disappointed at first. The city had no character at all beyond the character of a modern town, with galvanized iron roofs situated on a cold tableland. If it had lain 9000 feet lower down not a soul, he assured himself, would waste a word on La Paz. For all that, he still had the odd thrill of excitement in his blood that La Paz had at first sight stirred in him. Curious, he could not tell why. The thrill did not wear off.

Goehrs walked across the little square and suddenly stopped dead in his tracks as if struck by lightning. Two German cuirassiers were on guard in front of the big building, in their helmets with neck-guards, with the big cavalry swords in their hands, and in high knee-boots.

Pre-War Potsdam—with Indian features under the helmets. On a sudden Goehrs became quite alert.

The Plaza was swarming with folk. Most of them were Indians squatting on the ground. The women wore many gaily coloured petticoats, one over the other. The more prosperous they were, the more petticoats they wore—just as in Goehrs's native place, Vogelsberg, on the Schwalm. They wore a poncho over their shoulders and a coloured shawl on top of that. All aniline dyes. Very crude. Very bright. They wore amazing headgear. A tall, brimless chimney-pot of panama straw, a tall panama pot hat, varnished white. Several had hard felt hats, turned up at the brim. These hat monstrosities were so grotesque that they gave Goehrs the impression that every woman had to concentrate all her attention to balancing the thing on her head. Almost every Indian woman was supporting her right or left breast with one hand while in the other she held a suckling infant. They were a different type from the Quichuas. Not as intelligent, but healthier, more reminiscent of Tyrolese, less pathetic. With short, rather stumpy noses. Aymaras.

Aymaras. The aboriginal indigenous races of the Bolivian plateaux, of the salt steppes with their hurricanes, of the tropical Yunga valleys brimming over with coffee and coca, the dwellers on the shores of Lake Titicaca. Aymaras who always had been a highland tribe of Indians, at home among glaciers and snowstorms. And these were the people who were wearing white panama chimney-pot hats, stiff with white varnish, that were manufactured only in Europe and expressly for them. Men wearing green uniforms with red stripes on their trousers were walking in and out among them. They wore peaked caps and trouser-straps under their patent-leather boots. Prussian uniforms and Prussian movements. Goehrs was profoundly moved and horribly scared. But the faces of these Prussians were dark. They were Bolivian officers with the eyes of Indians. With Indian faces, single eyeglasses, and Prussian mannerisms.

In the " Paris " restaurant Goehrs saw an announcement that a " social tea " would be served there at five o'clock. Goehrs went in. It was cool. But there were no folk representing Bolivian " society "—in so far as it existed in the European or North American sense of the word at all. There were no natives and no ladies. A band churned out jazz music in a gallery above the company's heads. When the band was quiet, Goehrs heard the few officers who, in addition to himself, had dropped in to tea, talking German. And the few other people seated in this solitary place of recreation in La Paz were doing the same thing.

When Goehrs left this notable gathering and went out on the Plaza, he came out on the side that was already in shade. He immediately began to shiver. The menacing dusk followed hard on the heels of the scorching noon. Goehrs crossed rapidly to the other side of the street and suffered from the heat.

As he did so, his eye caught a hairdresser's establishment which, like all of its kind, was called " Peluquería Royal." It lay on the shady side, but Goehrs very badly wanted his hair cut. Seven hairdressers who were enjoying the sun on the other side of the street followed his tracks into the chilly shop. All of them Indians in white coats. No human being looks more comical in a white coat than an Indian. They all looked on attentively while one of them cut Goehrs's hair. Goehrs discovered, to his surprise by this time, that not one of them spoke German. At the critical moment when the Indian was holding the scissors upside-down to trim the hair round his temples, a shot was fired outside in the Plaza. A ringing, sharp staccato shot. All seven Indians shivered, turned pale, and dashed out into the Plaza. For some seconds Goehrs was sitting alone in the Peluquería Royal and wishing he, too, were outside in the sun. The cold fairly filtered up his marrow like a chemical fluid.

Then the seven Indians and the proprietor of the peluquería came back chattering and laughing.

" Well ? "

" A tyre burst."

They all breathed their relief long and loud.

" Tell me, señor," Goehrs turned to the proprietor, " why
is it that no one has ever tried any heating in this town ? "

" There never has been any heating in this town," said
the Indian, with an expression as if Goehrs had asked him a
question conveying an affront to public morals.

Mislaid—A President

" THEN what is really behind the President of Bolivia's
resignation ? " Goehrs asked the representative of the
other South American State after dinner. There was an
electric heater on the floor thawing their legs.

" You have arrived in Bolivia at a very interesting juncture," said the diplomat, drumming on the tablecloth with
his fingertips. " President Siles's four years of office had
expired in January. He ought by rights to have left in
January and proclaimed a new election. It was illegal for
him to be elected for a second term. But Siles stayed in
office ' in the national interests ' to organize an ' unbiased '
election. That, naturally, annoyed every one who hoped
to come into office, enormously. For not a soul, of course,
believed that Siles was going to go. That Leguía, who has
been ruling in Peru for the last ten years, has already turned
the heads of a lot of Presidents in South America. They
all of them want to be President, like old Leguía, for life.
In the case of Siles, this mimicry is absurd because he is not
a man of Leguía's calibre by a very long way. You have at
least to be a bit more than a little morphinomaniac, to play
the part of Napoleon—even in Bolivia. To cut a long story
short, Siles at length realized that that cock would not fight
and the other day he therefore staged this full-dress
resignation ' in the national interests.' That, of course, is
bluff. He ought, in accordance with the constitution, to
have handed over the reins of Government to the President
of the Senate until the election. But Siles did not do that
because the President of the Senate is one of the few decent
people there are in this country and would never have run
elections on the Siles line, that is to say, elections at which
only the supporters of Siles could, for obvious reasons, have

reached the ballot box and every one else have been shut out. Siles therefore handed over the government *ad interim* to the ministry ; which is constitutionally impossible, in fact a barefaced violation of the constitution. His ministry is, of course, made up of his hangers-on. And this ministry at once proclaimed election for a plebiscite to decide first on the re-election of Siles, secondly, on the abrogation of the law under which Siles can be President for four years only, and thirdly, on the consequent establishment of a dictatorship. . . . The whole position is, of course, impossible, nor have we any of us yet paid our calls on the present Government. We are marking time."

" What are you marking time for ? "

" To see whether there are going to be any elections at all."

" And if there are ? . . ."

" If there are, Siles will be elected."

" And if not ? "

" If not—I am waiting to see Siles standing outside my front door one morning and asking to be taken in."

" That would amount to revolution."

" Undoubtedly."

" And by whom ? "

" By his enemies," said the other smiling. " Every one is his enemy who wants to get at the reins of Government himself. There is an agitated ex-President in Paris and another in Mollendo, both of whom are hard at work, and a regular stock exchange has been opened at Buenos Aires of Bolivian exiles to bring about his overthrow."

" And what is the programme of these people ? "

" Don't talk about programmes," said the other. " All programmes here begin with ' free elections,' but no soul dreams, when the time comes, of having free elections. Nor are there any parties on the European model, though there may be factions that are labelled by similar names."

" I should have liked to have seen that man Siles," said Goehrs.

" No one knows where he is," said the diplomat. " Not even his wife. There is a little estrangement between them, arising, they say, because her ladyship recently left her handbag at home when she was going to see her dentist and, when she returned unexpectedly, had a painful shock that threw doubts on her husband's fidelity. But that may be gossip. I believe Siles is lurking somewhere, safeguarded by the henchmen of his faction and waiting for the elections.

For in their own interests his people must take measures to prevent Siles being shot before the elections.

" Is Siles really white ? " asked Goehrs.

The representative of the country that considers itself to be wholly white smiled.

" Hardly any one here is entirely white. Every one therefore makes such a point of being looked on as immaculately white. Nowhere in the world do they hate the word ' colonial ' as virulently as here. Consequently, the most amusing *contretemps* occur at times. The ambassadors and ministers, coming to La Paz on appointment, have a very ceremonious reception here. They make their entry with a military escort and so forth. When the new French ambassador arrived, he made his entry in a white tropical uniform. But that stirred so many ' colonial ' memories here that all the official crowd were furious and wrote indignant letters to Paris. For that reason not a soul here dare wear a solar topee, which would be deuced pleasant during the daytime."

The diplomat paused and listened intently. Two or three shots in succession rang out outside. Then all was quiet again.

" The Indios are enough to drive one mad with their everlasting firing," he then said, and leaned back in his chair.

" So the crux of the situation at the moment is the army," said Goehrs. " Whom is it supporting ? "

The diplomat looked shocked.

" No one knows that."

" Who's in command ? "

" A German general. I can imagine how every one at the present moment is bringing pressure to bear on the man by wires or proposals to cause the army to vote this way—or that. For the army is the sole organized power of the State—and any one who has the whip-hand of it after the President's retirement can do as he pleases."

" Really ! " said Goehrs. " And now, please tell me just one thing more : what is the real reason why there is no heating in this town ? "

Goehrs crushed out his cigarette and stretched his legs out as far to the heater as they would go.

" There is in point of fact, no coal," said his host. " In view of the cost of transport, to stock coal or wood would be so grotesquely expensive that no one could afford it. There you have got the whole country in a nutshell. The richest mineral land in the world, a country with vast virgin forests, cannot have any heating. At bed-rock it lacks only one essential : motor roads. But it hasn't any money to build motor roads. The people cannot think straight. They are thinking of revolutions instead of the country. They are thinking of themselves instead of the country. And what good does the money they extract from the public purse do them, if they have not even motor cars ? Funny, isn't it ? By the way," he added, as Goehrs rose, " look out if you do happen to have any official invitations. A few years ago all the fur coats were stolen from the President's palace on the occasion of a big show."

INDIANS IN LA PAZ

THE following morning was Whit-Sunday. The Indios fired their guns off in the churches, let off squibs at the altar, and littered everything with confetti. They were wearing their carnival masks as well.

Goehrs was living next door to a bank, and there was a church adjoining the bank. When he left the house, Goehrs therefore found the street congested. A drum-and-fife band was standing in the middle of the street. But they remained unseen because some two hundred Indians in fancy dress were revolving round the bandsmen in the street.

There were two parties of Indians.

On one side they were all wearing white pleated coats and white brocaded waistcoats adorned with a lot of scraps of looking-glass and gold lace. As a headdress they wore bundles of feathers, several feet high, and gay balls of wool on wires. They carried masks of wood or paper. Among them, too, were women in long skirts. The women carried white handkerchiefs in front of their faces and wore a bandeau supporting four feathers on their heads. They carried sticks ornamented by plumes.

The Indians of this party kept on going round and round in a circle to the lilt of the drum-and-fife band. They changed step, stopped, side-stepped, stopped, changed step again. Dully, but rapt. And always round and round in a circle. They took no notice of the traffic of the street, fifty yards away from the Plaza. The motors could not get through, and their drivers drove back or into side streets, cursing.

The second party was assembled twenty yards above the first one in the steep street. They had their own band.

And they were dressed quite differently. The Indians of this side were wearing breeches trimmed with coloured fringes and leather shirts. They were wearing a martial headgear similar to that of the Sioux—and to that which Goehrs, at the age when he revelled in Fenimore Cooper, had worn for his games. The Indians wore big red, yellow, and blue feathers on their shoulders and back, sweeping almost to the ground—plumes of the parrots of the virgin forests. They were stuck in a crown into which many scraps of looking-glass were inset.

Goehrs was quite nonplussed by the spectacle.

So far as he knew, none of the civilized Indian tribes had ever worn the barbaric war-paint of the North American Indians. Goehrs had seen many traditional portraits of Inca and pre-Inca princes, processions, and proletarians. None of them were dressed in this hunting attire. The Indian nobles of the pre-Spanish era had worn a sort of turban, or something like a Roman fillet, or perhaps a sort of feather coronet like the Persian satraps—an exotic, but a significant, unostentatious and virile ornament. Goehrs had seen many of the mummies wearing it.

But whence had these Aymara Indians of the Bolivian highlands derived these stage trappings of the North American buffalo-hunters ? The leading man in this second Indian section carried a little toy musket in his left, and a little wooden sword in his right hand.

It was quite a witty idea.

Yet all his movements as well as the tune he followed were instinct with real dignity. He passed down the street in long strides, and his whole party followed him. Like many Indios, he turned his feet pronouncedly inwards, that lent his gait a hint of feeblemindedness, but he soon reached the merry-go-round where the first party was revolving. He broke up the ring with his musket and sword, and swept it aside with magnificent gestures, bisected it once or twice and then returned, again in slow-march step and followed by all the members of his party, to the spot higher up whence they had set out. There they, too, danced in a ring.

The movements of the second party were curiously spasmodic. The chieftain always made three change-of-foot steps and then raised his arms with the musket and sword. He stood still, drew one leg up high, dropped it again, and fell on his knee. He then bowed low, rose in wrath, and advanced tempestuously, changing step. His followers were holding lances in one hand and fireworks in the other, which sputtered away like machine guns and showed no inclination to stop. There was something martial, something degraded, and yet something stately in the steps with which these people came dancing up. At the same time there was something pathetically ludicrous about it.

Nor on close inspection did it escape Goehrs that everything the Indians wore was made of cardboard and collected from the Lord knows what junk heaps. For the forbears of these Aymaras had never possessed glass, or rifles, or paper.

But the performance as a whole, together with the music, and as danced by those fanatics, represented after all a dim memory of the past, a melancholy harking back to something imposing, was a fascinating reproduction, even if under the influence of alcohol, of some millenary ceremonial, distorted, it is true, with things that the Indian had in the meanwhile adopted from the Europeans. And interwoven, too, with the things the Indians had taken over from the Catholic Church.

A little later the first party went to church, danced before the Madonna, ordered their band to play in her honour, and kept on with their incessant firing. They were nearly all of them horribly drunk and had their quid of coca protruding from their left cheeks.

" What are these people making all this to-do about ? " Goehrs asked the little know-all boy from his hotel, who was standing beside him in a sort of confirmation suit. The boy was a thoroughbred Indian.

" It's an Indian festival," said the possessor of the black suit, laughing. The Indians tickled him immensely.

AN ART CONFERENCE

WHEN, a little later, Goehrs was driving across the Plaza with Pando, the planter, he saw that the sentries outside Government House had big, white, full-dress plumes on their helmets. And fixed bayonets.

Pando owned coffee plantations in the Yungas, the tropical valleys that intersect the Cordilleran plateau. He was half an Indian and fond of Germans—he could not tell you why himself. They drove together to the little museum which Fritz Buck, a German who used to sell jewellery and watches in the Calle Comercio, had founded. Thirty years of excavation and research work on the part of an enthusiastic amateur, of a man with a taste for these things and pleasantly obsessed by them—far more obsessed than a scientist can ever be. In the little private gallery Goehrs saw old Indian fabrics, which, in their draughtsmanship of animals and in the spacing of these animals, were among the most exquisite things he had ever seen. He then inspected the ornaments, the vases, the silver masks, the knives and maces, and the figures of animals, which the German, long before most people, had excavated in Tiahuanacu.

The sight of these many tangible articles reminded Goehrs of the theory that Tiahuanacu, with its astronomically schemed temple, must have been an immensely populous city 13,000 years ago.

"How old do *you* take the ruins of Tiahuanacu to be?" he asked the collector.

"Perhaps a thousand years older than the Incas," he answered.

"The devil!" said Goehrs.

So there was a discrepancy of 12,000 years between the theory of the man with the motor boats and that of the man with the jewellery. How small the world was after all! But in what a spendthrift way people threw thousands of years about. Everything our civilization covers, thought Goehrs, everything we can really know and properly use is comprised in four thousand years, at the outside. If we limit ourselves to the Greeks only, we need only count twenty-five hundred years. And if you throw in Homer and his era, beginning to become misty by this time, and the myths and legends, say three thousand years. And yet here, between two pure estimates, lay four times that number of years.

"How do you determine the time in your calculations?" asked Goehrs inquisitively, gazing at the image of a little goddess.

"By my studies," said the collector simply. "By my study of those vases."

That was very plain. And very plausible. And not in the least complicated. But that was no reason why it should be right.

"As far as I am concerned, I don't worry about a few thousand years or so," said the planter, amused. "Coffee takes four years to grow. Then the crop comes along. Year after year. I only count by crops."

Pando was a slight but powerful man. He had travelled

a good deal in the interior of Bolivia. That was noteworthy, because the majority of educated Bolivians had not the faintest notion of the interior of Bolivia.

The collector's vases were very beautiful. All the older specimens had the condor painted on them, delightfully severe, often cubist in execution, sometimes with hands and feet, sometimes holding the triangle symbolizing the three phases of the position of the sun. The sun was always on its wings. Surrounded by all the symbols, as the primitive people knew them. Moons, Maltese crosses, key patterns, and pumas—pumas that signified moon and night. The decoration of the vases was very geometric.

"The condor," said the collector, "is dragging the Sun over Mount Illimani, across the earth, indicated by steps, and the puma's head that indicates night."

That was a very ingenious interpretation of a tangle of dots and roughly if cleverly executed heads of animals. And a rather complicated interpretation to boot. Almost the reading of a picture puzzle. But if there must be interpretations, a possible interpretation, and a pretty one, too.

Many vases from Lake Titicaca had regular heads. They were perhaps portraits, for they were very lifelike. The portraits all had a protuberance on the left cheek—the quid of coca. Many of the heads had straight, flat noses. They were the Aymaras. A little negroid and not very intelligent. Many had arched Arab noses. They were the Quichua. Other heads were without doubt Malayan, which some wind of chance or other in some stray century had jettisoned on the American coast.

Wonderfully inlaid knives with llama heads for handles. Of the utmost daintiness. A glorious silver mask as thin as parchment, with closed mouth and closed eyes. Dating from the year 400 or from the year 12,000 before our era? wondered Goehrs. No matter, the exhibits were very ancient. In the case of peoples like the Indians, legends and traditions of events lingered interminably. If even the Incas knew practically nothing about the ruins of Tiahuanacu, it meant that a long and dark period did in fact intervene between the two civilizations of the Indians. But it perhaps furnished the explanation of yet another mystery. Goehrs remembered that wharves had been built in Tiahuanacu and that at one time this vast ruined city had been definitely on the shore of Lake Titicaca, but to-day it was nearly twelve miles inland.

There was a good deal to suggest that this metropolis had been destroyed within the space of hours. Unfinished buildings, the midden-heaps, the craftsmen, tools—exactly as at Knossos in Crete, where owing to an earthquake and the outbreak of fire the most highly cultivated Mediterranean people had simply been wiped out of history, so thoroughly, so terribly, so finally, that even the Greeks only knew of a catastrophe occurring a thousand years before their golden age by way of a timid legend.

The South American continent, too, was probably at one time visited by a great catastrophe. The lake swallowed up the city and then retreated. Perhaps there were great eruptions under the surface of the waters, or the continent sagged in on one side—a theory which the remarkable coastal lines of its sea favours. In any event, Tiahuanacu disappeared with dramatic suddenness, and the Inca peoples, even more astounded than we, were confronted by the giant skeleton of the city, the ruins of which were spread over the highlands of Bolivia as if they had fallen from Mars.

Another notion struck Goehrs.

" Have you ever thought whether the climate may not have changed on the plateau ? "

" No," said the connoisseur, and gazed lovingly at his vases.

" I have always had a feeling that, in spite of the altitudes, a Mediterranean climate must have prevailed here at one time," said Goehrs thoughtfully. " Greenland, too, at one period had its hot spell. Perhaps there were hot springs in Lake Titicaca—perhaps the lake was a sort of sea, too."

" How did you hit on that idea ? " asked the planter, whom the new topic interested more than the discussion about the vases.

" First of all, it's intuition," said Goehrs. " The whole lay-out with terraces facing the lake, the culture—in short, nothing here seems to go with the cold. That is a question for one's own skin, señor. And then—well, you can see this vast lay-out of agricultural terraces to heights that overtop Mont Blanc. Such an immense amount of settlement, such an immense amount of labour—I can only picture all that in a more equable climate and not with heat by day and several degrees below freezing-point at night."

" Possibly," said the planter. " But it need not necessarily be so."

Possibly—but it need not necessarily be so. That was

like everything else here. Everything was perhaps open
to explanation and everything remained unexplained.

CRUCIFIED INDIANS

AS Goehrs, in the company of the planter, came upon
the big modern avenida in the newer quarter of La
Paz, the modern hurly-burly with its motor cars and young
Bolivians in plus-fours struck him as an unreal world. This
world seemed unreal and out of place to such a degree that
he could hardly remember having come across anything as
jarring before. There were two worlds on this tableland,
and there were two worlds in La Paz, and it seemed to him
that the 12,000-year-old world of Tiahuanacu was real and
true while the world of to-day was a nightmare and
impossible.

A few minutes later they turned into the market of La
Paz, which was held in a large roofed enclosure like an
Oriental bazaar. Only the flower market, a hundred yards
round the corner, was in the open.

Goehrs saw a gay scene, but not nearly as full of colour
and exotic as Cuzco. He had already learnt all sorts of
things in La Paz about the Aymara Indians. The most
remarkable was the table of social precedence as it applied
to Indian women.

The pure-bred, unadulterated Indian women of the highlands wore a soft felt hat ; the half-breed women, the
Cholas, wore tall, stiff, white, varnished top-hats. And the
señoras, even if they were anything rather than white,
adopted European fashions.

This law of the hats was not codified, but it was obeyed
more rigorously than any public or moral legislation. It
stood for the social co-ordination of the three classes. It
might happen, of course, for one class to climb. Thus there
were mothers in soft hats who arrogated the varnished
chimney-pot hat for their daughters. The child had then
climbed (not the mother) and had maybe attended a convent
school. For the centenary of the Liberation of Bolivia all
these class distinctions had been abrogated for the space of
a single day ; the nation had fraternized in its celebrations,
and all classes had experienced social advancement. The
women of the soft hats had become pretty Cholas in
chimney-pots, and the pretty Cholas had gone about
dressed up in European style as señoras. But that was only

the daydream of a red-letter day. By the morrow it was all over. But the most dire offence you could give a genuine tall-hat Chola to-day was to call her not a genuine but a " jubilee " Chola.

For they are absurdly fond of dressing up. The whole of the Calle Illampu was full of shops of the hard-working Indian traders who provided the most ridiculous stuff to pander to the Indian's rage for dressing up. Goehrs saw the dancing-masks of indescribable grotesqueness being made of wood and cardboard ; weapons, feather ornaments of flamingo and parrot plumage—but other stuff as well. He saw Indios running about as Yankees, in check trousers and grey bowlers—but also as Spanish pages in knee-breeches and flat caps.

They were very fond of watching their fellow-creatures, too. All the women sitting in the market-place would squat on the ground as if in church. They gaped at the buyers.

" How much are the paltas ? " Goehrs asked an Indian woman.

" They are not for sale," said the woman. She was there, as were so many of her fellows, with poultry or garlic on the ground in front of them, for the sole purpose of enjoying the bustle of the market. The paltas and the chickens and the garlic were a pure pretext for being allowed to squat there. And how they sat ! They were expert in the art of sitting on the ground. They had a contempt for chairs. And when they sat down, they dropped as though hurled to the ground —but they broke their fall deftly on their heels, erect as statues. A striking bit of technique, that of sitting down.

Their bearing is pretty self-assured, thought Goehrs. He had heard that the Indios from the Altiplano used to be abominably treated. In earlier days the townsfolk would allow them to deposit their wares in their houses, and kick them out without paying them their money. Nowadays they were at any rate paid something. But in the trains, any lout of twelve, provided he wore a collar, could make any old Indian woman in a soft hat get up and take her seat himself—even if the aforesaid lout was himself three-quarters Indian twenty times over.

The Indios did not really understand European mentality and European ways in the least, and could not become accustomed to them. Goehrs was a guest in a house where the " boy " whom, although he was consumptive, they had taken in out of pure charity to wait at table, and had dressed up in a linen jacket, went on strike because he got

Russian soup for dinner—although his master and mistress were having the same Russian soup themselves. He had previously been in the Brazilian legation and claimed to have received three courses there, but he included potatoes, vegetable and dish water as separate courses in themselves. He was being fed ten times as well in his present situation—but he went.

"Look over there," said the planter. "That's a Chipaya."

Goehrs saw an Indian woman in native garb, who had plaited her hair into forty-two pigtails. Twenty-one on the right and twenty-one on the left.

"When they marry, they tie little images at the end of the pigtails."

The Chipayas were a small tribe, living outside on the great salt steppe where from time to time the great hurricanes sweep the land. The roofs of the houses were therefore made fast in nets. They lived in complete isolation up there, five days' journey from their nearest neighbour.

Wonder how many days she has been on the road? thought Goehrs. And how long will she want for the return journey? You could travel from Paris to Bagdad in less time. But it really amounted to nothing more than a shopping expedition for her. These Indian tribes have no conception of time.

"And that is a Callahuayo," said Pando, tapping a man on the shoulder, who turned round and stood as expressionless as a corpse. "You ought to have a look at the pattern on his wallet and on his poncho," said the planter quickly. "Do you see the upright rhomboid? This fellow is undoubtedly descended from the caste of the physicians attached to the Inca court. They had a sort of plaid like the Scottish clans. You can see it on his headdress, too. It is easy to recognize. And not a soul except these direct descendants would wear that pattern. That's simply unwritten law."

The Indian passed on without moving a muscle of his face.

"They are very conservative," said Pando.

"Yes, but just because they are so conservative, I can't help being surprised that they don't object to the treatment they get."

"The Aymaras were always the slaves—even the slaves of Indian tribes that were more intelligent than they," said the planter. "They never have offered any resistance—except on the occasions of slave revolts."

"I should not be surprised to see an Indian rising," said

Goehrs. " And I can't understand why the Russians have not got a foothold in what was at one time a communist community."

" The Russians aren't the least bit dangerous, for the Indians don't understand what they're all about. They couldn't understand the language or the ideology of the Bolshevik. They'll never be stirred up to strike a blow on any social grounds. When the Indians strike, it is only when torture has reached the limit where even the Indio can't stand any more of it."

They had reached the Plaza Murillo.

" But if ever the Indians do rise, then the Lord have mercy on us. I've had one experience of it and I should not care to repeat it. On that occasion a few hacienda owners had nailed an Indio to a cross—it's not so long ago—and the fellow died, which is normal under the circumstances. That started a big slave revolt on the Altiplano. The Indians murdered the ringleader, trepanned him, mixed his brain with chicha in his own skull, and drank it. They forced the Catholic priest to drink and dance with them. They then carved up the body into several thousand little bits and sent the bits all over the highlands with the message : " This will be the fate of all who torture us." The message stirred up a devil of a rising. The Government had to send up troops from La Paz to stamp the blaze out."

" Poor devils," said Goehrs. " So they were all shot down besides ? "

" What choice have you when the State is in danger ? " said the planter, shrugging his shoulders. " I believe the general who ordered the soldiers up did not like the job at all. By rights one ought to be fighting on behalf of the crucified not against them. But the State has to keep its house in order. If the Indians start murdering, we are all in for it. There's only one white man to every nine Indians."

Six Categories of Bolivians

GOEHRS in a short time became fond of La Paz. He liked its customs, too, which the climate there changed as hardly anywhere else in the world. Goehrs loved it all, carried off his feet by the stark tragic primitiveness of Nature and life—although he was cold.

One evening he went to look for a letter-box to post his mail, and discovered that La Paz did not possess any letter-boxes. He looked up the General Post Office. It was a little remote building, where a lady was selling stamps and doing her knitting. The post office was a side show in Bolivia and was not, as in other more communicative countries of Europe, honoured by buildings of distinction.

Goehrs went in quest of concerts and plays.

There were none. Not a soul cared to go out at night in that cold. Any one who contracted inflammation of the lungs up here and did not get a special train to the coast of Chile—that was the quickest route, but it took as long as a journey from Paris to Rome—in a few hours' time, was done for. There were people who, having reached La Paz after long voyages and weeks of travelling in order to take up appointments there, had after two days to hurry back to the coast and take the long sea voyage home again because they could not stand the climate. In the case of most people this manifested itself in the usual guise of the soroche ; others succumbed to suicidal tendencies and eczema. Others could only crawl about like disabled flies. There were mountain-climbers who came to La Paz and shortly afterwards recovered consciousness on the coast. They could not stand it. There were even people who came here from Europe and had double windows put in. But that gave rise to scandal. Bolivia regarded it as an unnatural vice. Why double windows ? they argued. If the weather is cold, you go to bed earlier.

There were a few cinemas, and Goehrs envied the Indios who frequented them for being able to sit so close together to keep one another warm. The wealthy were much worse off ; when the ladies in " society " came to late dinner, they divested themselves of their furs for a second in the ante-room, entered the room where their host and hostess were awaiting them, shivering in evening gowns with bare arms, and then sped back to their furs. Goehrs was on one occasion sitting opposite a young Englishman who had just learnt that he had been transferred to Algiers and was almost speechless with delight. It was only when dinner was nearly over that he put a question that was worrying him :

" Do the servants talk Arabic or French there ? "

" French."

" Splendid," sighed the young fellow, relieved. He did not, it is true, know a word of French, but it was a relief none the less.

" You are pleased, I suppose," said Goehrs.

" Of course. I shall enjoy basking in the sun again. The sun, of course, shines here all right during the daytime, but then it's a bit dangerous. And at night—my dear sir, I want to be able to read a book in bed again without having to put on gloves—yes, and without wearing a hat, if you can understand."

But although the climate is a sore point all round, it obviously does not disable everybody.

" I have played in tennis tournaments in my fifties," said a lady. " The only thing you must not do here is to let yourself get exasperated. It is only annoyance that pulls you down. You have an intermittent pulse as soon as you are annoyed."

Goehrs made the acquaintance of people who drove every day from four to six to the golf links a few hundred feet above the town and played their eighteen holes there.

" It keeps one fit," one of the cheeriest players told him, " and yet every ripple on board ship makes me sea-sick." By the way, these are the highest golf links in the world. About 13,000 feet.   The links are indeed wonderfully situated. On the Altiplano. The vast desert that leads down for weeks and days to Chile, full of salt, borax, and saltpetre, full of storms and of a solitude such as Asiatic deserts do not know. Breathing a silence, under the spell of which every living animal fell. Even the alpaca herds had an air of grandeur. Even the donkeys and most downtrodden Indios became imposing and great in its setting.   There was probably no scene more wildly savage and sublime than this desert with La Paz in its dip and towering above it the Illimani, pale and gently flushed, just beginning to soar on a pediment of 13,000 feet of Cordilleras and rising over 21,000 feet in a vision of glowing, unreal jagged crests.

Goehrs was fond of lounging about La Paz. The Plaza was very small and the Calle Comercio hardly worth mention. But the longer he strolled about it, the more certain he became that La Paz was a sort of city in the moon. After a short time he learnt to distinguish six types of Bolivians :

(1) Bolivian Indios in full national costume.
(2) Bolivian Indios in national costume.
(3) Bolivian Indios in slashed breeches with panama hats.
(4) Bolivian half-breeds without collars.
(5) Bolivian half-breeds with collars.
(6) Bolivian half-breeds made up as ministers, as lawyers, as gentlemen in motor cars, etc.

Each of the castes had the deepest contempt for the one below it. From day to day the whole of the population, however, was kept at ever-growing nervous tension. Something was brewing; no one knew what it was, but every one was aware of it. The temperature became feverish.

One evening two young men were walking in front of Goehrs down the Calle Comercio when the little Indian lads were yelling out *Ultimata Hora* and *El Diario* like mad.

"Officers' leave is stopped and the police are heavily armed as from to-day," said one of the young men. He hailed undoubtedly from Bremen. Judging not only from his accent. The reddish blond was not a common type. There were, moreover, several German business houses in the street.

"Don't know whether they ought to give the officers revolver ammunition. If there is one thing I should funk, it would be the officers. Mestizos as officers—good Lord! And on top of that every third will want another President according to the way he has been canvassed."

The young man made a gesture, the significance of which there was no mistaking.

"They say," said the other, "that Kundt has left his villa outside in Otrajes, but is living at the General Staff."

Then they halted and bought a ticket for the "Lotería Nacional" that was to be drawn on the morrow.

Goehrs spent that same evening at the German Club. The German Club had a membership of over a hundred, for, because of the mines and because many big Peruvian firms had branches in La Paz, there was a curiously large number of Germans there. Goehrs knew his overseas German well enough to know that the feuds dividing Germany were sure to recur in their midst with tenfold acrimony. There was, above all, the question of the flag, and there were big businesses that sacked their employees if they did not adopt the same politically intransigent attitude as their employers; there were the clubs that were in opposition to the Reich and to its diplomatic representatives; there were ambassadors and associations sent to Coventry. It was, in short, a thoroughly unedifying and infinitely painful spectacle to watch the *querelles allemandes* being fought out before foreigners.

The evening at the German Club in La Paz was, however, delightful. The evening had been very tactfully arranged and effectively organized by Frau Marckwaldt, the wife of the minister. Goehrs felt at home without having, as usually

210

happens, to suffer under the sentimentality and songs of the programme. Everything was simple, in good taste, and full of cordiality. He made the acquaintance, in addition to that of the minister, who had ample opportunity of safeguarding German interests in particularly difficult cases on particularly difficult ground with a great deal of tact and firmness, of a number of sound men and of their views, and he could have wished that Germany had had the good fortune for many of her public men to possess the perspicacity of these simple citizens.

The German Club was a bower of flowers and foliage, and there was plenty of laughter. Mining men, merchants, officers, and airmen who were piloting the Junker machines of the Lloyd Aereo Bolivano, a German concern that had worked wonders in Bolivia. On many of the flights across the Cordilleras and the forest valleys, which the passenger covered in a few hours, he saved days, in some cases three weeks on muleback. The only thing that hurt Goehrs was the fearsome things there were to drink. Although there were very good German breweries in Peru, the Germans in their club in La Paz drank a hock cup. This cup was compounded of essences and was about the most horrible thing Goehrs had ever tasted. But the company was charming—whereas it is ordinarily the other way about.

"Who is that man over there?" Goehrs asked in the course of the evening and pointed to a guest in a blue suit who looked half a diplomat and half a soldier. A big, powerful man with a clever head who was rather like Ludendorff.

"That is the chief of the General Staff."

"Kundt?"

"Kundt."

In this way Goehrs made the acquaintance of the man of fate for un-presidented Bolivia.

At two o'clock Goehrs drove home. But all night long cavalry and mounted gendarmerie clattered in the streets of La Paz. The patrols kept each other informed by long-drawn whistles that they were still keeping awake.

THE YUNGAS

THE Yungas are ravines in the Cordilleran plateau, and these mountain clefts descend very rapidly. They are the quickest lift in the world for exchanging one climate for another. In the course of a single day you can drop from the glaciers in six climatic storeys down to tropical heat. From Norway to the Congo—with all intervening stations.

A minister sent three telephone messages, and Goehrs felt reassured that there were no difficulties in the way of his journey to the Yungas. For there were all sorts of obstacles. First and foremost, at one point of his journey he would have to engage mules. For everything available in the way of mules was urgently needed there, and the nearest farm where he might perhaps have got some was a good distance away. But Goehrs had sprained his ankle and could not walk. There was, it was true, a little railway as far as the Yungas, but the railway was bankrupt. It was bankrupt although it was a State line. Moreover, only three quarters of it was finished. A motor road was planned at the same time, but that was even more in arrears. It was not as simple as it looked. When it ran short of money for the railway, the State had found a way out. It had left the trains standing where they were, had dismissed the staff, and instituted an autocarril service for as much of the line as was in working order. The autocarril is a motor car on wheels that runs on railway tracks.

" At the railhead two mules will be waiting for you," said the minister. " I have given orders to that effect." Goehrs expressed his profuse thanks. He got a letter to the station-master in the virgin forest terminus who was to provide him with the mules. Then with the letter and two saddles and saddlebags full of gear, he had pushed off in the autocarril. He was looking forward to being warm that evening by way of a change, some twenty miles deep in the forests of the Yunga valleys.

The autocarril had a forty-horse-power Ford motor. There were two ladies in silk stockings and silk frocks in the same carriage, each of whom had a saddle in one hand and a bridle and a blanket in the other. Planters' womenfolk from the Yungas. Then one or two Indian women with their offspring.

The Cordilleras looked at times almost shorn, as if someone had cut big squares out of their green hide. In between were patches of snow. The Ford reached an altitude of 14,000 feet. Herds of llamas raised haughty heads in annoyance, indulged in a gallop or two with the movements of antelopes, then stood still and looked down contemptuously.

At 14,000 feet the Ford was allowed to cool down for ten

minutes. The second halt was La Cumbre, 15,200 feet. The motor was allowed another breather. The Ford was by this time close up to the barricade. Glorious black blocks with slabs of ice. In between little plateaus here and there with peat trenches. With frozen lakes under a hot sun, and an atmosphere that was like a thin, sharp glass. Black pigs running in and out of the Indians' earthen huts. Every now and then one Indian caravan after the other plodded devotedly across the plateau. Red petticoats. Red mufflers. Smart mules with packs. The colours looked most attractive against the greyish green turf.

And all this at about the height of Mont Blanc.

One of the houses of piled stones displayed the placard :
" It is the duty of every Bolivian to die for his country. The murders of Fort Vanguardia cry for vengeance." That's a long time ago, thought Goehrs. It alluded to the war that had all but broken out with Paraguay a few years ago, a war it must have been very difficult to wage because both the armies would have to penetrate the Chaco to get to grips, which seemed to Goehrs an impossible feat. Kundt, it is true, had told him it would have been possible. When this war with Paraguay was imminent, and all the European newspapers, who knew nothing whatever about Paraguay and Bolivia, were writing very comic stuff about them, the Bolivians fetched back Kundt from Germany whither he had previously retired in dudgeon. For it was the third time Kundt had earned Bolivia's ingratitude.

Goehrs read the placard a second time. A devil of a language for Indians, he thought. He watched a convoy just coming up out of the Yungas and trailing past in silence. Did these folk in fact really know that they were Bolivians as well as Aymaras ?

Goehrs paced up and down until the motor had cooled its forty-horse-power down.

The barrier of the Cordilleras appeared to be insurmountable now. Polished black, veined with snow. Quite firm rock. Goehrs made sure of this particularly, for the Cordilleras were not always quite honest. At times they mixed rubble and sand into huge formations, faked a whole range of everlasting hills, and then whole mountainsides would suddenly slide away for miles round and take whatever happened to be clinging to them in the way of roads along with them. But here everything appeared to be wrought iron. The solitude of these heights defied description.

Goehrs read *El Diario* for a bit. What a lot of things there were going on in the world, to be sure—tragic—cheerful things . . . he felt entirely out of touch with them here. . . .

The German ambassador, Baligand, had been shot in Lisbon. The Zeppelin was about to start for Cuba. Carol had landed near Bucharest from an aeroplane and had been proclaimed King after all. Nehring, the glider, had come down in the Rhine. . . . Relationships between Poland and Russia broken off. That was Europe and that was its news.

Goehrs looked about him in surprise. The black pigs were snuffing about his boots. The Indian women were changing the napery of their babies and putting their index fingers into their mouths to keep them quiet. The Ford mechanic was sucking an icicle. . . .

The motor moved on again and then the tunnels came. And then the glaciers hung down straight over Goehrs on the right hand and on the left like hanging gardens of ice, rigid, blue, sparkling. They were going downhill now.

Again the autocarril headed downhill for quite a time under the ice blocks and snowfields towering above it. And above them, higher still, rose the peaks of the black mountains, made sleek by glaciers. Sometimes the rocks were modelled on the lines of flutes and then of a sudden they all began to steam. The Ford serpentined down the narrow cañon like an aeroplane. For three hours it had been groping its way along the foothills of a sea of mountains, now at last it was to find the ravine. On the right rose a nightmare wall. On the left, too.

Below, however, there were signs of vegetation. Below there were red skirts and alpacas clustered round stone houses that looked exactly like blocks of rock. Goehrs was sliding down into the Yungas. In half an hour into the climate of Switzerland. In ten minutes into that of Italy. In half an hour into that of southern Spain. All this came about in a narrow ravine that was gradually widening out. Goehrs slithered through undergrowth and scrub all unexpectedly into a forest climbing the mountainside. A dense forest, a little primeval forest.

Goehrs slithered down to Hichuloma. There the Ford came to a standstill. Goehrs got out. On his right the abyss fell sheer, and the sweet aroma of virgin forest was wafted up from below. The precipice rose plumb on his left. A man in a pullover and riding-boots was standing before a galvanized-iron shed. Goehrs handed his letter to him. The man was the stationmaster. The man shook hands genially with Goehrs. " The mules will be here in half an hour," he said.

Goehrs worked out that he would have a five miles' ride to the nearest finca. His foot was hurting. And he would not be able to help arriving after dark now, which was not exactly pleasant because the path would head straight downhill all the way. Goehrs seated himself patiently on a bench in front of the iron shed and studied the eight stout beams rammed into the ground and connected by a few thin laths. So this, he thought, was the " *Gran Hotel in Construcción*" that the posters were advertising all over La Paz—with modern bedrooms, cuisine de luxe, and choice wines.

He smiled. People took themselves and everything about them so seriously here. But his eye darkened at once when he saw four horsemen in riding-boots with big old Spanish spurs riding up from the Yungas. They dismounted and went into the shed. One of them was unable to walk. He was shaking all over under a bout of malaria. Goehrs glanced down the slope. A little river, a tangle of creepers. The mosquitoes were sure to come with the dusk. He went into the shed where the stationmaster was enjoying a meal.

"Where are my mules ? " he interrupted brusquely.

" It is a hard climb for the beasts in the heat to get here," said the stationmaster without putting himself about. An hour later he had finished his meal and the mules had not put in an appearance. He strolled comfortably past Goehrs, who was sitting on his bench in the broiling sun, without further reference to the mules.

Goehrs was boiling with indignation. First of all, mules had been waiting for the two ladies in silk stockings. An Indio had brought them up from a finca twenty miles away in the Yungas, and the ladies had saddled and ridden away— the minister's mules could just as well have been on the spot, too. And now the sick engineer's four mules were browsing a few yards away from him in their trim English saddles, stripping green branches of leaves. And in front of him lay the Yunga defile, fragrant with moisture and vanilla. The great primeval forest. And beyond it lay the coffee plantations, the fincas whose names, scribbled down on a slip of paper, he had about him—and farther on still, tropical heat and steam stealing through the crests of palms. And he was without transport.

After half an hour of it, not a sign of a mount. Other people

215

from the station mounted the four mules and rode away. Goehrs then took the stationmaster by the shoulder. The fellow pretended to be busy, bustled about, and with it all had nothing to do beyond seeing an autocarril arrive once a day and standing by when another went out.

" Here, señor ! Where the devil are those mules ? "

The stationmaster shrugged his shoulders.

" Do you know who ordered those mules ? "

" Certainly."

" Your own minister. . . ."

" Yes . . . very influential man. . . ." The fellow laughed. In a flash Goehrs was aware that the scoundrel had never had any intention of ordering the mules, that he hated him, that he was making a fool of his minister and that he was obviously jeering at everything, including the fact that he had to dispatch two autocarrils a day. Goehrs looked the man between the eyes. He was the common type of Bolivian with a swarthy face. Pretty mixed.

" Bueno," said Goehrs quietly. " I am going back to La Paz by the autocarril."

What else could he do except go back quietly and not manifest any annoyance, since he was not able to walk and it would in any case have been criminal folly to go on foot. When Goehrs at length left, the stationmaster and the manager of the Gran Hotel of the future with the choice wines were greatly diverted by the " gringo " who was returning to La Paz in riding-boots and with his saddle-bags. . . .

" Tell me," Goehrs asked the man who represented the other South American State that evening, " what was at the back of that chap's mind ? He must have known he was in for a row."

" Not necessarily," said the other imperturbably. " Every fellow is a protégé of his minister and every minister is dependent on his protégé. But apart from that—just let me give you this tip—it may quite well be that the stationmaster fellow has better information than we two have, that the minister on whom you are counting will not be a minister much longer. But for the rest, you can see how the average man in Bolivia hates the foreigner. The people are gradually beginning to grasp that they are reaping no benefit from the wealth of the country but that the Yankee is . . . and all foreigners are Yankees. What do you expect ? "

" It's all very well. But to promise a thing and not to keep it and then not even to express regret," growled

Goehrs, who was still haunted by the stationmaster's impudent expression.

"Nothing to worry about," said the other. "It will help you to understand what one of us feels like when, not some wretched railway hooligan, but the President of the Republic, promises us something and keeps his word no better. And it is not a case of a couple of mules, I assure you."

He poured out some mineral water.

"You surely don't drink ordinary water, señor ? In spite of an altitude of over 12,000 feet, it is dangerously contaminated by the mines lying higher up still. A fair percentage of Europeans die of typhoid in La Paz every year. There are an extraordinary number of facilities for dying here. A lot of miners have been discharged on account of the unfavourable prospects of the metal market and they are without food but have plenty of dynamite. And then there is this gap in the Government which a President used to stop. And the old President is lurking in Mollendo like a savage tiger and making trouble. . . . The army is pretty sure to be split, too. Don't be alarmed if guns should suddenly take to going off."

IN THE TIN MINES

THE mountains of Bolivia are in innumerable places perforated by tunnels. Many a mountain is drilled by hundreds of shafts. Bolivia is one of the wealthiest mining countries in the world. Its mines lie very high. One of them is in a mountain, Chacaltaya by name. After a famous battle in the War of Independence. About 16,000 feet high.

It is a tin mine. Tin is Bolivia's sacred metal. Bolivia is the second tin-producing country of the world. Ninety per cent. of its export is tin.

Goehrs was riding with two engineers on three mules up the mountainside to the centre of the mine. One of the mules was yellow, another was red, and the third was like a tiger.

"I bought the brute from a smuggler for 500 bolivianos," said one of the young engineers. "My last animal died under me of heart-failure, and that let me in for a broken leg with a triple fracture." The youngster was, to Goehrs's astonishment, a German, and his eyes filled with tears when he learnt that Goehrs knew the Feldberg. The youngster had been a student in Freiburg, and was insanely in love with the Feldberg. Eight years previously he had done a ninety-five-foot jump on skis on the old Feldberg run.

"When I go on leave next year for the first time after seven years, I am first going to California, going to buy a Ford, drive straight across the States, sell the car in New York, and go straight via Hamburg to the Black Forest. I've been up here for two years, never see a soul—well, you can imagine how I look forward to the Feldberger Hof. Have plenty of time to think it all out. Let's send a post-card to Herr Schladerer. Guess we are about four times the height of the Feldberg. But I can't do any more jumping with a triple fracture."

If Goehrs gave his mule the reins and imagined it might blunder, the thought of broken bones struck him as entirely natural. The mules, fresh from the stables, scrambled up the steep slope, sprinkled with rocks as sharp as needles, at a sort of trot. The other man on the yellow mule was the Bolivian inspector of six mines all belonging to the same combine, Señor Patino.

The sun was hot. No snow was lying at a height of 14,500 feet. Then a cloud came sailing round the peak of Chacaltaya, cut across its bald crest, and five minutes later the three wayfarers were in the thick of a sharp flurry of snow. The mules panted in the rarefied air. After a while they came to a mound of stone. On the far side of it was a little lake in colours such as are only to be conjured at such a height—a lagoon of reds, yellows, and greens. Indian women were squatting round the lake and washing their fabrics of the same vivid hues as the water. The bridle path led straight past the lake on to a dark hole. To the right and left of the path squatted Indian women, breaking up the rubble spewed out of the hole on little trucks. The ore.

The Indian women sat on the ground without shoes or stockings, cracking ore in a wind that was just about a freezing-point. In the lee of the mountainsides stood their dwellings—piles of unhewn stone. There they slept a night on the ground, wrapped up in blankets, at 18° F. Goehrs thought with a shudder of the home life of these people. What comforts could they have in life in dwellings like those ? How were they to love, to nurse, to instruct ? What was there to differentiate these folk from the beast at all ? Hardly anything.

"What do they pay the women ? " he asked Patino.

"Two bob a day."

" And the hands in the shaft ? "

" From three to five."

A bob was just about equivalent to a Dutch guilder.

Goehrs continued to watch the women working for a while before he entered the black hole, into the shaft. The pay, taking it all round, was not bad. But the social legislation in Bolivia was very bad. At one time a thrift law was in force in accordance with which every workman had to pay in five per cent. of his wages. That was designed to build up a reserve fund for the Indios. The Indios did in fact pay in for a year or two, then they bribed an official, drew all their deposits, and spent them on alcohol in a twinkling.

Then there was at one time a law according to which, in the event of an employee losing an arm or a leg in blasting operations, the employer company had to pay the employee a pretty stiff sum, about 3000 bolivianos. If this sum was paid out, half of it went to the lawyers, for every other man is a lawyer, and no one buys a hat without consulting his solicitor. The other half of the 3000 bobs allotted to the employee was gone in a fortnight, and the man, minus his arm or his leg, was cumbering the ground for the rest of his life. These laws were well meaning enough, but useless for practical purposes, and had therefore ceased to be operative. The human beings squatting on the ground here, and hammering ore barefoot among the glaciers, were left to the mercies of chance almost more completely than beasts. At the same time, they conveyed an impression of contentment, laughed, and showed their teeth. Strange, poor slave race, content if it be only permitted to sit still ! These women would go on cracking their nuggets of ore to three-inch rubble and continue to sit still and look on if you were to bring up a field gun and lay it on them.

" How many tons of ore do you move a day ? "

" Fifty-five," said Señor Patino.

" Small mine ? "

" Yes, the one here is a small mine. The greater number of the mines have shut down. Come along down the shaft."

The head engineer was a man of sinews and muscles that moved with disciplined energy. The shaft began where that black hole in the snowfield was ; the tunnel and its adit were so small that Goehrs had to bend double. But the picture they revealed was fantastic. The shaft was cut like a crystal. Huge planes were romantically scattered about in the darkness and flashed in the miners' lamps they carried.

The Indians' eyes that met Goehrs's flashed wildly. Goehrs had the characteristic odour of Indians in his nostrils and saw the curious light in their pupils ; which is altogether distinct from that of the light in the faces of Negroes and white men.

Still doubled up, Goehrs climbed on into the shaft that at some points dropped sixty feet and rose ninety at others. At a height of 16,000 feet, it wound into the bowels of the snow-covered mountain. Trucks slid noiselessly past him. Shadowy Indians, boring the blast holes, flitted past. Goehrs picked up a lump of stone—it was very heavy. His heart was beating at racing speed, but he was able to talk as usual. When they were in the open again, the ski-man of the Feldberg grinned and said :

" By Jove, nothing the matter with your heart ! We were, to tell the truth, trying to knock you out. There's a bit of sporting satisfaction in knocking out a visitor."

Goehrs gazed for a second at the cheery humorist. Then he could not help laughing. The boy really meant to play the game. But Feldberg people have a way of thinking that, wherever they may be on the face of the globe, they are on the Feldberg.

" What does tin really look like ? " he asked, turning to Patino.

Patino handed him a stone in which a glittering dark crystal about the size of a pea was embedded.

" Almost like a black diamond."

" That was the reason we had had ideas of having the crystals cut. But there are already more diamonds than enough in the world." Patino laughed resentfully. " But there is, as things are, too much of everything in the world. Bicycles, human beings, tin, gold, corn. Whatever you may be trading in, there's a surplus."

" The tin crystal would be too light for cutting," said the German. He dropped the slab of stone to the ground.

They were now standing exactly in front of the hole of the shaft, and Goehrs suddenly felt the icy draught issuing from the mountain in the small of his back.

But before him was an immortal vista, hundreds of Cordilleran peaks. And above them, higher yet, towered the pale Illimani in a pink flush. Near him squatted the gaily coloured Indians on the frozen earth round the gleaming lake. What colours ! What a scene ! And what a fate !

THEY scrambled and slipped down three hundred yards of the mountain slope to the spot where the works lay where the ore was treated. An aerial railway ran alongside. When the ore came down from the galleries above it was transferred to trucks which slid down the three hundred yards while the empty trucks were taken up. The sheds stood below, the cantonments alongside.

" What is the percentage of tin in the ore ? "

" Four."

The ore was first treated in rolling-mills, where it was crushed to the size of grains. It was then sorted in drums according to its size. Then it was brought under hydraulic pressure that deposited the heavier metal and washed away the lighter residue. The deposit was then scooped up on to slanting tables, kept under continuous vibration. The tin was roughly separated from the other ores mixed with it which were tilted to one side because they were lighter. And the tin that remained behind was yellow in colour. The residue of the tin porridge was carried on—and here the most ingenious idea of the whole process was applied. The tin mess was conducted into a basin, where a screw was working at five hundred revolutions a minute, creating a great deal of froth. The water was mixed with turpentine, which increased the froth tenfold. Any remaining foreign matter was pretty thoroughly separated by this lather and removed. The solid matter left was drained of water and dried off. It lay about in heaps. It was a blue sand by this time—tin.

" There—this is 60 per cent. tin," said Patino. "That is as far as we take it here. We pack the dust up in bags and ship it to England where the stuff is smelted."

" And in its final state it looks white," said the German laughing.

Goehrs inspected the process again. The drums, the mills, the vibrating tables, the lathering basin, the hydraulic pressure. Nearly everything in the open air. Only scantily roofed in. So here the ore was refined from 4 to 60 per cent. He took a pinch of the blue sand in his hand.

" The fate of Bolivia depends on that dust," said Patino.

" On that dust," he repeated bitterly. They walked for a bit along a little dam.

" What was the reason that made you close down most of your mines ? " asked Goehrs.

"Half a minute," said Señor Patino, and did some calculations on his fingers. "The price of tin per ton via Liverpool was in

1928—260 pounds sterling,
1929—180 pounds sterling,
1930—140 pounds sterling.

It surely is obvious that on these figures any one owning tin mines where the cost of production amounts to more than 110 pounds per ton must close down.

"And where they can be worked cheaply the output consequently increases?"

"On the contrary," replied Patino. "The world is economically all to pieces. It wants much less cheap tin than previously it used to want expensive tin at twice the price. At the present moment Liverpool is holding stocks of 50,000 tons of unsold tin."

"Is there no international agreement for the distribution of the work? No quotas? No controlling syndicate as in the case of diamonds?"

"Not yet. The world output is about 185,000 tons of fine tin per annum. The British and Malay countries produce about 55,000 tons of it; Bolivia 45,000; the Dutch in Sumatra 35,000. The rest is pretty well equally distributed. Now follow me carefully! If all these countries, which almost all can produce more cheaply than we, knock out Bolivia, they can just about cover the world demand for tin."

He kicked a stone into the water.

"The worst of it is that it's not a purely economic problem but a big political issue. It's not the case of a handful of mine-owners fighting the world in this metal slump. Bolivia, as a whole, is involved up to the neck."

"Really!" said Goehrs, who had frequently heard the same sort of thing before, where in other countries it undoubtedly had not been true.

"Half a minute," said Patino, and went on counting his fingers. The tin exports amount to 90 per cent. of the Bolivian exports. There are dues on this export. From these dues Bolivia draws 60 per cent. of its revenues. Its budget is therefore balanced on the tin dues. The tin dues, however, are based on a price of 260 pounds sterling per ton. And the price per ton to-day is 140 pounds sterling. Follow? The tin slump, of course, means national bankruptcy. Bolivian revenue is cut in half. The question is not whether the tin industry keeps its head above water ; the question is now is Bolivia going to keep afloat ? "

" Bolivia has survived plenty of slumps," said Goehrs. " The quinine slump, and the rubber slump. It will survive the tin slump as well. To-day's prices are rock-bottom prices and will right themselves as every cycle in international finance rights itself."

" I don't believe that these prices are temporary," Patino insisted obstinately. " For the problem is not exclusively a question of international finance. There is another factor in the case of Bolivia. Bolivia is an industrial country, but it's not thoroughly organized from the transport point of view. And if its transport isn't on an efficient footing, and before there are funds in hand for putting it on such a footing— everything else is waste of time."

He gazed for a moment reflectively at a couple of Indians washing their gaudy ponchos in the glassy water of many colours.

" A machine costs me $5000 down in Arica, on the coast. By the time I have brought it up here it costs me $8000. Timber brought all the ridiculously long way from San Francisco is cheaper than timber from the Yungas, from forests the crests of which you can see in front of you over here. The spirit distilled in the tropical districts of Bolivia, which is brought here on muleback, is packed in cases of beautiful timber, equivalent to the finest mahogany. And you can't market these fine timbers, trunks as thick as that front door over there, simply because their transport is too expensive. In the Yungas they'll give you a whole basketful of oranges for 50 centavos. You will get only two instead of a hundred for the same price here. That surely is lunacy."

" That is lunacy," agreed Goehrs.

" It's the fault of the system," said the engineer. " When they start making a road here, the beginning of its construction falls within the term of office of one President, whose job ends in four years. Not a soul dreams of completing the job in the next man's term of office. For if one President is all enthusiasm for some scheme or other, let us say roadmaking, he raises a public loan without worrying how he is going to pay it off. And the new President, in whose term of office repayment falls, worries still less about repaying his predecessor's debts—he simply raises another loan. And where do these public loans come from except from the Yankees ? In this way Bolivia is pretty heavily mortgaged to the Yankees—and has no benefit from it."

" Then Bolivia is more or less a colony."

" Yes! it is a Yankee colony—not to put too fine a point upon it."

" And is it possible for this state of things to change ? "

" By one of two alternatives, señor. Either the Yankees, who have the State entirely under their thumb financially, will hoist the Stars and Stripes over Government House (but there is no likelihood of that at the moment—the Yankees are not as premature as that) or there must be a long presidency, a dictatorship, prolonged well beyond four years and in the hands of a man who has energy and clean hands."

" Is there such a man to be found ? "

" Not likely. But we want one badly. And there is only one single individual who could discover him and put him in power."

" Who ? "

" Well, the man who has the power to do so. The Chief of the General Staff. General Kundt."

TWO PRESIDENTS

FIVE of them rode up the slopes to the icy summit of the mountain where more than a century before the battle of Chacaltaya had been fought in Bolivia's War of Liberation. A battle on the scale appropriate to those days. A few hundred Spaniards on one side and a few hundred Bolivians (who were themselves Spaniards—or rather half-breeds by Spaniards with Indian women) on the other.

The four men accompanying Goehrs were Bolivian engineers and inspectors.

" Twenty people were banished to Buenos Aires yesterday," said one of them.

" Among them the only opposition candidate to Siles left in the country."

" That's not true, señor," said the third, " for the man in question is my brother-in-law, and I talked to him on the telephone this morning."

" There you see how much you can believe," said the first.

" The situation is quite peculiar," said the fourth to Goehrs. He had smallpox scars, was almost black, had studied in Chile, and was very well informed. " President Siles has resigned after trying to keep his seat in the saddle after his term of office in order to put through the match agreement with Kreuger and so on. But at last things

became too hot for him. The Government now only consists of the ministry, which, of course, ought to have
resigned office with him. The ministry has now proclaimed
the election of a convention as in four weeks' time from
to-day (after Parliament has been sent home) to resolve
that

(1) the Constitution be amended;
(2) it is open for the President to be elected twice in
succession; and
(3) his term of office be prolonged to six years.

The black man closed a trifle abruptly because his mule
blundered and nearly came down.

" Pretty sensible," said Goehrs.

" But illegal," exclaimed the second.

" Not even quite that," returned the black. " Only in
constitutional law. The whole thing is, of course, impu-
dence—but the people will regard the manœuvre as legal.
Nor would there be much to complain about if only the
elections were free."

That was the crux. For as long as Goehrs had been in
these countries he had heard the same plaint. Every reform
of the constitution was always turned into a lever to enable
a gang to keep in office.

" Nothing is better organized than the methods whereby
the party in power shoulders the weaker one off the ballot
boxes. No one will get near the polling-booths who is not
voting for Siles."

" The dangerous time for Siles is just now, immediately
before the elections," said the third, " for something may
happen at any minute. The former President Bautista
Saavedra is lurking in Mollendo and spending a lot of money
to make the army amenable and in publishing pamphlets to
stir up the people."

" Saavedra was President before Siles—until 1926," said
the black man, " and had banished the troublesome Siles.
Of course, the banishment was disguised as an ambassador-
ship to Lima. Later on the two came to terms. Siles was
allowed to return to La Paz, and there the two party leaders
came to an agreement to the effect that Siles was to become
President as soon as Saavedra's term was up. Then Siles
was to have his four years in office and make room for
Saavedra again. There was said to be an agreement in
writing on these points, that is to say an agreement in
writing between two men who, if not supported by entirely

different sections of the population, have two quite distinct programmes behind them. Is it proper there should be agreements of this kind, señor ? Do you call that government by the people ? And tell me, is not a sound dictatorship better for a nation than such business bargains between men whose supporters really amount to only three per cent. of the population ?

"And Siles is not keeping to his bargain now ? " said Goehrs.

"Of course not. That's the whole trouble. You can imagine the feelings of the opposition crowd for yourself. Very nasty temper."

"Whose side are you on ? " Goehrs turned round to the black man, who was now riding behind him because the track was very narrow.

"In reply to that," said the half-breed and pushed his horse forward, "I beg to declare as follows : Siles is a miserable, unpleasant morphiomaniac. His wife presides over his War Cabinet. His ministers are—well, one of his ministers has as his sole qualification the fact that his wife has a figure that appeals to Siles. For that reason the man was made a minister. As far as I am personally concerned, I should have no quarrel with Siles if only he were a man. But he isn't. He's a pinchbeck imitation of Leguía in Peru. He has photographs taken of himself in the pose of Napoleon —and all the while is busy with a hypodermic needle. I'm against him, of course."

"Your reasons," said the second, " are maybe just as much rot, in part at least, as that story about your banished brother-in-law. But you're right all the same. Siles is no good."

"And Saavedra ? " asked Goehrs. They had by this time reached the flat summit of the mountain, and his pulse was hammering like mad.

"Saavedra," said the second, " is at any rate a man of energy.

"And unpopular," added the first.

"The deuce," said Goehrs. "Poor country to have a choice only between these two. Which of them ought it to elect ? "

The black man rode past Goehrs. He pointed to a snow-field lying in front of them at a height of 16,000 feet. "That's the battlefield," he said. "I don't suppose that it all was very different then. What is there that has changed in the world ? "

GOEHRS had once watched an old Indian woman address General Kundt as he was getting into his big staff car with two orderlies on the front seat. The woman had addressed the general, and the general had laughed. He was still talking to her as the car drove off. It had been quite an affecting picture. Goehrs had frequently seen the general driving through La Paz, once on Whit-Sunday when the streets were crowded. The crowds had waved their hands and taken their hats off. The general was undoubtedly popular among the common people and the Indians, nor did he affect anything of that disastrous geniality that only exasperates people.

The general had invited Goehrs to have a "bite of bread and cheese" and, as he lived a goodish way out of La Paz and some nine hundred feet lower down, he had sent his car for Goehrs with the kindly intent of saving him ten bob in taxi fares—his big staff car with its military chauffeur—and for this very reason Goehrs arrived a little late. For as the car swung round the big avenida of the new quarter, it ran into a crowd of people moving down the avenida and uttering shouts of no uncertain meaning. The car was closely hemmed in by half-breeds, and only a smart move on the part of an Indian traffic policeman made a gap, and the car escaped from the close embrace of the demonstrators into a side street.

It was still daylight when Goehrs reached Obrajes, a valley looking like a bit of Tuscany, in which the general's house stood. Goehrs had been counting the milestones and reckoned that, if the demonstrators were to come straight through from La Paz, they could not reach Obrajes until after dinner.

The house stood in a flower garden. Goehrs passed through the gate and past a cage with a couple of singing starlings and a cage with a monkey. Beyond the house he caught a glimpse of the river that occasionally came along with a three-foot boulder, which it hurled at the little break-water sheltering the house—a gift of the State of Bolivia. In a hurried glimpse Goehrs saw the rock bombardment ammunition piled up there. Quite a romantic site for a house.

An Indian in a white jacket dashed up to stop the car outside, but it had passed him. The general came to meet Goehrs straight from the telephone in the hall.

"The students are demonstrating in La Paz," he said. "I have just had the report. They say the procession is three blocks in length."

Goehrs would have taken the mob bellowing down the avenida for anything rather than students.

"It's not as bad as all that. I drove through them in your car."

"Well, come on and let us have dinner," said the general, and presented Goehrs to his wife and daughter.

Seen at close quarters Kundt had a striking head. In uniform without his cap he really looked like Ludendorff. With his cap on he looked like Hindenburg. A tall, muscular man of sixty, with a delicate nose, aloof bearing, and clever eyes. He was the constructor of the Bolivian standing army, 8000 strong, of the officers' training schools, and of specialized arms, a talented organizer who went a good deal beyond his purely military province, for at the moment he was the only depositary of power. An ironic brain, by no means militarily atrophied, offhand and dominant, conservative and progressive at one and the same time.

The atmosphere struck Goehrs as easy and unconstrained. An Indian boy served the dishes from the left; he kept his right hand clenched behind his back with the expression of an assassin concealing the knife.

"Yes," said Kundt, glancing at the boy. "The Aymaras make excellent soldiers, wonderful performers on route marches, and, if you explain a military situation or problem to them in their own language, they will prove as efficient as any soldier in the world. Take my word for it. But when it comes to waiting at table, I assure you it would be an easier job for me to mobilize the whole army than for my wife to make the servants understand that they must not keep their hands behind their backs and must wear gloves for waiting. Rifles—very good. Gloves—not for your life."

"But they are good cooks," said Goehrs, taking a second helping of soufflé.

"The child looks after the sweets," said the ruler of presidentless Bolivia, and nodded to his pretty, fair-haired daughter. But before he could lift his spoon again he was summoned to the telephone.

One or two shadowy photographs of Bolivia, twilight mountains with droves of llamas, Sorata in the moonlight, the barren Puna, and palm trees in the haze of the Montaña, hung on the walls. In one corner was a cabinet with vases from Tiahuanacu. Antique Spanish silver trinkets on the tables.

Goehrs reflected why this should really surprise him. Like the majority of Germans, he had more definite and one-sided conceptions of the aspect and life of a general than of the member of any other profession. To judge by everything he had heard about Kundt, he would have expected this house to be different, more austere, with less taste for art, more uncompromising, with rough rather than fragile furniture, and barer instead of having the hallmark of a collector's taste. Whence comes the mental portraits Germans draw of their own generals ? Was it the fault of the generals or of the Germans ? He was unable to come to any conclusion.

Kundt had come to Bolivia as a German major before the War. Shortly before the War, he happened to be in Germany on leave—as a German major and a Bolivian general and army inspector—and by the end of the War had led his brigade of Guards from the field as a general officer. His relationships with Bolivia then became variable and curious but characteristic of the man. He had made the journey from Germany to Bolivia and back several times. As Chief of the General Staff he had maintained discipline for President Saavedra during his term of office. On one occasion he arrived in the middle of a revolution and had to turn back. On another a different President was in office than the man who had summoned him, and once, as a way out of a difficulty, he was appointed director of mines.

When the danger of war between Bolivia and Paraguay on the question of the Chaco became imminent, Kundt was summoned again. The Chaco is that wild, long subtropical steppe that until recently was hardly explored because it was only inhabited by savage Indians, a parklike steppe that some people hold to be valueless and others as a great reserve for cattle-breeding, and timber, and minerals. Kundt, who had put up with extraordinary humiliations, came back. His name proved to be an asset on the Bolivians' side in prospect of this war, which fortunately was, thanks to it, avoided. " It would have been a military walk-over," said Kundt, " but we did not go for the walk." His attitude throughout this crisis made him extraordinarily popular, although he was " gringo," a foreigner, which all South Americans, even if they are as black as niggers, look on as something rather contemptible. He had enemies. But he had devoted friends. And the people.

When Goehrs considered the diplomatic address the Prussian general had displayed, it made him thoughtful. Kundt had, as soon as the need again arose, entered into the service of people who had attacked him savagely in public. He had simply disregarded these attacks that had always been launched by individuals and not by the country, and had thus done a thing that is very rare in South America. He was matter of fact. He served Bolivia.

The general was now once again in an awkward predicament. The Cabinet, in which two officers sat as observers, had suddenly, after the President's resignation, had the functions of executive thrust upon it—a not altogether legally constitutional manœuvre. During the weeks that ensued between the retirement of Siles and the elections, Kundt was the only landmark in the void of State authority —a grand opportunity for an ambitious, but a hideous dilemma for a soberminded man.

Kundt had previously served President Saavedra, that is to say, a government of the broad masses which the intellectuals and the old families opposed. With the same adaptability, he had served President Siles, that is to say, a government of the small men, the half-breed interests, and the non-educated, who were trying to come to terms with the intellectuals and the old families, which proved infeasible. And Kundt became the victim of the tragedy of history when the intellectuals who, during the Paraguay crisis, had celebrated him as their hero, organized demonstrations against him. He had two banished Presidents, with both of whom he had kept faith, sending him very unambiguous telegrams more or less urging him to appeal to arms.

His position was very difficult. Whatever he did was bound to be wrong—unless he resigned. Why did Kundt not resign ?

The general came back from the telephone, at which he had been speaking for perhaps ten minutes.

" The Minister for War," he said in answer to an inquiring glance from his wife, " has expressed the wish that the Thursday evening concert the military band gives on the Plaza be abandoned. I have no objection. It is always as well to avoid incidents. The demonstration continues. It seems as if every one has taken leave of his senses. A colonel's daughter, who is a student, has made a speech against the Government and her father. Do you happen to know Butzbach ? I could never have

dreamt of such a state of affairs when as a company commander I was stationed in Butzbach. Grand times. The
Vogelsberg and Nauheim. I was once very nearly
cashiered because we went to the opera in Frankfurt in
uniform with toy balloons in our buttonholes."

"It's nice for you to have a visitor every now and
then, Papa," said the fair-haired girl smiling, "otherwise
I should learn so little of your nefarious past."

"Bless my life and soul," said the general, taken aback.
"Well, another pisco and let us go across for our coffee."

"An event is occurring this evening," said Goehrs,
"that is riveting the gaze of the civilized world more
firmly on Germany than any battle during the War did."

"Well?" said Kundt lazily.

"The fight between Schmeling and Sharkey," replied
Goehrs laughing. "I'm not the least keen on boxing.
But the Bolivian newspapers have gone off their heads."

"Nor am I keen on it," said Kundt. "But there is
a German in it this time." And he brought his hand down
lightly on his knee.

"Yes. A German," said Goehrs. "I remember as
late as 1923 an American woman stopping the lift in a
hotel in Lausanne when she noticed she was using it with a
German—on account of the babies' hands we lopped off,
I suppose. . . . After all, the world has changed—and
quite a lot. Doesn't your appointment here—as that of
a German ex-officer—clash with the Treaty of Versailles?"

"It does," said the general, "more especially as I
have retained my German nationality—which the rest of
the German officers in other South American States were
not allowed to do. A certain country in Europe, that has
no interests in Bolivia beyond keeping a look-out for such
things, addressed a note to Bolivia on this very point.
Bolivia thereupon sent a noteworthy answer :
"'We take note of your protest and would call attention
to the fact that we are a sovereign State that has the honour
to act as it thinks fit.' That was the end of the matter."

"Have you got the army well in hand?"

"Sure of it."

"You are talking of the rank and file?"

"The ranks are certain. . . . There is, of course, the
risk that the politicians may have got at the officers."

". . . Have you had any experience of a revolution in
La Paz yet?"

Kundt laughed. "When I had been back a fortnight
231

after the War, the Minister of War telephoned that a regiment had mutinied. Just such another night as this."

"What did you do then?" Goehrs asked, as the general went on chuckling.

"First pulled myself together. Then I dressed. Then I drove to the barracks of the regiment that had mutinied, but never reached it because the mutineers were simply sweeping the street, lit up as bright as day, with rifle fire. Might just as well have walked a couple of hundred yards on to a machine gun in a searchlight. Apart from that, the fellows had climbed over the wall of a non-mutinous regiment and had fraternized with them. I only had three cadets with me and did not want to send them to their death, and therefore went, since I guessed what was up, to my quarters—to the General Staff which was excellently adapted for emergencies of this kind, and waited for morning. Then I went to the barracks of the regiment that had not mutinied. I strolled across the barrack yard. There they were, and I said: 'What's the trouble, lads?' One of them stepped forward and said: ' Better rations, more decent treatment,' and so on. I said ' Boys, I am only just back. But you shall have everything you want. But if you hang about here much longer and play the fool, your womenfolk will begin to feel anxious about you.' Well, they began laughing then, and the mutiny was off. But the company of the mutinous regiment that had climbed the wall remained to be dealt with. They refused to clear out. I gave the order, ' Shoulder arms.' They didn't. Things were now becoming ticklish. In cases like these, you have to deal with the individual. So with an N.C.O. I went up to a man and asked him: ' What's your name?' The fellow gave his name. ' Write it down,' I ordered, and his name was noted. I thereupon told the man whose name had been taken down to fall out two paces. He did. I shouted: 'Shoulder arms.' He did. That was the end of that mutiny."

"Did the men not get their proper rations?"

"Of course they did. That was the thing I saw to first. But the men were, of course, egged on for political purposes; they had been told that their rations were bad, and they believed it. The men know me now—and not a man is going to mutiny."

"I hope," said Goehrs, "that the officers who look for promotion from a rising will behave in the same way."

The general raised his hand and brought it down a little harder on his knee this time. But before he could say anything, the Indian boy rushed in and announced the Minister of War who had just called. The general got up quickly and left the room. Through the glass door of the adjoining room Goehrs saw a shadow pass. The tinkle of spurs. Firm footsteps crossing the parquet floor.

The general was away for half an hour. For half an hour Goehrs was alone with the two ladies, who quietly, without outward nervousness, watched a more dramatic part being thrust on their husband and father in the drama of the revolutionary ferment—without any action on his part except to stick to his post.

Then Kundt came in again. "A cognac, please," he said, and jestingly held up his hands above his head. "The Minister of War has just informed me that Saavedra has finally decided I shall have to be shot."

"General," said Goehrs, "do you not think it would be right for you to declare for a new President?"

"That would mean a putsch. On no account."

"Then," said Goehrs, "I think you ought to resign. For you are in an ambiguous position."

"My dear sir, half an hour later we should have civil war in La Paz."

"But you will perhaps have it in any case—and under unpleasant conditions for yourself."

"I do not think so. But even if we were to, fate and Providence, and not I, would have to shoulder the responsibility for it." He took up his position before the fireplace. "I am only human and my sense of responsibility only prompts me to stick to my post. The country needs law and order, and I am going to preserve them as long as I can." He examined his nails carefully. "You see," he went on with a curious smile, "there is always the temptation to play the part of Wallenstein in a situation like this—and I might be able to do as I liked and put in any man I backed as President. But a more urgent duty as I see it is to safeguard the country that needs peace and quiet against upheavals that always set it back by twenty years. I'm devotedly fond of this country that deserves a kinder fate than it gets. I have devoted a good many years of a life that is not growing any longer to instil the sense of discipline and civic spirit I brought with me out here from home. I have not educated it only in the military sense for the purpose of waging war against it, but in order to inculcate certain qualities a nation needs if it is to hold its own in competition with others. This appeals to me as more important than to cast oneself for a heroic part. For this reason I have eschewed war wherever I could eschew it. Exactly as I want to avoid civil war today. Don't worry if people say that my position is illegal. In this country illegal and legal have a different meaning from what they have in other countries. I am firmly convinced that, if I were to resign the chief command, the situation would not only be far more illegal but far more alarming as well. I'm not clinging to this appointment and I'm giving it up next spring in any case; but I'm standing by my job and for what I feel for this country. And don't worry if people say I'm ungrateful if I refuse to attempt a rising for the sake of my old friendship with Saavedra. Didn't I earn my old friendship with Saavedra by safeguarding him against risings?

"And don't worry if people say that no one in this country is worth my running any risks for him, or running risks in my capacity as a German. Hang it all! it is just because I am a German that it becomes my duty, even in moments of difficulty to take risks for the sake of a job I have taken upon my shoulders, and to continue to stick to my post. Otherwise I might just as well have pottered about Wiesbaden after the War, or settled down in Berlin, or have been gardening in Butzbach. It would have made life easier, the Lord knows."

"Well, we shall get over this fortnight, too," said the general's wife.

"As over everything else," said Kundt, contemplating his fingernails.

QUITE A SUDDEN DROP

GOEHRS remembered that every one described a return to the coast from La Paz in terms of exuberant relief. They ceased to have to keep a check on their heart. They lost their dread of dying of inflammation of the lungs or of some surgical mischance. They had not to stay in bed all day long after they had been out really late at night by way of a change. And there was no occasion for them to go on suffering from the cold when once, with a cry of ecstasy, they had reached the coast.

Goehrs had in the first instance assumed that he would

share these sentiments. But he did not. Far from it. For he had fallen in love with the fantastic solitude in which the Altiplano of Bolivia spread beneath the sky. And he had fallen in love with the strange, inflamed vision of La Paz that at first sight had struck him as a disenchanting town of sheds with galvanized iron roofs. He had become acclimatized. He did not even suffer quite so much from the cold.

When the train by which he finally left La Paz had worked its way out of the dip and reached the uplands, he had another glimpse of La Paz. It was bewitchingly sketched in a setting of such lavishness as only the Cordilleras can offer, in its severity, charm, and strangeness. And Goehrs felt his heart contract at the thought. And then, too, Goehrs saw the Illimani once more, with its regal triple summits. These crests, too, were unique. The first ascent of the Illimani was slow, leisurely, grandiose up to the first summit. The second rise was complete in line, short and final. And then the third began, bold, mighty, only hesitating once for a space before culminating superbly in the third peak. To such heights did the mountain soar. And then it broke off and plunged down in a wild line of snow worthy of Dürer.

Beyond it towered the thousands of other Cordilleran peaks, as Goehrs had seen them for the first time, crowded together like a herd of llamas that, with their half-inquisitive and half-startled heads, are in doubt whether to stand still or to speed on, in that moment of relaxation, which in the case of animals as of mountains is the most fascinating of all.

Goehrs travelled across the tableland for the greater part of a day and a night. He came to Oruro, the mining centre. A mining town with a population of 30,000. Silver and copper. The Indians in their time had had their mines there. With an ancient fortress. At a height of almost 13,000 feet. Full of offices and mining people. He went on to Rio Mulato where the line branches off to Potosí. Potosí was an Indian word and signified din. Garcilaso de la Vega told the story how an Inca emperor once came here and learnt that the mountains were fairly bursting with silver. But when he began to mine the ore, a voice from the mountain warned him that the wealth was ordained for another coming after him. The Inca fell to the ground and kissed it and broke his works off, whereupon the mountain collapsed with a crash and

235

was given the name of Potosí.   Then the Spaniards came
and were not to be deterred either by a voice or by the
Indians, from opening up the silver mines.   For a time
Potosí grew into a great city.   With a wonderful old mint,
with old Spanish palaces and mansions and churches.
A fair, cold town, over 13,000 feet above sea-level.

To the north lay Chuquisaca, renamed Sucre since the
War of Liberation after the general.   Four thousand feet
lower than Oruro and warmer than La Paz.   With a
university, banks, nine squares with churches and gardens.
The old capital of Bolivia.   Pizarro had resided there, and
it was he who had founded it.   The soil on which Sucre
was built was gold bearing.   The golden foundations of
the town supported 30,000 inhabitants.

Everywhere in all these towns there was something
menacing in the atmosphere.   But Goehrs saw nothing
definite that he could earmark as revolution.   But revolt
was for all that in the air.

Goehrs was still within the ring fence of the Cordilleras.
Still upon the plateau.   Amid towering mountains,
tunnelled like ant-heaps.   Between the silver mines of
Huanchaca and the copper mines of Calama.   The great
borax lakes were beginning to open out and volcanoes
to be mirrored on their dull gelatinous surfaces.   Not a
living thing, not a human being, for hundreds of miles.
The salt steppes extended as if there were no other scenery
on earth.   And mountains at length began to lag behind.
They had less snow and became scraggier and more shy.
It was only on the skyline that they showed rosy red with
snowy peaks, flushed, hundreds of them, like fretwork
minarets.   Goehrs was conscious of a constriction of the
chest, as if he were deserted, now that the mountains with
which he had lived for many a week began to fade.   He
grew languid and depressed.

Instead, the plateau lay glittering under a white powder—
but it had ceased to be snow, it had turned into salt.
Hundreds of miles of saltpetre pampa opened out, vast
and mournful, but imposing in its way : that flat, salt
tableland where the nitrates lay hid in their holes.   The
chimney-stacks sent out their smoke to meet him.   The
nitrate factories came and reeked into the air, the soil
of the pampa was upheaved.   The plain was torn by
dynamite charges on every hand.

The terrain slowly began to fall away.   The Puna dropped
lower with the salt steppes.   In the course of the previous

night the frost had been so hard that the carriage in which Goehrs slept crackled continuously with the cold. The weather was becoming milder now. Goehrs dropped down in one whole day from 13,000 feet to sea-level. At first storms had continued to sweep the upland steppes and the salt pampas with inexorable severity. Now towards evening there was a savour of the Riviera in the air. Too mild at a plunge. Too relaxing. How often had Goehrs longed for the balm of the paradise of the coast when the cold of Bolivia was chilling his blood like a poison. But now, when the gentle airs of the subtropical plain were being wafted in over him, the abruptness of the change made him restless, he felt an aching homesickness for the wild, rough fugues of the high mountains.

Out of humour and ill at ease, he was just in time to catch sight of the sea through the dusk. He saw a P.S.N.C. boat with her green load-line. He saw another liner with the red funnel of the Compañía Sudamericana de Vapores. Goehrs was, as a rule, as responsive to ships as a marine barometer. Ships stirred his imagination. Stately ships kindled him to enthusiasm. But that evening the sight of ships depressed him.

In the meantime he had long ago crossed the borders of Chile between Ollague and Chiguana. Across the Chilean frontier with the white-and-red flag and the star on the blue canton.

Part IV

CONCERNING CHILE

NITRATES

THE haven which Goehrs, coming down from the silvery frosted pampas, had reached, was called Antofagasta—and by the following morning he was ensconced a couple of miles or so outside Antofagasta in a little cove on the beach. Behind him stood a small bungalow, the automobile club. Goehrs with his companion had undressed on the beach, and was sitting on the sand beside his garments gazing along the coast—a coastline of over 2500 miles. The coastline of an enormously elongated country that on an average was not more than the run from London to Manchester in breadth. In spite of that a country almost twice the size of France, but with hardly more than one seventh of it suitable for cultivation. Goehrs looked along the coast. There it lay from where he was sitting, 450 miles of it ; the coast of the pampas. Desert.

The coastline was very narrow here, hardly more than a few miles wide. Then the Cordilleras rose as perpendicular as a wall for 1500 feet, and then mounted even higher to the tableland from which Goehrs had just come and where the nitrate fields extended in unbounded desolation.

The nitrates in the upland wastes did not lie continuously in reefs like, say, gold, but in pockets here, there, anywhere, everywhere. It was difficult to tell with the naked eye where nitrates were and where they were not. But the engineers knew. They blasted every pocket. Dynamite explosions crashed all over the mountain plateau, where not a soul lived except the engineers and the workmen. Huge pillars of smoke rose perpendicularly into the sky. The blasted soil was then conveyed to the nitrate works, which, with smokestacks reeking grimly, occurred suddenly here and there : the *oficinas*, the nitrate factories. In the oficinas the earth was ground and then boiled in big retorts. The nitrates were boiled out and carried off. The foreign matter still remaining in the fluid was segregated, and the sud then flowed into the *salinas*, big canals of iron tanks in which the salts slowly crystallized. In the desert these containers gleamed like white-hot molten metal. The nitrates were then filled into sacks and taken by rail over long distances to Antofagasta, or to other ports on the Chilean coast.

It was with mixed emotions that Goehrs, with the tang of the sea in his nostrils and its roar in his ears while the white rollers broke on the shore, recalled the vast solitudes on the tableland of the Cordilleras, the tall chimneys rising at big intervals, and the sheds and folk who eked out their lives among dynamite explosions and boiling retorts.

This desert was Chile's wealth.

" The trouble is," said the man lying alongside of Goehrs, the manager of a big Chilean works, "that the local people will, once and for all, not put big capital into nitrates. Whereas the Yankees chuck eighty million dollars about like a bagatelle. The Yankees don't worry in the least about difficulties. In fact they devise new processes for nitrate production which at first sight look insane. You have, of course, seen how nitrates have hitherto been produced. They blasted the sites in the pampas where they expected to find nitrates—they are immediately below the surface—and boiled the soil blown out. It was, of course, troublesome—one crater here, another over there. . . . The life of the nitrate deposits on our pampa was estimated at a hundred years. Then came the Americans and said it took too long and that it was too tedious to pass from one hole to another in that way. Let's simply plough up the whole pampa, dig the whole thing up, the muck, the gravel, the nitrates, chuck it all into one pot, and treat it by cold process. We won't do any more stewing. We'll put the whole mess under hydraulic pressure. Every one thought the Yankees were mad. The whole scheme, they said, was insane. But the Yankees unfortunately never go mad. Well, you've seen the Oficina María Elena. The process there is in actual fact cheaper than the other. And instead of a hundred, the whole pampa will be turned over in twenty years' time. And then it will be the turn of the other pampas. . . . That fellow Guggenheim, the leader of the Yankee nitrate group, is really one of the big men of the industry. He doesn't even worry about the world demand which, as you know, is dwindling every day. Guggenheim is taking as big a stock as he can carry on the coast and is stacking the bags in stores built on chemically sound principles to prevent the nitrates from deteriorating. Wonderful methods! Same thing with his plant. Once a machine in his oficinas is not quite A1, he simply scraps it. He doesn't waste time on repairs. Nothing matters to him except—waste of time. And in this way the Yankees have, to a greater or lesser extent, collared the nitrate industry."

The fair-haired young man by Goehrs's side was talking with a very embittered voice. Goehrs saw the seas outside breaking against the fragment of a quay that a storm had recently torn to ribbons. And beyond it lay the sun-steeped Pacific, in fragrance and blueness, and fraught with temptations of every kind. The whole of Chile, Goehrs reflected, has wretched harbours—the worst harbours all the world over.

" It's a calamity for my native country that the railways as well—everything in fact—is slipping out of the control of the local people and the British into the control of the Yankees," said the young man.

" Are you a Chilean, then ? " Goehrs exclaimed in astonishment. He had naturally taken the man, who spoke German faultlessly and looked like a German as well, to be a German.

" I have never set eyes on Germany," said the Chilean.

Goehrs knew that the young man derived of German parents. He had, like many of the descendants of German stock, become a fanatical Chilean patriot.

" I have done my year's military service in Chile," the Chilean continued. " I have, of course, like all Chileans, strong predilections for Germany. I didn't even bear Germany any grudge for the fact that it was she of all others that dealt Chile the most severe blow that was ever dealt her—I mean the invention of artificial nitrates. Stupid that this blow should have to be dealt by Germany while it was we who, almost alone on the face of the globe, stuck to Germany throughout the whole of the War. . . . Yes, that and the low prices ruling for nitrates, are a source of great anxiety to my country. For Chile is to a great extent living on the export duties on nitrates."

" Every country has a similar source of anxiety nowadays. Tin is to Bolivia what nitrates are to Chile."

The young man rose to his feet and shivered with indignation.

"Bolivia . . . how can you draw any comparison between Bolivia and Chile ? Bolivia is in a chronic state of bankruptcy ; Bolivia is a chaotic country all the way through. Bolivia is in fact a Yankee colony by this time, gorged with Yankee capital. But we—we in Chile don't want to become a Yankee country. And we need capital. And capital is only to be had from the Yankees. And capital from the Yankee is more dangerous than an army corps with its heavy artillery in position."

Valdivia and the Conquest of Chile

GOEHRS was sitting in the lounge of his hotel that afternoon, on the common balcony which ran past all the rooms like a street, and looking out on the main street of Antofagasta. Goehrs had pictured Antofagasta as a second Buenaventura, as a ghastly hamlet where they shipped nitrates and copper—and nothing more.

This conception proved mistaken. Antofagasta struck him as human, familiar, and electric. Antofagasta ceased to be medieval. There was nothing suggestive of the atmosphere of another planet in Antofagasta. Here he found the good old world again. And Goehrs had a foreboding that the most interesting part of South America lay behind him. This was Europe.

Seventy thousand inhabitants. Imposing public buildings. Palm gardens. Police in khaki and solar topees. Shops, compared with which those of Lima were suburban. Pretty girls who had the backs of their necks shingled, whose complexions were touched up, who walked about on long legs moving freely from the hip joints. Public gardens on the beach. Here it was again, the good old world. Wearisome, and yet affecting. Goehrs felt almost at home in this nitrate township, from which he could escape only by sea. And this, agreeable as it was, was by no means what he had come for.

At the sight of these fashionable girls, who looked half like Scandinavians, half like fair-complexioned Indians, at the sight of these sleek, handsome, tall creatures, who lounged rather than sat in their automobiles—the little black girls of the highlands of Peru and Bolivia, who had looked down through the harem screens of their balconies, seemed improbable. The glassy air on the Altiplano of upland Peru, on the glaciers of Bolivia, seemed as improbable as a myth, a dream, in this bright, matter-of-fact machine-driven world. The patter of the bare feet of the Quichuas and Aymaras on the frost-bound surface of the streets of Cuzco fell on his ear as some faery, puzzling, hardly credible sound. Goehrs felt at once that the Chileans were a race apart.

"What is their descent?" he asked himself. "Surely, too, from Spaniards who intermarried with Indian women?" But the Spaniards in Chile had been a convict settlement, not the flower of the nobility as in Peru, Ecuador, and Bolivia. Nor had the Indians in Chile been the cream of the Indian race as in Bolivia, Ecuador, and Peru, but an uncivilized, savage, predatory tribe, the Araucanians. A sort of South American Zulu, a kind of Patagonian Sioux. In Chile, therefore, there had been effected a fusion of two social types and races, both of which were of a patently warrior bent.

On December 28th, 1534, the Spanish officer Pedro de Valdivia had a conference with another man in Pizarro's banqueting-hall, the outcome of which was an agreement for the purpose of the conquest of Chile. The name of Chile, it is true, had not at that date been minted, but the conquest aimed at the territories that make up present-day Chile—a conquest that not even the Incas had wholly achieved.

Pedro de Valdivia was a man of thirty-nine years of age. He set out on this adventure with rather fewer followers than had Pizarro for the conquest of Peru—with 150 men and some thousand Indians. He set out with porters and priests as for an expedition against a Negro tribe. In his train he had one solitary woman, his mistress, Inez Suárez. Valdivia knew, geographically speaking, precious little of the venture on which he had embarked— just like Pizarro a little earlier. He did not know that the coastline of Chile was of such grotesque length, and he believed the Strait of Magellan to be considerably farther north than it really was. But he had the same zeal as Pizarro and as Almagro, as Balboa, and as Colón— and he had the same good luck.

The fighting with the Indians was fierce. But as early as 1541 Valdivia founded the capital of Santiago. He proclaimed himself Lieutenant-Governor of the "*muy ilustre*" Don Francisco Pizarro. During his lifetime the foundations of Valparaíso, La Serena, Valdivia, Villarrica, Imperial, of one or two forts, and Concepción were laid. It is not difficult to visualize the size of the populations of these towns when it is borne in mind that 150 soldiers set out on the expedition and that, later on, 200 Peruvian reinforcements joined them. Eight years after its foundation, Santiago was a village with a population of 500.

Chile was carved up among these people like a stag's hide. It was carved up in strips of territory with, and strips without, Indians. No one was permitted to leave the country again for fear of its becoming depopulated. No one was allowed to dispatch uncensored letters abroad at pains of a fine of a thousand gold pesos and the lopping of his right hand, to prevent the repute of the colony, that wanted immigrants badly, from being injured. A German historian, A. Wilckens, records that fifty years after its foundation Santiago had 200 wretched huts, Concepción 76 houses, 36 of them of thatch, and that the status of a town was conferred on Castro when once it could boast of twelve thatched huts.

A woman's gown at that date cost three pesos, a pair of riding-boots the same sum, as did a leather jerkin. A short sword cost two pesos. It cost fifteen pesos to have a requiem mass read. A Spaniard's funeral cost twenty pesos, an Indian's six. One peso was the price of five sheep or one cow. So a mass cost fifteen cows or five pairs of riding-boots. A curious scale of values. An infantryman on the other hand is valued at one thousand pesos, a horse at as much as two.

The laws to keep Valdivia's gang of adventurers from scattering were severe. Any man found loitering about the highroad after dark was fined, any one initiating drunken orgies was flogged, fined, put in the stocks, and deprived of his weapons. An Indian injuring a horse had his hand cut off. In addition to that they colonized, in other words they despoiled the Indians of their land. It was annexed in the same business-like way and with the same enthusiasm as Pizarro and Balboa had annexed it in the name of "God and of the King," and there can be no doubt that the Spaniards, who could neither read nor write and who were the most unblushing scoundrels in Europe, were greatly and genuinely proud of their mission. This, probably, too, gave them their irresistible dash. They were murderers and saints at one and the same time.

" Pacificación y Población" (Pacification and Population). Destruction of the heathen, conversion and the settlement of the country. That was the same battle-cry as in Peru, the watchword of the kings, the popes, and the Inquisition, and it was carried into effect with unprecedented zeal. True, the situation in Chile was more difficult than it was in Peru. The Indians put up a fight and held out for centuries in the south. The Indians were almost continuously at war with the new masters of the country, the half-breeds of the intermarriage of the Spaniards and Indian women. In the course of the wars the Indians frequently burnt the towns and wiped the Spaniards out.

Valdivia, too, with his little force, fell in a battle in which the Indians proved the abler and more successful fighters. On January 10th, 1554, a horseman drew rein in the middle of Santiago. He had ridden up from Concepción in eleven days, and announced that Valdivia had fallen. The Araucanians appeared to be in a position to reconquer the whole of Chile. But the Spaniards held on although they were only a handful and although it happened when sometimes for two years in succession no Spanish ship touched the coast. . . . It was from these forbears, Spaniards and Indians, that to-day's Chilean race has derived.

Goehrs had another look at this tapeworm of a country, on the map lying on the balustrade of his hotel balcony.

He judged by eye its coastline to be as long as the distance from Stockholm to Baghdad. The narrow strip of coast lay squeezed in between the sea and the Cordilleras as Egypt is between its two deserts. Only the centre portion, the stretch between Valparaíso and Puerto Montt, the " Vale of Chile," was fertile. In the north Chile extended to the tropics, in the south as far as the glaciers overhanging the sea. In the north it was a desert with nitrates, iodine, and copper ; in the south it was virgin forest with lakes and volcanoes. Untilled country. An amazing hodge-podge.

This country had won its independence from the Spaniards a few years earlier than the majority of the South American States at the beginning of the nineteenth century, and had loaned its generals and fleet to the other States. It had plunged unhesitatingly into war with its neighbours and had conquered them. The war with Chile had cost Bolivia her coastline together with Antofagasta. The same war in the 'eighties of the past century had cost Peru, which plunged in to the aid of Bolivia, the provinces Chile annexed, the provinces which gave rise to that Tacna-Arica question by which Europe, that never felt quite sure where these places really were, was bored for decades until this matter, too, was disposed of by an amicable bargain in which Peru had, it is true, the worst of the deal.

This country, which hardly has any Indians left, but has an inborn capacity for navigation by air and sea, has the best army of South America to-day. And that with a population of hardly four and a half millions. For a century Chile has had a history made up of conflicts between its Parliaments and extraordinary figures by way of dictators. For some long time it has had a constant flow of a good type of immigrant from Germany, an influx that has almost left a hallmark on the south of the country. A German general, Körner, organized the forces of Parliament against the dictatorship of Balmaceda and beat him in 1891.

" The Chileans seem to like Germans," thought Goehrs. From the balustrade of his hotel he could see that the shipping company opposite had given itself the name of " Germania " by way of a recommendation, and he had just seen in the paper that a sports club which had not a single German member had adopted the same name. Childish as it was, it was gratifying.

After all, thought Goehrs, in spite of their long, unprotected coastline, the Chileans really never did declare war on us.

CHILEAN YUGOSLAVS

BUT Antofagasta had not only a German, it had a Yugoslav element as well. And Goehrs was going to be made aware of it. He was surprised at first to discover, while yet on the lounge of his hotel, where a good deal of the domestic life of its visitors was enacted, that the building opposite was styled " the Yugoslav Bank of Chile." He was still more surprised that the German Transatlantic Bank was lodged in a sort of annexe to this monumental erection.

Goehrs, however, did not allow this modest domicile to deter him from visiting this establishment for the purposes of cashing his traveller's cheques. For though they were traveller's cheques of the American Express, he was glad for a German bank in the first instance to have the scrap of profit on the rate of exchange these cheques earned in South America. But what was his reception ! The fact that a German had cropped up desirous of having his cheques cashed at a German bank met with resentment and distrust. The cashier's office did not open before ten, and Goehrs had to wait for several minutes. He was treated like a criminal, asked to produce his passport and papers, and snubbed by the young clerks, who obviously had nothing to do at all, for an unwelcome intruder—although his cheques, his passport, and his credentials were in order, and, to crown everything, his cheques were forgery proof. This German disillusionment upset him a little. But patience ! Just before going on board he suffered his Yugoslav defeat as well.

To reach Valparaíso, some 720 miles to the south from Antofagasta, you either had to take ship or travel by air. The day Goehrs proposed to travel, two boats left simultaneously, the *Oroya* of the English P.S.N.C., and the S.S. *Aconcagua* of the Chilean Compañía Sudamericana de Vapores. Goehrs chose the latter, a vessel of 8000 tons. Then he called for his hotel bill.

The hotel was built without windows on a gallery round a courtyard. The rooms only had doors, and were lit by skylights. Only a few rooms gave on to the street and the famous lounge. But the bedrooms on the ground floor did not even do that, but on to " salons " built out in front of them. Goehrs, who did not care a damn for the moth-eaten and dingy hangings of the smelly salon, had, on the night of his arrival, agreed on the price of a single room with the manager and the son of the proprietor. He had been given a room with a salon because no other was available, and he had agreed upon a price that seemed to him fair and, as in the East, each party had confirmed it by an oath. The manager had already left on the *Oroya* that morning because this promoted waiter thought too much of himself to travel by a Chilean vessel. And the proprietor's son seized this opportunity of the missing witness to double the price of the room. Nothing availed to induce him to desist from this brigandage, not even when Goehrs, who was alone in the office with him, made a quite unequivocal gesture with the palm of his hand. At this moment Goehrs for the first time saw the proprietor's name on the billhead. It was Ivan Razmitic. Goehrs remembered that a celebrated Yugoslav congress had, during the war, held its meetings in Antofagasta, that Chile was a huge reservoir for Serbian emigration, and that the richest mine-owner in Chile was a Yugoslav. All of these people had worked their way up the ladder in a short time. (Goehrs remembered the biggest mining magnate of Bolivia, Patino, who happened to be, by way of rare exception, a native, a Bolivian, who had not, it is true, been a crossing-sweeper in Oruro, as the story went, but at any rate as a small clerk had collected accounts from house to house, before he had hit on the notion that there might be ore here and there in the mountains.) In short, Goehrs appreciated that he was being robbed, not by a Chilean, but by a Yugoslav. And that this robbery was cleverly stage-managed, tactically well organized, and unscrupulously carried out, because Goehrs's boat was leaving in half an hour's time, and he either had to sacrifice his passage or pay.

So he paid. He paid for a room with a "salon" which he did not want and for which he was not by agreement chargeable; he paid for a dirty room without a lock to the door or glass in the window; he paid a price for a room that had never been aired and could never be, with a tin basin to wash in, a price he would not have been expected to pay for bed and bathroom in a first-class hotel in Europe.

Goehrs could not help laughing. He had always regarded the Yugoslavs as an efficient nation. He was laughing still when he went on board. As an old traveller he had never thought that it would be possible to catch him in such a simple booby trap.

To make up for it the *Aconcagua* was the more enjoyable. Goehrs suddenly felt in paradise on board, lapped in undeserved good fortune. After the cantonments of the Puna, the hutments in upper Peru and Bolivia, after his exhausting weeks of cold-weather campaigning in unheated rooms, the smoking, reading, and card rooms, the promenade decks, the pretty South American women, suddenly struck him as a fairyland. Everything as clean as a new pin. And the meals beat the monotonous bills of fare of an English liner.

" Efficient nation, the Chileans," he thought, leaning against the taffrail and viewing Antofagasta from the sea. And the sight took his breath away once more. For the Cordilleras came much closer to the sea than they had seemed to from the shore. An immense brownish grey rampart confronted him, a bastion of the mountains descending to the chafing blue sea. The Cordilleras stood on guard like an awe-inspiring, smoothly polished mound, as regular as though drawn off by a ruler above and below, like an almost flauntingly safe barricade of Nature. And on the tiny shore between this mountain range and the Pacific the Chileans had raised their town.

But Goehrs could hardly believe his eyes. These efficient Chilean folk had bedaubed the 1500 feet of the towering polished Cordilleran ramparts from top to bottom with advertisements in huge letters. Vast and hideous. And with it all, to no purpose. They were announcements of little cafés and of shops for photographic requisites—and these announcements in letters ninety feet long were only visible from the sea.

Quaint folk to have progressive notions of this sort. Half an hour later Antofagasta was only a beehive of lights overshadowed by the barricade of the Cordilleras, but they were well-drilled bees and the lights fell into line—like regiments.

Shortly before, several hundred pelicans had flown towards the boat in the dusk. With their huge wings and big heads they sped low over the surface of the water, scanning it like learned spectres as soon as the fish began to rise in the half-light. Goehrs could have watched them for hours. For months, wherever he had come across them on sea or on board ship, pelicans, owing to their paradoxical appearance, had exercised a particular fascination on him. They looked as if they had been predestined for a higher walk of bird life than just to catch fish. Goehrs could never make out how these clumsy birds, dropping like a stone into the water to spear a fish, managed to turn right round in doing so. The movement was a contradiction of logic and of the mechanics of falling and was undoubtedly uncommonly difficult. One minute the pelicans were flying away from him, plunging into the water, and the same instant were turning their beaks towards him again. However closely Goehrs might watch he could not discover how they did it, nor could he find an explanation for the reason of the right-about-turn trick. It was obviously part and parcel of the enjoyment of their evening meal, Goehrs finally decided with resignation.

LIFE on board the Chilean boat was charmingly boring and delightfully comfortable. He could have had both on board the British liner, too, but British boats were boring and stiff, while the Chilean liner was, in a pleasant way, happy-go-lucky. The *Aconcagua*, called after the highest mountain in the country, hailed from New York, and was one of the two big, handsome passenger ships Chile possessed. It was crammed full of children with their Indian, negroid, and Malay nurses. The vessel was full of dainty, young, porcelain Chilean women between the ages of twenty and twenty-five, who had four or six children apiece and were travelling without their husbands.

There were a few men on board, but they were in the suite of Señor Carlos Davila, a little undersized man, Chile's ambassador in Washington. On board every other ship of her class in the world, every one would have dressed for dinner. The South Americans, however, hate anything that looks like a dinner jacket or tails—at any rate those hailing from the West Coast do. Everything aboard was well done and in good style, but even the ladies did not dress in the evening. And after every one had assembled and ordered dinner, the senior steward and the members of the band sat down to dine in the saloon at the same time. That would not have done at all on board an English ship but, as things were, it was quite pleasant. And every one was charming to the children. All the stewards loved the children. They were striking-looking children and they called the tune. They fairly clung to the coat tails of the band, and, when the musicians were not playing on their instruments, they were playing with the children. And when the ambassador was not on shore and visiting parts of Chile he did not know, or dictating a report to his secretary on the promenade deck— and if he did not happen to be playing deck golf with the junior ship's officer—he was passionately fond of playing hide-and-seek with the children.

It was a cheerful, easy life, with excellent meals and only slightly torn bed linen.

During the past weeks Goehrs had seen silver mines and copper mines, nitrate oficinas and the borax lake ; he had visited María Elena and Calama and Potosí and Chacaltaya, Chuquicamata and Chanaral, Coquimbo and La Serena ; he had seen pears as big as cucumbers and oranges the size of pumpkins ; he knew the percentage of nitrates Chile contributed to the world's stock and the percentage of iodine Chile prepared for the world's market—huge figures—and he knew the millions of litres of wine it exported to Germany.

But what a lot of good it did him, and how pleasant it was, after all these grave and reverend matters, to be faring on board a floating nursery, *via* Valparaíso!

DIPLOMATIC SHUFFLEBOARD

THE ambassador who came from New York on board the *Aconcagua* had visited the nitrate oficinas all the way down from Antofagasta. Playing deck golf with Goehrs he discussed these oficinas and the hot and cold processes of nitrate production with him. The Chilean Government had just concluded a pooling arrangement with the owners of the big and smaller nitrate oficinas. Fifty per cent. of the shares were held by the Government, forty per cent. by the Americans, and ten per cent. by smaller holders. The Government had contributed the real estate to the pool and received from the Americans in return a round, agreed revenue in place of hitherto variable export duties. Payment for the first four years was as follows : $22,500,000 for the first year ; $20,000,000 for the second ; $17,000,000 for the third and fourth years. The ambassador, imparting this information, was highly pleased with this deal because it was sound business. " There is hardly any sound business," said he. " But by this deal the costs of production of nitrates are not only reduced, but the budget is stabilized as well."

" Excellent," said Goehrs. " What does the budget amount to ? "

" A hundred million dollars."

" If nitrates yield a fifth at most," suggested Goehrs, " you must have a lot of other resources."

" No doubt," said the ambassador, without enlarging on the subject, and drove his disc a good thirty yards in the direction of the fourth hole. Deck golf was played all round the promenade deck, nine holes out and home. The holes were rings of chalk. The ambassador had approached to within a foot of the fourth.

" Do you know what I have now discovered to be a fact in Washington, though I am quite unable to account for it ?

A pro-German tendency. All of a sudden a regular change of front."

Goehrs drove his disc but unfortunately missed the ambassador's, whereupon Davila reversed his club to push his disc on to the ring with its handle. He succeeded to a nicety.

"Exactly the same thing struck my colleagues in New York. We none of us had any explanation to offer for it. But the change of front is none the less a fact. The enthusiasm for everything French has passed away overnight. The Yankees are a far more sentimentally susceptible nation than people think. They do not, really, know much about politics and they have a very poor opinion of us diplomatists. When they hear the word ' ambassador ' mentioned, it suggests not a diplomat but the hotel to them."

The ambassador smiled, took a shot at Goehrs's disc, hurtled it into the scuppers, and with a gentle shove approached the fifth.

"What is your candid opinion of Mussolini ? " Davila inquired, after making sure that he was only half covering the fifth.

"I put the same question myself to Leguía in Lima not long ago."

"And what did he say ? "

Goehrs played his disc out of the scuppers with his handle.

"That such a modest man as he could not pass an opinion on so great a personality."

The ambassador shook with mirth at the idea of Leguía's modesty. " We have achieved the same ends in Chile as the Fascisti in Italy. And without having any Fascisti. Good government. Équipoise ! " (The ambassador was talking of the faction of General Ibañez, who had become President of Chile by a sort of bloodless military putsch. He had for the first time paid the *medio-pelos*—the people with moderately long hair, i.e., the military caste—who were looked down upon in Chile, decently, supplied them with motor cars, and promoted them to responsible offices. Carlos Davila was his ambassador. " Ask your compatriots whether I am telling the truth. The population is pro-German in Chile—I tell you frankly—we do not do anything to encourage it—but it is a fact. During the War we interned thirty-seven German ships in our harbours and did not declare war on Germany. Try to find another country

251

that would have resisted the temptation. . . . It's your turn. . . ."

That evening there was a farewell dinner.

The big saloon of the *Aconcagua* was draped with flags, and as a compliment to Goehrs the German naval flag was displayed. The children were allowed to have their supper in the dining-room that evening. The coloured electric lights, which normally were not used, were lit along the wainscoting. Every one wore a paper cap with plumes and aigrettes. There were tin trumpets in front of every grown-up. And all the children had rattles in their little hands. Whenever the band, playing for dear life, knocked off for a moment, the children with their rattles and trumpets fell in. The din was deafening.

The Chilean children were rather pale, not tan or darkish like the Bolivian and Peruvian; they were if anything a little sallow, like the Italians, and their eyes had a far-off Indian look. They began to throw paper streamers about. The dining-room soon looked like a gay paper tent. And as an accompaniment they shouted the ship's chanty. Every ship has its *canción*. The *Aconcagua's* canción was unusually peculiar. It was called " Las Pelotas de Carey ":

> *Las pelotas, las pelotas,*
> *Las pelotas de Carey.*
> *Es un baile muy de moda*
> *En Pekín y en Camaguey.*
>
> *Carelmapu, Camarico, Pailahuque,*
> *Chiguayante, Quilicura, Pitricufquen,*
> *Son de Chile, pueblos ricos, pintoresco*
> *Con olor a Yerba Buena y a Pequen.*
>
> *Las pelotas, las pelotas,*
> *Etc. . . .*

They shouted it as if nothing else in the world mattered except this song and they made their treble voices hoarse to make it go with a swing. Every family party had its own table. On Goehrs's left all the children of the Flores family of Arica were singing it. Their names were Carlos, Cleopatra, Aída, María, Oscar, César, Diana. On Goehrs's right sat the cherub choir of the Serrano family of Iquique. They were called Belarmino, Alicia, Alberto, Ricardo, Marializ, Ignacio, Hector. . . . All the heroes and all the saints had blessed these children's names and their song.

252

Before the dessert the ambassador with a high dunce's cap on his head passed Goehrs's table. " The revolution has broken out all right in Bolivia," he said, laying a telegram on the table. " Have your coffee with us in the bar afterwards ! " " With us " meant his charming wife and the foreign correspondent of the *Nación* of Santiago, with his wife, and Mr. Lee of whom no one knew anything.

" On the Argentine-Bolivian frontier," Goehrs read, " some forty men, led by the ex-secretary of embassy Hinojosa, have torn up the railway line at the frontier station La Quiaca, and, with the unemployed who joined up with them, have advanced on Tupiza." (Tupiza was a station in the interior of Bolivia in the direction of Uyuni, the junction of the Argentine-Bolivian and the Chile-Argentine railway systems, in the neighbourhood of the silver mines of Huanchaca.) " The rebels have destroyed the telegraph and telephone services, have looted, and have issued a communist manifesto, and in the course of it have left no doubt that they intend to have President Siles and General Kundt shot. The Bolivian Government has moved troops from Oruro and has ascertained that the banished ex-President Saavedra is the moving spirit of the rising."

Goehrs laid the telegram aside. It was of no importance. A communistic manifesto. . . . In Bolivia, where not a soul had a notion what socialism meant. Kundt would make short work of a ridiculous affair of that kind, Goehrs felt sure—provided the whole thing were not an astute red herring on the part of the Government.

Goehrs got up and went to the bar, passing through the length of the vessel, which rang with children's voices shouting " *Las pelotas.*"

VALPARAÍSO

ON the following morning the liner ran into a bay. In the bay rose a town like Genoa. As fragrant. As hilly. Valparaíso ! Goehrs left the vessel, from which the ambassador was just being escorted by thirty persons on the lines of a Roman triumph. Goehrs was not surprised, for Davila was the shrewdest brain in Ibañez's government and one of the men best qualified to mobilize American money for the benefit of Chile. On the other hand Goehrs was surprised when, although the Chilean exchanges was only worth a third of the Bolivian, on disembarking on the quay he found that he had to pay the porter, in accordance with a printed scale of charges, eighteen pence for every single one of his ten pieces of luggage. He considered that, even if a military Government had carried the day against the old families and looked for support from dock labourers, and consequently was bound to have a tenderness for porters, this Government was being too generous to dock labourers.

Valparaíso was rather a European town. A little depressing when once one was there. About 200,000 inhabitants. Tolerable shops. Goehrs had a lot of German friends in Chile. That same afternoon he drove out with a young man, who insisted on showing him the Sports Club, to Viña del Mar. Viña del Mar was the place where all the " best people " lived and at the same time the watering-place where the whole of South America of the West Coast were wont to forgather.

The Sports Club was really a unique institution. It was enclosed like a park by a ring fence. You drove in at the gates past the porter in livery with a certain sense of awe. And then you saw a racecourse as well as a succession of tennis courts, golf links, hockey matches for ladies, and people doing gymnastics—all in action at the same time.

" The whole show is a limited liability company," the shrewd little German explained. " The share for participating in all the sports costs 5000 pesos (half that in marks). For golf alone only 1000. For tennis only 300. Do you see that flock of sheep in the vacant space ? That is the dividend. I get mutton every year at Christmas time for my golf share. Neat, eh ? "

And he climbed into his Buick again and drove Goehrs along the beach to Con-Con. The doubling of a word signifies the plural in Indian. The road to the extreme limit of Valparaíso Bay was very good in some parts and very bad in others, which meant that in patches the road had not been made at all.

" Funds ran short here every time," said the little German sarcastically at these patches. " But the road in which pretty well three million pesos have been sunk will have to be finished off by the unemployed. The unemployed are very dangerous everywhere."

" I thought General Ibañez's Government was as stable as a rock," said Goehrs.

" As long as it can go on paying the high salaries for the officers, it is. The officers' caste is in clover. You can see that by the market there is in motor cars. What officer in the past would have dreamed of driving about in his own car ? As long as the strong men's Government is in funds, it's got its supporters: if it hasn't any, well, it goes bust."

Valparaíso was, after the capital, the biggest city of Chile and it was of especial importance as the port of Santiago. The road along the seashore was fascinating. After a drive of some twelve miles, a single royal palm suddenly rose on the beach. This was where the Aconcagua River flowed into the sea, for it was not only the name of a ship ; there were a mountain, a river, and a province all bearing the same name. They drove along the river far into the country. Thatched huts, grazing land, palms, and ponds. A blend of Sussex and Holland—on the shores of the Pacific. The cattle had coats as silky as catskins. Towards evening they were back again on the beach of Viña del Mar.

" Now look out," said the little man, " the next bend is called Miramar."

Four hundred handsome, smart cars were drawn up across the road behind a chalk line bisecting the road, with their bonnets towards the sea—like horses aligned for review. In most of the cars well turned out, long-legged girls were sitting or lounging, many of them quite fair. They were smoking cigarettes with amazing aplomb—painted Madonnas with an open-air breeziness. They were all dressed with an eye to Paris fashions and with a suggestion of the sporting touch. And they were not in the least chary of making very merry at the expense of the German and English ladies strolling past, a reckless, provocative, and handsome crowd.

" What are all these cars doing here ? " asked Goehrs.

" They are watching the sunset," said the little man. The majority of the ladies were in fact gazing fixedly out to sea, seeming lost in thought.

Goehrs laughed. He was not at all sure whether the performance were a sort of impudent romanticism or a freak of sentimental vogue. How could one tell what was going on in the heads of these conceited, pretty girls who, for all the Indio blood in their veins, looked down on English and Dutch women as too underbred to associate with them.

" Very clever girls," thought Goehrs. " Very clever, in view of the fact that their forbears were a convict settlement."

ONE day Goehrs had taken the little funicular railway up one of the hills of Valparaíso. For Valparaíso only consists of the width of a few streets filched from the sea with an effort—and for the rest, of hills crowding down to the beach. And these hills were very steep. All day and every day the funiculars were travelling up and down these hills because it would be madness to climb such steep slopes on foot. On the hilltops little terraces were laid out among the houses, and any one who cared to could leave his house at any moment to enjoy a gorgeous view of the Bay of Valparaíso.

"Is there really any anti-Semitic feeling in Chile?" Goehrs asked the little German, although there was not the least occasion for the question.

"They don't worry about anti-Semitism—they simply don't understand what it's all about," said the little man. "Anti-Semitism had first of all to be elaborately expounded to the Chileans by Germans."

Goehrs knew that, despite the labours of its official representative, the Germany colony, numbering about four thousand, was at daggers drawn on the question of the flag. The feuds, as in other South American countries on the West Coast, had assumed proportions it was difficult to realize even in Germany. It had proved impossible to give a reception for either the ex-Chancellor Luther, or the former head of the Defence Force, General Heye, at the German Club on the occasion of their visits to South America, because, twelve years after the Treaty of Versailles, they had not yet amicably settled the flag dispute in Valparaíso. The colony had on one occasion addressed itself to Stresemann to get a lead from him. "Only the man who stands by his present colours abroad," Stresemann had wired back, "is worthy of being a German."

"I can understand that Germans who have built up their prosperity in Chile under the black, white, and red flag do not want to scrap their old colours," said Goehrs. "And Stresemann's telegram has no doubt induced them to respect the flag of the Republic, whether they like it or not."

"Not a bit of it," said the little man. "Even in the capital, Santiago, the German Club has offered as its extreme concession that it might fly the commercial flag with the republican canton on official occasions. Twelve years after Versailles."

They went down in the funicular again.

" In the old days," said Goehrs, " England was the strong man in Chile, was it not ? "

" Yes," said the little man, " but England is dropping out of South America everywhere nowadays—even in Argentina. England has no money left and has its hands full with its own colonies and dominions. England is taking a step to the rear wherever it comes into contact with the Yankees. The Yankees are the only people with money to lend and, when they do lend it, they know why they are doing it and what they want for it. The American banks have instructions to incur substantial losses every year, only to remain in business. And in this way the Yankees are scooping out the whole of South America. It is a regular system of economic colonization—and any one who knows the Yankees, knows that this colonization by cash is far more formidable than the English methods which tackled it with rifles. That's the reason why all Chileans without exception hate all foreigners—because all foreigners are people who are making money in Chile and taking it out of the country and have all the natural resources of Chile in pawn. Don't you allow yourself to be hoodwinked by yarns about pro-German feeling. The Chileans' pro-German feeling probably is there right enough, but it's a sentiment not a fact. The only fact is that Chile hates foreigners and is bound to hate them, because its economic necessities make it inevitable."

SANTIAGO

IN Santiago, Goehrs at length reassured himself that there was such a thing as rain. And it was on a rainy morning that, after being looted and despoiled of his money in staggering fashion by a baffling organization of hotel boys and porters—by porters and taxi-drivers—and then by more porters and more hotel boys, and finally by railway guards and porters—that he reached Santiago. Santiago, the capital of Chile, the fourth biggest city of South America, had a population of from six to seven hundred thousand inhabitants. Its site was such that Valparaíso was really its port, and it was setting out to devour its own port.

Goehrs travelled in a comfortable railway carriage through an attractive landscape of woods, rivers, meadows, grazing cattle, galloping horsemen—not very different from, say, the country between Salzburg and Trieste. Charming but not very novel. And no Indians. In the train, Goehrs read the twenty-eight huge pages of the *Nación*, the biggest Chilean newspaper. It was a very political organ because it was the mouthpiece of the Government's policy—after the Government had bought out its former proprietor, or rather had banished him, which amounted to the same thing. On the front page of this important political organ, Goehrs saw five uncommonly pretty girls' heads, almost life-size. That and nothing more on the whole page. A few lines of print informed Goehrs that these five most attractive débutantes were going to be introduced into society that very day— that is to say, they would thenceforward go out to balls ; which they previously had not done. The first of the damsels, Señorita Blanca Eyzaguirre Lyon was, in honour of the occasion, giving a party of four hundred at the Club Hípico, and the four other girls had accepted invitations to it. On the margin of this page of the *Nación* was a note to the effect that at five o'clock in the afternoon there was a tea-party at the Savoy Hotel as on every other day, and that yesterday among other guests present were the Señoritas (about fifty names followed) and, in conclusion, that at six o'clock that day about twenty friends (mentioned by name) of a Señor Luis Herrera Cortínez were giving him a little entertainment in honour of his birthday. Goehrs received the information of the social life of Santiago with all the keener interest because he appreciated that kindred news-papers of the world would be giving voice to the troubles of the nation in similar prominent positions. The Government organ of Santiago substituted for this the portraits of attrac-tive Dianas about to enter the social circles of the nation. Delightful, thought Goehrs, but has Chile no other pre-occupations ?

In Santiago, Goehrs reached a really big city, the main area of which was occupied by village purlieus, a city whose principal business streets were gaudily illuminated by blue, red, and yellow sky signs. At the end of these streets of flashlight advertisements rose pink-tinted walls of an immense height—the snowfields of the Cordilleras that seemed to be draped like fantastic curtains behind them.

Goehrs's car pulled up in the middle of the main street, which was lamentably narrow. Thirty cars behind it hooted in wrath. Three boys dodged like fencers in and out among the flitting cars to drag his luggage from the middle of the main street into the hotel. Amid the strident din of protest-ing cars piling up behind him, Goehrs made his way to the

Savoy through the rigid rampart of taxis, parked along the pavement. But he did not reach the hotel as quickly as all that. He did not succeed in crossing the pavement. For the pavement was hedged by a double row of young people all standing with their backs to him. And between this double row of young men, the girls of Santiago strolled the whole length of the street in couples, tightly wedged together owing to the narrowness of the pavement. And the young men, dazzled by the passing vision of so much female loveliness, refused to budge for Goehrs. It was only after breaking through this cordon that he reached the Savoy. But the hotel was so small and its hall so tiny that the ladies of society of whom he had already read were almost crowded out of it to take their tea in the street or at any rate at the desk of the reception office. After Goehrs had at length negotiated this obstacle and had secured the number of his room, a chain of twenty youths wound in single file round all the tables out of the tiny bar in the corner into the hall.

"Ah," reflected Goehrs, "Señor Luis Herrera Cortínez and his friends, who have been entertaining him to celebrate his birthday." He looked at the clock. It was half-past six. The festivities could not have lasted longer than a couple of whiskies and sodas. From six to half-past, thought Goehrs, and it had occupied the most prominent position in the *Nación*.

"A little shoddy," thought Goehrs, as he studied Señor Luis Herrera Cortínez's oiled and curled friends. The ladies at the tea-tables, on the other hand, were very well turned out. Their complexions were the height of fashion and so were their silver-fox furs. They were smart, supercilious, and very pretty. Goehrs, one is sorry to say, enjoyed this thoroughly. It was such a long time since he had been in a well-found hotel with central heating, and so long since he had seen these bewitching, expensive creatures with the features of painted Cleopatras and that expression of coy aggressiveness that young girls affected that season.

THE CHILEAN CORDILLERAS

GOEHRS had driven out from Santiago by car for some miles into the Chilean Cordilleras, and then had walked on with a couple of German friends. He had reached a corral enclosed behind a circular wall, in which untamed mules were just being broken in. The mules were racing madly round in a circle, and four men with ropes were standing in the centre and fetching them out one after the other by lassoing the animals round their forelegs and throwing them with a jerk. As soon as the animal was on its feet again, it was again spilled, until it was so worn out that it behaved itself. Then one of the cowboys would mount the beast and ride it out of the corral. Tall eucalyptus trees towered above the corral and snowclad mountains above the eucalyptus trees.

Goehrs and his friends climbed a hill lying in a valley surrounded by many Cordillera ranges. A quarter of an hour later a dog joined them and proposed to dispose of the remnants of their lunch on the summit, a bulldog with the head of a toad and the eyes of an honest woman. They climbed through the scrub and for two hours inhaled the strangely intoxicating aroma of its undergrowth, a blend of salt sea, vanilla, jasmine and shellfish. Just as in Corsica. When the three men reached the top, they divested themselves of their dripping shirts and sat down in the sunlight of a Chilean winter. Facing them rose a pretty mountain, about 11,000 feet in height. Where the divinely fragrant scrub stopped short, the snowline began. Beyond it rose a yet loftier mountain. And from a snowfield, veiled in gleaming, translucent haze, the Aconcagua, 22,800 feet high.

Goehrs looked down on the maze of the valleys of Chile as you look down from the Arc de Triomphe in Paris on the streets radiating from it. The mountains of Chile were not as shiny, not as unreal, not as fretted as those of Peru and Bolivia, but majestic, and spacious and deep. . . . More deeply echeloned in more sublime symmetry than any part of Switzerland. The valleys were very varied. One might be as misty as the North Sea. Another full of blazing sunshine. Yet a third as chock-full of murk as if a blasting charge had just been fired. Many valleys leading down to the plain of Santiago ran into a barrier of silver foam out of which many triangles rose, triangles of mountain peaks piercing the haze like sharks' fins.

" Jolly to be hiking again," said Goehrs, bringing his hand down on his bare chest.

" The Chileans are fond of saying that Germans and dogs go about on foot," said one of the Germans, and gave the dog a chicken bone. " You'll never meet a Chilean on foot in the hills and are safe in addressing any man you may meet here in German. It's sure to be one of the thirty thousand domiciled in Chile. It's funny with what contempt the

Chileans look down on pedestrians. Englishmen, if they do walk, are at any rate playing golf. But there are fewer Englishmen every year. Their big firms are going, and the English are going with them. They are retiring, business keeps on growing worse, and I would not give a peso for the future of South America."

" The Chileans are going smash, too," said the other and, in his turn, gave the dog a chicken bone. " The old Creole families keep on growing more impoverished and more standoffish and more exclusive. And the women keep on growing smarter and prettier, and no one gets any fun out of it."

" Pity ! " said Goehrs amused. " But what do you mean. . . ? "

" They are too chaste," said the other, " although to judge from the way in which they sit a horse and wave their legs about in the Savoy you might think the reverse. As a matter of fact no one has any fun with them unless he marries them. No one has any fun with them for one thing because they think too much of themselves even to fall in love, and for another, because this is after all still a colonial country. A woman still commands a big price. In the beginning, of course, there were no women here at all, only Indians—and that sort of atmosphere lasts. Woman keeps up her price, but she has to be careful that her market value does not depreciate. The girls even at long entertainments don't touch alcohol for fear of anything untoward happening because, if anything should happen, not a soul will marry her. To make up for it, they dance very alluringly at parties and turn the heads of their fiancés and friends—but they keep their price up.

" That's why the brothels of Santiago used to be so famous and numerous and attractive as no others in the world. True, thanks to them, eighty per cent. of the population was diseased, but people do not make much of a fuss about that out here. . . . No, I'm not trying to be sarcastic. The mentality of the race happens to be averse from taking these matters very seriously. A Yankee chief of police, who once took charge, prohibited the brothels one fine day with the result that everything went on as heretofore except that the police force had to be doubled on account of the danger and the bribery. The prohibition was cancelled in due course, but the old times are over. The youngsters are not making enough money nowadays to be able to spend any. The gay times are over for good and for all. Good Lord ! it was a life, too, when at the time of the big boom in nitrates there were even Chinese brothels in Antofagasta, and the engineers who came in from the desert oficinas to Antofagasta every few months on three days' leave used to ride their horses into the houses of the pretty Chinese women. There were high jinks in the oficinas, too, in those days, and the lads, even in their desert exile, had a bit of fun out of life. All drinks, for example, were free, and the oficinas consequently had plenty of visitors. Three years ago it was only beer that was to be had for the asking— and now there's nothing. No doubt hard times promote morality, but it does not make this infernal life overseas any gayer.

"Now . . . do you expect me to believe that these Chilean girls, who sit in the hotel bars drinking cocktails all day long, live the lives of cloistered nuns ? You only have to look at them . . ."

"There's really nothing in that," the second German interrupted as he donned his dried shirt. "The young people of Santiago cannot even meet anywhere, they're kept under perpetual supervision. There was a scandal two years ago. After some entertainment or other, a party of boys and girls drove out into the country and had an orgy including alcohol in some obscure hostelry. Mine host had a peep through the keyhole and to his consternation discovered that the girls were members of the Chilean aristocracy, that is to say that they were wealthy girls, whose photographs appear in the newspapers like those of film stars at home. Mine host rushed straightway to the telephone and rang up their fathers, who came out at once. After some short altercations, four marriages were celebrated forthwith. The two remaining boys, who did not want to marry, fled to Argentina exactly like political offenders. But that sort of thing only comes off once and then only among Chileans themselves. . . . A European never succeeds in having a liaison with a Chilean woman. In fact, even to be invited to their houses is almost out of the question."

"Invitations . . . that wouldn't worry me," said the other, "and I don't care a damn what Chileans do or leave undone as among themselves . . . what worries me is what is going to happen to me. I haven't any money to allow me to marry and brothels aren't to my taste. I get in a pretty rotten state in the course of time. And even if I could marry, I wouldn't marry a Chilean, for these marriages between Europeans and Chileans never turn out well."

CHILEAN GAUCHOS.

They had all three resumed their shirts and made ready to descend through the haze of the scrub. Goehrs, it is true, was far from taking all his young companions had told him without a grain of salt. The Aconcagua had drawn a light cloud round its crest. The dog, having disposed of nearly two chickens, trotted off sleepily and well content in front of them. From one of the valleys, just as if it had been expelled out of a trapdoor, a column of fog rose, filled it to overflowing, rose higher, and trailed up the side of the precipice.

" Pity that you probably won't be able to get to South Chile," said one of them. " It's raining cats and dogs down there now ; you'd see nothing except rain and all the country between the lakes is waterlogged. It is one of the prettiest landscapes in the world. Lakes with volcanoes, volcanoes with lakes—quite German. The houses, the towns, the farms, the habits—all German. Down there you can really see how the German spirit can inform and mould things once the German leaven be given time to work, and if it be introduced in propitious conditions. Just imagine, even the Indians down there are learning to speak German instead of Spanish."

" Quite right," agreed the other, " but it doesn't do to attach too much importance to these symptoms. As a matter of fact, Germans, at any rate in the towns, surrender their German nationality damned fast. In the second generation they become Chileans and talk Spanish. The exceptions are, although people are fond of quoting them, by no means the rule."

The descent was more difficult than the ascent, for there was hardly anything that could be called a path, and they were all glad to be standing close in front of the corral wall again. The gauchos had by this time mounted their horses and were picking out the mules from the saddle. Half the animals that had been in the corral were broken in now. But the rest were still raging round in a circle, and every now and then came the thud of a body on the ground as one or other of them was flung by the lasso. The wall of fog in front of them flowed down like a cascade over the low hill triangles in the plain of Santiago. But behind them the snowy peaks of the Cordilleras rose red and clear-cut against the sky.

On the way back to Santiago, which took hours, the car pulled up five times in the dark. A car was always at a standstill in the road on these occasions and the two

Germans always inquired anxiously whether they could be of any service. This attentiveness struck Goehrs as a little overdone. The people, he suggested, could surely signal if they wanted assistance.

"No, no," said the German. "I must pull up and inquire. That is the least the courtesy of the road demands here. If I were to fail to do it, the people would report the number of my car to my club, and I should forfeit my reputation for being a decent fellow."

A CHILEAN COUNTRY MANSION

GOEHRS drove with a young Chilean of the name of Vicuña Ossa to an old estate which in its time had been as big as the properties of the first Spaniards were wont to be. That is to say, it had at given breadth extended from the sea to the Cordilleras, straight across the whole of Chile. At first these estates had held their own. But in time they had dwindled ; so, too, the estate to which Goehrs was on a visit. The family, in the second half of the nineteenth century, had, as was customary at the time, lived in Paris for many years. And the property had now become a wine-growing estate, the vineyards of which did not extend up the hillsides, but, as was usual here, were laid out over the flat ground between the Cordilleras. It was still a big property and one of the biggest wine-growing estates, with a yield of 250,000 litres a year.

The mansion stood in a park, a one-storey building with two wings, with a colonnade in front of the portico and two classical friezes. The park was old with the delightful scent characteristic of old gardens, beguiling and melancholy. Eucalyptus trees to the height of 195 feet, astonishingly slender trees, beside araucarias almost equally tall and in between palm trees and roses. A lake and yew hedges. Busts of Diana and Ceres stood on the lawn, of the nymph veiling herself and of the nymph in flight, and the statues of nude handsome men, aiming their bows into the shrubbery.

Away from the house was stabling for racehorses ; facing it pergolas and fragrant flower-beds. In the centre of the terrace stood a Chinese tea-house, where Goehrs was taking tea. He looked out across the park and the pond and between the eucalyptus and the palm trees on to the gold background of the plain, which in its turn ran out into the white wall of the Cordilleras. A prospect at once tropical and arctic, bearing witness to the subtle refinement of the tastes of the inmates of the mansion.

But where were these people ? Goehrs had noted that the park was neglected, that the stables stood empty and were in bad repair, that the rooms were untenanted, and that the most recent French pictures to be hung in the drawing-rooms were portraits of beautiful women in the modes of 1890.

" Your people are in Paris, I suppose ? " he asked the young Chilean.

" They are living in Santiago just now," the latter answered, and finished his tea.

The estate was half an hour's run by car from Santiago. There were no plays nor concerts in Santiago and hardly any entertaining of families among themselves. What could induce the family to live in town instead of in this attractive mansion ?

" It is too boring out here."

Goehrs found a suspicion he had entertained for some time confirmed again ; it was that the Chileans manifestly had no taste for nature. What had become of their ancestors' taste for the amenities in general that had at any rate schooled nature to downright sensuous luxuriance round their dwelling-places ?

The young Chilean, too, seemed to be relieved when they were seated in the car to return to Santiago. They arrived just in time to dine at the Union Club. Ladies and gentlemen sat in a little separate room. The club house was for the use of men only and women had only recently secured their unobtrusive admission to this annexe to the dining-room. As a rule ladies did not go out at night, and the men, who in consequence did not have their evening meal served until a very late hour, were tardy about turning up at the club. But wherever the women did appear, they were smart and unusually full of charm of manner—even the plain ones carried themselves remarkably well. Goehrs remembered having seen a bewitching bevy of beautiful women who moved well at the races. And the racecourse of Santiago was really a setting the ordeal of which only the most highly qualified could stand—the racecourse with its big grandstand, its green lawn, and for its immediate background the snow-capped Cordilleras, so close as to seem not half a mile away.

" I can't imagine," said Goehrs in the bar, " these pretty,

lively, and knowledgable young women living such retired lives as every one tells me they do."

" But who told you anything of the kind ? " asked the young Chilean in amazement. " Things are, apart from one or two domestic customs, not the least different from what they are in polite society in Europe. Except that in our case, civilization as a whole developed a little rapidly. In 1910 not a lady in Santiago had yet worn a hat, and half Santiago was still open country. But nowadays . . . well, nowadays," he added smiling, " every one is wearing a hat and does everything that conforms with the wearing of hats."

" UNFORTUNATELY . . ."

ON the following evening Goehrs went with young Vicuña Ossa to the La Bahía restaurant to eat some sea-food that were particularly luscious and popular in Chile. On the way they were held up by a half-frantic crowd pouring out of a picture theatre into the open. The crowd of some three hundred had misinterpreted some noise and thought an earthquake was in the offing. Every one in Valparaíso was suffering from a neurosis as from a nightmare that the whole town might collapse—as indeed had happened before—and earthquakes were of frequent occurrence. The people were continuously in the state of nerves that Goehrs had seen during the War in the case of towns over which enemy aeroplanes appeared every day.

On the other hand, the men were unusually reckless and behaved as if life were of no account. In the nitrate mines they made bets on who would hold a blasting charge with a burning fuse longest, or, as in Santiago, a young man would jump from a balcony only because some one dared him to do it, and break both his legs in consequence. This mixture of virile daring and cynicism was always a puzzle to Goehrs. There was one thing, assuming that he had got the hang of it aright, he never understood. On ceremonial occasions, after the usual " *Viva Chile !* " they used to shout " *Mierda !* " This strange word was probably an abbreviation for "*Mi hermosa patria,*" that represented a long fanatical panegyric of Chile, but the word " *mierda* " in slang was nothing other than the famous expression General Cambronne used in a sense in which no man of good breeding would use it. Goehrs came across a lot of incompatibilities of this kind among the Chileans.

La Bahía was one of the few restaurants there were in Chile. There was a soup with choros, mussels as big as your hand which you had to eat roasted with a knife and fork. There were full-flavoured fresh- and salt-water crayfish of a delicious aroma, and little oysters served in wooden vessels. There were black, sweetish crabs, jaivas, and baked mussels, ostiones, that had a big red tongue and tasted like lobster. And finally there were the finest lobsters in the world. These came from Juan Fernández Island, a day's run by boat off the coast. It was there that the prototype of Robinson Crusoe had sojourned in the guise of a deserter. But the author who made Robinson Crusoe one of the most famous figures in literature subsequently transferred the scene to the West Indies. But this did not deter the great liners on a round-the-world trip, stopping off at Juan Fernández, and their English passengers left hundreds of visiting-cards there every year in honour of their great compatriot. The lobsters from this island were so juicy and aromatic that Goehrs persuaded himself he had never tasted lobster before. Later on he noticed that the express across the Cordilleras to Buenos Aires reserved a special compartment for the beast— an honour not even accorded to crowned heads on their travels. Yet the lobsters are not even mentioned in the programme of the three things no man must miss on a visit to Chile. First, the Cueca, a dance with a pocket handkerchief. Secondly, chicha, that awful Indian fusel oil made of corn. And thirdly, the Chilean damsel herself, the most risky experiment of all, for Chile has for a long time held the record for syphilis.

" And yet another record," said Vicuña Ossa, bending his sleek black head and handsome sallow face over the table with an air of mystery. " For a time it had the biggest turnover for champagne."

" For all that, the race is strong," said Goehrs. " It must be the strongest race in South America."

" Yes," agreed Vicuña Ossa, " a docker of Valparaíso port on one occasion beat the world's champion Sharkey."

" So the Indian strain seems to have been a success here by way of a change," said Goehrs.

The young Chilean shrugged his shoulders and assumed a frigid look.

" Strain ? . . . The cross was very slight and a very long time ago." (Like all Chileans, he claimed to be pure white.) " I consider the Indians to be a wretched race. When he conquered Chile, Valdivia fortunately massacred so many of them that there are only a few of them surviving in the south." (He calmly ignored several centuries of war.) "Valdivia unfortunately only made one big mistake," he said slowly.

"What was the mistake he made, señor?"

"Unfortunately he did not kill them all off."

General Ahumada's Plans

WHEN Goehrs called on him General Ahumada was standing with the *Mercurio* in one hand and a cigarette in the other in the front garden of his villa in Santiago. He was wearing a dark coat and striped trousers. His tanned complexion, his grey hair, and eyeglasses were all of a piece. In European eyes he looked the typical head of a civil service department. But the general was a genuine general, for in Chile the title of general is not a complimentary soubriquet as in Venezuela; it really stood for high and earned military promotion.

"Good morning."

"Good morning."

The general had been military attaché in several countries, among others in Germany and Bolivia, and spoke several languages, including Japanese, and was a man of many interests, which included the value of real estate and immigration problems. He was the brain of the "Caja de Colonisación," a State institution to encourage immigration, to which General Ibañez's Government had allocated an annual grant of twenty million pesos for ten years. Goehrs was keenly interested in the settler problems, more especially in Chile where the climate so closely approximated that of Germany.

"Why do you put yourself to so much trouble in connexion with immigration?" asked Goehrs as they went into the house. "Most of the other countries of South America simply tell the immigrants to go to hell. But you, for a nation with a population of from four to five millions and with a budget rather severely strained, are spending very considerable sums on it."

"You have taken my answer out of my mouth," said the general, playing with his eyeglasses. "Please do take a chair. Chile has had a population of four millions for only a few decades, and we have got to populate the country properly—with the right sort of stuff."

" And you have a preference for Germans ? "

" I shall be very careful not to say so," said the general smiling. " What would the ambassadors and representatives of several other countries have to say to that ? However, if there is any element of the immigration that has left its hallmark and tradition in Chile, it has been the British and German immigration."

There had, of course, been a big influx of Italians and Yugoslavs, too. The Italians as a rule were in a small way of business, the Yugoslavs in big ones. But they were at bottom no more farmers than the British. The south of Chile, on the other hand, consisted of German peasant farmers, a type of immigrant that does not, it is true, fuse readily with the nation as a whole, but neither does it ever deteriorate to the level of the cross-bred Chilean cultivator. It is a conservative peasant type that has raised the standard of the Chilean peasantry as a whole.

" Very true," said the general, crossing his knees, " we only want the best we can get and we are prepared to spend money to get it. Nothing is too expensive for that purpose."

Goehrs did in fact know that Chile wanted a lot of new blood. He had seen something of the housing shortage of the poorer population and the consequently ghastly returns of the tuberculous, for whom there were no sanatoria. He had seen tenements in which the tenants had, out of sheer want, used the flooring and window frames for fuel. But in the country there were still vast building-sites and a lot of elbow-room for human beings. There were quantities of building-sites that were good enough and quantities, especially in the north, that only wanted irrigation to become good. And for this purpose the Chileans wanted sound, stable, qualified folk. That was at any rate sound common sense.

" The colonization funds are purchasing half a million sterling's worth of real estate every year, and we are carving the estates up. We are buying land in the north and irrigating it. We are buying land in the south and bringing it under cultivation. We are developing three categories of work to offer. Under category A we offer good land with a house, stabling, and fencing—as a going concern. Forty acres per head. For $10,000. Ten per cent. payable on occupation. The balance repayable over 33 years. . . . The other categories are rather more complicated. In the case of category B for example, there is no house, but more land and twenty per cent. down is required. All the land is within access of civilization. No virgin forest. We really are not asking for pioneers who first of all have to eradicate malaria and kill themselves in doing so, but we want to settle good land situated in the heart of Chile and not occupied yet."

" Sounds almost too good to be true," said Goehrs, with the Peruvian jungle colonies in his mind, and was not quite convinced. " But aren't there any difficulties about the sites ? " he asked suspiciously, for he had heard that the acquisition of real property in Chile often meant long-drawn legal proceedings, because there were always a number of owners of the property who all had " titles " to the same plot of land—dating back to the old days when they had first pegged out the country.

" I beg your pardon," said the general, slightly shocked that a question suggesting that there might be snags should be addressed to him. " The government surely conveys the land without any legal jokes. As regards ' titles,' any man who bought land without us earlier on ran the risk, of course, of burning his fingers, but all that has been stopped now. A separate Government department has been instituted for settling these matters, and before long there will be no more disputes about title in real estate. Is there any thing else I can do for you ? "

" I should like to ask you to let me see Peñaflor."

" At once ? " asked the general, eyeing the telephone receiver.

" Please."

" With pleasure."

A German Settlement

SANTIAGO was an unusually sprawling town and looked, in consequence of the nature of its site, like an interminable Innsbruck—like a beautiful mountainous snowscape in which houses happened to be scattered about. After a two hours' drive, Goehrs reached the neighbourhood of the German settlement Peñaflor. The country reminded him of the landscape between Heidelberg and Frankfort. Only some horsemen in dark ponchos gave the scene an exotic note. But when Goehrs at length saw little red-roofed villas in the German style peeping above the hedges on the blue-black ploughland, his heart beat a little faster. It really was a bit of Germany.

The villas of Peñaflor were not one-storeyed like those of Chile, nor thatched, but they were the facsimiles of villas in Hessen, in Baden, and in Swabia—and every villa stood in its own twenty-five acres and was manifestly pleased with itself.

Goehrs pulled up for a minute before he drove through the barbed-wire fence that enclosed the settlement. He was an enthusiastic disciple of the climatic theory, though not for the sake of the theory, but by dint of his own experiences. He had observed that people from one country will feel thoroughly at home for any length of time in any other country and really prosper only if the new climate corresponds with that of the place whence they hailed. Ecuador, Colombia, Peru, and Bolivia had therefore presented no conundrum to Goehrs so far as immigration was concerned. Germans in large numbers would never be able to feel at home and prosper there. After all, even dogs and poultry deteriorate there. But the climate and the landscape of Chile corresponded with that of Germany ; in fact the climate of Chile was more favourable because the winters were milder. It happened to be winter, and Goehrs was driving an open car. The weather at times had a nip and at night the thermometer went down to round about freezing-point, but in the day-time it was mild in the sun. The south of Chile had therefore attracted thousands of Germans in the course of centuries. There were at least 5000 living in Santiago alone. And they had become acclimatized. The German stamp imprinted on the landscape of Chile remained indelible. Here Germany had in fact not arrived too late as everywhere else in the world.

All on the alert, therefore, Goehrs drove through the barbed wire into the colony of Peñaflor. There was a house standing on its own field every few hundred yards. The colony had only been opened up by the Caja some three months previously. The thing as a whole looked like a latter-day model-village community, a garden suburb. Very slim almond and fruit tree saplings only three feet high skirted the main road—the leafy main avenue of the future.

Goehrs asked a man, ploughing a field on his right, for the administrator's office.

" Across the market place and to your left," said the man, shading his eyes with his hand and gazing in astonishment after the retreating car whence a voice unhesitatingly addressed him in German.

The " market place " was pathetic. It consisted of a

circular plot of trodden earth in the middle of the fields. There were as yet no buildings, no school, no town hall, no factory, nor even a club yet. Only flattened earth. But every one was already living so entirely in the vision of what was to be, that every one saw the market place as it was going to be. Exactly as every one saw and treated the track through the ploughland as a stately drive.

Goehrs found the administrator, a young man in riding-boots and a khaki shirt, in a little Ford, on a little hacienda far on the skyline. A young German who, born in Chile, had been educated in Bavaria, an alert, resolute young man, grave for his years. They drove in and out and round about the settlement. When they came back to the market place, the administrator again explained all that was going to be spent on that spot. Goehrs knew all about it.

Many of the settlers had sold their furniture in Germany. The Chilean consuls had picked the men and had made a good many mistakes in the advice they gave them. Thus many arrived without furniture, without the ten per cent. instalment, and without working capital. But the Caja proved helpful. It paid them a subsistence allowance, paid for their stock and the bulk of their furniture, and even paid for their hay. Goehrs was surprised. Was not that rather overdoing it ? What was at the back of it ? he asked him-self, for he was accustomed to see immigrants without money being treated like muck all the world over. But there was really nothing else at the back of it beyond the fact that the Chilean Government really did want to settle qualified men on the fruit farms within the vicinity of the capital—and had corrected the mistakes that had been made in setting about it.

There were not only peasants, but erstwhile intellectuals, land-owners and commercial men, among the settlers. They had bade farewell to Germany that had let them in for reconstruction and bankruptcy and had made up their minds to produce fruit and vegetables on their own farms within a few miles of Santiago for the rest of their lives. Was it a hard decision ? Goehrs looked out over the wide, sweet, clear landscape. Every now and then the rampart of the Cordilleras showed up like a marvel through the grey weather.

The car had stopped just in front of a plantation in which a gentleman in knickerbockers, a soft shirt, and a béret was at work. He introduced himself :

" Paul Puhlmann."

Paul Puhlmann was one of the intellectuals. A stoutly built man.

" Going on all right ? "

" Well—I have planted my peach trees and a few bush trees. That will give us some shade before long." He looked across at his five-roomed villa, standing fenced off by railings in the forty-acre field of ploughland.

" The factory will be ready next year. As you know, we are all working for the pot. Fruit. The factory is going to make it into jam. The vegetables are to be marketed direct in Santiago. Co-operation—well, there's no escaping that sort of thing any longer. But to make up for it, it's pleasant country."

" Does the colony pull together well ? "

" On the whole they do. A few had to be fired. You see, it is only possible with people who do not run counter to the common objective."

" Can you really ever pay off the sum the land has cost you ? "

" I think it is possible. In thirty-three years' time . . ."

All three men pursued the same train of thought. Thirty-three years . . . Goehrs realized that there was not a longer interval of time between a world that had had neither telephone nor electric light, nor steamships nor wireless, nor railway nor telegraphs, and an age that had them all, than between his grandfather's generation and his father's. What might not happen within the next thirty-three years ? How many governments ? How many systems ? Perhaps half the amount would be remitted . . . Perhaps they would let the settlers off altogether. There was really nothing to worry about.

Goehrs's glance scanned the fields where German men were guiding the plough and herding cattle on the soil of Chile. He felt happy about them. How different was their destiny from the destiny of the German emigrants who had been flung like manure over the coffee plantations of Brazil and about the forest colonies of Peru and Bolivia ! This colony was perhaps a particularly attractive show colony, but it was, after all, part and parcel of a genuine scheme of colonization, operating on the same principle.

The less exacting the antecedents of the settlers were, the more comfortable, Goehrs reflected, they were sure to feel in their five-roomed dwellings. But the more educated they were and imbued with Germany's culture and the amenities of European life, the harder must be the decision to spend

S

the rest of their lives irrevocably on a plot in a Chilean plain with a road frontage of 150 yards by 750 in depth.

" But don't you miss a good deal ? . . ." asked Goehrs hesitatingly. He was thinking of the theatre, concerts, friendly gatherings, the morning paper, all of them conditions of life to which Herr Puhlmann must have been accustomed and which he must have enjoyed. Herr Puhlmann, resting on his short spade, smiled—the smile of the disinherited who had faced it and got over giving up amenities that were without meaning to him or to his real life. But with a rapid glance Herr Puhlmann surveyed his land, only a quarter of which had been planted, and his trees that reached as high as his knee. His look had a new and real affection. He was already coming to love this land which he had only owned and tilled for three months.

" But have you not the sense of being in an alien country ? " asked Goehrs, who had caught this look and understood it.

" No. In Germany," replied Herr Puhlmann in a low voice.

BOLIVIA IN REVOLT

COLONEL VON KIESLING was one of the many German officers who, after the War, had taken service in other countries and was to a certain extent in Chile what Kundt was in Bolivia, except that his functions were not those of a commander, but of an adviser. He was an organizer, one of twenty others.

Kiesling had during the War seen service in Palestine, Syria, and Iraq and at the same time had conducted some excavations and written about them. For the past half-hour in the lounge of the Union Club he had been endeavouring to make Goehrs appreciate that there was no such thing as Moorish art. " The odds and ends of stalactites in Granada are only a bore," he insisted. " It all hails from Persia. So do the ideals of chivalry. I have discovered caves to the east of Baghdad with portraits of Oriental knights in full armour."

" In view of the torrid climate of those parts, not an innovation of any importance," said Goehrs. " Richard Cœur-de-Lion, at any rate, found his armour so heavy, considering the costumes of the day, that he was brought down with it."

" Nonsense ! " exclaimed the colonel. " The man succumbed to a regular attack of undeniable malaria. By the
way, Bolivia seems to me to be in full revolt."

" All I have heard points to the contrary. Hinojosa has
fled back across the Argentine frontier after publishing a
manifesto to the effect that, if he were to come into power,
he would in the first instance refuse to pay the Yankees the
debts due to them, and then would have Kundt and Siles
shot as lacking in intelligence."

" Contradicted ages ago," said Kiesling. " Quite a new
version. But authentic this time. I just got the telegram.
Oruro in the hands of the insurgents. Street-fighting in La
Paz. Eighty killed. The police had shot a student during a
demonstration, and his friends paraded the corpse about the
streets for hours. And then there was the devil to pay."

" Isn't that a bit exaggerated, too ? " asked Goehrs, who
remembered certain despatches from the same news agency's
correspondents in other kindred circumstances.

" No—it's a military putsch, starting in Oruro and
spreading to La Paz. If you doubt the newspaper men, read
the list of passengers arriving in Antofagasta by the last
train from Bolivia. If you study these lists, you can always
tell what's up. Rats leave a sinking ship. The train that
left Chile for Bolivia to-day was turned back at the frontier."

" I fancy Kundt is prepared for something of the kind,"
muttered Goehrs.

" I fancy so, too," agreed the colonel. " But Kundt is in
a very awkward political predicament. He is the representative of a Government that has come to grief completely—
and if a new Government should come along with a decent
programme and there ceases to be a Government to back
Kundt, he will have to order ' cease fire.' Of course, if Siles
had not resigned . . ."

Goehrs contrasted Kundt's position with Kiesling's.
Kiesling was a military official. An instructor pure and
simple. He had had to renounce his German nationality.
Everything was so thoroughly organized, so carefully
checked and counterchecked in Chile, that a foreigner, even
against his will and thrust into the limelight by circumstances, could never have attained such political and
personal power as Kundt had in Bolivia. That anything of
the kind was unthinkable was the main difference between
the two countries.

" The Bolivian soldiers are said to be good."

" Sure they are," said Kiesling. " The Chilean soldiers

are the strongest fellows in the world, with a dash of Indian blood. They can live on next to nothing and yet bring down a bull. One of them got Sharkey. . . . Oh ! I see you have heard that. Chile has, if not the biggest, the most efficient army in South America, 25,000 establishment strength. And 20,000 police. The Argentines have perhaps rather more. Look at the history of the South American wars ; wherever Chilean troops . . ."

At that moment, Goehrs saw a group of ladies and gentlemen passing him. In Chile, as on board the *Aconcagua*, no one likes dressing in the evening, and foreigners dining at the club did not dress for that reason. The Americans who had just passed, however, were in full dress and the ladies in low gowns, and they were all very noisy, very unobservant and very parrot-like. Goehrs noticed that all the Chileans followed this group with a peculiar strained look in their eyes. Goehrs had often seen this look following the Yankees. This look meant that the Chileans might very well have the best army, 25,000 strong, in South America— but that this army would not be worth two dollars if staked against American capital. And here through the Union Club, with its Chilean members in morning dress, passed in full evening dress, talking " Yankee " at the top of their voices, not any chance American party but the real rulers of the country—inconsiderate, without any adaptability, without any sense of it.

The Yankees, thought Goehrs, are in a fair way to becoming the best-hated nation in the world.

" In 1909 there were not four Americans in Santiago," said the colonel quietly. " How quickly conditions change. There are thousands of them now." He thrust his right hand in his broad belt, which he wore in French and American fashion in place of dirk or sword across his otherwise almost entirely German uniform.

" The navy is probably honeycombed by English instructors," suggested Goehrs.

" Yes," said the colonel. " You often meet with a lot of fair play at the hands of the English. Not long ago I came into touch with the British naval attaché. We had fought on opposite sides in the Dardanelles and swopped reminiscences. Bueno ! Three months later he turned up again with the unprinted manuscript of the British Government's official report of the campaign in the East, Vol. II. He requested me on behalf of the Government to look through the MS. before it was put into print with a view to determining whether it was unbiased enough. I looked it through and wrote ' admirably impartial.' It was not until then that the book was published. . . . Well, well, the army has German training and the navy English, and the two departments do not overlap, and that has its economic reasons, contracts from England, contracts from Germany. . . ."

" Unfortunately, the English are dropping out of South America," said Goehrs.

Kiesling got up. The guests for whom they were waiting had arrived, and they all went across to the dining-room. They took their seats there in the members' room, but heard the Americans talking in the adjoining room reserved for ladies. As the Chileans do not speak such pure Spanish as the Peruvians but clip it a good deal, the " Yankee " next door with its slowly chewed vowels sounded all the harsher.

The Union Club was a huge building. Although there was no night life in Santiago, and although most Chileans went to bed after their evening meal, and although bachelors of forty lived with their parents and continued to do so even when they were occupying big positions—in spite of all that, the Union had for a long time been the stronghold of men against a world of women. As until recently women were not admitted, the Union Club was the excuse and the pretext for every dissipation the Chilean spouse could and did perpetrate. The club at that time was the most exclusive in the world.

" Señor X. is playing chess and cannot be disturbed," the porter would say when the Señora rang up—and became a wealthy man for his pains. And Señor X. had his alibi.

Never again.

Ladies had now taken an entrance of their own, a lift, and a portion of the dining-room by assault. They were right, thought Goehrs, as he reviewed the tables of their Chilean husbands. There was very little difference at bottom between the Chilean husbands and the husbands in Lima, in the Balkans, or in the south of Italy. But the wives were on the average among the most beautiful and most charming women in the world.

THE TRAGEDY OF A GOVERNMENT

AFTER dinner the company drove out to the Cristóbal. That is a hill in Santiago round which the town had sprouted, although not very long ago it was not particularly easy to reach on horseback. From the top of the Cristóbal you looked down on Santiago and its lights at your feet, the vast city quite isolated in a vast plain which it broke with an incredible flood of light. The long streets trailed for miles beyond the city like comets until they ran out into other towns dimly luminous on the skyline. It looked as if Santiago had fallen into the sea like a meteor and was still shining brightly and clearly. Santiago nursed an ambition in common with many South American towns, to be not only well lit but superlatively well lit. It was a town that spent more money on lighting than any great city in Europe. There was something attractive and rather hectic in this luminousness.

The Government that spent fifteen millions of pesos on electric lighting was inspired by a feverish ambition to be clean and bright and to develop the country. It had a progressive programme that outbid all others. General Ibañez was admittedly a man with clean hands, but he was often compelled to change his team and he was fighting a heroic battle against the corruption that was once and for all innate in the political constitution of these colonial countries. Roads, railways, nitrates, public buildings, light, sanitation —an extraordinary effort. Goehrs had seen a square that was to be enlarged. Santiago was to have a big, handsome new square. The houses obstructing the site were to be pulled down and the houses for the purpose had already been earmarked. One of these still had its scaffolding round it ; it had only just been built. The scaffolding would now have to serve the purpose of demolishing it again. A scheme on really big lines and a grandly conceived object-lesson for a country with an intimidating budget.

And yet in the long run it was all going to drop into the lap of the Yankees.

Goehrs began to hunt for all the landmarks of Santiago he knew in the beautifully broad rays of light below him : the Alameda de las Delicias and the houses of his friends, the grandstand on the racecourse and the museum he was not allowed to enter because it was so full of cracks that in the event of sudden earthquake it was bound to collapse. Goehrs felt sure with every sense of assurance that the country was now being steered on a course that was designed to promote its advancement and that it was in the long run all useless as against the might of international capital-ism that was simply doing what it liked with the country. The Government was working for the good of Chile—by means of American money. The Government was working to advance Chile to the hegemony of South America and was working on behalf of an American colony. The Government was exhausting itself in converting Chile to a European civilized state at furious pace and was wearing itself out on behalf of the Yankees into whose possession it was all, sooner or later, bound to fall.

Goehrs felt this tragic destiny of a nation as keenly as he would have felt the tragic destiny of a family that was confronted by a similar fate. It was a new phase of tragedy not easy to grasp, but thrilling in its intensity.

ACROSS THE CORDILLERAS

GOEHRS would above all things have enjoyed seeing the southern extremity of Chile, but he got no farther than Valdivia. He did everything that doth become a man to see the south of Chile, but he did not see it for one very absurd reason. This reason can only be appreciated by people who have taken a car round the Bavarian Tyrol into Austria, or have arranged a tour through the heart of the English Lake country and have seen nothing of Ullswater and the fells, have throughout seen nothing but rain.

It was raining from above and from below, and the strips of country between the famous lakes of the Switzerland of Chile, which would have to be crossed by automobile and mule, were turned into an impenetrable swamp.

There lay the beautiful lakes—the Lago Llanquihue and the Lago Todos los Santos—and alongside of them rose the beautiful volcanoes, the volcano Calbuco and the Osorno—and Goehrs was well able to imagine how beautiful they were, pointed like the Misti and covered in snow with forests and clouds climbing their flanks, and little steamers crossing the lakes in the sunshine. And then he would have gone to the Argentine portion of this southern Switzerland and have crossed the Lago Nahuel Huapi, would have driven by car in a few hours from Bariloche to the station Kilometre X where he would have caught the train from Argentine Patagonia to Buenos Aires, forty-eight hours via Bahía Blanca.

It was a wash-out. It was raining.

He saw neither the lakes nor the volcanoes, but he was convinced he knew exactly what they looked like. He had seen so many mountains for months that he could get over it ; he skipped this chapter and set about crossing the Cordilleras by the Transandine Railway and cutting across the width of the South American continent.

It took thirty-six hours and it cost $150. But there was a snag.

The trains during the winter at times got stuck in the snowdrifts. There were people who had to wait for weeks to get from one side of the continent to the other. For that reason there had sometimes been desperate whites who had gone on board at Valparaíso, had sailed for three days to Antofagasta, had travelled for three days to La Paz and for another six days from La Paz to Buenos Aires because there had been such a heavy fall of snow in the Cordilleras that the train that only took thirty-six hours to do the journey could not get through. Even the Prince of Wales, who was accustomed to travel more smoothly and expeditiously than most mortals of this world, had been marooned for a week in Mendoza and even he had not succeeded in prevailing upon it to stop snowing.

This train left twice a week. The last train but one had been two days late and had been snowed up for two days. The last train had struck a patch that was entirely blocked, and its passengers had had to cover a mile or so on foot and carry their own luggage to boot. Goehrs, therefore, for the two days before he left, studied the heavens continuously to see whether they remained serene or whether a storm were piling up on the mountain tops.

The whole of Chile at this date went clean off its head about an airman who, in charge of the mail across the Cordilleras to Argentina, had crashed among the glaciers. He had, together with his mail bags, been written off as missing and forgotten, when he cropped up again. He had come down on a glacier, lost his rucksack, tumbled down a crevasse and had sacrificed his medicine chest. He had no compass, nothing to eat, was without snow goggles, was half starved and wholly blinded—yet after a week he turned up again to be the hero of South America between Chile and Argentina for another week.

Goehrs caught the train in Santiago, where it was the property of Chile as far as Los Andes, but then became the private property belonging to the Argentine and Chilean Transandine Railways. Snow began to lie at a height of 3000 feet. Snow was quite a different proposition here from what it was in Bolivia, where there were cornfields at altitudes of 12,000 feet. The train was electrically driven

INDIAN CHILD FROM THE CORDILLERA HIGHLAND.

and made its way a little timidly between two banks of snow to the right and left of it. It did not seem to have much pluck—nor had the passengers any to spare. But it was a train with a conscience ; it was only that things to the right and left of it kept on growing more and more insecure. Then the tunnels began. But they were for the most part tunnels of the kind that children make. Of wood and scraps of tin. On the right rose the wall of a steep rock. Above, sheds built of wood and roofing-paper to keep the snow off the rails. On the left there were occasionally holes in the shaky contraption—windows into nothingness or on to the snow barrier lying beyond. The train struggled on . . . through the sheds . . . under galvanized iron . . . in the end it was as if they were riding on a snow-plough. But the train did not give up.

Magnificent black and white mountains. On the left the Inca Lake, over 9000 feet. On the right, almost twice as high, the Cerro Juncal. The mountains crowded closer together, the ridges becoming like a dragon's back. Chimneys. Bridges. Then the station Los Caracoles. The station was a blockhouse. It stood above the masses of snow like a swimming-bath and, like a springboard over the water in a swimming-bath, a long, swaying wooden path ran across the snow to the railway lines. And proudly, for the last time, the Chilean flag fluttered above it.

A man in a leather jacket vaulted over the springboard, advanced to the shaft of the flagpole, and looked up at the flag. The colours were white and red. One quarter of the white field was blue enclosing a white star. The man raised his arm ; the train left the blockhouse and plunged into a long tunnel. In the middle of the tunnel it suddenly began to ring its bell in the darkness. That was the frontier. It ran through the middle of the tunnel. When Goehrs in his train crawled out into daylight again, he was in Argentina.

The name of the station at the exit of the tunnel was Las Cuevas. The Argentine flag was drooping from the station building. Blue, white, and blue. Below, a clock. Argentine time was forty-four minutes ahead of the Chilean.

Part V

CONCERNING ARGENTINA

ACROSS THE PAMPAS

AS he passed through the subterranean tube of the Cumbre Tunnel between Chile and Argentina, Goehrs had at the same time crossed the highest point of the trip. The Aconcagua with its full 22,800 feet came into view once more ; the mountain outlines became wilder ; on the right appeared the Tupungato that was a little lower than its big brother on the left—and then the track went downhill to an oasis, to the garden of the Cordilleras, to the wine-growing district of Mendoza, a green patch in the stony steppe.

Goehrs travelled through the rocky desert on the eastern ridge of the Cordilleras. It was as big as Germany. Then he passed through the pretty little town of Mendoza with its 70,000 inhabitants, many of them vintners, into the pampas country that was half again as big as Germany and yet was only a bit of Argentina. Argentina had almost a third the area of Europe. It was six times the size of Germany. It had a population of eleven million Argentinians, and they, in contradistinction to well-nigh all the other States in South America, were almost all white and for the most part immigrants. Argentina was a country extending 2300 miles from north to south, a distance from the North Cape of Norway to Sicily. Of its area of over a million square miles, a fourth made up the southern portion, barren Patagonia. To the west it ran up into the Cordilleras ; northwards it extended to the plain of the Gran Chaco, into which patrols occasionally rode but never came back—Indian territory. In the centre lay the grazing and grain country, its nucleus : the pampa.

Goehrs plunged into the pampa. Argentina became as flat as a board here. As though drawn with a ruler. The outlook grew balmy and green and clear. From the west eastwards it kept on growing brighter. Goehrs, who was not at heart a man who imagined he could only live in the mountains, thought this suddenly farspread horizon astonishingly refreshing. This clean plain struck him as enthralling.

In the provinces, on the slopes of the Cordilleras, Goehrs had seen *estancias* on which the cattle were still caught by *boleadoras*—lariats with heavy balls at their ends which were thrown so as to twist the rope round the beast's legs and so bring it down. He was now looking out on estancias where the milking was done by electricity. He saw gauchos as they are described in story-books and he saw modern cattle-guards. He watched the strange country dances and ate meat roasted in its skin on the camp-fire. Islands of tall trees rose continually above the flat plain. On every occasion there were houses on these islands, small houses, huge houses, houses for the accommodation of cowboys, houses furnished for the reception of house-parties of visitors. In between, the cattle were grazing for hundreds of miles all round. Here and there lay lakes for watering the cattle. Goehrs could not bring himself to take the masses of these beasts, or the peace and stillness brooding over the herds, the trees, the racing gauchos and the estancias, calmly and for granted. Goehrs had travelled from Panama to Valdivia, a huge distance from north to south, always in the company of the Cordilleras, always in the thick of the Cordilleras which invested these inspiriting expeditions with an ever-renewed sense of unity. He was now browsing along with the herds. Nature was calling a halt, and he had a notion that he was drawing breath more easily, more freely, more peacefully, and more restfully in this breathing-space of Nature.

As time went on, this restfulness went to his head a little. He kept on seeing millions of heads of cattle. Then came the confluence of the Paraná and the Uruguay Rivers and the spot where this new river became known as the La Plata, the River Plate, and was really as big as a lake even there.

There lay Buenos Aires.

Buenos Aires was the biggest city of South America. It had over two million inhabitants. It was the city that, as seen from the pampas, had co-ordinated and welded the whole of Argentina into one nation, and it was on the other hand, as seen from the Atlantic and from Europe, the city that had swallowed millions of immigrants in its monstrous jaws.

The whole of Argentina, from Patagonia to the plains

of the Chaco, from the provinces of mines and wine among the Cordilleras to the grain country in the east, was riveted to Buenos Aires.

Buenos Aires was not only politically a strange city. It had strange inhabitants, too.

THE PEOPLE OF BUENOS AIRES

GOEHRS, standing dazed and impatient amid the great wilderness of stone that was Buenos Aires, spent a whole day at the outset in searching for the Argentina he knew, its mountains and illimitable plains. He could not find it. Buenos Aires was quite other.

Something strange had occurred, too. The city was shrouded in a thick mist, and Goehrs, who, for the first time for many months, was plunged once more into a veritable metropolis, felt these chasms of buildings soaring away into the mist to be downright uncanny. Even Santiago had still kept touch with Nature, and Goehrs had, as a matter of fact, passed abruptly out of the medievalism of the West Coast into the purlieus of the skyscrapers of Buenos Aires. He was standing on a balcony in the seventh storey of the Plaza Hotel, which far exceeded his means (but he was inquiringly minded enough to be anxious to study the premier hotel of South America and its denizens), with a square of palm trees below and the sea on his right—everything in dim outline and faintly lit up by electrical sky signs.

Buenos Aires was the sixth biggest city in the world. Brand-new. As if made to order. Delivered ready for use. A wilderness of stone of which you could say anything except that it was not a wealthy city.

Goehrs drove about for hours delivering his letters of introduction, for what was a human being in such a city without letters of introduction ? For hours he saw nothing but small and big and very big palaces, handsome squares, big monuments, high towers to the palaces, and men-servants who came to the gates, flung them open, and then scurried back to the palaces. For several hours Goehrs laboured under the impression that the whole of Buenos Aires did in fact consist of nothing but palatial streets, interspersed by trees, of men-servants and motor cars. Many of the palatial streets were only opulent, others were Renaissance and many assumed the guise of Greek temples.

Not only frontages, but carried out right through in correct style. Overwhelmingly massive. And amazingly new.

The most diverting feature was the banking quarter in the City. Whole blocks here consisted of a single building. All styles had joined hands here to make the buildings huge and high. Many of these banks were quite ascetically austere in style. Others showed a slight leaning to the Renaissance. The Boston Bank, however, was triangular, but had a huge carved entrance like one of the church portals in Lima. The rest of its triangular bulk was smooth and naked like a bird that has been plucked bare except for a bunch of tail feathers left in the prominent position. They stood all huddled together like giraffes gone crazy in the murk of a city twitching with lights that did not seem in the least prepared for monsters of this sort.

The banks were only indulging in the usual competition of impressing a public, obviously trained to infer their capital resources from the monumental character of their premises.

Thus did Yankee frontages obtrude for the first time in an old colonial city, which was beginning to assume its third new aspect. Why not ? reflected Goehrs. The Argentinians, too, talked in an accent similar to that of the Yankees. They chewed their Spanish in exactly the same way as the Yankees chewed their English. To judge at any rate from the palaces and the smartly liveried commissionaires standing in front of them, Buenos Aires was bound to be a city in which, as in the United States, wealth was the standard by which everything was appraised.

In the afternoon of the second day that Goehrs was in Buenos Aires, one of the men to whom he had a letter of introduction called on him. Goehrs had a cup of tea with him and asked him some questions about another notable to whom he had an introduction.

" Don't fail to make this man's acquaintance," said his visitor, who had a name of repute in scientific circles, " he has a fine country place of 23,000 acres in the pampa."

" But is he otherwise a person of interest ? " asked Goehrs smiling.

The Argentinian looked at Goehrs a little resentfully. He did not understand what the question meant.

At this moment at lady crossed the hall of the Plaza, and the porter, the reception clerk, and the manager darted apart as at the muzzle of a revolver to give her passage.

" Who is that ? " asked Goehrs, who had seen the lady twice before and had been unable to place her type here, for it was very striking.

" Besanzoni."

" Who is she ? "

" The star of the Colón Opera," said the Argentinian nonplussed.

" Has she a good voice ? "

" Undoubtedly. Her jewels are worth a million and a half pesos. You are sure to see her. I hope you will come out and see us. Let's say Tuesday."

" Delighted," said Goehrs, " but I have only got your office address."

The Argentinian gave him his card. " We are living out of town. Tigre way. It's a new house. Two thousand pesos a month."

The man who had called on Goehrs at his hotel had proved to be a charming fellow. But when he had gone, Goehrs felt a little bewildered. When he had inquired about a man's character, he had had a sum of money for answer. If he tried to find out a man's mentality, the other had quoted the acreage of his estate. I shall have to be prepared, reflected Goehrs, wherever I go, to be asked, " What about your capital ? ' or " How is your income getting on ? "

He went to bed early. During the night the long-drawn howl of the sea-going liners from the New Harbour reached his room across the palm trees in the square. He suddenly succumbed to an acute attack of homesickness for the Altiplano of Bolivia, for the Puna, for the Indians of the Sierra, even for the desolate nitrate pampas of Chile. And yet he was powerfully impressed by this stone box of a capital, this city of two millions that simply reeked of wealth and was the hydrocephalic head of a country to which it was not in the least suited, this metropolis of icicles towering aloft, this capital for countless millions of cattle, for illimitable lowlands and for unexplored plateaux of *yerba* cultivators, for vast landscapes between fantastic rivers, for horsemen and Cordilleras, for grainland, for a paradise of horses for pioneers, for the granary of the world.

And yet this city, with its too narrow streets, with its impossible traffic regulations, its ostentatiousness, its grotesque prices, impressed him. There was something horrifying about it, something crushingly cruel about the way in which the inhuman wealth of the city was bound to impress the immigrants as they crawled from the bowels of the ships. Immigrants without money ? They were bound to be crushed by the sight of Buenos Aires.

But what was the population of which Buenos Aires was composed ? Was it the seat of the old Creole aristocracy ? By no means.

In the centre of Buenos Aires there was an Italian city with a population of 500,000—a little Milan ; there was a German city of 40,000 ; an English city of about 40,000. There were French, Polish, Syrian, Turkish, and Jewish towns. There were Hindu, Slovak, Russian, and Greek towns in Buenos Aires. Was this city Argentina then ?

No—and yes, thought Goehrs.

But in any case it was the wealth of Argentina.

No further wails from ships rose from the harbour. It had become quiet. The greyhounds of the lines with records to lose had left a minute or two after midnight to put a day to the credit side of their speed ledger by this little manœuvre. In this hush Goehrs fell asleep.

San Martín

BY the following morning the fog had cleared. In the Plaza San Martín below, the sun shone brightly on the equestrian statue of San Martín. The general with uplifted hand was riding his handsome charger gallantly into the circumambient air among the palm trees and the motor cars. Mars was at his feet. Round about him rose the allegorical figures of War and Victory, with reliefs depicting the battles of his armies from the crossing of the Andes to the pro-clamation of the independence of Peru. A far cry—the history of the War of Independence during the decades after 1800. A monument with a meaning, for without San Martín and Argentina the northern leaders of South America, Bolívar and Sucre, would never have settled accounts with the Spaniards singlehanded.

Withal, the wealthy and haughty Argentina of to-day had at that date been a bit of a Cinderella. At the beginning of the Conquest the Spaniards had never worried their heads about those great and fertile areas. They had no market for the vast cornfields and the huge stocks that could be grown and reared there. This country, therefore, was the last to attract them. The Spaniards wanted gold, and that was to be had in Peru. This gold was the ruin of Spain—for Spain did not invest gold nor use it for working capital, but simply spent it and became the more impoverished the faster gold flowed into the country and out again.

When the Spaniards were gone and the notion of Argentina was firmly established, the conception covered a number of provinces that were really States on their own account, more especially since they adopted, in 1825, the American constitution, which gave the several States a considerable measure of independence. It was very difficult work to weld these States into a unit. They fell, twenty years after their foundation, under the dictatorship of De Rosas who, more of a condottiere than a statesman, exterminated the Indians, fostered corn-growing, and, after seventeen years of tyranny, fled in 1852 on board a British man-of-war.

The first passenger dock in Buenos Aires was opened in 1855. Two years later the first railway engine gave its first snort. The bustle of international traffic began to stir in the harbour. The struggle between the party that aimed at a strictly centralized federal State and the party ambitious for powerful individual States continued in the history of the Presidents and revolts. Once the railway system was developed, the advantages of the centralist policy began to become apparent, because it was not until then that the great country could be surveyed and organized. In 1891 the peso fell to a fifth of its value, which in those days was looked upon as complete bankruptcy. After some shilly-shallying the exchange was stabilized again. In 1916 Dr. Hipólito Irigoyen, one of the most remarkable figures in South American history, was elected President for the first time.

The history of Argentina was the history of its capital. It culminated in the present spick-and-span, brand-new, restless Buenos Aires. Hundreds of picture palaces. Close on twenty theatres. Huge docks and the citadels of the banks. A brand-new city, divested of traditions. It was only the affectations of their architects that had, here and there, adapted a few balconies of the colonial era to its modern buildings. In 1880 Buenos Aires had a population of 300,000. Fifty years later, over two millions.

Goehrs reflected on the irony of history that kept the gold, silver, and tin countries of the west in medieval provincialism, undermined by the world slump, battered by dictatorships, harassed by revolutions of every kind, with populations consisting of huge proportions of Indians and half-breeds, while in this country, contemned for centuries, that to-day hardly numbered half a million gaucho half-breeds in an almost entirely white country, in a cattle and corn country, so mighty a city as Buenos Aires could arise.

Into the maws of the city, into the vast reservoir of this country, the millions of emigrants from Europe had rushed, had thronged city and country and had themselves prospered. At the date of the Franco-Prussian War, Agentina had less than two million inhabitants. Five-and-twenty years later, it had four millions. At the outbreak of the World War, close on eight. And by 1930, nearly eleven

This is a map of the provinces and territories of the country :

The province of Buenos Aires was in itself more than half as big as France, which, after the Treaty of Versailles, had (barring Russia) become the biggest State in Europe. And the province of Buenos Aires had almost three million inhabitants. The territory of Santa Cruz, on the other hand, which was not much smaller than the province of Buenos Aires, had only 12,000.

Goehrs, who was always fond of comparisons by map and of playing with history in terms of geography, saw that the little independent republic of Uruguay—which was only independent because, in the course of history, Brazil and Argentina had grudged one another possession of this scrap of territory—was lying on the other bank of the La Plata between Argentina and Brazil. The independent republic of Uruguay was not very much bigger than half the province of Buenos Aires, which was only a scrap of Argentina.

Goehrs's thoughts, exhausted by figures and calculations, harked slowly back to General San Martín who, amid the trophies of war and his victories, was cheerfully riding his handsome charger in the sunlight through the trees and motor traffic of the square. It was a Sunday, and the general appeared to feel quite at home amid the crowd of cars driving out round his monument to the races.

Goehrs went down into the lounge and asked the porter whether the racing was likely to be good that day. The races are, together with Colón Theatre, the place of all others where Buenos Aires has the best opportunity of preening itself. Goehrs was expecting to hear something about the quality of the horses running.

" The racing is very good," said the porter. " Usually 500,000 pesos change hands."

The Argentine peso was at the time worth about eighteen pence or thirty-six cents. On the pampas a horse on an average costs about ten pesos. A seat on the grandstand about the same.

What would this people feel like if ever the peso were to fall again, thought Goehrs. He never heard of anything that had not some connexion with the peso. Morality, manners, patriotism—everything in some mysterious way hinged on the peso. And Goehrs again became frightened lest the families he met might inquire what his income was. Because he did not know. Or what the acreage of his country place was. Because, of course, he hadn't one. . . .

THE RACES AND SOCIETY

GOEHRS drove into the Park of Palermo past villas and mansions, past gatekeepers in brown, blue and gold liveries,—he drove through streets that melted almost as gently into the Park of Palermo as Paris melts into the Bois de Boulogne. The Park was big and well groomed. Statues of men, greyhounds, stags and lions. Well-groomed lawns. Well-groomed palms. Just a little overdone, exactly as the houses of the city were a little too handsome and the doorkeepers a little too distinguished, just as if everything had become a little stilted owing to the accumulation of wealth instead of having become easy, thanks to wealth.

The stands disappointed Goehrs. They were not as handsome as those of Santiago. Santiago's grandstand was a narrow ferro-concrete hotel with a stand built on to the outside of it, a building where the members of society gave their dances and prided themselves less on their money than on the fact that they were members of the old families of the country. Goehrs had expected that Buenos Aires society, which worshipped wealth even more than ancestry, would have turned out its stands even more opulently. That was not the case ; he had made a mistake. He was, it is true, debarred admission to the most select stand, which was reserved for members of the Jockey Club only. To the right and left of this stand were two others. The one on the left was reserved for owners who had horses running, without being members of the Jockey Club. The paddock adjoined this stand, and the lady " friends " of the men who had their seats with their wives and daughters on the Jockey Club stand had access to it. These members frequently strolled from the Club stand to the one adjoining the paddock, where their friends were sitting. They went apparently to have a look at the horses, in point of fact to see their friends. Every one knew that and every one took it for granted—and by this decorous method of watertight compartments, these men enjoyed the society both of their family and of their mistresses. The world and the half-world were within sight of one another, but did not come into contact.

This procedure had almost the force of law. When the Negro dancer Josephine Baker, who by virtue of her marriage bore an aristocratic name, appeared on this stand one day as the guest of an enthusiastic member of the Jockey Club, some dozen other members gathered round her, laughing and chatting, headed her away from her escort, and bowed her out. The Club was not Argentina but it was very influential, controlled the racing licences for the whole of the country, and had a clubhouse on the walls of which French impressionists were hung as if they were nothing to boast about.

Goehrs, who had not the honour to have any horses

running or to be a member of the Club, had his seat on the stand to the right of the Jockey Club, on which the rest of the fashionable world was accommodated at the rate of four dollars a seat—and he was disappointed. It was not stylish. The porter had misunderstood him. It could not possibly represent the brilliant Argentine " society " he aspired to see. It did not happen to be a big racing day. And then he remembered having seen the Papal flag displayed from several villas. He looked into the *Prensa* and it at once became evident to him why it was so and not otherwise. A diplomatic reception by the nuncio and two other receptions had cheated him of the spectacle on which he had come to feast.

At any rate it was crowded. And if there were no snowclad Cordilleras for a backdrop as at Santiago, the centre of the course was made to look very attractive with its green lawns and pretty ponds. The stretch in front of the stands was sandy. It looked like a beach. As the weather had become a little overcast, great blazing braziers were standing on the beach. And a crowd of several thousands round them. On the right, adjoining his, was a fourth stand. It was less select and less expensive. And here, too, stood thousands, motionless, solemn, as if cast in bronze.

The starters paraded. The thousands scanned them, made notes, and then streamed away behind the stands to a huge totalizator to stake their bets. They then passed up in big lifts to the several tiers of the stands. When the starting bell rang, not only were the stands full, but there were thousands on the beach. Goehrs on arrival had backed No. 18. It was the third race. For three-year-olds ; distance eight furlongs.

There were false starts on the far side of the oval course. Then at length the little jockeys, hovering in their white, red, and yellow caps and silk shirts over their slender, sinewy mounts, came into the straight and strained towards the finish. Until the moment when the horses were level with the first stand, the crowd was silent, unsouthern, apathetic and impassive like any other South American crowd. The moment they entered the finish in front of the four long stands, a miracle happened. The thousands all of a sudden went clean off their heads. Dignified men, frigid young bloods leaped on to the seats and began to shout. The crowd on the beach waved their arms and swayed about as if caught in a hurricane. Every one was roaring a name, waving his card, becoming red in the face and behaving like a man in a delirium. Goehrs had never seen a similar attack of dementia. The moment the rush of horses had passed the winning post, the crowd became quiet. A murmur of excitement lasting a few seconds was only a faint aftermath. Then every one became impassive and solemn again.

Sport ? wondered Goehrs. No ! But business.

He had noted without emotion that No. 18 had finished seventh.

He took up his stand at the totalizator for the next race and saw that thousands of middle-class people were staking what was presumably the whole of their means of subsistence for the ensuing week—neck or nothing. Then he returned to Buenos Aires with a lighter notecase—with a hole in his wallet and with the conviction of having seen, if not the cream of the city's fashion, at any rate its greed for gold.

The women he had seen had all been pretty. But one was the facsimile of the other.

SOCIALISM

THAT evening Goehrs drove to the South Harbour. He drove for twenty minutes past paddle boats and thousands of masts moored there—swept by feeble lights, eerie, an almost endless tangle of timbers and shadows. Goehrs had heard that men and women died in the streets here from poverty. It was not as bad as all that. He explored the dockers' quarters and the brothel district pretty thoroughly. The public houses had for the most part American names, " White Horse " and so on, with painted transparencies at their doors. They were barns with a band, making music on a platform. The men sat at little tables in the middle of the room. All around, along the walls, like dogs in a kennel, prowled the little three-pesos cocottes. The proprietor, in his shirtsleeves and waistcoat, patrolled about among them like a lion-tamer. Negresses, Malays, Indians, Englishwomen, Chinese, Italian—Argentina. They revolved ceaselessly round in a ring. Some of them were very fat, seemed quite clean, and stroked the brows of the men at the tables. They were very made-up, had a long pointed curl in the middle of

293

the forehead plastered down and prolonged to the bridge of the nose, and did not seem to take the least offence if one of the patrons should prefer to give them the cold shoulder.

The general company consisted of seafaring men from every craft, of every nationality, of fellows wearing neck-cloths instead of collars.

On the wall notices : No dancing.

The squalor in the streets did not seem to Goehrs as bad as in many model cities of Europe. And the vice was not more gross than in other harbour towns—if anything, cleaner and better behaved. But it was, after all, in ghastly contrast to the streets of the city leading to Palermo Park. A ghastly contrast because it was obviously a case of either one extreme or the other—no middle class.

As Goehrs walked up the parade of the sailors' light-o'-loves along the water edge, on the right in the darkness the dimly lit ships, on the left the endless chain of little girls and the public houses with their noisy jazz bands, he saw a placard pasted against a wall. Headline : Socialist Party.

It was the first time he had seen that in South America.

THEATRES

IN Buenos Aires there were theatres again at last. They began at half-past nine and went on playing until about one o'clock. It was possible to see quite a number of them in the course of a single evening. With an Argentine journalist, Goehrs first went to an Italian play. Then he saw one act of a play in the Odéon where they were giving *Volpone* in French. Then he saw an act in the Yiddish theatre of a play called *The Smith's Daughter*, which was being performed by Schwarz's company of New York.

From eleven to twelve they went to a " one-hour " play in the Teatro Nacional. The play given was called *La Gringa Frederica*, by an Argentine playwright. It was an uncouth play and uncouthly acted, but it was a native Argentine play (not a foreign travelling company play as at all the other theatres) and represented a certain phase of Argentine mentality and something of Argentine literature. It was difficult to follow because Argentina is not, of course, Spanish. Argentine-Creole is a language so complicated with Italian, Indian, and English that Spaniards hardly understand it. Nor do the Argentinians claim that they talk " Spanish " ; they refer to their " *idioma nacional*."

The play depicted a wealthy Argentinian family. The father was a widower who was unable to manage his offspring not on the score of morality but because they had grown up like untrained puppies, the girls no less than the boys. The children were pretty well grown-up, but out of hand in behaviour, dress, and manners in a way such as only the most purse-proud wealth—that looked down, not only on foreign nations but on their manners as well—can produce.

The harassed father engaged a German governess, the " gringa Frederica." The word " gringo " in South America connotes a great deal : foreigner, contempt for the foreigner, hatred of the foreigner.

The children (in the play) received the German with howls of derision. The German governess was not even very violently caricatured. She only talked her Creole with a German accent. But things changed. Two months later the children were tamed ; they were brushed and combed, appreciative of beauty, well mannered, well groomed, well informed. In the debates that followed, the German told them some home truths about their inward uncouthness and their outward conceit. As a matter of fact they got this moral rubbed in, not by a German governess, but by an Argentine playwright addressing an Argentinian audience. It was this that made the play interesting, as indicating the educational influence the author took for granted to be embodied in a German governess. And finally it was interesting for the defects for which an Argentine author scarified his own compatriots. It therefore did not matter, reflected Goehrs when the play was over, that the company acted like Zulus and that the play was, in construction, as improbable as an American " happy ending " sketch.

The two men then went on to a cabaret, called " Bataclan." It was a man's show, full to overflowing. There was not a single woman in the stalls and the grand circle. The atmosphere and the interjections were consequently in accordance. The audience responded with gusto to the stuff the ladies on the stage said and sang—and the ladies were anything but ambiguous. Many a man in the front row of the stalls, when a diseuse advanced close up to the footlights, tried a resolute grab at her legs, or became even more familiar when the artiste in question, who was usually exceedingly full-bosomed, reclined in front of the footlights as if the stage were the seashore.

The turns were quite clever and entirely indecent. The male audience was thoroughly roused and a nasty atmosphere of concupiscence soon prevailed throughout the place.

Shortly after the two had arrived, a really unusual incident occurred on the stage. A diseuse who was rather stout, but none the less shapely, turned her back on the audience, picked up her short skirts and then waggled the right half of her hinder quarters while the corresponding left half remained motionless. This posterior and anatomically hemispherical dance brought the house down. The audience yelled, stamped its feet, and clapped its hands, and its enthusiasm became even more ebullient after the turn that followed. This woman was as a fact neither graceful nor pretty, nor could she sing, but she was an Italian. And half the audience was Italian, which went mad and rolled its eyes as soon as it heard its *idioma dolce*. The Italians are the most difficult race in the world to fuse and the one most constant to itself—next to the English and the Chinese.

As the two men were leaving the Bataclan, a couple of Yiddish, an Italian, a French, and the German *La Plata*, together with the Argentinian newspaper, were being shouted in the streets.

A really international city, thought Goehrs.

"Yes," said the journalist. "There's a paper to almost every language. And the sales of the Argentinian papers are quite big. A journal like the *Prensa*, for example, has a circulation of nearly half a million copies.

PRESIDENT IRIGOYEN

IT was close on one o'clock when the two men arrived at El Greco. The Casa del Greco was in the Libertad and it was a longish drive. Goehrs had all the evening been pondering over the placard in the South Harbour that had alluded to the existence of a Socialist Party, and during the last few days he had seen and heard a good many things that had a bearing upon it. There had not been any

296

indication in the theatres that there was any social unrest in the country—still less in the music halls—and except for the usual communist bogy, there was no trace of it in the Press.

It struck Goehrs as a little uncanny, and he did not understand it. He had been astonished at the time that the Indian proletariat in the western highlands had not given rise to a socialist movement, and he had found a partial explanation for it in the tragedy of the Indian race. In Chile the Government in the hands of a general would no doubt have simply strangled any movement of a socialistic character. But Argentina? On the one hand, life seemed to be flowing gaily and it seemed to be really the best of all possible worlds if you only considered the surface of things. But that could not possibly be the case in such a pronouncedly capitalist State. On the other hand, there was a Socialist Party, and it even had some efficient deputies— but was it just as strange that this should be the case in precisely an agrarian country?

What was the truth about the socialist movement?

Goehrs knew what the position was so far as the middle classes were concerned. The bourgeois parties of South America had adopted all the sonorous verbiage that sounds idealistic and was supposed to embody ideas just as it had done in Europe and North America—but they were in fact private factions with well-defined individual interests and, apart from that, tools in the hands of a few ambitious men and one or two greedy wire-pullers. Not a glimmer of any constructive idea anywhere.

"What form does the socialist movement in Argentina assume?" Goehrs asked the journalist in the course of the drive.

"It is in existence," said the latter smiling, "but that is about all. For one thing it exists in the big towns only— and that is not enough. The vast open country, the farmers and the gauchos, won't have anything to do with it. They couldn't be better off under any other organization of society than they are at present. And then the movement has not any ideal driving-power. You can't get the people to grasp the driving-power of the idea—the Argentinians only become conscious of it when it takes the form of "Criollismo," Creolism, of Argentine national sentiment. I am not a socialist and therefore I think it just as well. But it is, of course, a matter for regret. The communists have gained no influence at all. The Soviet propaganda

297

literature that gets smuggled in can't even be translated because all the terminology for it is lacking. That is a matter for regret because every movement is dangerous if it has no intellectual basis, but remains a matter of the belly. For this reason all the strikes are savage and undisciplined. Not horizontal but vertical, if I may put it in scientific language. Without co-ordination. Every man for himself. The bakers and taxi-drivers have the most pronounced communistic leanings—but what they are concerned about is increased wages. And every section strikes on its own account. The principal section of the socialistic movement are the dockers. And it is very much the same state of things there."

"Really! Then there are plenty of strikes?" said Goehrs. "In the west they were prohibited. And what about the censorship of the Press?"

"Its methods are not as high-handed here as in the west. That's no longer feasible," said the journalist, looking out of the window to make sure the car had turned down the right street. "Since the *Monte Cervantes* of the Hamburg Line ran on to a reef off the coast and a Buenos Aires paper reproduced a photograph of the ship stuck on the rock and faked a portrait of President Irigoyen sitting on her, with the caption 'The Ship of State,' there has been no Press censorship in Argentina."

"But every one I meet hates the President," said Goehrs, "and for an official organ he only has a gutter rag, and all the big papers must be against him and yet none of them really attacks him hotly. I can't make it out."

"Who can tell?" said the journalist, and shrugged his shoulders. They reached their destination shortly afterwards. The Casa del Greco was a curious establishment, a private house, from top to bottom decorated with blue azulejos. The tiles came partly from Spain, partly from Holland. There were Chinese carvings and the Tsar's double-headed eagle on the chimney-pieces. And all the rooms were little drawing-rooms, every room reserved for its own party. The journalist ordered a couple of whiskies when the waiter appeared as he touched the bell.

Goehrs had, of course, heard a great deal about President Irigoyen from the moment he set foot in Argentina, and he could judge from it the spell that the old man, with his round, striking head, seemed to exercise. The spell, it is true only affected a portion of the Argentinians, to wit, the small folk, the folk in the open country, the gauchos, in

fact any one who was not a member of the old Creole aristocratic houses (aristocratic in the sense of the old-established
families, for there was no nobility in South America, not
even in cases where the descendants of the old grandee
families could have claimed titles of nobility).

These people—the majority of the nation—would, even
during Irigoyen's first term of office, which began during the
War in 1916, have held by him through thick and thin.
And Irigoyen had been re-elected to his second term of
office, which began in 1926, by the same small folk who
also worshipped General Ibañez in Chile and Leguía in
Peru. Irigoyen himself did not derive from an old family.
He was perhaps of Basque, perhaps of mixed Turkish
descent. At any rate he belonged to a class that Argentine
society (and that did not mean " society " in its
narrow English sense, but the politically influential and,
from the very first, powerful factions) regarded as rabble.
The rage of the great families at this tribune of the people
who had divested themselves of power was extraordinary—
more especially as Irigoyen was far from being a Socialist.
In no country in the world, neither in Germany under Ebert
nor in Greece under Venizelos, had Goehrs seen such
insensate rage against the leader of the State as against
Irigoyen in Buenos Aires. The whole city was a fanatical
opponent of its President, who was, however, always
returned again by the supplementary elections in the
country.

Irigoyen was very nearly eighty, but a sturdy man who
seemed to be obsessed by his mission in an almost mystic
sense. His supporters treated him as a Messiah—and he
had some such similar notion about himself. He was, to
judge by his actions, a personality that bordered at times
on dementia, at others on genius, but probably the most
obstinate, the most purposeful, the most fascinating and,
with it all, the clearest brain in South America. He did
pretty well what he liked with his Parliament, his opposition,
and his eleven million Argentinians without overstepping
the law. He was a dictator of the stamp of Leguía in
Peru. But there were no broken arms and no islands like
San Lorenzo in Buenos Aires—and Irigoyen could stomach
criticism. An attack like that of the " *Monte Cervantes*
Ship of State " would have led to banishment and the
" purchase " of the newspaper in western countries.
Nothing of the kind happened in Argentina. Yet the old
man did what he liked—he prorogued Parliament if

Parliament did not come to heel, and he brought Parliament to accept things Parliament didn't like at all. Goehrs had talked to people who had seen Wilson, Clemenceau, Stresemann, and Mussolini, and who had approached Irigoyen full of distrust and incredulity—and had left his study with the conviction of never having met such a powerful, vital, and magnetic personality.

With it all, Irigoyen was a simple, poor man who did not live in a palace but in a small house and not even one of his enemies asserted that he was open to bribes. He was grotesquely obstinate. It was almost impossible to get to see him. He had at once, at the very beginning of his presidency, abolished a lot of ceremonial—such as the reception of foreign representatives. He sometimes kept ambassadors waiting for weeks before he received the letters accrediting them. He kept the Spanish ambassador, who was to invest him with the most exalted Order of Alfonso XIII, waiting with his most exalted Order until he included him in his reception of some delegation in connexion with aviation. He was terribly impolite, but impolite in the way of a sage who cannot spare the time even to acknowledge matters of no importance. He was *muy gaucho*—a wild dog.

Personally, he had clean hands, was not self-seeking; but like all the few men there are in South America who are not self-seeking, he had a crowd of people round him who admired him, whom he did not see through, and who were not themselves immune from self-seeking. As he hardly ever gave appointments, an audience with him was a valuable consideration for exchange and barter. Two days after his arrival in Buenos Aires Goehrs had a talk with a man who told him that he was in a position to procure an audience with the President for him for 200 pesos.

" I should not dream of it, my dear sir."

" Not even for a gold watch ? "

" Not even for that."

These people who were *muy amigo* with the President, and committed him to things that were neither straight nor savoury, irritated the people in Buenos Aires to white heat— together with other, more important, things Irigoyen did which were economically bad mistakes. Above all his insensate aversion from the Yankees and everything appertaining to the Yankees—from the Yankees who in a comparatively short time had raised their capital invest-ments in Argentina from an inconsiderable sum to a billion and a half, which was, it is true, counterbalanced by even more considerable British investments. Irigoyen was not afraid of the English, but he was afraid of the Americans. He was the one and only big man of South America who opposed them tooth and nail, deliberately and unconditionally. He hampered business and he hampered it in a senile, impossible, but logical way.

He had the bulk of the population with him. He could therefore afford to let socialistic views shape their own course. They did not seem to him dangerous in an agrarian State. Irigoyen, indeed, seemed in general to have no sense of the driving-force of views opposed to his own. The pretty well unrestricted powers of a South American President—if his hands were only half-way clean—induced in every one of them an exaggerated sense of his own personal authority, and this constituted politically an unpredictable factor. Even Leguía in Peru had it. Leguía, too, in spite of tortures and in spite of the corrupt dealings of members of his family, regarded himself as a Messiah. Irigoyen, to an even greater degree, believed in himself alone. The bulk of the small men in the country decided in his favour at the elections, and it probably needed only slight pressure to ensure this result. In the city every one was against him, and here the opposition was soon intimidated by a few shots, just a volley or two of musketry and a few killed. Irigoyen walked barefoot and smiling over the volcano that was his capital—even, as on one occasion, when the students had howled down one of his ministers. He believed in himself, while the whole of Buenos Aires regarded him as a disgrace to the nation, as a bandit chief, as a contemptible ruffian, and clamoured for a change of system. But how ensure it, Goehrs asked himself. The President's term of office lasted for six years. Revolutions were becoming very rare in Argentina, a purely white country which had a very complex, delicately adjusted economic system.

"Didn't Irigoyen prevent a declaration of war against Germany?" Goehrs asked the journalist when the two whiskies were set before them. "I have heard that. . . ."

"He certainly did prevent war," said the journalist, "but not for any pro-German proclivities. That sort of things sounds very pretty, but sentimentality of that kind never goes to make history. He acted on very magnanimous lines at the time. When the clamour for war arose, he said in Parliament: 'We Argentinians are not any hole-and-corner South American nation that plunges into war for the sake of grabbing a few ships as naval prizes. If the people and Parliament force me to declare war, I shall stake the whole strength of Argentina on the issue. I shall call up every man of military age without exception and send him to the battlefields. . . . ' Well, they were very proud words, and the demonstrations died down in view of this unpalatable prospect. Argentina did not join in the war. But history is not made up of proud words, and the motives of big political actions are not sentimental."

The journalist pressed the bell and gave the waiter instructions to let his office know by telephone where he was to be found.

"Why, in your view, did Irigoyen not go to war?" asked Goehrs with curiosity.

"He did not go in," said the journalist, gazing up contemplatively into his cigarette smoke, "because his predecessors in office, the gentlemen of the Jockey Club, wanted to go to war. . . . For they, of course, were pro-French. He further did not go in, because the Yankees did. In the third place he did not go in because neither the Church nor Spain did. And, fourthly, he did not go in because he, in contradistinction to others, had sufficient timber in Argentina to be able to hold out against the possibility of a coal blockade with which he had to count. Those were his actual reasons."

"They, too, do him honour."

"Perhaps," said the journalist, "but he would not be able to carry through to-day what he risked then. His halo is too badly chipped. He would to-day be immediately confronted by an opposition he wouldn't succeed in brow-beating. Have you ever heard of the chieftains of the western provinces? They constitute a really formidable opposition to Irigoyen. And the fellows take risks, too. Some of the western provinces in the Cordilleras are so remote and so inaccessible that they have an independence of sorts. Regular condottieri, leaders of clans with big bodyguards, are the rulers there, and the provinces obey them. Even military intervention would be dangerous, because a small army would simply evaporate there. That sounds comic from the point of view of a modern great city, but you at any rate know the country. The fellows with the body-guards, too, have themselves elected into the Senate, and the Senate is in opposition to the President, and they

actually make speeches against Irigoyen—under cover
of their bodyguards, of course. . . . They are the people
who frequent this Casa del Greco. No one takes it amiss
in their case. But they would take it very amiss if one of
Irigoyen's ministers were to celebrate his orgies here.
You can have anything you want. Apartments and
bathrooms."

Goehrs gazed with astonished eyes at the Tsar's double-
headed eagle, at the blue tiles, at the folding screen, and at
the Chinese bronzes on the mantelpiece.

"In the old days," the journalist went on, "when the
big brothels with their Japanese, Malayan, their black and
their white garrisons, were still going concerns, the big men
of the big estancias would go to these establishments
straight from the railway stations and stay there for days
together. Nowadays, when the palmy days of their
revenues are over, they only bring their visitors here
occasionally. The prices are, it is true, pretty stiff. In
many cases a dinner runs into 400 pesos."

"Then we were well advised only to order a whisky,"
said Goehrs, who did not aspire to enter into competition
with the big men of the big estancias.

There was a knock at the door, and the waiter called the
journalist to the telephone. He was away for five minutes.
Then he returned.

"News, señor," he said. "A revolution has broken out
in Peru."

Goehrs felt as if the ground of South America were
reeling under his feet. In Peru—after ten years of a
dictatorship, the apotheosis of which he had just been in
time to see. "Impossible."

"Not at all. The garrison of Arequipa has mutinied."

"Arequipa is nearer to Bolivia than to Lima."

"Yes," said the journalist. "The revolution is naturally
sliding downhill. General Ibañez and Irigoyen won't
get much sleep to-night."

BOLIVIAN INTERLUDE

SOME little time before that evening, the course of
events had taken a turn unfavourable to General
Kundt. The frontier rising with Hinojosa's communist
flavouring had, as Goehrs had guessed, proved only a

303

comic-opera incident. On the Sunday in question, which has attained a horrible significance in La Paz as " bloody Sunday," the students had organized another demonstration—against Siles, against Kundt, against Siles's re-election and his plebiscite. The students fanned the revolutionary embers into a flame. Then a crowd of a few thousand assembled in the Plaza Murillo and came into collision with the police. The police opened fire. On Monday and Tuesday La Paz was dead. On Wednesday the revolution broke out in Oruro. General Blanco Galindo, in command of the Camacho regiment, proclaimed a provisional government. General Blanco Galindo was a Bolivian general trained in France and a rival of General Kundt as well. This was General Galindo's declaration of war against Kundt as chief of the General Staff, who was of equal status with the Minister for War. The declaration of war by one section of the army against the other. Civil war and revolution.

If the revolution had broken out under the lawful rule of a President, Kundt's position would have been straightforward. He would have mobilized his forces with his usual military skill and without responsibility since he was only doing his duty in safeguarding the Government against disorder. But the fact was that there was no regular Government behind Kundt—nor a personality of any kind. The Government had collapsed, and in reality consisted only of a disembodied ghost that Kundt called law and order. This made the general's position very complicated. Since the rising was come that he had tried to prevent and against which he had issued an exceedingly severe manifesto to the army, a very stringent obligation to forestall bloodshed was imposed on him. For, all in all, everything the provisional Government raised in the way of demands and principles was reasonable—even if based on mutiny. But a mutiny against a not altogether lawful government. From a juridical point of view it was a game of blind man's buff. As a matter of cold fact, they had already begun to shoot.

Bolivia during these days was hermetically sealed against the outside world. No train, no telegram, not a soul crossed the frontier.

The revolution ran its course. Potosí, Cochabamba, Sucre, Tarija, and Santa Cruz went over to the rebels. As from Wednesday night no one in La Paz was allowed to leave his house. The police kept the streets under rifle

304

fire. Kundt occupied the high ground round La Paz with artillery and machine guns. On Wednesday night the French ambassador gave a dinner-party. Two of his guests, Bolivians, were shot in their car by the police on their way home. The police were not under Kundt's orders, but the crowd laid everything ugly at his door just as they had credited him with all the prestige Bolivia had won at the time of the Chaco agreement.

La Paz lost its head. On Thursday the students fraternized with the cadets of the officers' training college. The cadets mutinied and together with the armed students who had done their military service held the military college against the regular troops, until the regulars took the building by assault. No harm befell the cadets in the fighting. But the youngsters had behaved very pluckily. The greater part of the Press compared these boys who had mutinied against their general with the Greek lads who had died at Thermopylæ. The representative of the United Press, writing from Antofagasta, compared the Bolivian with the French Revolution. It was, of course, buncombe. There was at any rate this difference between them : in the French Revolution the mass of citizens rid itself of an effete aristocratic caste by which it was being sucked dry, whereas in Bolivia the old factions were trying to settle accounts with the Government by the new factions.

La Paz went mad. A rumour of 500 killed was hawked about. The cadets, it was reported, had been shot down to a man. Kundt had given orders to hang 50 civilians in front of the General Staff headquarters. Kundt had been bribed by Siles for an enormous sum to issue the manifesto to the officers calling on them to remain unconditionally loyal to Siles. The air force had mutinied and was flying over La Paz with bombs to drop them on the police. In the meanwhile the greater part of Bolivia had declared for the revolution. On Friday morning a great battle seemed to be imminent. Siles and his acting government engaged in long negotiations between themselves. Kundt was not to to induced to commit himself to civil war. He went to the German legation. President Siles betook himself to the Brazilian embassy ; the Minister of War to the Chilean. The revolution was over. Kundt had made a fatal mistake in believing that it would be possible to sidetrack the revolution. He capitulated the moment he realized this and thereby did the most sensible thing he could do. At noon on Friday the mob looted Siles's private house. Government House was attacked. A sister of mercy flung herself in front of President Siles's wife and got a bullet in her chest. The President's wife was wounded. General Kundt's house in Obrajes, which the State had presented to him for his services rendered to Bolivia, was wrecked and looted. Goehrs was the last visitor to see the monkey and the whistling starlings, the Spanish silver trinkets, the delicate photographs of moonrise in Sorata, the portrait of Hindenburg, and the glass cabinet with the vases from Tiahuanacu. Everything was smashed or carried off.

The whole of La Paz was jubilant. The airmen were, so the newspapers reported, dropping flowers instead of bombs. The victims were given a solemn burial at the expense of the public funds. Mobs of drunken Indians appeared outside the German legation and threatened to break in, but a company of infantry, moved up for the protection of the legation, put a stop to it. The German minister extended his hospitality to Kundt with his wife and daughter—and the German minister was an able and active man who knew exactly the tone to adopt that became Germany's representative in such a hideous predicament and in a country like Bolivia. Kundt was a German national. The minister could not possibly turn out a German, who had done his duty in difficult circumstances, into the street to be torn to pieces by a mob of Indians. He declined, as against the newly constituted Government, to discuss the suggestion. Kundt had protected the Government in being, and public safety. He was not responsible for the measures taken. Nor, according to Bolivian law, could President Siles be held responsible for any measures whatsoever taken in the course of his term of office. He was, therefore, with the knowledge of the new military Government, removed to Chile shortly afterwards. The new military Government was anxious to avoid the odium of Siles being assassinated. That spoke well for the common sense of General Blanco Galindo, who, in due course, appeared in La Paz and formed a Junta de Gobierno. A military dictatorship.

He at once published a " statute " of twenty-four points. All charges of corruption by the former Government were to be rigorously investigated. An amnesty for offences of a political character was announced in order to restore national concord. The administrative personnel of the

State was reduced by 25 per cent. Illegal imposts were annulled. State subvention of the Press was prohibited. Freedom of the Press was restored. A commission was appointed to report on the economic position of the State. Members of the army were prohibited from taking an active part in politics. No member of the military Government issuing the manifesto was allowed a vote in the elections of the national convention to be held shortly. No member of the military Government was permitted to stand as a candidate for the presidency.

When Goehrs read this manifesto at the time, he was free to admit that it was startlingly efficient and that it touched on all the sources of abuse that poisoned public life in South America. But he realized, too, that the new military Government prohibited and penalized a good many things it had itself just committed. Goehrs had seen and read plenty of manifestos of the same tenor. Every new Government made its bow in the name of liberty by similar methods and every Government turned its back on these cardinal principles as soon as it felt threatened or attacked.

These generals were perhaps unusually upright men. Goehrs, who had become attached to Bolivia for its climatic and racial tragedy and its scenic grandeur, hoped it might be so for the country's sake. But as things were, not even a demigod would have succeeded in maintaining these principles, where there was no one to meet the postulates they raised.

In any case, General Galindo, the head of the new Junta, took steps to have three million bolivianos, which were due by way of interest, remitted to New York. He was still a comparatively young and an able man with a brain trained not only in the military sense by French strategy.

For a time there was some talk of bringing Kundt to trial before a court martial. The minister, Marckwaldt, refused extradition. He declined even to discuss the suggestion that Kundt had been bribed. He brought all allegations against Kundt to the touchstone of facts, and the facts were all on Marckwaldt's side. A few weeks later he escorted the general and his family to the coast. A few months later the newspapers of La Paz were writing about the chivalrous German general again.

At the time the general was at the German legation he gave a representative of a news agency an interview which is characteristic of the man and his methods.

" Public opinion holds you responsible, General," began

the journalist, "for the massacres on Sunday and for fusillading the cadets."

"From the very beginning to the end I refused to employ troops against the civilian population. They have not been so employed."

"I saw the police firing recklessly on the crowd."

"I have stigmatized this incident as abominable. I had no authority over the police."

"And the cadets?"

"I did not give the order to employ troops against the cadets. The cadets mutinied and fired on the troops. It was only then that I permitted the troops to return fire on the cadets. Imagine this had happened in Washington, and what they would have called it there. The number of casualties is wantonly exaggerated. Five hundred are reported to be killed. The military hospital returns fifteen. Not a single one of the cadets whose massacre I am supposed to have organized was killed."

"Why did you issue the manifesto just before the outbreak of the revolution—the manifesto in which you took your stand entirely on Siles's side?"

The general brought his fist down on the table.

"Siles knew nothing about this manifesto. I had inquiries instituted among the commissioned ranks to ascertain whether the officers as a body meant to adopt a hostile attitude to me; if so, I was prepared to resign. The officers answered that they did not want to become embroiled in a revolution. And I therefore stressed the need for preserving law and order. That is the history of the manifesto. If they now assert that Siles paid me a big price for the manifesto—very good; in eleven years' service I have not drawn a centavo beyond my pay. The Government has the records where my pay is accounted. It will be enough for you if I give you my word as a German officer that there is not a word of truth in these slanders."

"I don't doubt it, sir."

"The people are yelling for my head. I am an old man. Even this setback does not make very much odds to me. But the people have broken my heart. I have resigned my appointment and am in this pitiable position now only because I refused to open fire on the people. I wanted to avoid civil war. When the new Government came into the open, I did not, although it originated in a mutiny, shoot it down, but I ordered my men to lay down their arms. The old Government had ceased to exist. The programme of the new one was good. I did not want to have any firing for the sake of a ghost . . . but believe me, sir, I could have had plenty of shooting. I had the situation well in hand until the last minute."

The general waved his hand.

" The revolution is victorious," said the journalist.

" Undoubtedly," agreed the general. " After all, I trained the Bolivian troops that won the revolution."

" Against you."

" Against me," Kundt confirmed bitterly. " For, after all, I offered no resistance."

" And what of your career for the future ? "

" After these attacks I cannot stay on in Bolivia," said the general quietly.

" But how do you propose to leave ? " asked the journalist, who knew that Kundt was a prisoner in the legation and that the Junta was contemplating court-martialling him.

" How ? " repeated Kundt. " Just as I am." And he pointed to the grey pullover he was wearing over a pair of blue trousers. " With the only property left me. . . ."

INDUSTRIALIZED ARGENTINA

WELL, Kundt had left Bolivia, had crossed Lake Titicaca. He had spent a week in Arequipa, had sat under the tropical trees of the Quinta Bates, had played with the three dogs and seen the Misti, that strange, smoking mountain, during the eruptions, of which the tension in the air becomes so strong that any man committing a crime during these meteorological conditions is given the benefit of extenuating circumstances.

And on the general's heels, on his track, the revolution had slipped down from Bolivia to Peru—a terrace lower on the Cordilleran stairway. From 11,500 down to 8000 feet. For ten years Leguía had been held to be unassailable. Ten years of dictatorship, and all attempts on him had failed. But the army had now scored a success. In the person of Siles in Bolivia, one of those pinchbeck charlatans who was not up to Leguía's measure and had tried to ape him, who imitated Leguía's methods without a trace of his character, had been pulled down. The Peruvian soldier has smelled blood now, and an ambitious general who took risks and succeeded in overthrowing the dictator would have a free hand to do anything he liked.

The Peruvian generals had become hypnotized by the success of the Bolivians. The first of the dictatorships that had not relied on the support of the old factions had fallen—and the old gang sniffed the dawn of a new day.

On the following day Goehrs could gather no news beyond what he already knew. The garrison of Arequipa had mutinied. The Government in Lima had sent warships to Mollendo. Goehrs worked it out : three days up to disembarkation at Mollendo and thence to Arequipa—that depended on how much ground on this desert slope of the Cordilleras the insurgents had by that time contrived to occupy. It might take a long time if Lima remained quiescent. Leguía was a man of sixty-seven, suffering from a disease for which he ought to have undergone an operation years ago. He could not afford to have the operation, because as soon as he was under an anæsthetic and the knife at work on his body, the revolution would have broken out.

Everything depended on Leguía's power of resistance and whether he were successful in scotching the psychological suggestion that, after Siles, Leguía too might be mortally wounded.

On the following morning, Goehrs had a conversation with a man who was a professor at the university, president of a big company, a lawyer, and Argentina's most eminent statistician. He had a Scandinavian name and looked like a Yankee.

" South America," said this authority, " has ten countries : Argentina, Peru, Brazil, Bolivia, Chile, Ecuador, Colombia, Venezuela, Paraguay, and Uruguay. If you really want to understand South America aright, you will have to devote half your time and half your attention to Argentina alone for the following reasons :

" Of the ten States and of the whole of the superficial area of South America, Argentina has

50% of the foreign trade,
43% of the railways,
60% of the goods traffic,
56% of the passenger traffic,
45% of all telephone installations,
58% of all motor vehicles,
60% of postal business,
61% of all telegraphic despatches,

55% of the consumption of newsprint,
　　72% of the total available gold.

As against that, Argentina has, as compared with the nine other States of South America, only :

　　16% of the superficial area of South America, and
　　16% of the population.

Of the 7,500,000 square miles of the total superficial area of South America, Argentina actually holds only 1,150,000 (which none the less is quite a lot when you come to think that Germany has only some 186,000).

" On this showing Argentina's achievements are extraordinary."

Goehrs kept silence, overwhelmed by weight of numbers which, like all figures, told a clear, logical, and convincing tale but, like all statistics, were probably misleading in the conclusions they suggested. He had a suspicion that these statistics, without necessarily being actually incorrect in figures, were a flourish of Criollismo, of national pride, and an exaggerated tendency to stress everything Argentinian for its own sake. Goehrs remembered that he had never seen a foreign flag by itself, the Argentinian was always hoisted alongside of it. Small children saluted the colours. And every Argentinian regretted that the Zeppelin had not been built in Buenos Aires nor *Faust* written in Bahía Blanca. Very vain, very lovable, and even a little impressive.

" If these figures are meant to convey anything to me," suggested Goehrs, " it would be that Argentina, being a corn and cattle producing country, seems to be well on the way towards becoming an industrial country."

" Let us hope so," said the professor, president, and statistician.

" Heaven help us," said Goehrs.

It gave him a downright shock. He had seen the pampas full of fruitfulness and cattle—vast areas uncontaminated by the curse of the industrial age. And now this country was to be put in the way of creating industries, setting up reeking smoke-stacks, of plunging into the murderous struggle of the old industrial countries. It was lunacy.

" We are, as it is, producing three pairs of boots and shoes per head of the population," said the statistician, " and we are producing them far more cheaply than Europe."

The word cheap always struck Goehrs as humorous when

applied to Argentina. A neat six-roomed dwelling in a nice quarter cost $450 a month, a cook $40 to $60. To have one's tonsils removed cost $225. A visit from a physician with a reputation cost over $75. Two seats in the grand circle at the opera cost $65. All this was, of course, to be had at lower rates, but the higher ones were the rule. The sale of foodstuffs was not organized on the same scale. A fisherman got at times a thirtieth part of the profit the middleman made. It was the same thing with fruit. Everything was dear beyond all rhyme or reason. And people spent an insensate amount of money without really receiving value for it.

And this was the country that was to become an industrial country.

"I should consider it a horrible fate," said Goehrs. "After the War a number of States that had not dreamt of such a thing before set about building up their own industries. And what was the upshot of it? The whole world is being swamped by overproduction."

"We shall see," said the professor smiling.

A GALA NIGHT

THAT same evening there was a subscription production at the Colón Theatre. It was not possible to attend these productions by simply buying a ticket. These productions were oversubscribed and were among the most fashionable and exclusive in the world. Goehrs had therefore put himself to some trouble to get a seat and in the end had been most hospitably invited to occupy a seat in two boxes. On this occasion Goehrs was looking forward to making up for what he had missed at the races, to seeing Argentinian society in full dress.

He studied the programme: *Madame Butterfly*. And then a Russian ballet. Either might be good or might be excruciating. The quality of the performance did not concern him greatly because for the first time in his life he was going to the playhouse, not to see the play, but the spectators. Nor did he ask any questions about the artistic standard of the theatre. For formulating questions was still a problem that presented considerable difficulties in Buenos Aires. At first he had inquired a little naïvely but somewhat on the following lines: "Is Rio de Janeiro really as beauti-

ful as they make out ? " And had for an answer : " Yes—
there are some very good families there."

But this was exactly what he did not want to know.

Or he had inquired : " Are those poplars over there ? "
and they had told him : " They cost fifty centavos apiece
and in five years' time fetch five pesos apiece. There are
30,000 saplings on that plot of ground."

Poor Goehrs ! He had asked for botanical information and
had again been given a business calculation. Once he had
also asked : " Does the Colón draw good houses ? " and he
had thereupon learnt : " During the season (about three
months) a box costs $1250."

It was for this very reason that Goehrs abstained from
inquiring whether the cast included any singers or dancers
of repute ; they would probably only have given him the
artistes' salaries.

So Goehrs went to the play that evening and he was
really carried off his feet. The house, decorated in a scheme
of salmon and gold, had six tiers and a capacity of 3000.
On all six tiers pretty young women sat in the front row,
and a man in evening dress was standing behind every lady.
The young ladies were very pretty and very dainty, and all
wore light, full-length evening frocks, short, fur-trimmed
little coats, and hardly any jewellery. They were very
unadorned in their beauty. They were, too, blessed with
faces of angelic charm, faces that expressed a gentle
harmony, a harmony not lacking in ardour but an ardour
that was, to all intents and purposes, remote from the world
of men.

" Where else would you find its like ? " thought Goehrs.

These young girls were all brought up at home on French
lines. They could not travel much in Argentina itself. For
mile upon mile there was only pastureland, plains and cattle
all round them. They no doubt went out to their estancias,
but they only rode horses and read French novels there.
Now and again they might go to Europe with their parents
and, for the rest, wait for the hour of marriage, which used
to remove them out of the world entirely and even now only
left them a fraction of the liberty that young married women
in Europe and North America enjoy.

In one of the intervals, Goehrs took up his position just
behind the orchestra to get the full effect of the house and
its occupants as a whole. Never had Goehrs seen so many
unvarying, dainty, and ethereal beauties as in that survey.
On his left he saw some capacious boxes with their black

curtains drawn. These boxes were reserved for families in mourning. As the period of mourning was very long in Argentina and the families were big, these boxes served a useful purpose.

The intervals between the acts were longer than the acts themselves. They were, too, of greater importance to the audience that strolled or stood about the grand foyer than the performance itself. Argentine society met and exchanged small talk there. As a spectacle, that, too, was very interesting. But from 9 p.m. to 1 a.m. was—well, was just a little long, so it struck Goehrs, for *Madame Butterfly* and a twenty-minute ballet.

But he felt far more enthusiastic about the intervals than he was about the production. It was only the voices of the young ladies that made him just a little scared. He had frequently had a shock on the telephone when, fully alive to the fact that he was talking to a dainty young damsel, he suddenly heard the bray of a tin trumpet in the receiver. The way in which the Argentinians enunciated their own idiom was in jarring contrast to the speaker's sensitively arched lips and the big, melancholy, but flashing eyes. They all spoke with a remorseless accent—coarse, distorted, chewed, and from the bottom of their throats. It always sounded, as he passed any particularly attractive group, as if a gathering of rusty weathercocks had just begun to creak.

But the spectacle . . . the spectacle itself was fascinating. The production, on the other hand, was provincial. Naturalistic and empty. The Russian ballet impossible. As if Reinhardt and Tairoff had never been. And painfully sentimental. And badly lighted. But Goehrs really did not worry about that. It would no doubt have been an all-too-perfect event if the performance had been as beautiful as the spectators that watched it. The beautiful ladies of Buenos Aires, it is true, thought the performance delightful. It was, furthermore, in keeping with their charming faces to be so unsophisticated.

CRUISING ON THE PARANÁ

ON the following morning, Goehrs had been invited to a longish trip on a motor yacht. A party of five of them proposed to work up the vast river system flowing into the sea not far from Buenos Aires. At this spot the huge Paraná River, so big that sea-going ships can make Rosario, flows down-country to join the no less huge Uruguay River. From their junction the new river is called La Plata. At first it has a width of rather over 30 miles, but by the time it empties itself into the sea it has increased to 150. A river mightier than the Mississippi. The country where the Paraná and Uruguay met was intersected by innumerable canals that linked the two rivers and their tributaries, so that this part of the country near Buenos Aires had become a prosperous, greater Holland.

About an hour's run from Buenos Aires some thousands of motor boats of every size lay moored in the little Tigre River. During the summer Buenos Aires society beguiled its boredom and its leisure on board these boats.

The boat on board which Goehrs reached the Tigre moorings the following morning was called the *Ycum-Go*. It was a particularly handsome boat, a regular whale of a boat with 600-horse-power engines, a saloon, and six little cabins and a bathroom fitted in, and the family to which it belonged would often cruise for a week up the Paraná and its tributaries, bathe, smoke, swim, fish, tie up where the fancy took them, and turn on the gramophone.

Medina and Kinkelin were at the engine board. The big motor boat was running its engines.

" Forgive me if I am late," said Goehrs, " but I didn't reach my hotel until two, and have only had four hours' sleep."

Medina was a young man of thirty, swarthy, with overbearing eyes and that lengthening of the face in Yankee fashion that is peculiar to many Argentinians. He knew England and France well.

" I've had even less," he said with a laugh. " The mother of a friend of mine has just died, and so we had to sit up all night with him. We still have some horrible customs here at times. That is Kinkelin. And now pay your respects to the womenfolk. They're in the saloon and have been playing ' The Return of the Gay Caballero ' for the last quarter of an hour."

Goehrs had been listening to the record all the time. It was being sung in English enunciated with a half-way Argentinian accent that seemed to amuse the two young ladies very much as Goehrs entered.

It was midsummer in Europe—early spring in Argentina. At night it went pretty chilly, but during the daytime the temperature that turns Buenos Aires into an incubator for the Argentine summer months was mild and pleasant.

Hardly had they entered the saloon when the engineer threw over the starting lever ; the stern quivered at the start, and then the beautiful craft shot smoothly down the stream. Goehrs took his seat with the two men in the stern, which was so flat that if you were not careful it was quite easy to slip down it into the water.

They dodged in and out of the innumerable canals. The country was fairly crosshatched by water courses, which all by some mysterious interconnexion served to link up the great river systems. There were orange trees growing on the islands. The houses were built on piles in consideration of the floods.

" Any news from Peru ? "

" Let's hope the revolution is going through," said Medina.

" Why do you want it to go through ? "

" So it will go through for us."

" Then you are going to have one ? "

" I doubt whether it can be done nowadays," said Medina. " We're too Europeanized by this time. It would do a lot of harm, too. But how is the tension going to be relieved if we can't get Irigoyen certified as mentally unsound ? "

" No news ? "

" The navy and the army in Lima seem to be standing by Leguía. But all that is only rumour for the time being."

Goehrs had seen nothing beyond that in *La Razón*. Neither of the men sitting beside him knew Lima or had a notion of the peculiarities of Peru. Kinkelin as a type was suaver than Medina ; he was more Italianate in appearance and had a fine forehead and scholarly temples. He had his offices in one of the skyscrapers of the city, and his company owned hotels, aviation concerns, banks, and big slices of Argentine estate. His company had the reputation for being one of the few companies concerned in settlements for immigrants that were at the same time fair-dealing. Kinkelin was in his middle thirties, and one of the important personalities in Argentina, without making it obvious and without trying to make it obvious. Medina had a big business in the export of several articles, and a big number of estancias in different parts of the country. Kinkelin affected European diplomatic society, whereas Medina was a member of the old guard of ancient Argentina aristocratic families, whose exclusiveness, so they thought, hardly allowed them to welcome a British ambassador under their roof. His mother-in-law owned a big palacio and on one

316

occasion told the wife of the American ambassador, who, as was common knowledge, was anxious to buy a big palacio and was prepared to pay a big price for it, because he chanced to express his admiration for hers : "*Oui, c'est un très joli palais—et le seul palais à Buenos Aires qui n'est pas à vendre.*" Other members of their set might in the long run sell a palace that had cost two millions even to a gringo for three, for business was business, when all was said and done. But Medina's mother-in-law simply declined to deal. Not even at four.

What struck Goehrs was that these two men, like every one else in Argentina to whom he talked, spoke of a revolution with the greatest reserve. The opposition in Argentina, that is to say, the opposition of the old families, of financiers and capitalists, talked of Irigoyen with abhorrence but full of national feeling, full of a sense of responsibility, full of moderation, wisdom, and affection for Argentina. In all other countries of South America, the few hundred or the few thousand persons who embodied the power of the State had talked of a revolution with little more concern than of a football match. Argentina was far prouder, far more civilized, far more conscious of the ramifications of economic life—in short, it was, even in the attitude of its inhabitants, "different." There was not only mileage, but there were centuries between the States on the other side of the Cordilleras and this country.

The ladies in the saloon were playing a tango. They then hunted up the wireless stations all over the rest of the world. It seemed rather weird on the river.

The following morning they pushed on up the Paraná without cruising about. At an early hour the women were playing " El Carretero." Carlo Gardel's tenor rang softly across the water and rose like an angel's voice—and between-whiles Gardel would whistle in a way that sounded very lighthearted and very melancholy, like everything else in Argentina.

Heavily laden, 10,000-ton steamers were beginning to pass them, coming down from Rosario, a few hundred miles distant from Buenos Aires, a town of 260,000, from which the yield of the Argentine cornfields poured straight into the ship's holds and floated some hundred miles of river to the sea.

Meadows and scrub on every side. It was too cold for bathing.

Goehrs sat with Kinkelin and Medina outdoors in basket

chairs in the stern, the blue, white and blue flag of Argentina floating beside him. It had a sun on the white field. That was the official naval ensign. All yachts had to fly the naval ensign, for all yachts, over and above their private ownership, were the property of the State that claimed them in the event of war. All passing craft therefore had to salute the yacht. Argentina had a navy, as had Chile ; it had in fact warships with heavy guns, and endeavoured, as did Chile, genuinely to enforce military service, whereas its enforcement in the majority of the other countries was little more than a farce. It took three months for students and brain-workers, if the latter could show a certificate of efficiency in musketry. And these people were soon given a commission.

" Steady on," said Goehrs, as he skidded with his chair at a twist of the boat—she was going all out—and grabbed the flagstaff just in time. " People's views on military matters differ widely. In Peru a father and mother would sink into the earth for shame at having an officer for a son, nor would they like it in Chile—whereas here, people are pleased at any rate to be an officer on the reserve list."

" Quite right," agreed Kinkelin. " And therefore there is nothing more foolish than to take South America as a collective term. The term South America is the silliest and most fatuous word I know. The Future of South America . . . the Situation in South America . . . the Rise of South America. . . . As if there were not a greater world of difference between Bolivia and Argentina than between Australia and China. Here, cattle-farming and corn-growing, white man's country ; over there, Indians, mountains, and mines. There is in fact nothing on this continent you can compare with anything else, and yet every one in Europe throws everything that happens in South America into one and the same pot. What would you say if we were to generalize on things occurring in Europe on the same lines ? Ought I to feel alarmed about Europe because General de Rivera has set up a dictatorship in Spain and failed to maintain it, or because revolutions still occur in Portugal . . . or because ugly things, quite beyond our understanding, still occasionally happen in Albania ? "

" Well, after all, there are still some things that South America has in common," said Goehrs. " For example, the common fate that associates you and the nine other States against the Yankees."

Kinkelin nodded his handsome head and trailed his hand in the water for a moment.

"That is a danger that need not perhaps occasion any great alarm," he said equably. "There are other unknown factors concerned in that. Supposing, for example, the countries which have borrowed dollars up to the brim were one fine day to refuse to repay the dollars—what then? Will the Yankees declare war then? I hardly think that in a glaring case like that they would have the moral courage to do so. I have always told the English that the crassest bit of stupidity perpetrated in the post-War era was for them to be the only people to begin repaying war debts to the Yankees. They ought to have borrowed more and then more still. To have drained the Yankees of capital—that would have been a more sensible course than, in their old-fashioned alarm about international credit, to have tried to bolster up their precious prestige. What does international credit mean to-day? Absurd! In fact there are no more old problems left, only new ones arising every day. Do look about you. A short time ago they thought they had solved the crux of the general economic situation by going on raising the output of production because the prices of raw material were coming down all the world over. By doing so the costs of production were, it is true, reduced. But too much was produced. There was not so big a reserve of new consumers as they thought. And there they were in a real mess. Overproduction all the world over is a problem that is more urgent than any of the old romantic problems. More important than war and peace even. War and peace, too, is a grotesque problem from our point of view. That makes you open your eyes perhaps. But we are quite a new country without any martial traditions. We are hardly a century old. We quite fail to grasp how you can hope to solve economic questions by means of heavy artillery. Just look back on the history of the past twenty years. Nothing but follies have been effected by means of artillery, never a solution. . . .

"I could never make out why European nations rush to arms instead of concluding commercial agreements with one another. Good Lord! supposing I were to have my trade competitors shot down! That is a reason, too, why I suffered so hideously during the War. I was at school in Germany for two years, for three in France, and then was in England for a long time. During the War I was in Argentina. Argentina is a prism of many nationalities—and these nations, who had in reality been Argentinians long ago, began to hate each other. This hatred for one another, this common folly, knew no bounds. And the worst of it was that it was the flower of the Argentine nation that wanted to plunge into war. The people and the old Argentinians did not of course want war. But the cream of the nation and the newspapers wanted it, but these two sections did not represent the people. In Argentina less than anywhere."

" Then what is the people ? " asked Goehrs, and gazed into the distance across the water that seemed illimitable.

" If we were to know that as accurately as we know what finance is," said the banker, " we should be a thousand times better off. The people ? Elections, newspapers, statistics do not tell us. If we knew what the people were . . . there you are, señor, that is one of the new problems our era raises, one of the most formidable riddles, in fact, perhaps the final riddle."

He sat silent for a while with the strained expression of deep thought over his eyes :

" And yet it surely was Irigoyen, whom you detest, who refused to go to war and obviously did what the people really wanted."

Kinkelin smiled sourly.

" It is conceivable that the pretty stories they are retailing about the reason for Irigoyen's neutrality are true. It would, I agree, have been intelligent to have thought on those lines. Still more to have acted on them. But this President of ours is far too mischievous a character to have been able to think so intelligently. Or do you consider it a mark of intelligence that, not long ago on the day of the cattle census in the country, he had the banks and businesses in Buenos Aires in a city of two million inhabitants closed down as well ? No, señor, that is Gauchoism, he is a *caudillo*, a bandit chief with religious mania and without a brain."

" I should like to meet some one who does like him," said Goehrs. " I failed to do so even in the South Harbour."

" You would hardly be able to communicate with the people who really do like him," said Medina, and both men laughed. " Come into the saloon for dinner. We turn back to-morrow. And the day after we run across to the Uruguay."

In the saloon the ladies were playing the " *Cariñosa*," a dance song like the cooing of doves, silvery, tuneful, passionate, and charming and intimate in rhythm. Dusk fell.

Argentina was going to bed. Señora de Medina, with the aid of her neat little wireless set, tried to get some news about Peru from the pampas, from the air, from the Lord knows where. But all the news she got over and over again was how the weather had been behaving all over the place.

No Room !

ON the morning when the *Ycum-Go* crossed from the Holland of Argentina through the innumerable canals —the map position of which remained a mystery even to Goehrs—into the Uruguay, Medina yawned three times in the course of breakfast. His wife looked at him three times, once with a laugh, once with a smile, and once with a rather reproachful expression. Then he confessed that he had spent the night with a *dorado*. It had, he admitted, been rather a chilly entertainment, and it was not the right season of the year for such a prolonged bout of dissipation. But he had at length hooked a thirty-pounder that kept him busy playing it for hours before he landed it. The dorado was a species of salmon with a very sensitive mouth. He had caught it with a spoon bait. There were Englishmen who arrived in Buenos Aires on board a big liner and went straight on to a motor boat and up the Uruguay to fish for dorados.

His wife sent him to sleep it off. He did not reappear until lunch.

" In the summer," he said, " it doesn't do one a bit of harm, but it's too chilly now. As a boy I once made a month's trip up river right into Brazil and fished every night on the sly."

It struck Goehrs how very much the young women kept to themselves. They had few masculine interests and took little part in conversations that kept the men interested, although there were topics on which they might well have taken part—on divorce, for example. For in Argentina and almost all the other States except Uruguay divorce was unknown.

" Is the influence of the Church very strong still ? " asked Goehrs.

The question appeared to embarrass both men a little.

" Yes and no," Medina decided finally. " And that is just as well. If its influence were to drop out suddenly, we should have European conditions in our domestic life here—

and that would not do at all. If women of a temperament such as they have here were to live as the women of Europe do, it would be the very devil—impossible."

Goehrs recalled the angelic charm on the faces of the young women in the Colón Theatre.

"Sixty miles or so higher up," said Medina, who obviously was anxious to change the subject at any price, "I saw a panther drifting down on a thing like that last autumn." He pointed to a chunk of meadowland, floating down the Paraná like an island, similar to the meadows Goehrs had watched drifting down the Guayas in Ecuador. That had been on the equator and had been a long time ago. And how hot it had been then! Goehrs became conscious of a great craving for warmth—for a regular tropical basting.

The boat was travelling past a horse pasture.

"Has the difference on the pampas struck you, between the way horses are handled in this country and in Chile?" inquired Medina. "In the west there are, of course, provinces where they work with the boleadoras, but they are relics of barbarism. On the slopes of the Cordilleras, too, we have a couple of estates where the beasts are always half killed in the course of being broken in. Otherwise they are only broken to the saddle in this country as four- and five-year-olds. But really and skilfully broken in then. The Argentinians know a bit about riding, don't they? They keep the saddle even if their beast puts its head between its forelegs and looks more like a bow than an animal."

"Nothing like them," said Goehrs. "Aren't you afraid that the half a million horse gauchos might not start a social movement one of these days?"

"Not a bit. On the contrary. There are 450 gauchos to every 100,000 acres of pasture. No social system in the world could make them better off than they are. Those fellows can only exist under the conditions in which they do exist and they can only live in the spaciousness they do live in. Not otherwise. They are really well off."

"As long as Argentina is not an industrial country."

Medina made a movement with his hands that looked as if it were meant to push a century back.

"Not a chance of it. Besides, we are up-to-date. You have seen it for yourself, surely. In the west there is one estate where they still handle cattle with the lasso—and in the east we have estates where 6000 cows a day are milked by electrical methods in half a dozen dairies. Shall we have tea in the saloon?"

ARGENTINE CORRAL.

"The ladies may be coming on deck," said Kinkelin. The river kept growing broader. Goehrs noted that the run was drawing to an end.

"In Europe people imagine, I suppose," asked Kinkelin, taking his pipe out of his mouth, "that there must be vast quantities of land unoccupied in Argentina, don't they?"

Goehrs nodded.

"It's a fatal mistake," the banker went on. "There is hardly any land that is worth anything to be had. All good farmland is firmly held and so dear that it can hardly be worked to a profit by the purchaser. The theory of Argentina as an immigrants' country is ghastly nonsense. The only chance immigrants have in Argentina is as tenant farmers—and then they usually lose their money. I am telling you this for a good reason and in spite of the fact that I am personally interested in a settlement and real-property concern. There is always room for individuals, especially in the Misiones territory. But there are a lot of ups and downs on the yerba maté plantations they have laid out there. And then there remains a third use for immigrants: as cultural fertilizers, and surely no nation wants that."

Goehrs had heard that story often enough before.

But surely it is a fact that the soil of the great estates is very far from having been fully exploited," he said. "The land is there still and the people are making such a lot of money that they do not farm half of it thoroughly."

"Perhaps," said Kinkelin, restoring his pipe to his mouth and lighting it. "But how are you going to expropriate people? And if you could, do you want to dump yet more overproduction on the world? Small holdings are all very well. Hitherto, Argentina has always either had big wheat harvests and low prices or small harvests and high prices. So the market adjusted itself automatically. But now all of a sudden it had a poor harvest and low prices. Does not that tell its own story?"

"From the point of view of economics, yes. To satisfy one's sense of justice, no."

"Rot," said Kinkelin. "Economics are always justice."

The river grew as broad as a lake.

"No," Kinkelin continued, "Argentina is a very big country, that is true enough, and would be well able to support six times its population. But at the moment there would be no good purpose served in doing so. Further, the Chaco, which has great possibilities, is practically unexplored, and there is plenty of room in Patagonia, where

323

there is hardly any one living, but it is room that has to be made. Room for pioneers only. Only for people who are prepared to live on what they wring out of the soil. Not for the crowds. Everything else they may tell you on the subject is legend and ignorance."

" There is business for you," said Medina, and pointed to an orange plantation, " 4000 acres of oranges yielding $125,000,000 a year."

" Yes. It's sad but it's still true," said Goehrs. " It takes a lot of money all the world over nowadays to make a lot of money."

" Or you should have none at all," said Kinkelin. " You can't lose any then."

" There's one thing that is worse than ever to-day," retorted Goehrs, " and that is to have a little money." But it seemed to him that it was only the people to whom this applied who ought to be allowed to discuss the equitable distribution of the world—in this case only he and not his two interlocutors.

The motor began to grumble and pant a bit. The engineer put it back to 35 miles again. They drove through a yellow sea—the La Plata. The Uruguay had swollen the Paraná into a river over 30 miles wide that kept on growing broader, a redly glowing, sweet-water sea. On the opposite shore lay the independent State of Uruguay, with its capital Montevideo famous for its bathing beach and amazingly more expensive than even Buenos Aires, a State one-sixteenth the size of Argentina and one forty-sixth of Brazil, which only contrived to exist between its two giant neighbours because it was so small, a South American Luxemburg, and neither would let the other have it.

The *Ycum-Go* was quivering with speed. She ploughed through the yellow lake for an hour, crossed behind a couple of buoys, and worked back along the shore to pick up the mouth of the Tigre, the home of the motor boats.

Medina's wife and her sister were on deck. Señora de Medina had beautiful reddish hair, half shingled, light eyelashes, and very dark eyes. She had an oval face and a well-modelled chin, and was of medium height. She turned on the gramophone. A tango started : " Clavel del Aire." The boat swung into the Tigre. The motor boats lay moored along its banks like an army in bivouac. The Tigre was very narrow.

" I could go on cruising like this for days," she said, smiling. Her merry glance was overcast by a mist, the

324

pathos that lies in every woman's eyes in South America. " What are you doing to-night ? " she asked her sister, who was the image of her, only a little taller and darker.

" Nothing," said the sister, " I am waiting to see what Augusto's plans are. He is coming to fetch me." " How attentive," chaffed Señora de Medina. " We are arriving on the tick," said her sister. " I wired him." Señora de Medina stopped her gramophone. " Look there." The motor boat slowed down and made fast. Medina's brother-in-law was on the landing-stage.

" All well ? "

" *Muy bien.*"

" Good time ? "

" Not bad," said Medina. " I got a thirty-pounder."

" Any news from Peru ? " asked Goehrs. The brother-in-law was just embracing Medina in South American fashion. They leaned chest to chest and patted one another's left shoulder several times over with their right hand, talking all the time.

" Yes. It's all over," said the brother-in-law above Medina's head. " Leguía has bolted to Panama on board a man-of-war."

" The lights and shadows of dictatorships," said Kinkelin with a sarcastic smile round the corners of his mouth.

The lights and shadows of South America, thought Goehrs.

PERUVIAN INTERLUDE

AT the time Goehrs was staying at the Quinta Bates in Arequipa, a company of infantry with its band playing used to march through the streets every morning and after-noon. The cornets and drums had quite a different ring among the volcanoes and on the mountain terraces than in the plain, and their strains, half Indian, half martial, had a note of enterprise. Goehrs had long ago accustomed himself to believing that their inspiriting style of playing had no particular significance—and it proved to have meant some-thing after all. It was with this band and with his garrison that Major Sánchez Cerro had launched his rising.

Two months previously a sullen silence in Peru had answered the mutiny of the Arequipa garrison. Now, after the successful revolt in Bolivia, a thundercloud began to pile up over Peru. All the remoter garrisons declared in favour of rebellion. No one cared to miss the big coup for which every one had been waiting after ten years under dictatorship. But all that did not matter if Lima held by Leguía, for Lima was Peru. The soldiers made dramatic speeches in Arequipa for a whole three days ; there was some looting ; and some one who was neither for nor against the revolt got himself shot by mistake. Then Lima swung round. The students held a demonstration. The troops wavered. Telegrams came in from one garrison after the other that had joined the rebellion. The big white club in the Plaza San Martín began to get to work. Every one had been against Leguía. Every family showed some gap of a member banished, deported, or mutilated. . . . Every curve of force, even the most clever, has its limits. For ten years the strength of the old man had kept under everything that was in opposition to him, to his rule and to his policy—the end had come.

Leguía was an astute grey wolf. He did not let go for a single moment. As soon as the students began to demonstrate and as soon as he became aware that the army was swinging round, he changed his tactics. He knew that in the case of every Government dependent for its support on the parties of the Left the end was in sight when the army intervened in opposition to the parties of the Left. The masses of the Left lacked the organization and the initiative to offer resistance. His Indians were far away and did not understand the rising, had hardly heard of it. His dock labourers could not stand up to machine guns. The police was not heavily armed enough. He was only sure of the navy. And a portion of the troops. Leguía staked everything on that. He resigned—until such time as the agitation should have blown over. He himself, against whom the putsch was aimed, should be no obstacle to the pacification of the country. One of his generals became a member of the Junta that had taken control in Lima. Leguía with his " hares " in front of him and his " hares " behind him, drove down his fine asphalt road to Callao at such a pace that it did not occur to any one to stop him to ask him to pay his toll or to shoot him. In Callao harbour he went on board a pinnace and ten minutes later was on board the battle cruiser *Almirante Grau*.

There had never yet been a crisis in Peru when Peruvian battleships had not been lying off Callao with steam up to pick up the President if the situation should become critical. Gómez in Venezuela and General Ibañez in Chile,

326

too, had had certain cruisers with steam up as their last card, off the coast for years. The navy was safe. The ships had big guns. Their countries had enormous lengths of coast-line. The army on shore was small. Everything could be rewon from the sea. It was possible to await the course of events on board a cruiser. Neither Leguía, Gómez, nor Ibañez had made a cruiser trip for the first time.

Leguía told his ministers and closest partisans to take cover in the legations—in some of them there were a round dozen of Leguía's men. Then he dispatched his safe officers into the revolution to stalemate the mutiny. After his "resignation" things would, he assumed, calm down. It was only the first shock that was dangerous . . . and that the " Old Man " dodged. For he had before now been dragged on to the square in front of the Congress buildings and had looked down a Negro's revolver and had said : " I am not going to resign. Fire away." And he had pulled the game out of the fire then. He changed his strategy. But a ten years' dictatorship had been a very long innings. Too many people remembered the losses their families had suffered. Too many were conscious of the dead weight imposed on Peru. Too many realized their chance had come. Too many had been boiling with rage too long at the extrava-gance of Leguía's myrmidons for which they had to pay. The men with the monopolies and with the many motor cars had been a constant source of irritation to too many. The students were furious. Thousands stood on the Plaza de Armas and clamoured to General Ponce for the " Old Man's " head. General Ponce promised that Leguía would not leave Peruvian waters.

Leguía had not the smallest intention of leaving Peruvian waters. He was biding his time.

Two days after his resignation, aeroplanes with the officers from Arequipa arrived. Major Sánchez Cerro had been gambling with his life. He had no intention of being deprived of the fruits of his revolt. He turned out Leguía's generals. Lima was jubilant. The prisons were thrown open. Many people who were forgotten returned from San Lorenzo. And many new tenants moved into the jails and casemates. The whole of the army threw in its lot with the new officers' Junta. The new provisional Government found staggering evidence of corruption. The revolution was over. The cruiser *Almirante Grau* put out to sea ; then the weather was foggy, and Callao soon lost sight of the vessel.

The " Old Man " had played his last card. His cruiser was heading for Panama.

In the *Prensa*, Goehrs saw that on board the man-of-war in which the fallen President was travelling through the Pacific as on board his private yacht were two members of the American naval commission. Leguía had not been a bad henchman of the Yankees.

Goehrs remembered how, on the same day on which he had seen the severed human head reduced to the size of an egg, he had called on Leguía. In the room where Pizarro had been killed. In the garden with the old azulejos Pizarro had seen, and the tree Pizarro had planted. It was the same destiny, the same fate, the same medieval mysticism that had inspired both men and to which by some mysterious fatality the country was subject.

Goehrs recalled the day he had seen the old man in a frock coat and his tall hat in his hand, standing between the Queens of Beauty of Chile and Peru, well groomed, with white hair and well-shod feet. Pizarro, too, had been fond of playing tennis and had many Indian princesses in attendance. In his mind's eye Goehrs saw Leguía at the bull fight, at the races, fearless, indomitable, confronting every risk. He thought of his son, whom he had disowned for dishonesty. He thought of an elderly, drab lady, beside whom he had on one occasion bought picture postcards in a shop—his daughter. He thought of his other son, who, because some one had once robbed him of 30,000 pounds in a business deal, was chivying his associate through Europe. He remembered an Argentinian telling him how a son of Leguía had offered him a monopoly of all fur-trapping in Peru. . . . . Fifty-fifty—an enormous bribe at the expense of the country ; for the fur yield of the Peruvian highlands, what with chinchilla, vicuña, and many other costly pelts, was a very big business. The Argentinian had not closed with the deal because the cash payment was more than he could manage and the bargain was risky because a revolution would at once annul it. His informant had at the time shed tears of distress not to have been able to take the risk. Goehrs thought of the risk of business deals that Leguía's dictatorship had involved and of the huge sums that, in connexion with guano, oil, railway construction, and mining concessions, had accrued to the house of Leguía. And then as he had seen him on that day when he had just signed the order for the deportation of thirty persons to San Lorenzo and torture for an attempt on his life, saying gently and with a smile : " Ten years . . . and not a single day off duty. People always form certain expectations of a man and of his work, and one has to live up to them, and in the long run one adapts oneself to them. Yes—Lima had to grow into a great new city within ten years' time, but my programme for the irrigation of the coastal deserts and my programme of colonization by small holders are much more important. My whole will is set on raising the status of the Indians."

" Seventy per cent. of the population," Goehrs had said, and borne in mind too that this seventy per cent. were living more or less in the conditions of slavery, exactly as they had lived under the rule of the Incas and the Spaniards.

It was the terrible tragic destiny of this country that this man—the strongest man Peru had had since Pizarro, the first man to take up the cause of the Indios and to aspire to rule by socialist measures, over a country that had not a trace of a Socialist movement . . . it was the tragic destiny of this country that such a man was constrained to rule as a tyrant and a dictator to give effect to his policy. And it was a South American tragic fate that this strong man, who aspired to give his best to Peru and had done an amazing amount, was ethically involved in conditions of corruption that made half a Renaissance princeling and half a criminal of him. So far as " liberty " was concerned, Goehrs knew too much of South American history not to realize that the strongest dictators are, as a rule, succeeded by the weakest dictators, and that the people who shout " Liberty " loudest have by no means liberty in their minds.

The revolution in Peru was a revolution against Leguía's merits, and against the little men and the Indios. Goehrs thought of Pizarro's mummy in its glass coffin, which was let into the walls of Lima Cathedral and could only be seen by the flame of a match. Pizarro's mummy with its gnashing jaws and the wounds Almagro's bastard had struck. He thought of Leguía speeding on board his cruiser northwards to Panama through the fog. What was going to be the fate of a land in which everything always counteracted and spoiled itself, where the good invariably only induced the evil, and where the evil was destined to obliterate the good, and where, taken as a whole, everything only remained what it always had been. This see-saw remained the eternal tragic destiny of which this continent was the prey. It was enough to lead to despair. And yet Goehrs felt sorry for that old man, Leguía.

"In Another Three Years . . ."

SHORTLY afterwards one or two aeroplanes from southern Argentina flew across Lago Nahuelhuapi and the volcanoes to southern Chile. Banished Chilean officers occupied the cabins. On the following day the garrisons of southern Chile came out in revolt. For four-and-twenty hours the Chilean frontier was closed, no telephones, no telegrams. Then the frontier was thrown open again. General Ibañez had weathered the storm. A general by profession held the reins in Chile—the officers had nothing to gain. They were very well off. The putsch had been squashed immediately after it had come to a head.

But Buenos Aires was in a state of extreme nervousness. It looked exactly as if the revolutions were running through the continent in accordance with some law of progression. Goehrs would have liked to have seen President Irigoyen, who, whether Buenos Aires were for or against him, was, next to Leguía, the toughest figure in South America. But as Irigoyen hardly troubled to receive even the ambassadors ; and as Herr von Keller, who presided over the German legation with ability and perspicacity, did not succeed in bringing it about ; and as Goehrs would not go to the expense of either a gold watch or 250 pesos, it did not get beyond a wish.

A week later, Goehrs received an invitation to a reception at the house of an ex-minister. Every one was talking about the two successful revolutions and nothing else. In the case of the Peruvian, every one only saw the intolerable autocracy and the unbounded corruption prevailing in Leguía's family and entourage. As to the Bolivian revolution, Goehrs noted every one held a wrong view about it, and nearly every one was entirely at sea in the reason to which he attributed it. Many thought it was the emancipation of the Indians ; others, on the contrary, that a people athirst for freedom, the masses of the poor, had risen in revolt. And no one really divined that the Bolivian revolution was the work of an ambitious faction whose methods had been no less illegal than the position of the Government had been irregular.

"There are, at most, ten Argentinians who have ever been

to La Paz," said an Argentinian general, " and that is probably overstating it." He was a man who had been one of the first officers to enter the Chaco, and mountain sickness had always made his nose bleed. " I always rode with my pocket handkerchief to my nose, which did not look very martial," he said. " I am not exaggerating."

Well, his estimate of ten Argentinians may have been an exaggeration, but metaphorically he was right. A discussion about Riga in a French provincial township could not have been less well informed than the way in which they talked about La Paz in Buenos Aires—as is in fact true of any South American country discussing another. Not one of the company present knew La Paz.

More interesting, however, than the critical opinions expressed about the country were the comparisons that were drawn between the situation in Peru and Argentina.

After dinner the ex-minister took the general and Goehrs aside and said with marked emotion :

" It is perhaps indiscreet to discuss such topics in the hearing of a foreigner, but I should like him to become acquainted with our point of view without beating about the bush. Do you believe, General, that anything similar to what has occurred in Lima is possible in our case ? "

By " in our case," on which three words the minister laid especial emphasis, he meant Argentina. And his native land Argentina meant to him, not a gaucho, not a medieval condottiere State, but a perfectly balanced, harmonic, law-abiding, democratic republic.

The general's brow clouded. " I hope not," he said emphatically.

" But will it be possible to ward it off ? " asked the minister. " The feeling against the President is becoming stronger every day. He does more insane things every day. He looks upon himself as a prophet and therefore prefers to discuss matters with his charwoman rather than with prominent men ; he receives—oh, well—young schoolteachers twice a week, while he keeps the diplomatic corps kicking its heels in his waiting-rooms. Have you heard the story about President Hoover and the new cable to Washington yet ? Irigoyen is suffering from downright megalomania. As soon as the cable was decided on, on the occasion of Hoover's visit to Buenos Aires, Irigoyen told every one of his supporters that Hoover was only having the cable laid to be in a position to ring up Irigoyen at any time to ask his advice. You need not laugh. He believes it for a fact. The inauguration of the cable was bad. Hoover very politely rang up first, a fortnight before the official inauguration. But Irigoyen thought it was incumbent upon him to show his aloofness and to give another exhibition of his antagonism to America and sent a message that he was out. Hoover was, of course, annoyed; and when a week later Irigoyen took it into his head to ring up, no one was at home at the White House. Finally, a few days before the inauguration, Hoover, as the custom is, sent in a copy of his speech and requested Irigoyen to send him one of his. Irigoyen held his up until ten minutes before the ceremony, to forestall Hoover from making any alterations in his speech. Hoover's speech embodied the usual neat periods about mechanical science being a beautiful thing, a great and wonderful thing that brought nations closer together. . . . Irigoyen then answered officially, after the President had spoken in Washington, to the effect that it was true that science was a beautiful thing, but that it was not science that made nations happy and made them friends. Only grace from above could do that and without that we never could be happy. ' Science, for example, did not prevent you, Mr. President, from becoming involved in a terrible war.' Do you not consider that in grossly bad taste ? "

Goehrs hesitated a moment. " I consider it extraordinarily to the point," he said. " That was the Irigoyen who moves multitudes. He did not answer by platitudes, nor politely, but with a certain note of grandeur. The Messiah pose ? But it was the voice of the only great champion South America has against the Yankees. This man hated them, obstructed them wherever he could ; he would have preferred to wipe them out—but the Yankees happened to be stronger than he."

The minister was put out for a moment.

" You are quite right," he said then, " but surely it is not the sort of thing one says in public ? " He turned to the general. " But you have not answered my question specifically. Do you consider a revolution in Argentina possible ? "

" No," said the general, and looked the minister straight between the eyes. " Nor must it be. A revolution in Peru is a revolution against Señor Leguía. But a revolution in . . . Good Lord ! Argentina is a nicely adjusted economic country and, if revolution should become a habit here, Argentina is played out."

" Is that the opinion of the army ? "

"It is the opinion the army holds, although the army cannot see how things are going to work out. We are drifting further and further every day towards a veiled dictatorship, and a system of favouritism that ought not to be is already gaining a hold on the army. If destiny does not come to our aid we shall perhaps be having a revolution in another three years—but not before three years' time."

"Three years!" said Goehrs, amazed at the vast period of time on which the general counted. "If you admit the possibility of a revolution at all, it is already upon you, you will have it to-morrow in that case."

"There is one point you overlook, señor," said the general. "We do not want a revolution."

A Veteran

THE general then went up to a map hanging on the wall beside him. He pointed his finger to Argentina, and indicated the big space it filled on the map. Then he pointed up to the right in the flank of South America and ran his finger round Venezuela. It was a small country in comparison.

"You can govern a country by the methods with which Gómez governs Venezuela," he said, and made a curt motion with his hand that admitted of no misinterpretation. "Some years ago I went to Gómez on a mission. That is the man for the job. He simply kills off anything in opposition to him. He has built a railway for the sole purpose of ensuring his own safety. I have actually seen a road that is laid out in such a way that it is practically concealed—only for his own purposes, in the event of his having to bolt— and it leads straight down to his warships, always kept under a head of steam. The property that man owns is simply incredible. After all, he can always have what he wants in the long run. When I reported to him for the first time, he was in the country. He received me on foot, standing in front of his hacienda in uniform, but in a soft shirt open at the neck and a civilian hat, at seven o'clock in the morning. 'Let us get on at once,' he said. His staff was round him, scattered about the grounds. He jumped into his car. Forty other cars with his parasites and fellows who wanted to get something out of him followed in his wake. If he stopped, the whole convoy stopped. If Gómez stretched his legs the whole company stretched their legs. The road was bristling with bayonets on either side. . . . Well, all I mean is that that is one way of governing a country. But it will not do for Argentina. Argentina is a white country ; it is a progressive and self-respecting country."

Goehrs studied the general's face closely while he was speaking. He was impressive, perhaps a little sardonic at first. Then it became the face all Argentinians have when they are talking of their country. Proud, obsessed by national feeling and devotion. It was rapt, more especially striking in the case of this race that no doubt is temperamental, but even to a greater degree self-controlled.

" What is Leguía doing ? " inquired the minister.

" The Junta has ordered the cruiser to put back," said the general. " After the whole of the navy had gone over to the revolutionaries, what was the cruiser to do except to put back ? She could not go on cruising about on the high seas on her own account. Leguía is back in Callao. When dictators go bankrupt, it is usually a pretty handsome smash."

" I agree," said the minister. " Has it ever struck you that there is the same sort of poetic justice in politics as there is on the stage ? "

" Certainly," said Goehrs. " They will get rid of him by sending him to his penal settlement, San Lorenzo."

" They have already done so," said the general. " But not before two American airmen had made an attempt to rescue him on board his cruiser."

" Lord ! " said the minister. " What has it to do with us ? Shall we join the others ? "

The others were scattered about the reception-rooms, with their hands in their pockets, a little stiffly and aloofly, but polite, as if their aloofness were only self-protection, a defensive attitude against dangers that they were not certain about themselves. " Curious," reflected Goehrs, " that this antagonism against the Yankees and this aloofness should have become most ingrained in the case of a nation that is more than half made up of European immigrants." He was thinking of the solid German, Italian, Russian, and Jewish towns that had grown up in and round Buenos Aires.

" I am going to introduce you to a wonderful veteran," said his host, and led Goehrs across to a white-haired man, who raised his finely cut aquiline face and narrow light-blue eyes to receive him. The minister, with a manner expressing the highest regard for the aged man, introduced the two men to one another. He was one of the Germans who was old enough to have crossed the seas in a sailing ship in the sixties. These men, as Goehrs knew, loved Germany all the world over as something supersensuous. Germany was endowed in their imagination with a strength and a permanence in the face of which every fact, every reality, counted for nothing. A wonderful affection that hated everything that was against Germany and loved everything that was for Germany, and that was of an unfairness beyond all bounds. In the eyes of these gallant veterans, Germany was still the country it had been when, after the war of 1870, it had for the first time in centuries come forward as a great Empire, and the crown that had united it was in the eyes of these men quite as sacred and symbolic an emblem as the flag. Goehrs knew this devotion that was in one respect unquestioning and passionate and in another refused to face facts, without weighing, without even wishing to see them. This devotion was a burnt-offering to a Germany that did not exist, and it set itself up to sit in judgment on a Germany writhing in torments such as no Germany has suffered since the Thirty Years' War. Goehrs bore them no grudge. They knew no better, these poor overseas Germans. They had not lived in Germany, had not suffered in Germany ; they were dreamers, but they loved Germany. Goehrs made it a principle to respect and pay them homage, but not to take them seriously.

Legislation had in many countries placed the Germans in awkward quandaries. In Argentina the State laid claim to every child that had been born in Argentina for an Argentinian national, recruited the child for military service, and enrolled it as an Argentinian. And they became and grew up as Argentinians. There was no doubt about that. It was a fact.

The handsome old man to whom Goehrs was talking now had sons, and these sons were no longer young men. They had played—and were still playing—a prominent part in Argentine political life. As Argentinians. They loved their father as their father loved Germany. But they were Argentinians to the core. Their father had been a member of hundreds of German clubs. He was the oriflamme of the old-time German spirit, whether the foeman were the French, the British, or the world at large. Above all others, he hated the French with a refreshing, unreal, senile hatred—without knowing anything about them.

335

"Now supposing a quarrel between Germany and Argentina were to spring up suddenly," Goehrs asked him finally. "Let us assume this unlikely event, you surely would have to make your choice. In this case there could hardly be any other alternative. For whom would you decide?"

For a moment the veteran with finely cut eagle's head had that troubled expression Alsatians used to have when confronted with a final issue.

"Merciful heavens!" he said, exhausted and distressed, "my ties here are too strong. I should have to decide for Argentina."

But from the expression on his face, it was easy for Goehrs to see that the decision would be his death warrant.

Part VI

CONCERNING BRAZIL

A Tangled Tale

THERE is so little of real interest that one knows about Brazil, thought Goehrs, as he began to read a history of Brazil on board ship. He had just travelled a few hundred miles from Buenos Aires, having crossed the La Plata. The bar was so high that the ship all but scraped her bottom. And Goehrs was now on board the *Sierra Ventana* on the way from Montevideo, the capital of the Republic of Uruguay, up the coast of Brazil. There was no doubt a cross-country railway connexion, but the length of Brazil from south to north was some 2700 miles, and to try to get on by rail in these circumstances would have been like attempting to play tennis on stilts. So Goehrs was sitting on the promenade deck of the *Sierra Ventana* of the North German Lloyd, a passenger liner of 11,000 tons, on his way to Santos.

One knows so little . . . he thought. It was by no means warm at sea, and Goehrs was consequently attuned for mental exercise. One or two things at any rate he had known approximately. He knew that at the time of the conquest of South America, the Pope, in his capacity of arbitrator, had awarded a definite geographical area, not to the Spaniards, but to the Portuguese—the present-day Brazil.

He knew that Brazil was bigger than Australia, a country like China, an area like the United States of America, and that it called itself the " United States of Brazil." He knew that, in contradistinction to the rest of South America, its language was Portuguese in lieu of Spanish, and he also had a vague notion that towards the close of the Middle Ages the European powers had at one time engaged on a great imperialistic race for dominion here. British, Frenchmen, and Portuguese had competed for Brazil.

In fact, towards the middle of the seventeenth century it had looked as if the Dutch were going to turn Brazil into a great Dutch colonial empire. They had held it at the time for quite a while, but not firmly enough.

Goehrs knew that the Amazon that traversed Brazil was the most glorious river in the world, at times almost 70 miles wide, with hundreds of navigable tributaries practicable at high water for traffic over 60,000 miles, that its basin was five times the size of Germany, a fairy-tale virgin forest, less than 40 square miles of which were really opened up.

Goehrs had known that at one time half of the world's rubber consumption had been met by the forests of the Amazon, and that in some years three-quarters of the world's coffee consumption had been covered by Brazil as well. He knew that the twenty States in Brazil could be sorted roughly into three groups : those with a mean temperature of from 60° to 70°, those of from 70° to 80°, and those over 80°. A country of illimitable possibilities—and pretty hot.

He knew that the Portuguese had in their time imported Negro slaves, and that they had intermarried without restriction with the Negroes, and that there could hardly be an Indian problem here, but an almost complete absorption of the white man in the Negro strain. He remembered that, even before the final settlement of Brazil, a very stalwart Portuguese in the hinterland of the São Paulo of to-day had fathered a whole cross-bred tribe by innumerable Indian mothers and that this tribe under the name of Mamelucos had played a similar part in the history of Brazil as the Arabs had played in that of Africa, that of the warrior race, the slave-hunters, the legionaries and lansquenets, and that this tribe had even threatened and alarmed the almost Communist realm that the Order of the Jesuits had founded in Paraguay and in southern Brazil.

Goehrs knew that the several States of Brazil had in the course of their history waged war on one another, as Europe had made war against herself ; and that this analogy did not hold water, only because Europe did not speak with a single tongue. He knew, too, that the Portuguese, unlike the Spaniards, had not conquered Brazil in any spirit of fanaticism, of religious fervour, or in an orgy of colonization, but had slowly permeated the country by private enterprise and trading instinct, not in any spirit of overweening arrogance or zeal for conversion. He knew that one fine

VIRGIN FOREST IN BRAZIL.

day slavery had been abolished. He knew that there were Indian tribes living in the virgin forests who had never yet come into contact with a white man.

Goehrs knew that the population was based only on estimates. It was estimated to be 17,000,000 in 1900 ; twenty years later at 30,000,000, and ten years later at more than 40,000,000. But there were people who called these estimates moonshine and declined to make any estimates at all, and others again who estimated it at between twenty-five and thirty-five millions for the year 1931—entirely in the light of their experience and personal predilections. Goehrs knew, too, that he could reckon on two millions of Germans, or perhaps only one million, for the same reasons as set forth in the case of the total population. He knew, too, that the twenty States of Brazil had to apply eyewash freely not to fall apart altogether, for, in spite of a common Senate, Parliament, and President, the several States had in turn Presidents of their own and plenty of autonomy.

So Goehrs knew this, that, and the other thing. But there were heaps of things he did not know.

Among others he did not know that slavery had not been finally abolished until the year 1888. Nor did he know that in 1889, that is to say, twenty years after the Franco-Prussian war, and only a few years before he was born, Brazil was still an empire. It gave him a bit of a shock to find that he had never realized that.

Nor had he known that the coffee plant that yielded a crop three years after planting and may go on yielding one for twenty years and might attain a height of fifteen feet—that this tree, with which Brazil's destiny is bound up, was not introduced into Pará until the year 1727. Nor had he realized that three-fourths of the population could neither read nor write. He certainly ought to have worked out some of these facts for himself. But that slavery had only been abolished quite a short time before his own birth—that really gave him a severe shock (although he ought to have known it on the strength of his own experiences in Zanzibar). What small progress certain generally accepted humanitarian axioms had made in the world ! He considered that that ought to make him more tolerantly minded when the humanitarian advance of his own age struck him as unduly deliberate.

On the other hand Goehrs had pictured Brazilian administration and government as inclined to laxity. His view on this point had already been amended by the Brazilian

Consul General's office in Buenos Aires. He had secured all his visas for South America in Germany and in the most obliging and kindly fashion withal, in fact several States had endorsed them by letters of recommendation. Only the Brazilian visa had he failed to obtain in Europe. And when he wanted it made out in Buenos Aires, he felt as if he had been sent back to his nursery governess. Three times did the official in the little room, in which some thirty people were herded like sheep, return his form of application to him. Once, because Goehrs had filled in the extraordinarily inquisitive questionnaire containing fifty queries or so with his spare fountain pen—that is to say, in red ink instead of in black as prescribed. A second time, because Goehrs had in inadvertence committed the unpardonable offence of filling in the space reserved for his religion with his age and the space for his age with his creed. And the formula was turned back a third time because Goehrs had given Rio de Janeiro as his destination whereas his passage was made out for Santos. It was one of the most difficult visas among the fifty-odd he had succeeded in obtaining on his passport, and had called for the greatest amount of self-control.

Goehrs, sitting on the deck of the *Sierra Ventana*, recounted this story to the airman beside him who had for a time been manager of a German air line in Argentina.

"Worse than Prussians," he concluded with a laugh, though he had not felt the least like laughing in the Consul General's office.

"Not a bit of it," said the airman. "They are so stringent because a short time ago they found a dozen dead bodies lying round the wreckage of a crashed plane on the Brazilian coast. The dead were unrecognizable, but it did not take much guessing to ascertain that they were deported Brazilians who were trying to return to Brazil surreptitiously by this route—nor was the purpose of their return a mystery for long. Do you propose to travel by air in Brazil?"

"Probably."

"The Germans and their air lines have had to put up their shutters. The Yankees with their lines that are subsidized by America have simply squeezed us out. The German aviation policy is to blame for it, for hopping from one manure heap to the next in Germany instead of organizing a big bold representative German air service in

Argentina and subsidizing it from the start. It would soon have paid its way—exactly as our service in Bolivia is paying its way. That would have been more valuable to us Germans than the Prince of Wales's visit here can be to the British. At any rate we are holding our own with the German Condor syndicate in Brazil. Don't you think it is unusually chilly ? The weather must grow warm in a couple of days' time whatever happens. Santos is hot under any conditions."

"Let's hope so," said Goehrs, watching the coast. " Let's hope it will be as hot as Hades once again. But I can hardly believe it can be. I have been feeling chilly for nearly a year."

The Coffee State

IT was growing really hot. Four days after leaving Montevideo, Goehrs was looking out of the porthole of his cabin one morning. The water round the North German Lloyd's packet was remarkably calm.

"Sixty-six degrees," some one sang out.

Goehrs saw cliffs, mountains, and little hillocks running down amicably to the water's edge, and the cliffs and hillocks were overgrown with palm trees, plantains, and climbing plants—quite densely overgrown, untrodden by the foot of man.

The liner pushed inland up a tropical canal almost in a circle—she might have been on a river—and then reached the harbour of Santos. Santos was the port for the town and State of São Paulo. Santos was a town with a population of 150,000. The State of São Paulo had one of over six millions. São Paulo, the capital, lying a couple of hours' run inland at a height of 2600 feet, had a population of over a million. São Paulo was one of the most important and politically one of the two most influential States in Brazil, although it was only about half the size of Germany. In earlier days São Paulo had been one of the most dreaded haunts of yellow jack in the world. That had been attended to.

Close behind the quay Goehrs saw endless rows of sheds, echeloned one behind the other, endless storage huts, close, narrow, like battalions advancing on the town. They were the storehouses for coffee. Coffee in this State was produced on industrial lines. (For this reason it was not the best, and Ecuador and Peru turned up their noses at it in contempt.) Brazil was dependent on the prices of the coffee produced in São Paulo. It meant an export turnover of sometimes as much as $375,000,000. Brazil depended for its prosperity on coffee as Argentina did on its wheat, Chile on its nitrates, and Bolivia on tin. The country prospered or declined with the prices. It was sometimes within an ace of being plunged into disaster at the wrong end of the tariff. Sometimes these storage houses were empty. Then the price of coffee was high ; it meant that the world was drinking plenty of coffee ; and ships were lying at the wharves in dozens taking in coffee. At other times the storehouses were full ; then the price was low, the outlook for Brazil was threatening, the world was drinking less coffee than was being produced, and there were no ships taking in cargo then.

When Goehrs reached Santos, the storage houses were full to bursting. For some time this had been the normal state of things. Brazil was overproducing. As long ago as 1901 the world's coffee crop amounted to some twenty million bags of 150 pounds each—and the world demand had been for sixteen million bags. The tragedy of Brazil and of the State of São Paulo lay in this discrepancy. By 1902 there were already close on 700,000,000 coffee trees on the coffee *fazendas*. Coffee simply wolfed the soil and used it up, and the plantations pushed deeper into the country and encroached on the primeval forests—but the world refused to drink more coffee than it was in the habit of doing. Coffee prices dropped lower and lower—and production increased. There were even then over two thousand million coffee trees.

The world stoutly declined to drink up a few more million bags of coffee. It was too much of a good thing—the crop was left ungarnered and the exchange was bad.

In 1905 the States most concerned in coffee-growing put their heads together to find some means for remedying this state of things. They proposed a big loan to enable them to restrict the output with this capital, that is, say, to buy up the surplus coffee and to sell it when the market was more favourable. They also proposed an export duty to cover the interest—it was complicated by political considerations in connexion with the exchange—but this scheme did not get through Congress because the Rothschilds had criticized it adversely. The State of São Paulo therefore raised the funds required on its own account.

The plan experienced a good many ups and downs, but, at a time of overproduction all the world over, the slump in coffee was pretty severe. Prices fell although the storehouses were brimful with surplus crop bought in.

Goehrs saw the sacks of coffee sliding out of the sheds on the conveyancer belt, going up in tubes, passing across the deck, and then being automatically and noiselessly lowered into the ship's hold. In the background lay Santos, a town with automobiles, tramways, and mules, with Negroes, browns, and whites, and standardized houses. The colour of its inhabitants was very varied. In 1871 there were still two million slaves left. They had propagated and intermingled promiscuously. With Chinese, Portuguese, Mulattos, with half-breeds of Indians and whites. The progeny of these hybrids were now romping amicably about the streets.

A different tint was sitting in the window on every storey of the houses. The Portuguese were the only nation on earth that never displayed even the slightest trace of embarrassment in these matters.

Beyond Santos rose a belt of banana plantations. Goehrs passed through it up the mountainside to a height of nearly 3000 feet through a forest of orchids, lianas, flowers, palm and fan trees. It was traversed by a handsome motor road, which after a two hours' run led up to São Paulo and the plateau. São Paulo was the biggest city bar one in Brazil, with a population of over a million. It was the capital of the State of São Paulo. A modern, hectic city. Very new, very bloated. With a bigger number of motor cars than Rio de Janeiro. With more energy and business enterprise. Held in higher esteem for its financial operations than for its architecture.

There lay the coffee *fazendas*—with São Paulo lying like a leech in front of them. It had grown fat on the plantations. The air was good at this height. The avenues of the suburbs luxuriant. And from São Paulo a railway in a day or a night's run took you to Rio de Janeiro. A road, too, ran to a famous snake farm. Goehrs let himself off the snake farm. He let himself off the railway journey as well.

To the westward the huge areas of coffee trees extended, the plantations on to which the bulk of the immigrants was dumped to demonstrate by tending the trees in the blazing sunlight whether they would stick it or would go to the wall. The least exacting, the Italians, stuck it. People who claim to be well informed have described the life of these labourers as awful.

Eastwards lay the sea. And Santos. Goehrs had been told hundreds of times that the crowning moment of his life would be the approach to Rio de Janeiro. He therefore drove down to Santos to go to Rio by boat. The beach at Santos was crowded with vultures. Behind the vultures rose the big hotels. The cars drove round the bay on the wet sand. The wet sand furnished a magnificent practice track. A motor race was just being run in between the vultures, which took no notice of it, and the hotels, which did not mind it.

The bay shimmered southerly-wise in the background. The many canoes had cargoes of golden oranges. Goehrs felt the cockles of his heart growing warm again. The tropics were wheeling back.

RIO DE JANEIRO

PEOPLE had told Goehrs a hundred times over that the great moment of his life would be his entrance to Rio. But he saw nothing of it. His vessel entered the bay as early as six o'clock and on top of that it was raining. When Goehrs was called, the ship was inside the bay and he had to go up to the smoking-room to present himself with his vaccination certificate, his personal credentials and bill of health, with his passport, photograph, and disembarkation permit from the Consul General in Buenos Aires. He had to do it all in his bathgown—then the vessel was cleared and was free to make fast. She berthed between the *Highland Prince* of the Nelson Line, the *Mendoza* of the Transports Maritimes, and the *Almanzora* of the Royal Mail. Three big passenger liners. Three big steamships that left for Europe the same day. What busy traffic as compared with the West Coast—and it was not the season, and boats were consequently empty. The handsome Scottish *Highland Prince* looked like a warship, grey and lean. She was a 15,000-tonner, a blaze of lights, and had steamed past Goehrs's boat in the course of the night. She was sheathed in ice above her load line, for the whole vessel below was a huge refrigerator, shipping frozen meat from Argentina to Europe. The other vessels had small cargoes of coffee. These were the notes Goehrs made and the thoughts that occupied his mind on his first arrival at Rio.

A taxi thereupon took him to his hotel in half an hour. In the course of this drive the lay-out of Rio puzzled him. He only realized that his car kept on along the bay or along the shore, across the Praia do Flamengo, along the Avenida Beira Mar ; he saw the houses peeping above the palm trees like beautiful strongholds, and he kept seeing unsubstantially delicate mountains of oddly triangular contours rising out of the bay. At length Goehrs reached his hotel on the Copacabana Bay. An asphalt road led past the front of the hotel, and immediately beyond that the beach began. The beach was of sand as white as flour. Miles of it.

Many cars drove into the street and parked. Many ladies and men in bathing dresses alit from the cars and went for a walk along the beach. Goehrs had always noticed people in bathing dress on the promenades of Rio. No one took the trouble to look round at them. And the people in bathing costume had moved about as if it had been their habit from the dawn of time to walk across the Praia do Flamengo and along the esplanade in bathing-kit. It was delightfully natural. And this ensemble of the most reputable quarter, motor cars, bathing dresses, and of the beach of Copacabana Bay could not have been so charmingly possible in any other city in the world. And amid it all the waves broke crooning over the sand as they might in a bay of the South Seas, lavish and shoreless.

Within a quarter of an hour of his arrival Goehrs was on the beach in his bathing-kit. Here and there a mast broke in the semicircle of the bay. Lashed to the mast hung a basket and in the basket sat a man. In front of the man the surf rose green and steeply, and behind this wall of green foam a boat was moored. The surf had a backwash and it was deadly.

Although it was the end of the winter season for Rio, a fair number of people forgathered on the beach. But there were no huts, no cabins, and no basket-chairs. Every woman had a groundsheet of some striking colour which she spread on the sand to sit on, and attached to the ground-sheet was a wooden frame for a roof. The roof of the frame-work that supported the back was of the same distinctive colour as the groundsheet on which she was sitting, and the fabric floated about her like a sail. Quite improvised, well adapted for its purpose, and quite pretty. The majority of the women were dark brown, but not from the rays of the sun. All the men in the lifeboats behind the green foam were swarthy. And all the fellows squatting in the baskets at the mastheads were regular Negroes.

Goehrs ran up the beach in his bathing-suit before taking to the water. The sweep of the bay curved in sharply on Fort Copacabana. And then he first saw the Sugarloaf, hitherto hidden from view by an intervening hillock, the Pão de Açucar, the divinely slanting thumb that the Creator of this glorious landscape seemed to have left behind as a memento when he had finished it and was himself amazed at its wild loveliness.

Goehrs looked back. He realized now that Rio de Janeiro, which was not far short of having two million inhabitants, was built half inland from the sheltered bay and half in the open sea, so that like a star of many rays it ran out into the sea and back again, and that no one had worried if the forest had encroached into the town — everywhere, even among the villas of Copacabana Bay little hills rose, curious pyramids that had never been climbed, dense with palms and climbing plants and swarming with monkeys—and without regard for them the city had continued its mushroom growth all round them . . . the brightest, the most verdant, the most petted by the sea, the most radiant, most tuneful city in the world. Goehrs realized that in a flash. Skyscrapers and diving birds, aerial railways and lianas, omnibuses and beautiful fish went side by side, as if it could not be otherwise. Nor could it be otherwise, for this medley was harmonized by all the graces of Nature.

THE KING'S PALM TREE

IN the course of the following days Goehrs got to know Rio from a bird's eye point of view and ceased to be astonished when, after a twenty-minutes' drive, the Sugarloaf seemed to be nearer to him than it was after a drive of forty. And then he got a view of the entrance.

The entrance to Rio Bay was a little less than a mile in width. On the left rose the Sugarloaf, on the right Fort Santa Cruz. But between the two the little Fort Lage intervened. It was only then that the bay of Rio de Janeiro opened out, a bay with seventy tropical islands, a bay into which forty rivers ran out. On the left shore of the bay lay Rio darting and withdrawing the star rays of its fjords into the water and in the end seeking its outlet beyond the bay along the coves on the open sea. On the left shore of the bay lay Rio de Janeiro, the capital of Brazil. It lay in a Federal district as in a capsule, in neutral territory, insulated, cut off from contact with the rest of the States, like something particularly precious. . . . And on the right shore of the bay lay Nictheroy, the capital of the State of Rio de Janeiro that was quite distinct from the city of Rio de Janeiro, a little complicated but prudent.

The circumference of the bay was about ninety miles. And the entrance through the narrow channel between the natural fortifications fashioned of polished rock, the Sugarloaf and Fort Santa Cruz, was genuinely fascinating. Nature had given expression to at once a grandiose and a joyous inspiration by making this entrance channel so narrow and of such heroic proportions, so exotic and at the same time so delicious.

But not only the avenidas along the coves were designed with taste, wisdom, and vision on the shore of the bay. Even the main street, the Avenida Rio Branco, pulsing with hurrying motor cars and flashlight sky signs, was green with foliage. The big, sweating thoroughfare was embowered in trees. It seemed as if the city of two millions had only come into the primeval forest on a visit and had remained only as a vision of a metropolis. Even the great liners lying within the shadow of the skyscrapers on the Praça Marechal Floriano Peixato and the Praça Maua, even the ocean greyhounds lay among trees just as if they were some strange marine monsters that had sought the shade to rest under.

Driving out to the Botanical Gardens, Goehrs skirted a Negro encampment of galvanized-iron huts in the heart of the city. It stood at the foot of a little virgin forest crag, round which the city had flooded as it expanded. Resplendent, unsullied, the primeval forest descended close to the grandstands and the racecourse, and at the foot of the crag was a patch of Central Africa where the naked black children were rolling about in the sand in competition with the dogs.

The Botanical Gardens were a vision of tropical delights. At the entrance gates rose an avenue of royal palm trees like obelisks, simply majestic. It led into a jungle of bamboos as tall as a house and of trees bearing strange fruits and blossoms, and of beautiful pools with water

347

lilies, steeped in fragrance, linking up with rocks with which the virgin forest penetrated even here.

One tall palm tree in a little open space was called Palma Mater. Beside it stood the bust of the man who had planted the tree, in side whiskers and a Mozart pigtail. Dom João VI. Brazilian King Anno Domini 1820. This King, thirty-eight years old at the time, had in 1808 disembarked in Brazil with his court numbering a thousand persons. He had been convoyed to this country by a British squadron after Napoleon had deposed his dynasty in Portugal. The royal house of Portugal therefore sought refuge in the colonies. The King declared the independence of Brazil as a kingdom in 1815. Therewith Brazil, for the first time, began to breathe freely. Trade flourished. It became a nation on its own account. In 1820 this obliging monarch planted the palm tree in the Botanical Gardens. A year later, when the outlook for Portugal seemed promising, he returned to Lisbon and left his heir to the throne behind as Prince Regent. In the following year this amiable royal gentleman proposed to show his gratitude for his kindly reception in Brazil by repealing all the rights he had granted to her. Brazil was to revert to the status of colony and milch cow for the refreshment of the court at Lisbon.

But this proposal was doomed to failure. The heir to the throne who had been left behind in Brazil himself turned against the King and against the proposal. This inspired the Brazilians with such enthusiasm that they elected him their Emperor under the title of Dom Pedro I. But that was a century ago.

The palm tree planted by King João VI had grown out of mind in the course of this century. It had become thirty times as tall as the man who had planted it. It had survived the kingdom, the empire, and a crowd of dictators, and was now taking the republic under its wing. It had in the meantime founded its own dynasty, for all the other palms in the garden are descended from it as is the magnificent obelisk avenue of palm trees, the pride of Rio—that almost unending, majestic roadway where every tree is a peer to its fellow, equally tall, equally handsome, a genuinely imposing and tropical street. These palms were one and all giants and smooth as columns. Only quite at their top they displayed a delicate, handsome ring of leaves, a crown of foliage that rustled discreetly and serenely in absolute aloofness. It was bewitching music.

THAT evening there was a fête of the Argentine colony at the Hotel Copacabana. It was a flag day. In the hall on the first floor several hundreds of gentlemen and ladies invited by three members of the Argentine colony were assembled. Every man was wearing a blue-white-blue ribbon in his buttonhole with a medal the size of a silver dollar. There were included many influential, handsome, and wealthy people, ministers, deputies, ambassadors, industrial magnates, coffee kings, and railway kings who convey the coffee. Planters and diplomats and business men. They were standing about with their womenfolk beside them waiting for dinner to be announced.

The ladies of Brazil were not, like those of Chile, predestined by nature to lead the fashions; nor, like the Argentine women, trained to take the lead—but they were more natural than either, natural in the sense that attractive animals are and they were endowed, too, with a grace of movement such as, except for animals, only Negro women have. Almost all the ladies had a distinctive shade of colouring that pointed to a fusion of strains. The " pointing " presented some pretty puzzles. You were " pointed " in such a number of directions. For the Portuguese had been very catholic in their liaisons, first with the Indian women, later with Negresses. But the Negro strain had overlaid every other. A hint of Africa peeped out from them all. In the case of many it was confined to the corners of the eyes only. In the case of others it was painted all over them. Their Portuguese strain had in any case invested these Negro heads with sensitive, delicately arched noses. That was very attractive. There was a particular attraction for Goehrs, when confronted by these ladies, to puzzle out the Indian races and the negro mammies in the background of these pretty women overladen with rings and pearls, whose dusky necks contrasted so daintily with an ermine wrap.

Among this distinguished company was a Negro, almost a head taller than most of his fellow-guests. He was in full evening dress. His hair was almost white. He was still a fine figure of a man and had the most intellectual eyes Goehrs had ever seen in a Negro's head. Every new arrival went up to the Negro and greeted him with every mark of distinction. The generals, the diplomats, Chileans, French-

349

men, Argentinians, and Englishmen. Goehrs opened his eyes wide. It was quite a new experience. He had seen Negro rulers in South Africa, even an aristocratic Indian like Gandhi, being turned out of their train or their hotels because they were men of colour. He had seen the representative of African labour to the League of Nations being debarred from dining in the saloon of a vessel where only newly rich hairdressers had their meals. He had seen Americans insisting on leaving an Italian boat on the high seas before Egypt because a black scholar had intruded into the smoking-room. He had seen African cities where the black population was not allowed to walk on the pavement. . . . And Goehrs therefore did not trust his eyes. For the folk assembled here were Rio " society " and the whole of the diplomatic corps. And Goehrs knew that in every country of the world these people are the most pretentious, the most timid, and most supercilious—not individually, but as a caste.

Goehrs made the Negro's acquaintance, thanks to the kind offices of a man, who, although he had red hair, did not on that account unworthily represent, as an attaché, the diplomatic dignity of Germany on this occasion. The Negro was the most eminent psychologist of South America. He had graduated in Germany. His wife was Hamburg-born with a white skin and fair hair. " Simons . . . Cassierer . . . Goldstein," said the Negro, with a smile, in German. " I know all the German psychologists and psychiatrists, of course."

His wife mistook Goehrs, since he was privileged to know some of these very distinguished physicians personally, for a medical man himself. When he informed her of his ungrateful and rarely correctly practised profession, she said animatedly : " Then you are sure to have made some interesting studies of racial problems. In many parts of the world people are stupid enough to commit the mistake of looking on half-breeds as bad from the start. But everything in the world is surely a blend. Only think of the Spaniards who are one quarter of Moorish-Arab and one quarter of German descent along with their Celtic and Basque constituents. People really are ignorant. When I was in Germany with my husband every one took him for an Indian, Moroccan, Abyssinian—for anything rather than for a Negro of Brazil."

" For all that we must give the world its due by admitting that in many parts it has sound, dispassionate objections to raise against any intermingling, even if the reason for these objections is not altogether ideal," said Goehrs.

" But people are not even logical. Look at our Minister of Transport. He is half pure German, half Brazilian. He has all the good German and all the bad Brazilian points. Well, and what about the people ? " She laughed. " The people do not love him in the least for all his German virtues, but for his Brazilian shortcomings. That is the world all over."

Goehrs had no answer ready for her. In no part of the world, he felt sure, would any one have dared to dismiss the racial question in such a detached and airy fashion, and so sarcastically. That was a fact. But it was by no means a fact that this attitude was also the right one.

The " Misses "

A RACING motorist is an interesting acquaintance but, as far as the preservation of one's bodily safety is concerned, of doubtful profit. But why should one not risk a run with him—after dinner to the Lyrico Theatre—more especially as the evening was mild, the stars deep set, the bay under a magic spell, and Praia do Flamengo veiled in a fairylike silvery haze ?

The twenty queens of beauty of the twenty states of Brazil had been invited to the Lyrico Theatre that evening. Each one had her private box and displayed herself to the audience therein—and the audience was holding a sort of private view in anticipation of the great competition to be held shortly, at which the Queen of the State of Brazil was to be elected. Some silly stuff was being played on the stage, as in most of the theatres of Rio when a good foreign travelling company did not happen to disturb their stagnation. It was, too, a matter of secondary interest, for no one had gone to the theatre for the sake of the play.

There was a shield fixed to every box and on the shield was the name of a State, to wit :

Alagóas	Maranhão
Amazonas	Matto Grosso
Bahia	Minas Geraes
Ceará	Pará
Espirito Santo	Parahyba
Goyaz	Paraná

Pernambuco	Rio Grande do Sul
Piauhy	Santa Catharina
Rio de Janeiro	São Paulo
Rio Grande do Norte	Sergipe

The fronts of the boxes were furnished with these neatly painted names, and Goehrs in his mind's eye outlined the map of the Federal State of Brazil from the pretty girls sitting in the boxes over the names of their States.

In the interval the light was turned full on, and the audience began to move about. They passed in separate companies of about fifty along the gangways in front of the boxes and kept up a clapping of their hands before each until the beauty appeared. The beauty in question came out into the corridor and took her stand a few feet away from the applauding, shouting, and enthusiastic crowd, and smiled. The company then moved on to the adjoining box, and another took its place and again fetched out the pretty specimen on view that had in the meantime retired into its box.

The heads of the " Misses " were really beautiful. Most of them had bad legs. But each of them represented a different type. The queen of the State of Rio was very brunette but had a dazzlingly white skin. She was rather Spanish with a slight cross, the source of which it was difficult to determine. Miss Pará, from the northern State on the equator where fifty per cent. of the population is Negro, was almost English and of that unexpected fairness which, even if it has called in the aid of chemistry, is always alluring, and that not only in the case of a Southerner in the tropics. But Miss Bahia of the State of Bahia, which, if not quite so close to the equator, had fewer natives—Miss Bahia was quite negroid. Deep black. Very dark. A pretty mulatto, appealing to the genuine Brazilian taste, a type of which the young bloods of Brazil averred : " In the early morning there is nothing more refreshing than the skin of a mulatto." Miss Bahia, too, earned the tribute of the most enthusiastic applause. In the adjoining box sat Miss Rio Grande do Sul, of the southern State bordering on Uruguay. She hailed from the town of Porto Alegre, a city of over 200,000 inhabitants in which no fewer than three German newspapers were published, from a State on which the German element had left an abiding imprint. Rio Grande do Sul's queen of beauty was a golden blonde. She was a German.

"A people without prejudices," said Goehrs, as he got into the Bugatti again with his companion. "And a really great country. A country that contrives to be so varied as to admire European women and Negresses at one and the same time. . . . Some country!"

"Some country," said the great racing motorist, who, like many of his kind, was much too big for the little space at the disposal of the driver of a racing car, "but after all, everything is topsy-turvy here. The moon appears the other way about. The farther you go south the colder it gets, and the farther you go north the more infernally hot it becomes. The palm trees are thin at the bottom and thick at the top. But the worst of all is the sand." He pointed from the Avenida Niemeyer, amid whose rocks and palms the Bugatti was shooting like a streak of lightning, to the beach. "The sand in Rio is so fine that you can't drive on it. Whereas in Santo it is so firm that, when wet, it furnishes the ideal racing surface. I do 103 miles an hour in the Bugatti down there."

They had turned into the avenida of the Leblon quarter out of the Avenida Niemeyer. The esplanade here had been wrested from the sea by pumping-work and huge sand embankments, but a spring tide had washed half of it away in the course of the previous year. Nature here was either gentle or savage—or both.

"Listen!"

The driver had switched off the motor. There came a hum as of wild beasts from the Lagoa Rodrigo de Freitas, the surface of which shone like a mislaid lunar lake. They were the crickets round the lagoon and round the Negro camp.

"They chirp till they burst," said the motorist. "They literally split, so hard do they chirp. But what of it— they chirp at any rate."

They had reached Fort Copacabana by this time. The bay of Copacabana, with its rows of lights, swept in a semicircle towards the mystic sugarloaves gleaming eerily in the moonlight. The fort stood at the extremity of a curve that for sweep and size beat Nice many times over. The fort was a unique curiosity of Rio. A few years ago its garrison, twenty-four strong, had mutinied and had turned its guns on the town. The fort bombarded Rio. Then the garrison of twenty-four had sallied forth in skirmishing order to take by assault a city of two millions, the hub of which was about half an hour's drive by car away from the fort. In this gallant exploit the mutineers, it is true, went under and disappeared without leaving a trace. It was perhaps heroic of them to open fire with their big guns on the town, but it was ill-advised to attempt to rush so big a city with a couple of dozen bombardiers.

Pondering over this incident, Goehrs realized that he was not in a fairyland city, but in South America.

HILLS AS SHAPES ONLY

GOEHRS had no idea of the real grandeur of the scenery of Rio de Janeiro until he saw it from the Tijuca. He had driven up this hill through the residential quarter of Santa Thereza. This high-lying quarter used to contain all the hotels situate on the beach to-day, and used in the past to comprise almost all the private residences of foreign and Brazilian notables. But many of these people were living on the beach of Copacabana nowadays and spoke of the Santa Thereza quarter as a jolly little Negro suburb.

From a summer-house, the Vista Chineza, five hundred feet or so high, with little monkeys and birds all round him, Goehrs saw a large number of promontories jutting out into the bay below, and all of them had a curious triangle on their extremity, a triangle moulded in such a way that its peak rose above it in a rounded swelling. These rounded triangles were the pillars of Rio ; they were everywhere ; they trooped down, arrayed in forest livery, fragrant with orchids, into the bay and into the outskirts in their hundreds, in that mystic shape that always melted into the silvery haze, but none the less with clearly defined contours. The hills here had no suggestion of roughness—they were only shapes.

From the Tijuca Goehrs had a view of the greater part of Rio and of many of the phantom rounded triangles that pierced the silvery haze over the bay like the dorsal fins of floating fish. Between five of the biggest of these mystic sugarloaves Rio crouched and then thrust out another promontory—one that was destined to become immortal. It surpassed all the rest because it was the promontory on which the Creator has left his thumb behind as a memento, that wedge of rock unreasonably beautiful and bewilderingly strange, the Pão de Açucar, a moon mountain, a fragment of Venus's star, a jewel of the planet Mars. Goehrs looked down in the twilight on to the virgin

BRAZILIAN HARBOUR. VICTORIA.

forests and across the forests to the bevy of rounded triangles floating on the metallic haze of the bay.

At this juncture some one or other in Rio must have pressed a button.

Thereupon the City first of all sprang into light, and became a close cone of light. Then a ring of light leapt up round the lagoon lying in the heart of the town ; then the parts of Rio lying in between the pillars of rock became luminous. And then the fuse darted along all the coves, a tenfold string of it in loops. The light poured down like rain, but rain suspended on strings. It beaded the outlines of the fjords in an instant. Yet the dusk retained light enough to make every house in Rio still stand out distinctly—in spite of the distance—as if cast in bronze, and then the moon rose. The moon rose over the crests of the palm trees in the Avenida Niemeyer—and the hills, the palm trees, the coves, the seventy flat-beaten silver islands melted into a vision of magic harmony, into a scene that was at once clear-cut but unreal. It was redolent of flowers, of the song of birds, and of repose. Of repose as of the ineffably delicious intake of Nature's breath that only issues from silence and stands for the acme of delight.

THE NEGRO PROBLEM

ONE night the wealthy young men and the wealthy young women of Brazil who forgather to dance in the hotel of an evening came out every now and then to take the air on the terrace, twenty yards away from the opalescent sea, and every now and then put their fingers to their mouths and whistled on this exceedingly primitive instrument. Their object in doing so was to exasperate the taxis in which " society " drove abroad every evening. The majority of them drove on, unresponsive to these whistles. But occasionally there might be a nervous or a polite driver who would pull up. But it did not repay him for his trouble, for the bright young things only waved their handkerchiefs to him and thought themselves great humorists.

Goehrs had made friends with the racing motorist. At first sight it might appear that a racing motorist's profession would be a rather conspicuous way of earning one's living in Brazil, but this man as a matter of fact had another profession as well, which was reassuring from a social point of view. His mother had been a Czech, his father a Brazilian, and he was an uncommonly shrewd man. They were leaning against the balustrade of the terrace and gazing out on a sea that was breathing serenely and restfully.

" If you are right," said Goehrs, " every one here would have Negro blood in his veins."

" Myself among them," the motorist nodded in cheerful acquiescence. " Don't you think that is just as well ? It makes for a clear understanding and every one knows where he is."

Goehrs cast a side glance at the crowd of whistling nincompoops. " Society," self-styled, was very small in Rio. Every one knew every one. Goehrs had been bored stiff listening to all sorts of stories about the bright young things, about their marriages, their mothers, their fortunes won or lost, and all the rest of the gossip that furnished the approved topics of conversation of a society that deemed itself superior to every other section and, by virtue of this benumbing belief, was, of course, really displaying its inferiority to those other sections. The bright young things had at length succeeded in making an omnibus draw up ; the black driver was gazing up nonplussed ; and the whole gang left the terrace well content to return to their dance.

" There might be some of the old aristocracy left," said Goehrs, stretching his arms ; it was very warm although, thank the Lord, it was only early spring in Brazil.

" In theory there is. There are still men whose grandfathers were barons, in fact even bearers of hereditary titles dating back to the days of the Conquest. But it is a precious small stable, and all the runners are in poor condition. The folk inside there say acidly that the members of the European diplomatic corps prefer dancing with pretty mulattos, and look sour about it—but that cuts no ice because they have no money. That is the acid test. The new big landowners in coffee, cocoa, and tobacco are rather highly coloured. And it is the same elsewhere. Any man who has lost his money automatically steps out of the limelight. People cease to take their hats off to him ; he becomes trash. This is, in fact, the only country in the world where it does not matter what colour the neck may be, but only whether the neck have a collar— or not."

" That is really astonishing," said Goehrs, who still failed to become acclimatized to this utter disregard of pigmentation. After his experience he could, it is true, appreciate that it was possible to rid one's mind of the prejudice that black was inferior ; and he could understand that one tolerated black—but he could not grasp that it was possible to regard it as making no difference, in fact, not to be aware of it. For, after all, it *does* make a difference, he assured himself.

"It is not so astonishing," returned the motorist, "if once you realize how it all came about. The erotic interests of the big landowners used to cover a lot of ground, and they then brought up their numerous black progeny along with their white offspring. If a black child displayed any gift or intelligence, they did everything they could to encourage it. Many of the big men of Brazil have been pure, or very nearly pure blacks, and Congress to-day runs, as it always has done, up and down the whole scale of colouring. The Vice-President would not occasion comment in Liberia.

"In the case of the pure blacks an echo of the slave days occasionally breaks out. I remember an incident at the dedication of the monument to Rio Branco. The Rio Branco law of 1871, as you may know, provided that all issue of slave mothers were emancipated on attaining the age of twenty-one. There were a lot of fine speeches at the unveiling of this monument, and no doubt this struck a Negro gentleman, who suddenly got on his legs and, without being included in the course of the proceedings, was moved to make a speech. What he wanted to know was what had really been done for the Negro after his emancipation. Nothing ! And what of North America ? . . . In North America they simply massacred them. . . . He repeated the word ' massacred ' three times and shouted it louder each time. And that was rather embarrassing because Mr. Morgan, the American ambassador, was standing straight in front of him. Well, one of Rio Branco's relatives put an end to the incident by embracing the Negro and thanking him for his kindness in having spoken and for his generous sentiments. But the following morning neither *A Noite*, nor *A Paiz* nor the *Jornal do Commercio* had a line about the incident."

"And the American ambassador ? " asked Goehrs.

" What do you mean ? "

" Well, didn't he leave ? "

" He did not know a word of Portuguese and had had not the remotest idea of what it was all about."

Goehrs laughed. " I always regarded it as convenient

not to know the language of the country you are living in,"
he said. "You have the opportunity of making
observations you would not have made if you had known the
language. And you do not hear anything it is convenient
not to. Is there much American capital in Brazil?"

"Not so much as there is British. And it has only been
since the War that the dollar has been hard on the heels of
the English pound."

Goehrs nodded.

"This racial peace is really rather strange," he said
thoughtfully. "It has made a wide-awake, liberal-minded
nation of Brazilians. And that is an enormous advantage."

"No doubt about it," said the other. "Especially if
you look one or two decades ahead. . . . Look at Africa
where there is nothing but the colour problem . . . and
where the machine guns are bound to have a word to say
in the quarrel between whites and blacks one of these days.
We are never going to have that. Never. We are going to
get round that racial war."

IMMIGRANTS

AFTER this remark of the motorist Goehrs gazed,
lost in thought, down the esplanade where more and
more taxis were driving past to refresh Brazilians with
reinvigorating sea breezes. A new party of the bright
young things had strolled out of the lounge and had just
settled down on the balustrade to whistle. One of these
days the grandchildren of these people would really be
spared this racial warfare between the coloured races and
the white man that was going to make up the history of
Africa, Asia, and all kinds of islands for perhaps a whole
century.

Goehrs thought over the type of government of this
country, which had such an astonishing advantage morally
over other continents. Goehrs found the methods where-
under Brazil was governed to be, not ideal, but resembling
in simplicity the manner in which it had solved its racial
problem. He did not discern much idea in these methods,
beyond some notions of "progress" and "development,"
which were not really ideas. There were quite 37,000
miles of motor roads, only some 6000 of which were first
class. Round about 32,000 miles (there were only 1200

in 1880) of railways, 50,000 horseless vehicles, and 100,000 telephone installations. It did not amount to much.

It did not amount to much in the case of a country that comprised almost half South America and was so big that, when it was one o'clock on the island Fernando do Noronha, it was twelve o'clock in Rio, eleven in the Amazonian provinces, and ten in the Acre districts of the west.

The country was in fact administered in a very curious way. There were in the main two big parties, one of which certainly outweighed the other. And this party now in power, which was supporting President Washington Luiz Pereira de Souza, was the party of the São Paulo people and of the coffee magnates and capitalists. Washington Luiz's term of office was coming to an end towards the close of 1930. The elections for the new President had just been fought, and a henchman of Washington Luiz, a São Paulo man of the name of Prestes, had been elected and was at the time, just before taking up office, on a triumphal progress to New York, Paris, and London (and not to Berlin; which the Germans in Brazil took very much amiss). The other party comprised the country, the southern States, and the smaller folk, the people who accused Washington Luiz and his faction of being international capitalists, of squandering Brazil on the Yankees and of being Syrians and Italians, anything rather than Brazilians.

Well, then, the new President, who was to begin his term of office in a few weeks' time, was in Europe. But his opponent, the President of the State of Rio Grande do Sul, who had been beaten, had stated that he did not care a tinker's curse about this defeat, that the elections had been " faked " by the São Paulo crowd, and that he would make himself President of Brazil and rid the country of the gang that had been ruling it for the past forty years. And Brazil was, as Goehrs knew from the forms he had filled up in red ink and from the story of the crashed aeroplane, on the brink of a revolution.

And what was the nature of the differences dividing the two opposing parties? Purely economic. There were no others. For the time being Brazil was still under the thumb of the coffee interests. This party had hitherto manipulated the elections, nominated the several Presidents, and made all appointments to office. These matters were arranged and the appointments made before the elections. Almost in the Russian style.

There was no regular Socialist party in Brazil. The ringleaders of the strikes were locked up, maltreated, or thrashed. That was their solution of the social problem. On the other hand, the national festivals included the anniversary of the storming of the Bastille, Labour Day, and a day celebrating the Emancipation of the Slaves.

But the ruling caste was composed of men who had been ruined by the emancipation of slaves and still cursed the day.

Yet Brazil did not, for all that, fall to pieces, this State of twenty separate States, this huge hodge-podge as big as eighteen Germanies. Why not? What was the common bond between these several States? What was it that attracted them to one another? Language, history, the magnet of great enterprises effected in common, the same temperament? Probably a mysterious distillation of all these considerations. Further, a State like Rio Grande do Sul would have been in a position to make itself independent or to join up with Uruguay. Or the northern State, Bahia, that had everything with the exception of coal and iron within easy reach, would have been able to exist independently. But it never entered their heads.

Immigration, too, was a factor to be taken into account. In the course of the first century of Brazil's independence, since the big palm in the Botanical Gardens had been planted, it had had an influx of three and a half million inhabitants, a third of whom were Portuguese, a third Italians, together with half a million Spaniards. From 1908 to 1925 a record flood of one and a half million had poured into Brazil, and in 1927 alone over 100,000 people had disembarked in Santos and Rio to try their luck. And Brazil absorbed them. The Germans had a number of big and, in part, quite old-established colonies, and remained loyally German within these settlements. Immigration had, so far as land was concerned, better prospects here than elsewhere, because there was still a grotesque amount of room. But the Government, as a general rule, did not keep the promises it had made, and the virgin forests presented difficulties with which emigrants from civilized Europe were not qualified to cope. The majority of the immigrants, too, however forlorn their plight, raised claims the country could not meet. People who came without money had to spend three years on the broiling coffee plantations before they could save enough to purchase a small holding in the great forests. But the Italians stood life on the plantations better than the Germans. It was a ghastly training school.

There were some very old German colonies. When the soil was played out, they laid out a new settlement. The eldest son succeeded to the homestead after his father's death. His six or possibly sixteen brothers and sisters got the money to buy the land for new little homesteads and eked a livelihood out of them. It was a hard life, but the people were a free peasantry on their own land, a condition that had become rare in Europe. And in the meantime more room had been made for new settlers, who brought fresh blood and new ideas into these peasant colonies, which had become quite atrophied in the course of the decades they had spent in grubbing tree stumps out of the soil in virgin forests, remote from the outside world.

In any case there was a big discrepancy between the huge bulk of Brazil and its, comparatively speaking, sparse population and the difficulties the forests presented to settlement. An eminent man of science had calculated that the Amazon territories alone should theoretically provide room for a thousand million settlers. Unfortunately he was wrong. The inundation areas of the Amazon were unfortunately not like those of the Nile, fertile mud, but of Cordillera sand. In the same way everything in this mammoth country, even where things were plain sailing, was full of incongruities, and, where they were not, they became overwhelming and bewildering.

These were the thoughts exercising Goehrs's mind as he gazed down on the esplanade where the society of Rio that hardly gave these problems a thought was enjoying a drive. The group of wealthy and bright young things beside him, with their fingers in their mouths, had in the meantime continued to whistle for taxis. Nor did they stop when a sallow gentleman, accompanied by a horde of nieces and kinsfolk, appeared on the terrace and began walking up and down to enjoy at any rate the draught created by his own movements. The Prefect of Rio. Rio de Janeiro, the city, was, it will be remembered, surrounded by a zone of neutral territory and had no connexion at all with the state of Rio de Janeiro. The Prefect was subordinate to the Federal President direct, and ranked on a footing of equality with the twenty Presidents of the twenty States. The motorist had been at school with him, and they exchanged greetings as the bevy of nieces passed on.

"In our young days," said the Prefect, who had the reputation for being one of the soundest men in Brazil, "there were still plantations over there." He pointed in the direction of the steep Corcovado hill. "There are bananas there now. The trend of coffee is ever westwards. Is it not amazing? I often look back on our young days. We are pushing ahead at a great pace. What was Copacabana in those days? An unkempt foreshore. And now . . .?" He pointed down to the bay that looked like a huge, tautly drawn arc of lights.

"We are getting on," agreed the motorist, and carried the curt gesture the Prefect had made on towards the direction of Fort Copacabana, prolonging it along the coast towards the south. "This coast between Santos and Rio will change in the same way within the next fifty years. It will become the Riviera of the world. And what a Riviera !"

The night was as mild and as bright as a dream when Goehrs went up to bed. At four o'clock the storm broke, driving a hot, sticky atmosphere laden with sand on to the coast. It became so hot that the pages of a book, lying open in the room, began to curl upwards. The gusts shook the whole building and made Goehrs think the windows were going to be blown in. He became anxious about the roof. He remembered what the Leblon street had looked like, and he fully expected to see the Copacabana front torn to ribbons by the next morning. At five o'clock the electric light failed, and the thunderstorm took over the illumination. The skies shrieked and were so slashed by lightning that the illumination was almost continuous.

Goehrs looked out of the window on the following morning.

One or two young girls in big straw hats and bathing dresses were already walking about the beach, trailing after them those little canvas seats with their charming, brightly coloured roofs and smart gay groundsheets, on which the pretty little mulattos were going to deposit their own little seats.

The beach was beautifully white.

And the sea, the monster, was calm and placid, almost without a trace of surf. Everything Goehrs had forecast had failed to occur. It had been a sandstorm. And the sea had superciliously declined to have anything to do with it, and had remained neutral.

It really pretended that there had not, three hours previously, been any disturbance at all.

362

IT had often struck Goehrs that the more republican the attitude the United States of Brazil adopted, the greater the fuss they made about their last Emperor, deposed on November 15, 1889. Everything that wanted to draw attention to itself adopted his name, if not in a monarchical, at any rate in a romantic sense.

So Goehrs drove out to Petropolis, the last Emperor's summer residence. It stood at an altitude of some 2500 feet in the heart of a virgin forest. It was not a very old forest, had been recently laid out, but it was a virgin forest in the sense that Goehrs, who knew many ancient virgin forests, acknowledged to be entirely legitimate. It had grown up on the same lines as the primeval forests of Africa. All the trunks had been in a hurry to grow tall and to develop at their top to prevent themselves from being suffocated below. They had grown up wonderfully slim, and were overgrown by climbing plants and quite impenetrable. And finally the forest was bisected by a handsome motor road which republican Brazil had taken out for miles to the seat of its last Emperor. The Brazilians were pastmasters in taking dead-straight cuts of asphalted and cemented roads through forests that a couple of paces to the right or left became impossible to penetrate.

The forest of Petropolis had grown on the same lines as the primeval African forests, but without the panic-stricken terror characteristic of the latter. There was something delightful in the permeating scent, in the liana swings and the clumps of orchids perched on them like birds of vivid plumage. It was the same charm the coast had and the same graciousness characteristic of the race that was often not beautiful, too stout and too short, but attractive. Petropolis stood on its hill above the forest like a Brazilian Kissingen. The image of it. Imperial Brazil.

The first Emperor was Pedro, the prince regent left behind by João VI, a young sportsman of twenty-four, who, on hearing that Portugal was proposing to relegate Brazil to the status of a colony again, had gallantly, straightforwardly, and decently ranged himself on the side of Brazil. " Independencia ou Morte " were the words of his that became famous, that led up to his proclamation as Emperor, but did not safeguard Pedro from abdication nine years later under pressure of a revolution. At the age of thirty-three he abdicated in favour of his son Pedro II, a boy of six. Nine years of regency ensued. The men governing the country made it undergo its baptism of fire to put its cohesion and unity to the test. At the age of fifteen Pedro II was proclaimed Emperor and was crowned in 1840. He then reigned for forty-nine years.

His reign lasted from 1840 to 1889. During this period the world began to take shape more rapidly than for centuries before. During this period railroads were built, steamships began to ply, and slavery was abolished. In the meantime wars against Argentina and Paraguay were waged. The people accepted the railways and the steamships willingly enough and also the outcome of the wars with Argentina and Paraguay, but the question of the abolition of slavery brought about the Emperor's fall. The final decree was issued on May 13, 1888, and reduced almost all the great landowners to bankruptcy. In the following year the palace was surrounded and the Empire abolished. Pedro resigned and died in Paris two years later—and Brazil became a republic.

Pedro's fall was a tragedy, and later on Brazil never forgot it. He was a fine man of business in the interests of his country, a commanding intellect, a diplomatist and a sound psychologist. He had lived in critical times for Brazil and had consolidated the State ; he had suppressed several rebellions in the individual States and had trained them to act in concert to such good purpose that, diverse and remote from one another as they might be, they would have to live and die together.

Goehrs strolled about in Pedro II's park in Petropolis for a while. It was the same atmosphere that characterizes Baden-Baden and Kissingen, resorts too where Emperors used to stroll about, and where the atmosphere is still that of the imperial days of the 'eighties.

" Are there any mementos of the Emperor's days left ? " Goehrs asked a photographer from whom he bought a roll of films.

" Oh, yes. The American ambassador has got them at his country place," the photographer answered in German. Every one talked German as naturally as he would have in Baden-Baden, and it was all so in keeping with the atmosphere of the place that any other language would have sounded foreign.

Even the imperial relics have passed into the possession of the Yankees, Goehrs reflected.

" Business is bad," the man went on. " It's hard luck,

SCENE IN BRAZIL.

because I'm in debt. During the War the Brazilians burnt my house down. It's difficult for us Germans to make headway. As soon as we've got anything they bash our heads in. We are artificial manure, sir, cultural manure—nothing else."

The town was a German foundation (it has a population of close on 80,000 to-day). All the valleys had German names. They were called Bingen, Worms, Mosel, Wörrstadt, Rhein, and Ingelheim.

Goehrs drove back through the virgin forest with a sense of heaviness at heart. Germany had risen before his eyes in these valleys, beautiful Germany, but always tragically mangled, whose destiny in the world seemed to be to have its full strength brought to bear prematurely or too late—Germany that was always too big or too small but never, in tune with its spirit, quite harmonious and definite.

At a distance above a great stretch of forest, Goehrs saw Rio and the sea. He saw the pillars rising round Rio and the seventy islands of the bay, the Ilha Paquetá, the Ilha Governador, the hill above the Praia Gavea surmounted by its extra special little table-mountain, the Sugarloaf inclining towards the right, and the Corcovado opposite it, posing with a rope-dancer's daring to the left—a box of Nature's giant toys by a lotus pool, in a light of such delicate mystery as Nature lavishes but once, so unreal, so sweet, so wonderful, so entirely otherworldly. Between Goehrs and the sea lay the virgin forest, the orchid-scented, jealous virgin forest that mildews everything and remoulds it into stretches of woodland that become vanilla-scented clearings, and into little patches where every tree trunk at once furnishes the bed for hundreds of plants until the bodies of the dead trees against the green background often become more vivid emblems of the wilds than the living trees themselves. There was something akin to it in the way the sea swept in between the Sugarloaf and Fort Santa Cruz and in the way the forest flowed in from the plain between the rocky hillocks—or rather it was all of a piece. Just as gloriously as the sea rushed between the pillars of the bay, so sweetly, irresistibly, grandly, purposefully and tenderly did the virgin forest flood up to the rampart of the hills and stream up to the tableland over the knees of the outlying hills. It was marvellous. Everything in this landscape was in accord.

IN the course of these three days the following had occurred in Argentina : The Government had called out the military arm at night. The troops had opened fire on a students' demonstration. Thereupon the Government had occupied the more important public buildings. Irigoyen had ceased to come to the Casa Rosada, but stayed at home in his little house. The Casa Rosada, the Argentine Government building, was garnished with machine guns. But neither the inhabitants of Buenos Aires nor Martínez, the Vice-President of Argentina and Irigoyen's closest friend, knew why. Buenos Aires was being kept under duress, that was all.

The *Crítica* demanded Irigoyen's resignation. The *Epoca*, that no one ever read, thereupon demanded the suspension of this gutter rag. Irigoyen had never had a good Press; he had only the *Epoca* on his side, and the awful *Calle*, and, at best, the neutrality of the big newspapers. He had to pay for it.

Martínez, the Vice-President, went to Irigoyen's modest house and asked him to declare a state of siege. Irigoyen was seventy-seven years of age and in ill health. He transferred the Government to Martínez and gave him his state of siege. The *Crítica* was thereupon suspended overnight and a censorship imposed.

" Are you afraid of a revolution ? " inquired Irigoyen, the old man with the big square head and upright, sturdy carriage.

" Perhaps."

" The people are on my side," said Irigoyen indifferently. " My personal enemies are perhaps scheming an attempt on my life. I am not afraid of it."

In two days' time the provinces had come to an understanding. On the morning following the night on which the state of siege had been proclaimed, twenty aeroplanes appeared over Buenos Aires. They were military machines, and their appearance over Buenos Aires had hitherto been prohibited. First they dropped proclamations. Irigoyen, who had another four years of office to run, kept to his private house and heard nothing about it. Martínez endeavoured to arrest the leaders of the opposition. He could not even prevent the *Crítica* from appearing.

At midday one or two regiments marched into the city from the Campo de Mayo. The man who had organized everything, General Uriburu, a brown man of about sixty with a fine head and a dark moustache, followed them in mufti. The loudspeakers shouted the news through the city. The regiments, accompanied by artillery and escorted by thousands of private cars, marched slowly on the Casa Rosada. One or two cannon shots echoed along the Avenida de Mayo. Shortly afterwards Uriburu entered the Government buildings. Martínez came forward to meet him. Uriburu, after saluting, introduced himself. He requested him to sign his signature.

"I cannot and will not do so," said the Vice-President, "you are free to have me shot."

"The matter is too serious for me to oblige you by permitting you to live on as a martyr and a hero," said Uriburu.

The Minister of Public Works, José Abalos, came in.

"Better resign," he said to Martínez.

Martínez hesitated. Insurgents, smashing the portraits and busts of Irigoyen, were tramping through the Casa Rosada.

"Will you agree," said Martínez to Uriburu, "that I am not betraying any one or anything by resigning?"

"You cannot betray any one," Uriburu replied. "Your party has betrayed you long ago."

Then Irigoyen was to be arrested as well. He had disappeared in his car with the hue and cry at his heels. Irigoyen had been at his private address all that morning. The telephone wires to his house had been cut at an early hour; otherwise no one interfered with him. They really had staged this revolution as if they were trying to lay a man by the heels of whom they were not sure whether he was a crazy saint or a sainted criminal.

That evening the Plaza Mayo was illuminated. Uriburu took an oath to the people not to play the part of a dictator but to restore peace to Argentina. Irigoyen's papers were burnt in the public streets. Some one dragged a bronze bust of Irigoyen from the offices of the *Epoca*, knotted ropes round it, and haled it through the town. His house was looted and everything near it. The white flag flew from the Casa Rosada. The airmen dropped flowers. Irigoyen was done with. "Acabó el peludo." The "shaggy wild man" was done with.

The peludo, the armadillo, the caudillo, the bandit chief, Argentina's great gaucho, had really been brought down. He was run down by car near La Plata, arrested, and conveyed to the barracks. Thence he was taken on board the coastguard ship *Belgrano* and from the *Belgrano* to the cruiser *Buenos Aires*. The Argentinians had brought down their biggest man, the man they called a condottiere and a cowardly dog in the same breath, the man the country had idolized, a simple but great veteran, who fled with inflammation of the lungs and hardly knew what was going on, the great Yankee-baiter who only recently had had the audacity or the crazy inspiration to appoint a pugilist as consul in Washington.

The wheel was more and more approaching full cycle. There were regular generals ruling everywhere in South America now. And Uriburu's Government that pledged itself to early elections was forthwith offered credits amounting to 100,000,000 pesos at five per cent. by foreign banks.

Who was in fact the hunter and who the hunted in this game that history was always playing over and over again on this poor, harassed continent ? The general who doubtlessly meant well by Argentina ? Or the dollar ?

Buenos Aires did not ponder the problem. It was jubilant. It went off its head, looted, and lit bonfires in the Avenida de Mayo. No nation in the world, when it is once overtaken by fateful crises, sees the background of the moment. It only sees fallen idols and new heroes. Uriburu knew that, when he refused to have Martínez shot but laughed at his heroics instead.

Argentina had not had to wait three years for its revolution. It had slid across from Peru—all the way down the Cordilleras to the pampas this time. All the world had been wrong. And all the world was quite pleased to have been.

WITH—AND WITHOUT—COLLARS

WHEN Goehrs on one occasion went by ferry straight across the bay to Nictheroy, he discovered that there were really hundreds of Rios—hundreds of aspects in which Rio presented the whole picture of itself. But Goehrs was on his way to Nictheroy and ought by rights not to have been thinking about Rio. For while Nictheroy was only twenty minutes' run by ferry across the bay, it lay in another State ; it was the capital of the State of Rio de Janeiro and had a population of over 100,000. The State of Rio de Janeiro was a small State, smaller than Ireland—a

State that had the huge inland state, thirteen times its own size, in its rear and bore encysted within it the Federal district and the Federal capital of Rio de Janeiro. What chance had Nictheroy, even supposing it had been a town of marvels, when it was only twenty minutes across from Rio?

It was a Sunday. Goehrs had taken tea at the Brasileiro Yacht Club, which was really a German sailing club. The clubhouse lay hidden up a deep inlet of the bay, in the Sacco São Francisco, and its quarters were the old Castello de Jurujuba, with its immense walls in which the rings of the ordnance still remained. It was in the dungeons of this fort that the slaves used to be deposited, weighed, and distributed.

From the terrace of the Castello Jurujuba, you had a view of a little gap far across the bay, and its palm-edged setting framed the silhouettes of Corcovado and the Pão de Açucar clashing like poised daggers.

While a thunderstorm came and went, Goehrs had a look at the clubhouse, in the dungeons of which had cowered the mothers of many of the people who were that very day sipping their tea on the terrace. The thunderstorm returned, and Goehrs raced for the tram that stopped outside the gardens of the club, for it was half an hour's walk from the Sacco to the ferry.

It was a Sunday, and the train was so full that Goehrs had to stand on the outside platform. When a cloudburst poured down again he had to slip inside the train, drop the tarpaulin curtain behind him, and stand wedged in among eighty loving couples of Negroes and their fidgety knees. On Sundays, Rio in general appeared to be a Negro city; on Sundays it was blacker even than Cairo, and there was hardly a white man in sight. In this train, Goehrs had a particularly good opportunity for studying the interplay of colour. Not all the folk were black. They were infiltrated by Spanish, Italian, German, Portuguese strains—but they were Negroes. It was a proletarian excursion on its way home, and they were all carrying little aluminium cups. There were mothers among them who, it is true, were dark but had sleek hair and prominent, finely arched noses; but they in their turn had children who could easily have passed muster in a kraal on the Zambezi. There was every shading from yellowish-white to soot-black. There were almost white men with almost black women. And there were men with Portuguese foreheads, eyes, and ears, who suddenly became possessed of thick-lipped Negro mouths. There were Negro mammies

2A

who had entirely white children. There were Negro mammies who had pretty yellow Malay children.

But no one in the whole company seemed to take the least notice of the uncanny differentiations that distinguished them from one another, or even to be aware of them. They were sitting in one another's arms exchanging caresses, balancing their aluminium cups, pressing their knees against one another, rubbing each other with their thumbs, and were for the most part quite smartly dressed—and were talking Portuguese.

On the ferry to Rio the scene was the same, only enlarged by several hundreds. In Rio, Goehrs boarded the tram again. He noticed that the tram had two compartments ; one first, the other second class. The conductor was sorting his fares on some mysterious principle, and it gave Goehrs some trouble before he grasped the basis of his method of selection. The conductor passed all the men wearing collars into the first-class compartment whether they were white, yellow, brown, or black. He relegated all men without collars, regardless of their pigmentation, to the second class. He only looked for a collar. He sent a black boy with a collar but without boots or shoes into the first, and he relegated a handsome English lad in a low-cut jersey to the second class.

Goehrs was once again a little startled by the simplicity of this method of solving the racial problem and gaped at the artless way in which this levelling-up process was effected.

That evening Goehrs discussed the upshot of his observations with the Minister of Transport, Victor Konder, next to whom he was sitting at a dinner-party. Victor Konder was during the daytime domiciled in the Praça 15 de Novembro, in a handsome mansion with two royal palm trees in front of it, a mansion of the Empire period when it had been innocent of a minister of transport because there was nothing very much to transport. If you paid him a visit there you were put in a corner against the wall, while he talked to his other visitors in turn in another corner of the room. Which was very diverting.

Konder was of German descent with a Brazilian admixture and plumed himself on being a Brazilian " from the interior."

" Well," he said, " this regulation by collar has a deep and conciliatory significance. People usually take a wrong view of the slave system nowadays. Slaves, it is true, were bred like prize stock, and strong males were put to pretty female slaves, but, when all is said and done, they were inmates of the homestead and members of the household. That even in those days relaxed the colour bar. My nurse and my nursery governess were both of them Negresses. I loved them as nothing else on earth. I was not aware they were black. And they loved me. How they loved me ! The result is a lifelong bond that refuses to consider prejudices.

" Furthermore, the Portuguese does not regard this inter-marrying as a problem in the very least, but as a matter of taste. He does it with exactly as little intuitive hesitation as you would take a cold bath or eat cheese, both of which practices many millions of human beings hold to be some-thing entirely unnatural. And are we not right to live in this way ? Have we not got a prosperous present and the prospect of a peaceful future ? And what is the outlook for the rest of the world all round us ? England—India ! America ! Egypt ! South Africa ! They are burning and shooting all round us. We are at peace. We are not going to have any racial warfare. But fearful things are going to happen in America and Africa because racial war is not going to cease until the issue, once raised, has been fully and finally settled. We have our difficulties here, of course. But only in connexion with coffee. And difficulties arising out of coffee pass. . . . Good Lord."

And Victor blew something or other on his open palm away with a single puff.

" MY FRIEND THE SUGARLOAF "

GOEHRS now set about to climb the Pão de Açucar— which had hitherto, until the funicular was running, proved impossible. Late in the afternoon he went on board a little car that was still pretty well enclosed by the houses of Rio. The car was attached to a rope and with its assist-ance ascended some six hundred feet on to a rock, called the Urca. On the ridge of this rounded and insignificant rock, Goehrs walked a short distance and then entered another car that shot him into the air anew. He had often seen this car from below at the end of its rope, dangling between the two rocks—it had looked ridiculous and criminally dangerous.

Goehrs sat in his car that was to lift him from a rock of 600 feet in height to the top of one of 1200 feet, and his course lay above a virgin forest in a state of complete decay, of which he got a bird's-eye view. Goehrs was never likely to forget that journey, not only because it gave him a horribly painful sensation to be suspended at the end of a rope, of a South American rope, that might give at any moment, but also because the huge column of rock, on which the car was rolling like a ship in a gale at sea, burst through the untrodden forest with a directness, a force, and a beauty that took his breath away.

This was the Sugarloaf, his friend of weeks' standing by sight, on the top of which he got out. On the top of this column of rock was a little platform. It was like being on rockers to stand on it because the Sugarloaf was leaning over the navigable channel at such an acute angle that it seemed to be half-way in the act of falling into the sea.

But behind him Goehrs, for the first time, saw, since the promontory on which the Sugarloaf rose jutted farthest out to sea, the entire panorama of Rio as a whole, all its fjords, all its coves, all the lines of its well-planned streets, all the ridges that traversed and split it up, its lagoon, and its inland lakes—the whole arabesque decoration of the coast and the rounded hill formations that composed the whole scene of virile beauty. It was a vision of Nature's supreme graciousness, with all the evidence of the savageness it had just overcome, with hills that had in consequence become shapely pillars and pyramids, with virgin forests that, fragrant as hanging gardens, trailed from their slopes into the streets, with groups of houses that nestled against the heart of Nature, with streets that seemed to mark the triumphal progress of ordered landscape—a pastel of the highest unity human habitations can achieve with land and seascape. Perfection, beautiful beyond words.

The sun had set and was painting the mountain tops a dull red. The dream illumination of Rio then began. The ten pillars, the seven coves, the hanging forests—they all faded away, became a spiral, as drawn by the finger of the Creator and growing ever more beautiful and vibrating in its rhythm, became a breath that embodied every melody, rose and fell, and at length died away in a rapt remoteness that almost overpowered consciousness.

Everything melted into silver. Behind the screen of palms on the platform the moon rose over the sea. The bay was pink and white. The coves began to sparkle; the rows of lights along the fjords fell into clear-cut lines. The primeval forest at Goehrs's feet became a mysterious blur, above which he was floating as though severed from contact with the world. But the crickets raised their diapason from the depths, and the black vultures began to soar into the sky. A big passenger steamer, which looked quite small from that height, passed out of the bay under the Sugarloaf and exchanged signals with Fort Santa Cruz. The sea remained light for a long time. The moonlight then reached the forests and flooded them with radiance. And all of a sudden the houses, scattered about the neck of the promontory like angels' playthings, extinguished their lights, and then, on every side, searchlights began to play from the clocktowers, and to search the heavens in great wheeling arcs.

Goehrs had seen the Acropolis by moonlight and the Colosseum, Dar-es-Salaam at nightfall, Venice in her most magic moods; he had seen the Pyramids rise out of the desert at a distance of fifteen miles and then, close to, had watched the great cascade of stone descending from the skies; he knew Baghdad, Stamboul, Capetown, Damascus, Jerusalem; he knew Stockholm at night, when the Mälar was rushing through it like a hero of Nordic saga; he knew the Taurus, the Kalahari, the Kilimanjaro with its glaciers, the bastions of Rhodes above the Mediterranean; he knew Mount Lebanon, Chartres, Avignon, the Black Forest and the view from Cyprus across the sea, the view from the Castello dei Cesari on to the Palatine and the Sabine Hills, the view from Perugia across Tuscany to Assisi; he knew the Dead Sea and the falls of the Zambezi, and the gold mines of Kimberley and the view of the Alhambra from Granada; he knew the Rhine at St. Goar and venerable Würzburg and Lucerne, and Toledo and the Red Sea and the walls of Tetuan . . . the wonders of the world.

But this was supreme above all.

An hour later the wire rope slung the car into the dark again. A whiff of the scent of jungle rose from the depths. And then the rope again flung the car into the light and on to the Urca. The crickets roared as the wild beasts in the virgin forests of Mozambique in South Africa used to roar—but everything was perfect in its troubled harmony. Only quite at the far end of the vista glared the Rio Branco like the door of a furnace, a street of flashlight advertisements in glaring reds and greens.

The Rio Branco showed a fierce glare in the background like the campfire that the devout Lombard painters of the Middle Ages were fond of lighting on the margin of their pictures after they had devoted nine-tenths of their canvas and the whole of the foreground to depicting the joys of Paradise . . . of throwing it in when the picture was finished, as a sop to conscience to remind their fellow-mortals that, as a matter of fact, nine-tenths of life is made up of struggle, cruelty, and war.

A Spring Tide

A FEW days later the bright young things of Rio were on the terrace of the Hotel Copacabana again wielding little cameras and taking snapshots of the sea. The sea had suddenly taken leave of its senses. Without rhyme or reason, without a breath of wind, in clear, sunny, calm weather, it began to lash itself into a rage. It challenged the hotel in three sapphire green columns of waves of assault. One column was fifty, the next thirty, and the last twenty yards away from the hotel. Then one after the other the green columns dissolved in spray and spume—not all at once, but in countless detonations of high explosives with white geysers and volcanoes as high as a house. Fascinating but formidable.

So fascinating was it that after any conspicuously successful detonation the bright young things of Brazil would break into applause. The applause increased when the spring tide slowly overran the beach and at times raided the esplanade. By midday the waves were sweeping across the roadway, and a few thousand cars came out from Rio to drive over the flooded esplanade and to admire the spring tide.

Goehrs watched Nature's sensational performance a little glumly, for he had a ticket of the German Condor Airways Syndicate in his pocket for Bahia, some 800 miles away by a Dornier-Wal seaplane. This weather was bound to bring on fog, and in a fog Goehrs would not be able to see anything from an aeroplane, and there was nothing attractive in the prospect of flying across northern Brazil in a fog. He went back into the hotel and continued to grow glummer.

The big cardrooms of the hotel looked disconsolate. Copacabana had at one time been the Monte Carlo of South America. Argentinians and Brazilians, who really loathed one another, had amicably gambled their money away at the tables, but one day that stopped. The then President, Washington Luiz, had closed down the gambling rooms because the son of a well-known statesman deceased had gambled away his own money, his mother's money, and some more besides.   A lot of people considered the President's action as edifying but ill considered, for there were practically no distractions in Rio ; there was only one restaurant apart from one or two hotels, and they considered that, apart from the tables, there were plenty of opportunities for bright young Argentinians and Brazilians to get rid of their —and their mothers'—money.

The Argentinians would, in any case, have dropped out this year because the depressed state of business was compelling them to economize.   Goehrs had often noticed to what lengths the jealousy between these two nationalities would go.   They hated each other, not as the Bolivians and Chileans, as the Ecuadorians and Colombians, hated one another from time to time ; they simply got on to one another's nerves, and there was nothing to be done about it.   They were rivals.   They had both entered for the same stakes.   They both of them had an itch for the prestige of outstripping the other.   The Brazilians said that, when a man tried to talk Portuguese and failed, he turned out to be talking Spanish.   The Argentinians in their turn called the dead-heads who went to the theatre without paying for their seats Portuguese.   When they did not want to leave anything to doubt the Argentinians simply called the Brazilians monkeys.   The Brazilians were struck by the same zoological likeness in the case of the Argentinians.   The hearts of people in Buenos Aires went out to you if you were to talk of the Brazilians as niggers.   People in Rio were particularly gratified if you spoke of Buenos Aires as a city of dolts.

Goehrs had on one occasion in Buenos Aires seen Argentinian policemen making fun of Brazilian naval officers.   For both countries had, of course, a navy, even big, though obsolete battleships.   The Brazilian lieutenants were walking along the wharf in uniform and in cocked hats and the police made game of them.   One of the officers went up to the policemen and, anxious to close the stupid incident without a fuss, said : " We are strangers and want to have a look at your city and are therefore enjoying your country's hospitality.   It's not good manners to jeer at us."   The policemen went on jeering.   The officer thereupon changed his tactics, stood with his arms akimbo, threw back his small head in its cocked hat and said something very ugly in a very loud voice about the alleged moral perversions of Argentinians.   That wiped the police off the map.   And the

Brazilians, who had just been held up to derision for monkeys swaggered into Buenos Aires like cockerels.

Half and Half

THAT evening Goehrs meant to drive out to the suburbs where the final selection of " Miss Brazil " from among the queens of beauty of the twenty States was to be made in a stadium with a capacity of 30,000 spectators. The " Misses " were going to have their own President ; Brazil was going to have a representative whom no storm-cloud of revolution could overcast—and that would perhaps keep Brazil quiet. When Goehrs reflected on the way in which these twenty damsels had been spoiled during the last few weeks, how these hundred-and-twenty pound bits of attractive flesh had been fêted night after night at full-dress banquets and political gatherings, how they had dined every day in the company of ministers, foreign representatives, and Presidents, he did not look upon the notion that these girls might perhaps checkmate the outbreak of a revolution as an impossibility.

Just before he drove to the stadium, Goehrs read a violent attack on a German journalist who had been in Rio on the occasion of the first visit of the Zeppelin and had written some nonsense or other about a " nigger nation." The onslaught on the German journalist was very savage, and the scribe had, of course, not done the million odd Germans in Brazil any particular service by his article about the " nigger nation."

Goehrs, of course, did not claim to be fully and precisely informed about a country the size of China, the hinterland of which was as unknown to Brazilians themselves as Australia, in view of the fact that he had seen only five States out of twenty, but he did flatter himself he knew something about the psychology of the Brazilian in this his most sensitive point of all. For the Brazilian makes no secret, no secret at all, that he has Negro blood in him—in fact the best Brazilians regarded this strain as a stroke of good fortune, as an advantage, as a political blessing and a boon. But— the Brazilian was at the same time well aware that he, the primarily white man, had absorbed the Negro strain, that the climate of the country had been in favour of the cross,

376

and that he, the erstwhile white man, had assumed the responsibility of administering this proportion of Negro blood.

On the other hand, the Brazilian would lose his head as soon as any third party put the issue the other way about and put it as if the black slaves, imported from Angola in their time, had absorbed and superseded them, the erstwhile whites. No ! That was not the case. Quite the contrary.

That was the psychological position, and it called for delicate handling.

There were, as on the outcome of every experiment, two views to which one could not take exception on the quality of this half-breed race. There were people who regarded this hybrid race as the most untrustworthy, most obnoxious, and most intolerable thing in the world. There were just as many others who credited this black-and-white race with more possibilities than all the other States and nationalities in South America. They credited it with alertness, with quickness of uptake, with a sense of beauty, and big views for the possibilities of the country.

And the planning of Rio was undoubtedly unique—not altogether unaffected by German inspiration. German initiative that had installed the first telephones, electric railways, and wireless stations had been so signally successful that the pusillanimous alarm Goehrs had felt in the ascent of the Pão de Açucar was really a slur on the prestige which German enterprise had won in Brazil. Because, although Brazil—under very strong pressure on the part of the Entente—had during the War entered the lists against Germany, its belief in German efficiency remained unshaken. Goehrs knew that, because the plant on the Sugarloaf had been installed by a German, the rope attachment would not be subject to inspection. A German had made it. It would last to all eternity. Goehrs's belief in his fellow-countrymen did not go to quite that length.

The sanitary condition of the outer circle and the equipment of the hospitals were not, it is true, up to the standard of the excellence of the planning of the town. But did not that, so far as outer circles are concerned, hold true all the world over ?

So the car with Goehrs and his party drove up to the race course where Brazil's collective " Miss " was to be elected— and scored a popular success. Some hundred mulattos were gathered at the entrance and jeered. The function had been cancelled owing to the uncertainty of the weather—so

377

the ladies had to go on shivering in suspense for a few days before they knew who was going to become Miss Brazil. And until then the revolution of the southern States would not come to a head.

Goehrs walked through the quarter. It was a topsy-turvy district. What cross-breeds! What housing conditions! What scoundrels! What an impudent rabble! And what alluring, beautiful creatures did the girls include who, whether they had ten or thirty per cent. of white blood in their veins, had entirely distinct bodies, entirely distinct build, eyes, and hips. It was not only that the shades varied. That was the least important point of all. The bodies and the heads became distinctive. Many of these hybrid girls had the gracefulness of African movements—no woman had a more beautiful carriage than a fullblooded Negress of Central Africa—superadded to figures of a comeliness that appealed to European eyes.

But what a rabble it was! On the other hand the mulatto and quadroon ladies of the assemblage did not look thoroughbred.

Goehrs's party was furious that the show had been cancelled at four o'clock in the afternoon and that a city of two millions had afforded no facilities for making the fact known before eight o'clock.

" Pretty girls of eighteen like these are one of Providence's happiest ideas, but what's to become of these silk-clad damsels after having had presents showered upon them and being made much of for four weeks ? " asked a lady with very dark, beautiful eyebrows who was so thoroughbred that she had recently reached Rio by Zeppelin.

Thousands of people had poured out of the suburb and were now standing about to be jeered at by the hybrid mob.

" Half and half—like everything else," said one of the men, shrugging his shoulders. " The girls will marry—or do the other thing."

" You haven't lived long enough in a tropical country," said the lady with the beautiful dark eyebrows, " to have any right to be facetious about ' half and half ' offhand like that. Half and half is Brazil's watchword of destiny and a matter of course with Brazilians. I believe it's a European prejudice to think that half and half must invariably be a disability. Haven't we been hanging about outside this infernal circus long enough ? What about going to the Recreio ? "

378

THE Recreio Theatre was half in the open air, half under cover. A popular theatre. The audience was pretty consistently black. Many mothers had brought their infants with them, infants from one to five years of age. On the rise of the curtain, the children and their parents saw thirty to all intents and purposes nude girls on the stage. These nude girls were for the most part very pretty and, of course, varied in the colour of their pigment ; only their leader was stout, a type that still has its charms for South America.

The infants in arms and the children of five and their progenitors saw these naked girls and simultaneously heard the orchestra tune up. To Goehrs's speechless amazement they played the Brazilian national anthem, and the thirty nude coloured girls sang it from the stage with enthusiasm while the audience rose respectfully to its feet. The audience sat down again, and children saw a lady taking off her dress and a gentleman removing his trousers on the stage, and the gentleman devouring first his own straw hat and then the neckties of several of the bystanders—and then how life in consequence gradually became very obvious, very indecent, and very simple.

It was curious how soft the Brazilian tongue sounded after pure Portuguese. A Portuguese would hardly understand Brazilian. Brazilian had become a mellifluous dialect of the mother tongue.

The actors on the stage had not the very least style, but they were good in by-play, more especially when they did anything without words, when lost in thought or signalling with their eyes. Or when they became ironical. When they became ironical, they were first rate. When they parodied Italian comedy they were delightful. And when they gave glimpses of Brazilian home life they were splendid : that Brazilian home life, that like home life all over South America, still retained a good deal of pose and pride and posture about it even when there was nothing in the house for dinner—this incredibly ascetic home life that makes shift with salt junk and beans and was not one of the last reasons why a city so highly charged with sensuality as Rio could not boast more than one restaurant.

It was quite a cheery evening, but on his way back Goehrs could not get through the Avenida Niemeyer on account of the spring tide. He had to drive half-way up the Tijuca and saw Rio once more in its dazzling haze of light. It was, it is true, thick and there was some fog over the sea.

"Rio spends more on its street-lighting than New York does," said Goehrs peevishly. "But it would suit me better if the weather were finer. Flying is a wash-out."

The hotel, which he reached after half an hour's detour, was just being bombarded by the waves. Once the waves began to drain off, triangular heaps of white sand, looking like salt mines, were left standing on the pavement, and the main entrance was flooded. He had to drive round to the back. He made his way in by this side entrance and hurried out on to the terrace in front. The gilded youth of Rio were still holding the terrace undaunted. They were applauding with particular enthusiasm at the moment because two of their number who, in a lull of the breaker bombardment, had run down into the street and had taken up their position on a tall stone seat, had just, together with the seat, been entirely swamped by a huge roller. The stone slab of the seat was lifted off as if it had been a scrap of paper, and, when the massive wave collapsed, two hopelessly drenched mortals were left behind looking for their watches.

Frantic applause, in which the hotel staff joined.

The Vultures and the Lovers

BY the following morning half the esplanade was gone. Goehrs procured a special visa to leave Rio by not altogether unequivocal methods on the strength of Victor Konder's visiting card. He had had his experience of the Brazilian visa office and was not anxious to repeat it. He was just in time to catch a steamer at the very last moment leaving for Bahia in the north of Brazil. Goehrs was standing by the taffrail as the boat cast off.

"Why are the black vultures gathering so thickly over there?" a girl of sixteen close to him asked her escort, who, with a white moustache on a brown face, was obviously her grandfather. The ship had a lively wobble in the bows and was on the point of entering the channel between the Sugarloaf and Fort Santa Cruz.

"The vultures always gather together when a couple of lovers have thrown themselves off the Pão de Açucar. The police know their whereabouts then."

"Why do the police want to know that?" asked the girl hotly. "They ought to leave them alone."

" That would not be in accordance with the law and order that must be upheld in every State," replied the old gentleman. " The proper conduct of the State makes it desirable for the dead to be identified, and it therefore sends out a search party to bring them in."

The girl still did not seem to be convinced. But she made no answer and suddenly turned dead-white. For the current gripped the ship close under the Sugarloaf and tossed her about on such high steep waves that she groaned all over.

Goehrs looked at the Brazilian flag at the stern. It was green, with a big, yellow diamond in the centre. There was a blue globe emblazoned on the diamond, with twenty white stars that stood for the twenty States of the Brazilian Federation. And over them ran a white scroll with the inscription : " Ordem e Progresso." Order and Progress. And above that there was another big star. The star of Rio.

Standing beside the flag, Goehrs waved farewell to his friend the Sugarloaf.

BAHIA

AFTER a few days' run northwards along the coast, Goehrs reached Bahia. Bahia is the Brazilian State that possesses everything of which other States only have selections. It has coffee and cocoa, tobacco and gold, diamonds and oil, forests and orange groves, nitrates and zinc. It is bigger than Germany, has nearly four million inhabitants, and lies pretty close to the equator, although it is not too tropical. The city of Bahia, with a population of 300,000, is the third largest city of Brazil. It was at one time the capital.

Goehrs, of course, did not trust all figures. He knew that Peru is at times credited with four, at others with seven million inhabitants, and that even Brazil is credited by some people with twice the population estimated by other people. All returns were for the most part " half and half "—a little fanciful and very inaccurate. A jest that an opposition newspaper in Buenos Aires had perpetrated in the course of the cattle census of unhappy memory occurred to him. It had ascertained that in the Congress district 158 castrated rams had been returned. It came out with 158 castrated rams : Parliament.

Bahia was situated in the Bay de Todos or Santos, very beautiful, very mild, almost a tragedy of the tropics, with its dampness, with its coconut palms, its highlying new, and its lowlying old, quarters—the town of the slaves, of Negro majorities, of the reek of tobacco, and of churches. In the middle of the harbour lay a tramp that, as if by way of a joke, had sunk herself. Not only her taffrail but the whole of her upper decks showed above the surface. The tramp had literally rammed herself. She had put into Bahia one day when a Swedish man-of-war that, in accordance with an old pattern, was armed with a spur under the water-level, was at anchor in the harbour. The merchantman, unsuspicious of anything as formidable as that, ran gaily past the Swede and rammed the other's spur so deeply into her side that it was all over within five minutes. As she had among other things a cargo of sugar on board, the Bay of All Saints was for a time converted literally into a sweet-water lake.

While Goehrs's boat was making fast, he saw that Bahia was flying its flags. A Brazilian padre was standing beside him, and Goehrs asked him for the reason. He knew that the red-letter days of a country are often very characteristic of it and that those of Brazil were equally divided between political anniversaries and national pride. In addition to these there were the customary ecclesiastical festivals, but no more.

" One is never quite sure why they are flying their flags," said the padre cautiously as they disembarked side by side. " Last year a Dutch captain put the same question. The Dutch are a courteous folk, and the captain was quite prepared to flag his vessel. But they replied : ' We are flying flags to-day because on this day 275 years ago the last Dutchman left the town.' "

The padre smiled and hurried away through the wharves redolent with the acrid smell of tobacco and left Goehrs to his thoughts of Prince John Maurice of Nassau, who for twenty years had built up a Dutch colonial empire in a town where an enterprising, self-conscious nation had now taken root.

" Quaint nation," thought Goehrs, looking about him. He could see nothing but Negroes.

THE CHURCH AND THE SLAVES

THE sun was shining on Bahia. Then it poured as it can pour only in the tropics. Then the sun shone again. Then a renewed downpour. And quite suddenly on an overcast sky rainbows came drifting through the misty, pearly grey air.

When the sun shone for a while, it became palpable of what a high density of moisture the atmosphere was. Even in Rio, Goehrs had overhauled his wardrobe once a week. First, on account of the moths which, under an organized unity of command, raided and devoured everything, and secondly on account of the damp. A dark suit would be complete mildewed within a week ; in Bahia within four-and-twenty hours. Further, the climate of Bahia was pretty equable, whereas there were distinct variations in Rio. Rio, in the winter, was very much what midsummer was in Central Europe, and in summer it was distinctly hot.

The State of Bahia had a very long coastline, over 600 miles of it ; thence it rose from the coast to a tableland of several hundred feet in height, and passed on to mountains in the background and the vast river basin of the São Francisco. Nothing of it was as yet really opened up, and all of it was cultivated by primitive methods and remained full of infinite possibilities.

It was here that the first wave of European immigration had broken. Not warlike, as in the case of the Spaniards, in a succession of struggles of the commanders among themselves, not in religious exaltation, not in the spirit of callous imperialism, but in a middle-class, unheroic way, without palaces and armies. Colonization by *fazendas*, country homesteads, negro villages, and ecclesiastical buildings.

Goehrs saw seventy churches in Bahia. Including the private chapels of the old mansions, they amounted to 365. A different church for every day of the year. And what beautiful old churches, too ! And what centuries-old corners of the town !

In one of the old churches, Goehrs fell in with his little padre again. They went across to the great monastery that enclosed a little gem in the way of cloisters, cloisters with blue and white old tiles, azulejos of the finished perfection of Gobelins. Mythological scenes, full of monsters and goddesses, of Renaissance and Greek helmets. End of the seventeenth century. With the shadows of the sombre monks flitting past. Bahia looked like an Italian town seen from the diamond-paned dainty library. With grey-tiled roofs. Like Ravenna. Just as reposeful. But the church of the monastery was aglow with gold and baroque, of such a sensuous, wanton, opulent baroque style, of such a fiery, vivid, assertive gold, that the low sparkle of candlelight seemed to kindle the images to life . . . every inch was crowded with saints, women's bosoms, and weird monsters. The space was small, and all its furniture was of carved wood, of the rarest wood procurable, the only one the termite ants could not destroy.

" It all dates back to slave labour," said the little padre, stroking a figure in the screenwork, a variant of a Medusa, on whose beautiful wooden bosom little plates of gold leaf were inlet.

Goehrs started. There was something in the padre's voice that had rung like pride that the Church too had once had slaves to work for her. Monstrous as it sounded . . . from the point of view of these days, it was no more astonishing than that the Church should administer its property on a capitalist basis nowadays. Slaves in the service of the Church—that would have been taken for granted in those days, and the slaves had been well off in the service of the Church. It had indeed not been to the advantage of the Church to be so good to the slaves ; during several periods in Brazil as well as in Paraguay. The Jesuits had been evicted and the Jesuit realm in Paraguay, one of the most remarkable and instructive systems of civic life, destroyed. Goehrs recalled the humanitarian spirit of the Pope who had first of all espoused the cause of the Indians in a bull and thereby acknowledged them as human beings after they had, for some considerable time, been held as at a transition stage between men and beasts.

And yet—there was, all the same, something in the little padre's tone of voice that came as a shock to Goehrs. He did not know why. It was something in the inflection— there ought to have been a note of regret or of disapproval when a priest of to-day referred to " slave labour."

There were none but the descendants of these slaves, free and independent Brazilians, in the fantastic little gold church. They were at their devotions. There is something strange about Negresses at prayer. Their hands are fervent, and no woman in the world looks more beautiful on her knees. Only their woolly heads are too small ; they are not in the picture. But these black women of Bahia looked macabre kneeling in this dim glimmering church with its baroque images, with their black and brown bronze figures flecked by the glint of its gold. The majority of them in the intervals of their devotions hunted for lice, in the grand manner, quietly and indolently, with movements such as only tall, slender Negresses can boast.

They hunted for lice, cracked them, and went on with their devotions unruffled.

MANNERS AND MORALS

GOEHRS always had, in spite of all his experience in this direction, a sense of awe when, passing the seat of Government, he saw black, well-groomed gentlemen standing in the deep, open windows above him discussing the weal of Bahia—or possibly some other topic—with ample gesticulations. In the streets, in couples, college girls. Khaki skirts to the knee. Black stockings. White blouses and big hats. All that remained uncovered after all these habiliments were pretty little negress faces.

In the residential quarters of Bahia were some handsome colonial mansions in the early Portuguese style—as in Curaçao. Close beside them Negro villages under palm trees, with fat little Negro babies with banana tummies. Regular kraals. Not far off, a quarter with narrow, medieval streets, as in Portugal at the time of the Conquest. Goehrs was standing on a bastion of one of the old forts commanding All Saints Bay. Beside him stood a Brazilian, a man of weight and worth in the State. They had been chatting for some little time, and Goehrs, as always happened when he talked to Brazilians, was marvelling at the wonderful courtesy and delightful frankness of this man.

The Brazilians were the most courteous nation Goehrs knew. He had had the experience of the police staging a scene, a regular theatrical scene, of five minutes' duration, only to give him their advice where to park his car to the best advantage. He had known people who put their house, their cash, their country place at his disposal when once they had got over their initial stiffness. He had even heard Negro porters, removing heavy furniture out of a house on a sweltering day, addressing one another ceremoniously as "Senhor." On the other hand, Goehrs had been amused by the frankness with which Brazilians would discuss subjects to which a polite European would never even allude. Brazilian towns were, for example, infected by *lues* to such an extent that there were people who estimated this infection at 90, and some at 100 per cent. And there were Europeans in Bahia who, in consequence, would never touch a glass with their lips at a public restaurant. This disease was as rampant as it was in Egypt, where the general population was, among themselves, practically immune against it, and where, for climatic reasons, the more severe sequels so frequent in Europe and America did not supervene. But whereas people in Europe maintained absolute silence about a disease like *lues*—though discussing their rheumatism freely enough—people in Brazil talked about *lues* as they might about a cold in the head. Unsuspecting women from Europe swooned when Brazilians in high positions told them they were trying a new treatment.

Goehrs had long ago trained himself not to become fluttered when one part of the world regarded a subject as proper that another looked on as an abomination, and he knew that the same rule applied to morality, to manners, and to character, viewed in one light in one place, in another otherwise. But this frankness—on such a delicate subject—well, it still did cause him some astonishment. However, Goehrs had not been discussing with the Brazilian, the not irrational attitude of his compatriots on this matter, but politics.

" I have casually heard some mention in the south," said Goehrs, " that the north of Brazil was, at times, quite prepared to cut itself adrift from the whole Federation. Do you agree ? "

" By no manner of means," said the man decidedly. " They sometimes turn this sort of twaddle to account by way of a warning at the election of the Federal President. For there are always two opinions then—and I believe they trotted it out again on the occasion of Prestes's election a few months ago. A revolution—that is within the range of possibility. But no separation. No disruption, senhor. We are thoroughly loyal to Brazil."

" And when you hold your presidential elections for the State of Bahia, is there no talk of cutting the painter then ? "

" Never," said the man.

Then he laughed softly. " At presidential elections in Bahia the guns do, it is true, go off. We are very excitable among ourselves. But as far as Brazil itself is concerned, we are fanatically Brazilian."

Goehrs turned his back on the sea and gazed inland. Fifty yards away from the battlements rose the dark skeleton of a big building that had never been finished—the skeleton of a gambling casino for North Brazil that had been left unfinished. They had halted between two opinions for a long time and then had not built the gambling hell, but in

386

its stead, a little nearer the sea, had erected the monumental figure of a great Christ. Goehrs's gaze strayed from the one erection to the other. He again realized that a decided " either—or " would never grow from this soil, only a " half and half." He again turned towards the bay, with its beautiful beach, its palm trees, and its forts, below him. " Is the Yankee colony strong in Bahia ? " he asked, watching a Brazilian cruiser that was just making All Saints Bay.

" It is small," said the Brazilian. " But it represents a very big capital. The German colony is very big, but it stands for a modest capital. Look at that "— he pointed to an elevator that looked like a smokestack, one of the electric lifts that conveyed passengers from the low-lying coastal strip to the upper town in a twinkling—" that is American."

On the man's face Goehrs read the same expression of repugnance he had seen on the faces of many a man in Bolivia and in Ecuador, in Chile, Peru and Argentina, the resentment of men who were watching alien interests draining their country and its resources. It was a hatred heavy of fate.

" Did you hear anything in Rio about the story of the Yankees trying to buy British Guiana ? " inquired the man mysteriously.

The Guianas are a strip of territory above the equator between Brazil and Venezuela—and the last fragment of European colonization in South America. Part belongs to the Dutch under the name of Surinam, part to the French under the notorious name of the penal settlement of Cayenne, and the rest to the British, with the city of Georgetown. A torrid, terrible country.

" Are the English anxious to sell ? "

" At any rate the Yankees are anxious to buy. They are trying to buy every harbour in South America they can lay their hands on. And the English are dropping out—you can see that for yourself. But once the Yankees have got a foothold in Guiana, to the north of us, as well as in Panama, they will thrust their pincers forward and we shall have their knee in our back."

He opened his hand with a gripping movement and clenched it again. The next moment he was polite and affable as ever.

" But perhaps it may turn out differently," he said, and passed his hand across his eyes. " History, after all, offers so many possibilities for escaping from an impending doom. History is very resourceful and, above all, so fertile in ideas."

THE distance from Rio de Janeiro to Bahia was about 800 miles, and in the course of it Goehrs had passed the coastal State of Espirito Santo, lying between Rio and Bahia, a little State with wooded hills and fertile valleys, with potatoes and coffee and cocoa, with dense virgin forests and fever-haunted swamps. Goehrs had seen its capital, Victoria, with its fjords and its enchanting bay. Now when Goehrs was on his way northwards again from Bahia to Pernambuco, the fourth biggest city in Brazil, his vessel passed along the coasts of two other little coastal States, Sergipe and Alagóas. He arrived then at Pernambuco, the capital of the State of Pernambuco, the principal sugar State of South America. Pretty close to the equator. With 2,500,000 inhabitants, and 300,000 of them in the capital. There were Negro villages and attractive residential quarters in the capital, and the villa residences had a leaning towards the Moorish colonial style. There rose the pink, yellow, green, mauve houses with their striking ornamentations—an early Gothic style as if ordered at the pastry cook's. And apparently designed by an architect obsessed by a guilty passion for crochetwork. Everything, wherever possible, was openwork. With palms and fountains thrown in. A city with a few bridges. But without a trace of Venice to which, on account of the bridges, it used to be compared. Pretty, well-dressed women in the streets with the carriage of white ladies, who, when they happened to turn round, proved to be Negresses after all. A Jockey Club, painted sky-blue, a medley of churches, and a man dragging a pig along the principal street on a bit of rope. . . .

There was even a decent hotel. And there were newspapers. Goehrs always took a great interest in the provincial papers of every country. The newspaper of Pernambuco, in the absence of other things, interested him very much. On the front page of the *Jornal Pequeno* was, first of all, the picture of a thoroughpaced young Southerner, the portrait of " a young and brilliant " journalist on the staff of another paper, who had a birthday that day, as was being acknowledged in the most sportsmanlike spirit in these columns. Then there was not quite as large a portrait of, with an article about, that famous son of Brazil, Santos Dumont, who was also celebrating his birthday that day, and from the article it would appear that Brazil had inaugurated aviation for the whole of the world. Then came a portrait of a Portuguese general festooned in decorations and ribbons with an article overcast by sombre forebodings about the restoration of the monarchy in Portugal. And then there followed a picture of Hindenburg of the War era with a paragraph to the effect that he had just decreed a financial dictatorship. It was a portrait in uniform of nearly twenty years ago. How very different Hindenburg looked nowadays! thought Goehrs. What a world of wisdom and of destiny lay between the two pictures! The portrait reproduced in the Brazilian newspaper here made Hindenburg look like a Pilsudski. Under his caption the old gentleman looked exactly as if he had just come in from riding down to the Reichstag and affronting it.

Alas, thought Goehrs, folding up his newspaper, how close were the errors of history to its truths—and how easy it was to disseminate error, even though its author had not the smallest intention of doing so!

It was Pernambuco's boast to be the principal sugar mart of Brazil, and it was the town that challenged Bahia's claim to pride of place as the capital of the north. It was the town which, if ever aerial traffic with Europe should develop, would advance into the centre of the stage. Goehrs studied the life of the town without any overwhelming interest. For the golden sunshine fell on the façades of the old mansions about the bridge with the same reposeful radiance as on the palaces of Venice. Everything was already beginning to savour strongly of Europe.

And a white, spick-and-span liner of 8000 tons had just put in to the harbour with the red, white, and blue flag of Holland in the stern and the house-flag of the Dutch Lloyd at the masthead: the *Zeelandia*, homeward bound to Amsterdam.

Part VII

WHITHER AWAY, SOUTH AMERICA?

HISTORY SEEMS TO REPEAT ITSELF

GOEHRS passed a few minor Brazilian States at first, then South America suddenly dropped a curtsy—the coast fell away; it ceased to run north but fell away laterally, in an almost coquettish retreat to the West.

Beyond lay the vast State of Amazonas, one of the world's secrets, impenetrable, four times the size of Germany, a spellbound primeval forest, hardly a fraction of which was under cultivation. Indian country. Bisected by the mightiest river of the world, sometimes 70 miles in width, 1500 feet in depth, with hundreds of tributaries and with 60,000 miles of navigable waterways within its system— given a good head of water. Goehrs often used to wonder about this river that cut clean across South America. The river seemed to be in some way symbolic of the country, of the vastness characteristic of the whole of this continent, of that barbaric bulk that even in the most ancient myths always appeared in bonds, never wholly set free.

One day the jagged, narrow backbone of the island Fernando Noronha showed above the sea. It was the island where it was one o'clock when in western Brazil, in the Acre territory on the borders of Peru but still within the zone of the River Amazon, it was striking ten. The *Zeelandia* set her course dead on the island. Goehrs saw an airman passing over the *Zeelandia*, a triple-engined hydroplane, with every indication that it was a German machine. It was flying low and came down within the shadow of the island. It had hardly touched the water when a launch shot out from a big liner lying off the island. Through his glasses Goehrs distinctly saw the launch taking the mail bags from the aircraft on board and buzzing back to the liner again, and then he watched the big steamer making off full steam ahead. She was the *Cap Arcona* of the Hamburg-South America

Line. And the hydroplane belonged to the Syndicato Condor of Rio de Janeiro, the German air line that served Brazil with Dornier-Wal and Junker machines. It was the line by which Goehrs had intended to fly from Rio to Bahia ; he knew the pilot, who in a single night had covered the 1400 odd miles from Rio to Natal and thence back again straight across the ocean to the island that, though lying far out at sea, was still part of Brazil.

This performance was a pretty daring bit of German enterprise, for by this route the German beat the French line, which had hitherto been the fastest mail service, by a day. The mails left Rio on the German hydroplane two days after the fastest mailboat, caught her up off Fernando Noronha, transferred the mail to her, and off the Canaries a hydroplane of the Hansa Line took it over again—and the letters were in Berlin within nine days after leaving Rio. This happened twice a month and was meant to serve as the forerunner of a mail service to be organized one of these days with a squadron of Zeppelins and giant aeroplanes. The man who had elaborated these bold schemes for developing postal communications between South America and Europe by a squadron of Zeppelins and super-aeroplanes at German expense and for initiating it by German enterprise was the pilot Hammer, and Hammer had previously had another great scheme. He had landed in Colombia in 1920, had tested the Dornier-Wal for work in the tropics, and at a date long before Lindbergh had set out on his momentous flight and before the Yankees had worked out long-distance mail services, had made the first flight across Central America by way of Panama, Costa Rica, and Guatemala to Cuba.

Germany, having no political ambitions in South America, and not being under suspicion of entertaining imperialistic designs like the United States, might have had a great opportunity, but Germany was flying from one aerodrome to the next, twelve miles apart, in Germany, and missed her chance. She did not support the scheme for a world mail service—and the Yankees stepped in. They developed the line the first German trial trip had blazed ; they subsidized the services, and American machines instead of German were now flying from Florida by way of the West Indies to Panama. And from Panama they flew to Colombia and Ecuador and linked up with Peru.

At this juncture, Goehrs, as in a lightning flash, grasped the significance of this route—the tragic inevitability of its direction—the direction towards Peru, whence the history of

South America had had its source, the Peru of the Incas, the Peru of Pizarro, the Peru for which Vasco Nuñez de Balboa's expedition had set out, the Peru that had essentially been the goal of Columbia's quest—Peru, that had been the goal of all those epic, divinely inspired, lawless, daring, and predatory expeditions the Old World had sent out to the New.

And all these expeditions had taken the same route Goehrs had taken . . . the same route that, with a significance well beyond the reach of coincidence, Yankee capital was taking when it began to flow for the colonization of South America. By way of the West Indies. By way of Panama. By way of Colombia and Ecuador to Peru, Bolivia, and Chile, thence to Argentine and to Brazil.

It looked as if history were repeating itself. In other fashions and with men cast in different mould, with armies of bank clerks instead of retinues of mailed condottieri, by more suave and more insidious inroads, with the new, silent relentlessness of mechanization . . . but at the same hideous pace and with the same fell significance.

UNSTABLE AS WATER

THE captain of the *Zeelandia*, Captain Van Noppen, was on the bridge with Goehrs and took his ship quite close to the island of Fernando Noronha. He looked as slim as a boy with his blue Dutch eyes, an inquiring nose, and the rather quaint self-assurance that only Dutchmen have. He was wearing white drill and kept his left hand in his pocket. He murmured an order to one of the crew, who signalled it down to the engine-room. The brasswork on the bridge flashed ; the gold lace on the captain's cap glittered ; and the ting of the bell with which the engine-room acknowledged orders received sounded almost unnatural in the stillness that enveloped ship and sea. At times the smooth, rapid lilt of the " Cariñosa " on a gramophone drifted quite faintly from the promenade deck, and the captain cocked his ears on these occasions. Like all Dutchmen he loved the gramophone, and had three hundred records of his own in his cabin. Captain Van Noppen was an exceptional man ; he was neither tyrannical, nor vain, nor a sea-dog. He was a cheery man with ideas of his own, to which he gave voice—in whatever language happened to be handy.

Beside him stood an American, the representative of the

Standard Oil Company for Argentina, a man who looked like every other American, a Yankee with a square face and a firm chin. Goehrs was standing beside this man and beside Goehrs stood a Dutchman, who had been born in Pernambuco of a Dutch father and a Brazilian mother. He was an old, lean, narrow-chested man with a polished manner, a sensitive dark face, and white waxed moustachios. The *Zeelandia* steered 3.5° south past Fernando Noronha, and the island then revealed a peaked mountain, a cone that looked like the last reminder from Brazil of the Sugarloaf of Rio de Janeiro.

The man with the white moustachios shaded his eyes with a long, delicate hand, to which two races had contributed, and pointed a little affectedly to the island with the other.

" I do not know whether you are aware that Fernando Noronha belongs to the State of Pernambuco and that this State uses it for a convict station, and that except for myself very few people can have been on the island. I once had the honour of an invitation from the Governor and went out there on his little launch. Four hundred murderers are domiciled on the island, and most of the convicts have their families with them and, if well conducted, are permitted to live under their own roofs. And I assure you that, if you were to see the houses and their occupants, you would have to stop short every now and then to remind yourself that all the men over there are convicted murderers."

With the naked eye Goehrs saw the palm trees and the banana plantations on the coast of the island, which reproduced the delicious proportions of the praias of Rio, but on a smaller scale.

" It looks like a Garden of Eden," said the captain. " That is why I always pass it as close in as possible. . . ." He was about to add something, but the wireless operator was standing at the other end of the bridge with a message in his hand, and the captain went across to him.

" It really is a paradise," said the old gentleman with the white hair in the white drill suit and with the dark, greyhound head and the white military moustachios. " Five policemen are all they want . . . imagine it, only five policemen. The head cook was an artist—with two murders on record against him."

Goehrs smiled. A seagull stood poised on quivering wings, heading against the wind, just overhead. The first officer gave the seaman at the speaking-tube a low order. Slowing down in her course, the snow-white *Zeelandia*, beautiful, trim, and silent, sped past the island. Captain Van Noppen had come on the bridge again. He stood still for a while, breathing on a sheet of paper in his hand as if it were too hot to hold comfortably.

" Gentlemen," he said, at length, " a revolution has broken out in Brazil. . . ."

The Standard Oil man had hardly said a word during the whole of the voyage, but he made up for it that forenoon.

" It's damned well time," he said in the loud, strident voice of his compatriots, " that these countries were placed under an administration that would put a stop to this tomfooling."

" I can understand your point of view, senhor," replied the Dutch Brazilian with the white moustache, " the more readily as this revolution in Brazil must be inconvenient to you because it is aimed against your protégés in São Paulo and the money you have sunk in their coffee plantations. But on the other hand, there is not a soul in South America who is unaware that it was you who pulled the strings from New York of the revolution in Argentina six weeks ago."

" I should be delighted to hear it," said the American, " although the story is news to me. For there was no close season for us in Argentina. On the instructions of my company I have sunk twenty million dollars in Argentina only to have the oilfields prospected, and then I imported 15,000 tons of plant to get on with pumping it. Then the production that had previously been promised us was prohibited. Why? Because Argentina intended to produce oil on its own account. Sir, I am no bloodsucker, and I'm not a fool—but how and by what means did Argentina propose to produce oil? For it had not a red cent of capital. Well, then I heard, sure enough, that Argentina had been begging for a loan in New York to produce its oil at our expense. But, gentlemen, it is a stupid and impudent policy—to give us a slap in the face in front and to try to get money out of us behind our backs . . . not to let us get on with the work and yet to be unable to do it without our assistance. That sort of thing upsets business, and business can't stand it. And it's in the natural course of things for revolutions to come along if, in ignorance of the determining factors of the world, you go and block the natural channels of business."

Was it not to the accompaniment of similar discussions on revolutions and oil on board a Dutch ship that he had,

in his time, gone out to South America ? Goehrs reflected.
At that time it had been revolutions in Venezuela, Ecuador,
and Colombia that were exciting people—in countries that
were still living in the Middle Ages and where a grab at the
national purse still held out sporting chances for a man and
his partisans. And now he was leaving South America to
the accompaniment of similar discussions, but this time
they were concerned with revolutions in civilized countries
—this time it was the capital of foreign countries that, with
the callousness characteristic of economic struggles, was
plunging these countries into revolutions. There was a gulf
of five centuries between the significance of revolutions in
Venezuela and the significance of revolutions in Argentina
. . . but it was the same feverishness that destiny seemed
to have bequeathed to these countries in eternal token
of its helplessness, the same convulsions that had
kept these magnificent, unredeemed countries for tens of
centuries in an epileptic diathesis for which there seemed
no cure.

And what will happen to Brazil now ? Goehrs wondered.
So the many pretty little " Misses " from the many States
had, after all, not availed to sidetrack the insurrection, and
Senhor Vargas, the President of Rio Grande, had proved a
man of his word ; he was not going to permit Senhor Prestes,
the President-elect, to occupy the presidential chair of united
Brazil. The São Paulist faction would, after President
Washington Luiz, never again see the reins of Government
entrusted to one of its henchmen—the south, the north, the
inland States had risen to break the domination of the coffee
gangs and international financiers in the cities of the coast.
And Senhor Prestes, who had already paid his visits on
accession to office in Europe would have to fight for the
throne he had hitherto in no way occupied except, maybe,
in his aspirations.

*There was nothing durable on this continent. The people
were bound to have dictatorships and to smash them each time.
They were resolved to have democracies and they always got
dictatorships. They put themselves to all pains to organize, to
co-ordinate, to construct, and to mould—but at long last they
were bound to wreck it all again. They were unable to endure
any one or anything set in authority over them. Nor would
they even have endured Christ or Napoleon in authority over
them.*

" Gentlemen," said Captain Van Noppen, and now put his
right hand into his pocket as well, " it is growing rather hot.

Would you care to try a glass of cold tea in my cabin ? I can promise you that the tea shall be up to the mark."

He beckoned to the officer on watch. The engine-room signal became busy. The *Zeelandia* again headed full steam ahead into the ocean.

WHITHER AWAY, SOUTH AMERICA ?

THE *Zeelandia* was really heading for the shoreless, boundless ocean. Goehrs felt happy. He was being borne on board his snow-white ship into the indescribably mellow warmth for which he had yearned. He was being borne into his beloved heat, considerately tempered by a light breeze from Africa way. And now all the marvels that so mysteriously deepen the secrets of the equatorial zone were coming back again.

Slowly the unfamiliar constellations that had showed above the horizon as long as Goehrs was in South America began to fall away, and the stars of his boyhood and his home began to mount the heavens on the other side of the equator. How solemnly and coldly did the Southern Cross gleam as it fell away ! In what an ecstasy of bliss and beauty did the air breathe between the softly whispering sea and the low-hung magic constellation. And restfully ! How softly and brilliantly did the evening star rise !

Goehrs recalled that a statesman had once remarked to him that the League of Nations ought to be transferred to Venice to enable the statesmen who helped to shape the destiny of nations to share the delight of its fascinating atmosphere.

Pity, thought Goehrs, that it's not feasible to found a town of ships on the equator. A very great pity. Goehrs was crossing the equator for the fourth time—and on the fourth as on the first occasion it appealed to him as the focus of the generous sentiment of humanity, of the nobility of human nature, of tenderness and generosity of thought.

Goehrs went to the chart of the course to check the mileage they were making. The *Zeelandia* was doing her 290 miles a day—the currents were against her. She was wolfing 70 tons of oil fuel a day. She had a tonnage of 8000 and, generally speaking, would probably do 330 miles a day. And how gallantly she covered them, so slim, so graceful, so deeply enamoured of the sea. She was, like all Dutch ships, a well-found boat, everything about her was well balanced, everything on board her was good but not too good. She was a comfortable boat, and the passengers on board her were agreeably varied, Englishmen, Russians, Spaniards, Frenchmen, Brazilians, Dutchmen, Portuguese, and a little pianist of no nationality, but with a letter from Professor Einstein that read : " Fellow creatures : Do not ask this young man for his passport, but look into his face and hear him play." This was an effective introduction—except that he played rather too much. But the boat was not full ; it was between the seasons, and business was bad—and there was plenty of elbow-room to study the sea. Goehrs loved the sea ; he did not like missing a minute of its company, and from the decks of the *Zeelandia* he saw the sea everywhere. And that was an advantage of which very few ships could boast, for on the majority of them the sea was screened by bulwarks, by covered gangways, and by glass. Goehrs remembered a despairing passenger he had come across in the bowels of a great ocean liner who, strayed in the maze of gangways and decks, and prowling about between the covered swimming-bath and the lifts, was asking one steward after the other : " How on earth does one get to the sea ? " These leviathans, equipped with the very latest gadgets of mechanical ingenuity, appealed to Goehrs as triumphs of his generation, but he did not love them. He admired them profoundly as achievements, but personally he loathed them. He loved little ships, real ships, ships with the sea and open taffrail, in neighbourly communion with the waves, the moonbeams, the rollicking dolphins, the shark's fin, the flying silver-fish, and the screaming gulls. He loved ships that to some extent always shared in the rhythmic motion of the waves and snuggled into the sea and, as they rolled in really dirty weather, passed on their contact with the water as they had received it.

Goehrs followed the line of the equator from east to west with his finger. Passing a little above the River Amazon, his fingertip found Ecuador and Colombia. His finger on the other side of the continent came to a stop on the same tableland he had crossed with Patino and with Urquiza the prospector, who had probably shot himself by this time, with the young woman who had kept her pheasant coop beside the bull's loose box, those pheasants whose dynasty she hoped to found in Quito, and the half-Indian girl Rosita, who had once called out to him : " I should like to give you my hands to take down into the cabin to wash." On the same degree of longitude on the West Coast he had lain for a

397

year, so it seemed to him, on the Guayas River, watching the little eyots floating downstream from the interior of Ecuador. And on the same line he had caught his first clue to the problems and the riddles of that continent and had fastened on their track.

Once more, as then, his ship was faring serenely through the glowing phosphorescence round her prow, luminous jellyfish were floating past, and the Cross of the South hung low once more in the darkling sky. Big silver-fish were again leaping from the crest of one wave to the next, only to fall heavily as lead into the sea at last. Playful dolphins were again romping about within ten yards of his eyes and accompanying the ship in mythological good companionship. The day, half overcast, passed by in an atmosphere of soft, mysterious tension. The heavens towards evening were again arrayed in colours past all understanding, mystic golden figures again floated above the horizon, clouds like streaming lucent tresses above the masts, a lofty fortress of hammered cinnabar plates piled up in the background, and a gorgeous pageantry of sweet and tragic visions in pink and yellow swept across the African skyline. On the other side, above the distant South American coastline, those pure colours of fire, those rich purple tones of the shadows framing the pink highlights of fleecy clouds, appeared again. And again, in between them, lay, like the blare of trumpets, in the midst of a chorale of gold and fire, the ineffable stain of blood.

And the sea was again rapt in that ecstasy of supreme delight as it had been rapt on the Guayas River when Goehrs had watched the Indian fruit porters of Ecuador with their bronze arms raised over their heads and naked torsos, with the bunches of yellow-green bananas on their heads, coming down from the wooden piers of the fruit market, and he had taken them for figures symbolical of life, of peace and poverty.

Goehrs stared out to sea. What a gulf lay between then and now !

It swept down upon him like a cascade—an inferno of destinies, races, nations, men and women, laws and problems. An inferno not without its good angels, the angels of the mountains, of the volcanoes of Peru and Bolivia.

Goehrs endeavoured to recall once more what he had then expected to find in South America, on the Guayas River . . . he puzzled his brain with it for a while, but he failed to recapture it. He failed to recapture the hopes, the curiosity, the aspirations, and the expectations that had possessed him. Too much had happened in between.

But he did know what his experiences between then and now had been—he could recall them. He saw Lake Titicaca and the Sierra, and the Puna, the llamas and the Indios and the sun over Chacaltaya and its tin mines, the sun, " the poncho of the poor." He saw Leguía, the dictator, after ten years of despotic rule, at the age of sixty-eight, giving orders for people to be transported to San Lorenzo and for breaking their arms ; his smile, his gentle animal eyes, his delicate hands. He saw Major Sánchez Cerro of Arequipa, who brought him down and in the course of a few days rose to be lieutenant-colonel, colonel, general, and President of Peru ; he saw the serfdom of the Indians, the cities of the coast, and the roads begun into the interior. He saw the countries, seven-eighths of whose populations did not speak the language of their country ; he saw successful and unsuccessful crosses with Indian stock. He saw the nitrate pampas wreathed in smoke, the copper stocks for which there was no market, the wheat harvest of Argentina that had proved superabundant. He saw the mountains of the Altiplano, where people who contracted inflammation of the lungs were bound to die unless they hurried by special train to the coast. He saw the mob of Indian students yelling revolution in the streets of La Paz, the gamblers in the nitrate oficinas betting who could hold the fuse of a dynamite cartridge in his hand longest ; he saw the millions of cattle browsing on the pasturelands of Argentina, and he heard the gauchos dashing up and dancing the " Cariñosa " in the evening. He saw generals planning towns ; he saw strongholds where political prisoners were every morning flooded neck high by the tide. He saw the citadels and palaces of the Incas in the Cordilleras and the millions of Indians swarming in from the Puna, and setting stones on the edge of the mountains in homage to their ancient sacred city. He saw the blaze of light rising from Buenos Aires and the gentle Misti with its shapely plume of smoke and tropical Arequipa at its foot, the two thousand beautiful women in the Colón Opera and the metropolis near Tiahuanacu, at the altitude of 13,000 feet, of a civilization that was maybe ten thousand years old, and the monoliths and the gateway of the Sun with its undeciphered symbols, the gold masks, and the mummies with the parrot heads. He saw the lines of eternity recorded in the sickle dunes beyond Mollendo ; he saw the immigrants on the broiling coffee plantations of São

Paulo and the virgin forests of Rio and the pretty mulattos dancing with the foreign diplomatic staffs. He saw the proletariat of Chile using the woodwork of their tenements for fuel ; he saw the River Amazon and the aerodromes of the Americans on the banks of the Panama Canal. He saw the vultures perching on the houses of Valparaíso, the golf links of Viña del Mar, the cemetery of Buenaventura, the trophies of the headhunters of Ecuador, the country without railways, without roads, full of unexplored rivers and malaria, the desolation of the salt steppes of Bolivia, the racecourse of Santiago . . . and with it all he never lost the low cruel accompaniment of naked Indian feet pattering on the frozen ground of the capital of the Incas' empire along the streets of Cuzco past the palaces of the Indian princes and vestals.

Goehrs's eyes followed the deckhand who day after day used patiently to touch up the white taffrail of the *Zeelandia* from the same white paint pot. Then he again looked out to the sea that had become misty and silvery.

What a strange route he had taken through this land . . . and of what distraught, disconnected phantoms did not everything that made up the land consist ! What was going to be the fate of this incongruous continent, of this enigmatic bulk of land ? Whither away, South America ? Was this tangled, half-fused amalgam of different races, this un-fermented cauldron, this continent of intolerable and no less glorious conditions of life, this land full of gold and malaria, full of ore, wheat, cattle, soroche and *lues*, this patchwork of white, Negro, and Indian strains destined to become the continent of the future ?

Of the future ? Inevitably . . . but of a future of what nature ?

Would the new race arise from the mythical basin of the River Amazon in which a population of a thousand millions could—in theory—find room to live, and shake their heads with a disapproval that would make Europe shrink back into limbo, as in their day Byzantium, Athens, Jerusalem, and Rome shrank back, when the Nordic peoples flung themselves on their horses ?

Goehrs smiled. He did not believe it. He smiled because his was not the type of mind to become engrossed in specula-tions aimed some centuries ahead. For the moment he could see only one sole development. And this development hinged on the squadrons of aircraft he had seen ready for flight on the banks of the Panama Canal. This development hinged, too, on the streams of capital pouring southwards out of Yankee treasuries ; it hinged on the Yankees who were as surely determining the face of the world to-day as the Germanic tribes and the English race had shaped it in their day. Perhaps Argentina would one day in the natural course of events have the twenty million additional population it needed ; perhaps the Indios of Bolivia would cease to haunt the Cordilleras like coca-chewing, shadowy serfs— they might well have become extinct by then—and perhaps Chile would by then be a well-watered farming country and Brazil would have the two hundred millions it could comfortably absorb.

Why not ? But when—when ? And what problems would be engaging the world then and hold it breathless in suspense ? Quite other, no doubt, than those Goehrs had tracked out and pondered over . . . and no doubt of a kind he had not the courage to envisage today.

He looked out into the night and felt deep down and distinctly the pulsebeat of infinity, compared with which his whole range of thought, and that of his continent, were only a passing breath. He watched the moon rise, the moon that had its course four hundred times as far from the sun as the distance which separated it from the earth. He felt the stunning, invisible bombardment of the meteorites under which the earth cowered. He saw the 300,000 stars of the northern hemisphere and the forty millions of the Milky Way wheel into view. He saw ahead of him the whole star-flooded space of the northern sky, the light of which required three millennia to go from one end to the other. He thought of the eight hundred planets in their courses among the fixed stars and of the five hundred comets whose orbits took 150,000 years to circle but which he could not see.

He turned round and looked back towards South America. And then he saw the Great Bear, too, dark and beautiful, rising out of the waters again. It was low as yet and the pointers of the Wain were still trailing in the water, but its pole was boldly thrust out over the sea. And then came other stars, diamond Jupiter, red Saturn, soft, radiant Venus, and fiery Mars.

The Russian without a passport but the letter from Professor Einstein had just stopped playing in the saloon. The silhouette of the officer of the watch was pacing the bridge. The muffled music of his gramophone came from Captain Van Noppen's stateroom. The captain was playing one of his three hundred records, and the silvery lilt of the

" Cueca Chilena," which is danced with waving pocket handkerchiefs, was wafted for a second like the fragrance of some strong perfume across the deck. Abaft the ship, one or two gulls were following in the gleaming ribbon of the screw. It was extraordinarily still. Goehrs strolled forward into the bows to see whether a flying-fish, attracted by the *Zeelandia's* pyramid of lights, had not jumped on board. But even the fish were marking time. Goehrs held his breath and listened. Like all folk who often go down to the sea in ships, he could cut out all sounds that are inherent in a ship, the throb of the engines, the tremor of the bows, the slap of the water against her sides. It seemed rather to him as if at that moment the *Zeelandia* were slipping through the phosphorescence round her bows, as though through oil. She was faring, her nose set straight for Europe, into the overwhelming space with such assurance as if, even for a ship, even this space were instinct with law, with meaning, and with reason. . . .

Index

INDEX

Printed at the BURLEIGH PRESS, *Lewin's Mead*, BRISTOL